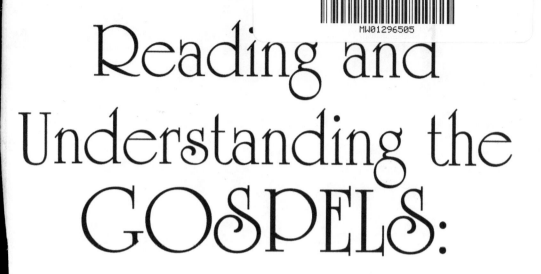

Reading and Understanding the GOSPELS:

WHO JESUS IS, WHAT HE TEACHES, AND THE BEGINNING OF CHRISTIANITY

Dr Thomas B. Lane

Outskirts Press, Inc.
Denver, Colorado

Reading and Understanding the Gospels:
Who Jesus Is, What He Teaches, and the Beginning of Christianity
All Rights Reserved.
Copyright © 2011 Dr Thomas B. Lane
v2.0 r2.1

Outskirts Press, Inc.
http://www.outskirtspress.com

ISBN: 978-1-4327-6823-2

Library of Congress Control Number: 2011924054

Outskirts Press and the "OP" logo are trademarks belonging to Outskirts Press, Inc.

PRINTED IN THE UNITED STATES OF AMERICA

*R*eading and Understanding the Gospels: Who Jesus Is, What He Teaches, and the Beginning of Christianity is the second volume in a three part series on reading and understanding the Bible. The first volume published is *Reading and Understanding the Old Testament: The Foundation of Judaism, Christianity, and Islam*. The volume to follow the Gospels will be titled *Reading and Understanding the Acts of the Apostles, the New Testament Letters, and the Beginning of the Church*.

I am dedicating these writings to Andrea, my very supporting wife, Lee Anne, and Lana my two wonderful daughters who for many years kept encouraging me to write, and to my best buddy, our first grandson, my little guy Samuel Lane Durkee, who was born three months early at two pounds five ounces. He was excited to come into this world so he decided to come early. May he bless his creator and the world as he has blessed us. My hope is that when he is old enough, he will read this humble attempt that begins to reveal the one God and will develop a relationship with that one God.

I am also dedicating this series of books to Lila Lane Fortier, our first granddaughter, who has not yet entered the world, but at this writing is soon to be born. I look forward to having her as one of my two best buddies along with Samuel. At some time may she learn from these books and be God's shining light.

A special thanks goes to my wife Andrea, who Samuel calls grandra, for the many hours she took going through the manuscript to help me proofread and correct my writing. Do not hold her responsible for my writing shortcomings. Also, a tribute is due to my loving, caring parents, Don and Pat, who gave me my first Bible and raised my sister Marsha and me in the church. A final tribute is appropriate to the one who originally inspired me to learn more about the Scriptures: Roy Ruckman from whom I took my initial courses in the Old and New Testaments at the University of Texas-El Paso.

Table of Contents

INTRODUCTION: PURPOSE AND METHODS OF INTERPRETATION

This book is written for anyone who is interested in acquiring basic knowledge and understanding of the content of the New Testament Gospels. It is primarily written for the beginning student who has never read through these four books or for anyone who wants to expand their understanding. Therefore it is not an advanced scholarly study but is designed to supply a foundation that will enable one to eventually read, meditate, and think about the content that is within the books, and possibly even motivate one to continue to a more advanced scholarly study. The goals are simply to help one gain a basic literacy of the content of Matthew, Mark, Luke, and John, to enable the reader to understand who Jesus is and what he teaches, as well as to help one better understand the books describing the beginning of Christianity.

This book is a canonical-synchronic study that takes into account modern scholarship. Canonical and synchronic means that the books of the Bible as they are completed contain all of God's inspired word, and that all parts need to be understood according to their structure and meaning, and in unity with the whole of all the books. The writer stresses a theological and religious approach rooted in the scholarship of historical and literary analysis and based upon the message of the content as understood by practicing Christians. A theological and religious approach is integrated with the historical and literary analysis because Matthew, Mark, Luke, and John were theologians. To ignore that aspect is to misunderstand the content. Here, the author accepts St Anselm of Canterbury's definition of theology as faith seeking understanding. This book is for anyone seeking to know who Jesus is and what he teaches, for Christians who have faith and are seeking a deeper understanding, but also for anyone who wants to deepen their knowledge about a person and faith that has deeply impacted the world in which we live.

Taking into account modern scholarship means that this writer attempts to utilize in a practical and applied way the principles of modern scholarship, even though this book is not about modern scholarship. In a beginning study of the content of the New Testament this writer does not want to overwhelm the reader with the methodology, intricacies, and debates of higher scholarship. It is preferable that beginning students see how a writer with faith applies scholarship in a practical way, as they read and attempt to understand the content. After the content is basically understood then the reader will be more prepared to deal with scholarship's intricacies and challenges.

In order to study modern scholarship's challenge to the New Testament such as historical and literary criticism, archeology, methodology and research, Hebrew and Greek word studies, who wrote the books, when they were written, why they were written, to whom they were written, how they were originally put together, and such debates, as well as other scholarly concerns, one will have to consult other works, and the reader is encouraged to do so.

This book will stay with the purpose of helping readers gain a basic understanding and application of the content of the Gospels. That means at times there will be an attempt to interpret and apply to our lives in a practical way some of these writings. This writer will do so in an attempt to clarify some underlying meanings and themes in order to challenge and enable the readers to begin to make some of their own applications as well as to perhaps disagree with this author. In disagreeing the reader is encouraged to show reasoning based upon Scripture and not personal preferences.

Until modern times the Bible was basically studied in order to better understand and serve God. With the coming of the Age of Enlightenment scholars soon allowed the historical critical method to dominate the serving God approach to the point that the Bible was broken into small pieces, dissected, and left there. Their primary purpose was to discover how the Bible came about and what was historically real and what was not.

This served a purpose and will continue to do so, but it is now time to put the Scriptures back together again into a unified whole to enable readers to once again better understand and serve God; thus the reason for the canonical-synthetic, theological, and religious approach. In the process we can not ignore the advances of biblical scholarship, and the fact that we now live on this side of the Enlightenment in a Post-Modern Age. The historical critical method continues to have an important part to play, even though it will no longer dominate.

It will be obvious to the reader that the writer is a Christian living in twenty-first century America. It will also be obvious that the author respects the historical method but sees the need to build upon that approach in a practical way, so that once again people can see that the Bible has much to say to people living in these times.

For Christians the Bible consists of an Old Testament and a New Testament where the word *testament* is also translated as law or covenant. In general Jews do not use the term Old Testament, for they do not accept the New Testament. For Jews, Torah, Tanakh, and Bible are what they call the Christian Old Testament. Torah means the law or the teachings. For Christians the New Testament is based upon the Old Testament but is also a reinterpretation of some of the old in the light of Christ. The New Testament also includes the addition of new content which is one reason why it is called the New Testament. Jesus came to bring the old to a climax, to fulfill it. God forming a people is like parents raising a child. Some things during infancy are permitted that later are prohibited or changed because of the development of God's plan and the increasing maturity of people.

This writer appreciates the statement made by the Second Vatican Council, in paragraphs 15 and 16 of the *Dogmatic Constitution on Divine Revelation* that says, "God, the inspirer and author of both testaments, wisely arranged that the New Testament be hidden in the Old and the Old be made manifest in the New. For, though Christ established the New Covenant in his blood; still the books of the Old Testament with all their parts, caught up into the proclamation of the gospel, acquire and show forth their full meaning in the New Testament and in turn shed light on it and explain it." Jesus said that he came to fulfill the law, to fill it full, to bring it to a climax, and to its deepest meaning and intention.

Jews reject the New Testament as Scripture since they do not believe Jesus was the Messiah, the Son of God who rose from the dead. For many Jews, Jesus was simply a prophet. Jews have a writing that is based upon the Torah but in a sense also reinterprets much of the Old Testament and adds to it. Talmud is the name they give to those writings. Islam accepts some of the Old Testament and New Testament, but only what the Qur'an accepts from both books. The Qur'an basically reinterprets those books for Muslims, and it also adds to it. This writer has discussed those things in detail in his previous book: *Reading and Understanding the Old Testament: The Foundation of Judaism, Christianity, and Islam.*

The writer's methodology is from the perspective of Catholicism and main line Protestantism, and those who call themselves moderate Evangelical, but it is not from the perspective of the Fundamentalist churches, or even the approach that some of the more conservative Evangelical churches use. The difference centers on methods of approaching the Bible and interpreting it. This writer does believe the Bible to be inspired of God, and he does take the Bible seriously but not always literally as defined by Fundamentalists and some conservative Evangelicals. Literal does not mean any of the following: "The Bible says what it means and means what it says," or "The Bible says it. I believe it. That settles it," or "Where the Bible speaks; we speak and where the Bible is silent we are silent," all of them meaning that there is nothing to interpret, or that it is not proper for a church to believe or do anything that can not be located in the Bible. This limits a church from applying and adapting the Bible to different places and different times.

All writing and all historical writings are interpreted writings. Even as translators change the original writings of Hebrew, Aramaic, and Greek Scripture to English, interpretations are often necessary. Another thing to note is that most writers when they discuss Jesus emphasize what his death should mean to his people. This writer will include that but will emphasize what his life should mean to his people. This will be understood better as one reads through this book.

Literal means the author's original sense, or as John Calvin said, the plain sense, as an attempt to understand the underlying meaning of what the biblical writers intended. The next step is applying it in today's world in order to better understand and serve God. This includes understanding the history, the different metaphors and literary forms the writers used to express their intention and purpose, and the theology of the writer. Consequently, the New Testament is seen as a living book not a dead historical document. It has as its purpose to tell the truth about God and the truth about ourselves with respect to our relationship with God, ourselves, others that God created, and his created order.

As we read the New Testament we must also keep in mind that the ancient writers did not write history as we moderns write it. Therefore to understand the ancient writers, we must understand their two thousand year old methodology and not try to force our modern day methodologies, ideologies, culture, and historiography onto their writings. In approaching the New Testament it is important to understand that the writings are more concerned with why things happened not how things happened; whereas we moderns are more concerned with the exact details of what or how things happened and chronology. The Bible is not designed to be an exact history or science book as moderns understand history and science, even though there is plenty of basic history in it. Exact historical and scientific facts, based on our modern day method of analysis and thinking, was not the way of thinking, methodology, or purpose of the ancient writers.

Even though many people could read and write, those early writers basically lived in an oral society where a narrative and story telling approach was the norm for expressing themselves to the masses. Through the narratives one learns their world view or story, and in order to understand Scripture, one must understand that form of approach. A narrative style was easier to remember and pass on. Villages would recite and pass on the information to others who would preserve the thrust of the story, and then adapt some of the smaller details to their particular need in order to make it more meaningful. Often drama and play acting were ways to pass on the main message in a way that is easier to remember. This can be seen in a structural study and comparison of the presentation by the four different Gospels of the parables, trial, crucifixion, resurrection and in the infancy accounts of Jesus.

The ancient writers were more symbolic and pictorial than we moderns. They were simply responding by faith to God working in their every day lives, and then expressing it in a manner appropriate with their culture. We are more concerned with the now, the present, the details of what happened, the chronology of something, and the immediate cause and effect. They were more concerned with underlying meanings, character formation and ultimate purposes. The biblical writers wrote to preserve the teachings and actions of Jesus. Their writings are how they remember it. They are faith documents based in an historical context to show that God is working his plan in history.

To express their faith the gospel writers use many different literary forms. They use historical narratives or historical stories, real history, poetry, hymns, parables, prophetic sayings, genealogies, eschatology, apocalyptic, religious myths, legends and much more. All of these literary forms are used by the different writers to pass on God's inspired truths, his theological truths, and his spiritual direction.

We must always keep in mind that the Bible is not a book to tell us everything we would like to know but to give us what we need to know. It is important to emphasize that the Bible is primarily a book of faith, a type of catechism, a book of theological and religious truths embedded in the context of the lives of real historical people. Therefore the Christian should look for the essential religious truths, the theological and moral themes, the ideas behind character development, the virtues and values God approves, and vices not approved, and God's overall vision, rather than a detailed chronology, exact historical description of events, exact rules to follow, and personal ideologies or moralisms. There are many issues that have developed in today's world that the Bible does not give exact answers to, but it does give us a way to help us begin to think through issues and find answers. The promise is that the Spirit will lead the church.

We will also see that many of the Bible's teachings will adapt and develop, then later be fulfilled and reinterpreted through Christ. In order to understand these fulfilled teachings as well as to apply them to our lives today, we need to see and understand their development. We need to see how they fit into history, and how they fit with the world view of God's chosen people.

It is also important to understand that the Gospels were written after the Apostle Paul's writings. He wrote in the AD fifties and sixties. The first New Testament book was written by Paul in AD 51. It was 1 Thessalonians. Most of Paul's writings are letters to churches dealing with local, situational happenings, even though there are many things in those letters that apply to believers of all ages. Many of the issues Paul wrote about are not even mentioned by the gospel writers. Possibly they were no longer issues, or it may also be that the Gospels were written to give a more complete and deeper understanding of Christ and his teachings.

As the reader goes through the books and chapters of the Gospels the exact verses that contain the information discussed will be used. This is done with the hope that the reader will get a sense of the Scriptures themselves, and at times open the Bible, turn to the chapter, and read the account, or at least some of the account in more detail and even meditate and reflect upon it.

There is no better way to learn about the Bible and be confronted by God's word than by actually reading it. Even though the purpose is to acquaint the novice reader with the Bible's content, this writer's goal is also to have readers eventually get into the books and read them for themselves. Most important this book will be ideal for group Bible study, and the books do not need to be read and studied in order.

This writer will have an introduction to each of the Gospels that gives the essence of each book. Therefore in addition to reading through the book there are other options. The introductions to all the books can be read first in order to get a sense of what each gospel book is about. Then, one can go back to a more in depth reading of the books to learn about their details. Finally, one can then go to the Bible itself and read it in an in depth manner. None of this needs to be done all at once, but accomplished at one's level of readiness, as one builds upon portions of knowledge gained. This book can also be used as a reference guide.

Reading and Understanding the Gospels: Who Jesus Is, What He Teaches, and the Beginning of Christianity is also designed to enable the instructor of Scripture, or the leader of Bible study, or the adult or young adult church school teacher, to take all of the students through a gospel while the students follow using different translations of the Bible. In that way the student gets more familiar with the transmission of the biblical text. This text book then becomes a secondary resource while the Bible is the primary resource. The instructor and the students can also use this book together as the instructor takes the students through its different parts.

Depending on the level of the students, the instructor may want to use the text as a reading assignment to discuss during class time. This writer has used all of these methods at many different levels, including adult church studies, as well as at the college and university level where he taught over a thirty year period. The way this book is structured is basically the way this writer taught Biblical Studies courses, always insisting the students be exposed to the actual verses of Scripture. This writer is convinced that there is a basic lack of understanding of Scripture because too many have no experience in using a Bible, never really reading the Scripture verses in context. They may have read books about the Gospels, and heard sermons on different ideas, themes, and Scriptures, but never experienced the Gospels for themselves. This writer is convinced that it is important for learners to open the Gospels and read them first hand, which is why this book is structured as it is.

Also, it must be stated that where this writer learned much of his information over the years is no longer remembered. Much of it is taken from professors in different courses as well as personal readings. The bibliography is an attempt to give credit to the information gleaned from personal study. Over the years many of the things learned were written into different Bibles and included within notes used in teaching.

These notes, accumulated over the years, usually do not cite the exact resources from which they came. This writer does not take much credit for original thinking about the text, other than the way this text is put together and apologizes when something in this text is taken from someone else, and could not remember where it came from. Hopefully, at the least, it is included in the bibliography.

A special appreciation is for the writings of Allen Verhey, NT Wright, James DG Dunn, Jim Wallis, Luke Timothy Johnson, and Marcus Borg, and the many thought provoking Protestant and Roman Catholic biblical scholars this author has read. In some places within the text, rather than long, numerous footnotes and endnotes, parentheses will be used to refer to the author listed in the bibliography of sources. This is done in order to produce easier reading for beginning students not yet ready to examine long footnotes.

On the other hand, most of the modern day applications of these verses are the thinking of this author. It is how the author applies Scriptures to the times in which we live. It is not expected that everyone will agree, but they are the thoughts and opinions of the author used to help the reader to begin to think about modern day applications. It will make for good classroom discussion as to why students agree or disagree with the author's comments on the Scriptures, but when they disagree, it is important to keep the discussion based upon Scripture. The author encourages this form of learning experience.

It would be nice to be able to write an objective account without any bias or presuppositions, but pure objectivity by anyone is not possible. Even so, this writer has attempted to read the Scriptures inductively, and as objectively as possible, apply them to our modern era. The goal was to go only where the biblical verses would lead attempting to view things today as Christ would. It is the author's hope that the reader will do the same, and when there is disagreement, let the discussion stay with reasoning based upon Scripture.

The author believes the Scriptures are still alive and will illuminate its readers in modern times. Group study is highly encouraged. This is so that one can bounce thoughts and ideas off others and have direction from church leaders, especially those who can lead students to think more deeply about the different verses and relate them to the vast storehouse of thinking contained in the church's long history.

In this work when this writer gives the Scripture or the sense of Scripture, the *New Revised Standard Version* is used. This version is acceptable to Roman Catholics, the Orthodox, and numerous Protestant groups, especially the mainline Protestant Church. Other than the biblical text, capitalization and spelling used in this writer's comments are from the *Society of Biblical Literature (SBL) Handbook of Style for Ancient Near Eastern, Biblical, and Early Christian Studies.*

As one reads it will be noticeable that the different Bible translations use their own system of capitalization, punctuation, and style that is sometimes very different from both the SBL Handbook and contemporary style. One example is the capitalization of (Sabbath) which the SBL Handbook uses a capital S, but the New Revised Standard Version does not capitalize (sabbath). The same is with the word Scripture, which is capitalized in the SBL Handbook but not so in the NRSV (scripture).

Because much of what is written is basically to highlight what the Bible says, there will not be quotation marks when the Gospels are quoted. This may be somewhat rare, but according to the *Chicago Manual of Style* (14th Edition) under alternatives to quotation marks it is acceptable. The reader will be able to tell most of the time what is from Scripture. Often what is quoted follows the word, say or said. The chapter and verses will always be noted in order for the reader to examine. Many times the reader will see a parenthesis ( ) with a number inside which will indicate the verse or verses referenced. This approach is taken in the belief that constantly looking at pages filled with quotation marks is too cumbersome for the reader as well as the writer. But where quotation marks are used in Scripture, they will be used in this book.

Dr Thomas B. Lane

MORE INTERPRETATION ISSUES

The New Testament is probably the most revered book in the modern world, but like the Old Testament its real content is basically unknown and little understood by the masses of people. This may be considered an affront by people who have heard sermons most of their lives, but listening to sermons does not necessarily mean one is now educated in the Bible. It may mean one is educated only in certain parts or certain verses of the Bible. Or it may mean one is educated in a certain clergyperson's theology and understanding of certain verses. It is apparent that most people are not familiar with the Gospels. Numerous recent studies show only forty-five percent of the people could even name the four Gospels.

The New Testament is a collection of twenty-seven books written by different authors over a period of about fifty years. The Old Testament covers a time period of approximately fifteen hundred to two thousand years. The New Testament covers about one hundred years, the first century AD. This is the time the Roman Empire controlled the area known as the Holy Land as well as most of the known world. The Old Testament focuses on the nation of Israel while the New Testament focuses on a person belonging to that nation, Jesus the Christ, a Jew, who established a church to which all nations are called. Christ is a Greek word meaning Anointed, while the Hebrew word for Anointed is Messiah. His first name is Jesus, but his last name is not really Christ, even though some write as though it is. He is Jesus the Christ. The first Christians who were Jews believed he was the Christ, the Anointed, the Messiah.

The word testament means covenant or law. So new and old covenants have to do with agreements God has made with his people. The old covenant was basically for one nation, and according to Jews there is still only one covenant. They are still looking for the Messiah and the new covenant. But according to Christians, Jesus, the Messiah, initiated the new covenant and a new age called the kingdom of God, and this new covenant for the kingdom is for all the nations in the world. Although there are different interpretations of Scripture, those serious Christian scholars of the different denominations, who are educated in Scripture, are in general agreement on a sizeable majority of the basic content and meaning.

There was a need for a new covenant for a number of reasons, one was that the teachings and prophecy in the first needed to be fulfilled or brought to completion. Another reason is that the Jews failed in their mission to bring God and his message to all the peoples of the world. In fact they had developed a way of thinking that kept the people of the nations from being part of God's people. The people of Judea were actually separating themselves from the world to the point that the people and the nation had become completely isolated from the world.

God had called his people to be a light shining in the darkness, a city set upon the hill, but his people rejected God's mission. Their attitude of pride and envy was expressed in the prophet Jonah, who did not want to take God's message to other nations. God's people were called to inform the world of who God was, and what his message was, and to be a moral example to the people of the world.

They were not to become like the pagans but a beacon of light to them. The new covenant for people of all nations was prophesied in the Old Testament, especially through Jeremiah (31:31-34) and Ezekiel (36:22-29, 37:24-28). The gospel writers inform us that through Jesus the new covenant and the new age are beginning.

The first four books of the New Testament, Matthew, Mark, Luke, and John are called the Gospels. Gospel is a word meaning good news. The good news is that God's kingdom is now breaking into the world through Jesus. The good news is that Christ, the Messiah, the expected Davidic king has come (Ezekiel 37:24-28). Jews from the second temple onward, from the time of Daniel, Ezra and Nehemiah, all post-exilic writings, believed as long as they were dominated by a foreign power, they were still in exile, and the sins of the nation had not been forgiven (Daniel 9, Ezra 9, and Nehemiah 9). This was true even though they were living in their land; it is more like a spiritual exile.

The good news is that the old is passing away, a new age has begun, the new kingdom is breaking into the world, just as the prophets foretold. The nation's sins are forgiven, the exile is over, and God has returned to his people. The problem is that none of it happens in the manner they thought it would. After the death of Jesus, the disciples will understand what he was saying when he was with them, and they will announce the kingdom, preaching Jesus as the king of the kingdom. The church then takes the place of the nation of Israel as the new Israel of God. Christ through the Spirit will then be the new Torah and new temple where God's presence lives, and where sins are forgiven. From Jerusalem the message of good news will be proclaimed throughout the world.

It is important to note that this kingdom begins with Jesus. Its official beginning seems to be confirmed in two parts with the fulfillment of two of his prophecies. After the death and resurrection of Jesus, he goes to the right hand of the Father and sends the Holy Spirit to his disciples as he said he would. This happens on the day of Pentecost when Peter preaches the first sermon and three thousand are baptized. On this day the Spirit is deposited within the church (Acts chapter 2). Then in AD 70 his second major prophecy is fulfilled when Rome destroys Jerusalem and the temple with its sacrificial system. This opens the way for the rapid advancement of Christianity. The Jews will have to reorganize, and the Judaism that develops will be mainly through the activity of the Pharisees and the development of a religion without the temple.

Jesus had warned the people to change their violent agenda toward Rome, or they would be destroyed. With the fall of the great city and the temple Jesus' prophecy is confirmed and he is vindicated. It will take Judaism a long time to recover. In the meantime the Jewish Christians and Jewish King Jesus will invite Gentiles into the new kingdom, and the movement will greatly expand. The Father will now attempt to rule the world through his Son and the kingdom he establishes. As we will see Jesus tells his followers that he came to preach the kingdom.

Colossians 1:13-14 says, He (God) has rescued us from the power of darkness and transferred us into the kingdom of his beloved Son, in whom we have redemption, the forgiveness of sins. This new beginning and hope for a sinful world that involves transformation and renewal of both individuals and the world in which they live, just as the prophets described, will be completed when Christ returns and all things are made new. This is good news and it all centers around Jesus, his life, death, resurrection, and the kingdom he came to preach. It must be noted that the kingdom is not just about eternal life in the future; it is about abundant life now. It is about the beginning of renewal of individuals and the world and its institutions now. It is about God's plan being put into operation until Christ comes again to complete the plan, making all things new.

These first four books of the New Testament, Matthew, Mark, Luke, and John, are called the Gospels. Even though each has its own emphasis, they are four complementary accounts of the life and teachings of Jesus. The book of Acts follows which is a brief history of the beginning, development, and advancement of the early church. Acts is followed by letters to the newly established churches from Paul, Peter, James and John, usually dealing with situational problems, but in the process there is much to learn about the new faith and its application throughout time. That will be the topic of the volume that follows this one.

All four Gospels are faith accounts and remembrances of what Jesus said and did. They are not intended to be exact detailed history or scientific biographies as people today define scientific, history, or biography, but they are biographies and history as defined by the ancient world. Matthew, Mark, and Luke have a different theological emphasis, even though they are united in telling the same basic story. Different theologies are a positive thing, for different people in different situations apply teachings in different ways. The unity in the New Testament is in diversity not conformity, but there is unity in the basics. Their similarities are as important as their differences. This will be explained later.

Ninety percent of Mark's 661 verses are in Matthew; fifty percent are also in Luke. But less than ten percent of the Synoptics is in John. Most scholars believe that Matthew and Luke used Mark's gospel as their outline. Matthew and Luke share about two hundred additional verses in common, which suggests they had a collection of Jesus' sayings that scholars call the "Q" source. The "Q" source has never been found.

Matthew and Luke also have their own source or sources called (M) and (L). Some of these may be written, but probably most were oral sources that had been handed down through the different communities. None of these sources has ever been found. Most of what has been stated concerning the oral and written sources and how the Gospels were formed are simply reasonable, educated guesses (*speculative theology*) developed by scholars analyzing the Gospels. None of the speculation really has a great effect on the basic story and Christ's teachings.

Matthew, Mark, and Luke are called Synoptic Gospels because they are similar. In one sense they describe Jesus from the point of view leading up to the crucifixion and resurrection, emphasizing a view of Jesus from his human side. Scholars call this a Christology from below. John's gospel views Jesus from his divine side emphasizing his divinity from a more theological and mystically oriented position. John looks at Jesus more from this side of the crucifixion and resurrection. Scholars call this a Christology from above. Both sides are true yet different. This explains to some extent the meaning of different theologies.

Before the Gospels were written, the teachings and actions of Jesus circulated orally and in writing for probably thirty-five plus years. It seems to be that there were many more oral sources than written sources. Then bits and pieces began to be put into writing. How the written sources originated and come together to form the written Gospels is called *source criticism*. How the oral forms originated and come together is called *form criticism*. Criticism is just another word for analysis. The four evangelists collected the oral and written pieces and combined them into their Gospels. *Tradition criticism* attempts to trace how the different forms developed until finally written. *Textual criticism* is making sure we have the best Greek text available for the complete New Testament.

Rhetorical criticism and *literary criticism* seek to analyze the different literary forms the writers used in putting their writing together. It seeks to understand the different literary forms and their purpose as well as who wrote them, to whom, why, when and how. This leads to *canonical criticism*, which analyzes how it all fits together into a unity and the whole of Scripture. Then scholars seek to discover how much of the book is written by a single author, and how much of the book is edited, and what the particular emphasis is of the author or editors. Each of the four Gospels has its own point of view (theology) adapted to the special groups to whom they were writing. The study of how the authors or editors used what they had and for what purpose is called *redaction criticism*.

It is also important to note that none of the Gospels tell us who the writer is. It was later that the early Christians added the names Matthew, Mark, Luke, and John to the writings. Another important point is that the chapters and verses were not added until the Middles Ages. In fact everything was in capital letters, and there was no punctuation, which makes adding the chapters, verses, and punctuation a human effort that involves not only translation from Greek to English but also interpretation. A quick example explains. The text would be as follows. The Hebrew or Greek text is written by putting all the letters together without punctuation such as GODISNOWHERE. Is that to be translated God is now here, or God is nowhere?

For the most part the Bible is basically a narrative, a story supporting a particular world view through the use of history, literature, and theology. The world view is God's written through humans living in a particular culture. Understanding the history, literature, and theology are also interpretation issues. All history, and all literature, and all theology are interpretive issues, which is why it is important to study the Bible with a learned believer associated with a church community.

Unfortunately, it is true that many university professors are not people of faith and consequently do not believe the Scriptures are God inspired. Most of them are historians trained only in the methods of modern scientific history. In their study of the Bible, most are only concerned with research in a very narrow area and are not really interested in how things fit together for inspired, theological purposes. This is usually what students study in the university. When lay people see on television information concerning the Bible, these are the people and their opinions they are most likely to hear. If anyone is interested, the bibliography includes numerous sources that explore in detail these different issues, criticisms, and translation issues. The issues are also easily googled on the internet. Their emphasis is not all bad, for it does serve a very important historical purpose, but it usually has little benefit for the average person who takes his religion and spiritual development seriously.

Christians believe the New Testament Scriptures are inspired by the Holy Spirit as the word of God, but they do not always agree on what inspiration exactly means. Even so, these Scriptures are written in the Greek language by humans using their own personal style. They are not magical books dropped from heaven written in sixteenth century King James English as some Fundamentalists seem to convey. As we explore these different forms of analysis in a practical way the reader will understand better the New Testament Gospels. Understanding the different Christian approaches to the inspiration and infallibility of Scripture is thoroughly explored in a book by Gabe Fackre, *The Christian Story: Authority of Scripture in the Church for the World.*

As we begin to read the New Testament, the serious reader will see what appear to be numerous differences and what are called apparent contradictions. Many of these, center on small details in describing incidents such as the accounts of Jesus birth, his crucifixion and resurrection, and some parables. In attempting to explain these differences, we will understand that ancient writers in an oral society did not write history as we moderns do. In looking at these differences, we will also notice how humans see things from different perspectives, and how this has its positive aspects. It is also important to understand that writings of Scripture labeled both human and divine do not always fit into rational analysis. Jesus and the Bible are considered both divine and human. We humans have difficulty dealing with that concept.

The perfect God inspired a message through imperfect people, and in the process allowed them freedom to express God's inspired message through their imperfections. But God preserves the world view and theology that remains infallible. It is also true that at the same time God is near us, he is also beyond us. Here we have two opposite ideas integrated. This is a mystery. Unfortunately, because of the Age of Enlightenment, scientific rationalism is the main methodology that many university scholars are concerned with, which eliminates the mystical, the theological, and the miraculous. This thinking also contributes to interpretation problems.

It may sound like this author opposes the work of university scholars in their historical and scientific methods, but that is not true. They serve a very important purpose. It is important to verify as much history as possible in order to show that faith is based in reality, but scientific history has a difficult time dealing with mystery, the miraculous, and the theological. Also, one must realize the purpose of many university professors is not to promote faith, even though some may have faith.

This writer's point is that in these times there are many factors to be taken into consideration in order to understand better and make sense of the Scriptures. We must deal with the fact that God is also mystery, and the writers of the Scriptures used different forms of literature to express their teachings and theology. Because of these numerous factors, anyone interested in learning the Scriptures from a holistic and in-depth perspective needs to study in a group with a leader who is informed in more than one aspect of the interpretation issues and one who takes the Scriptures seriously.

Along with this thinking is the theological diversity in the Bible. The New Testament documents not only express a variety of New Testament themes, but sometimes they speak in different ways on the same theme. As we will see sometimes a statement is true in one situation but not so in another. Understanding how different verses function in different contexts is important. It is like the root of a tomato plant that produces a number of different tomatoes; they all come from the same root, but are not always the same, even though they are still tomatoes. Context of a particular theme or verse in its different situations is the key to understanding, and is why it is dangerous to take anything out of context to prove a point. That is why it is very important to have a learned teacher in a church community as an instructor or group leader.

Stanley Hauerwas (1993,15-18) believes that when individual American Christians read and interpret the Bible without instruction from a qualified instructor apart from the church, manipulation and distortion will be the norm and not the exception. It is easy for the Bible to become a vehicle for a person's presuppositions, religion, ideology, politics, social, or cultural concerns that are quite different from the religion, politics, economics, social, and cultural concerns expressed within the Scriptures.

What happens in America is that many readers read their culture of a democratic republic, capitalism, and other interests into the Scriptures that say nothing about those issues. When that happens, the Scriptures become distorted, and then they are used for one's current ideology. In interpreting Scripture context is of utmost importance, and then from context one applies its implications for today. It is important to note that Jesus lived under a brutal dictatorship in a culture of slavery, yet said nothing about those two issues, even as he had much to say about certain economic and social issues.

As stated it is fact the there is much diversity in Scripture. George Forell in his book titled *The Protestant Faith* (1989, 57-61) explains that some of the diversity is best explained or understood by a concept borrowed from physics known as the principle of complementarity. Briefly stated, it means that the various ideas or pictures used to describe systems of atoms are adequate to certain experiments, yet mutually exclusive. For example, an atom can be described as a planetary system or as a nucleus surrounded by waves, whose frequency is decisive. These different pictures are complementary to each other. While they seem to contradict each other, they are both correct if used properly. Similarly, in theology we often get at the truth by saying two things simultaneously that on the surface seem to be contradictory, but the difference helps us to get a deeper insight into the Christian message.

In a book titled *God was in Christ* by DM Baillie (1948, 109-110) sums up the idea perfectly. Baillie says, The attempt to put our experience of God into theological statements is something like the attempt to draw a map of the world on a flat surface, the page of an atlas. It is impossible to do this without a certain degree of falsification, because the surface of the earth is a spherical surface whose pattern can not be produced accurately on a plane. And yet the map must be drawn for convenience's sake. Therefore an atlas meets the problem by giving us two different maps of the world which can be compared to each other. The one is contained in two circles representing two hemispheres. The other is contained in an oblong, Mercator projection. Each is a map of the whole world, and they contradict each other to some extent in every point. Yet they both are needed, and taken together they correct each other.

The different projections would be either misleading or mystifying to anyone who did not know that in their different ways they represent the surface of a sphere. But they can serve their useful purpose for anyone who understands that they are intended simply to represent in handy portable form the pattern covering the surface of this round earth which one knows in actual experience. The point is to illustrate that the Bible is somewhat limited in what it says because it is written in human words. That does not mean we can not understand it, but it does mean that we have to use words in different ways in different situations in order to try to understand the full truth that words can not really express.

So it is with the paradoxes of faith which often involve mystery. They are inevitable, not because the divine reality is self-contradictory, but because when we objectify it into an either-or analysis, all our judgments are in some measure falsified. The higher truth which reconciles them cannot always be fully expressed in words, though it is experienced and lived in the I-Thou relationship of faith towards God. Eliminating the mystery only falsifies and complicates the issue more.

The following are some biblical examples: The two creation accounts in Genesis where the emphasis in one is the transcendent God who is beyond all, while the emphasis in the other is the immanent God who is very near to us, even within us. Other examples are the Bible is human, the Bible is divine. God is love, God is wrath. God is just, God is merciful. One time it says, do not judge, but elsewhere it tells us there are times when judgments must be made. God has predestined, meaning God is sovereign and in complete control, yet humans have free will. Jesus is divine, Jesus is human. God is Father, God is Son, and God is the Holy Spirit. Salvation is by grace through faith and is a gift of God as stressed in John 3:16, Rom 3:19-26, and Gal 2:16, but salvation is by obedience and works as stressed in Mt 7:21, Mt 25:31-46, John 3:36, James 2:14-24, Luke 10:25-28, Rev 22:12. Christ came to save the world not to judge the world Jn 3:17-18, but Christ also came to judge the world Jn 12:48, Lk 19:11-28, Mk 8:38.

They seem to be contradictions, but they are not. It is not a matter of picking one and ignoring the other as some religious groups do. First of all, it is a matter of reading what is said in context. The four Gospels are an excellent example of how the principle of complementarity can function. Some see all this as contradictory, but only because they are not educated in the nature of Scripture and understanding the importance of context, how to interpret it, and they refuse to see Scripture as the inspired word of God. That does not mean everyone must see everything exactly the same, but there is much that can be agreed on, and even historically verified. The close reader will notice numerous differences as the Gospels are read. The challenge is how to make sense of these inspired differences.

In the previous comparisons we have a picture of opposites that historically have divided believers and non-believers, as well as dividing the different religious groups. One side is chosen as the truth while the opposite is ignored like it does not exist. The problem seems to be simplistic thinking while wanting to force God's truth or non-truth into preconceived notions or narrow boxes, as well as attempting to eliminate all mystery from Scripture. In our modern scientifically ordered society that tends to de-emphasize the humanities and the arts, we humans tend to attempt to fit everything into a rational logic that can be scientifically controlled.

The principle of complementarity says that there is truth in both ends of paired opposites. Both are needed to get the complete or total picture. They must be taken together in their different contexts, and they correct each other by integrating the opposite ends. The extreme ends that sometimes abuse the truth are defused, and one is able to get a deeper insight into the whole message. Often, a higher or deeper truth reconciles the paradox which sometimes is difficult to put into human words, but can be explained to some extent by thinking about the different map projections as noted. Ideas such as this are important in understanding the New Testament, especially the Gospels. In the end we are still dealing with the mystery of God.

By focusing on only one aspect, the total picture is missed. The different details expressed in the birth accounts, the trial and crucifixion accounts, and the resurrection accounts can be compared to an automobile accident where three people see it, but they all see it from a different angle or perspective. When they are called into court to explain what happened, their stories seem to conflict. Is one person telling the truth, and the other not telling the truth? Often times the answer is no, they simply saw the accident from different perspectives. Or even in telling the story they highlight different perspectives, because of their different contexts. It takes someone else looking at the total picture in the different contexts to put things together and make sense of the situation. Humans see things through different lens, but as they do, there are basic truths there, if they are open to learning from them.

When everything is put together for understanding, with the concept that these Scriptures are from a basic oral culture, a culture totally different from twenty-first century America, a culture that knew nothing about the individualism of a representative democratic republic or capitalism, and knew nothing or very little about a middle class, the main issues or major truths are more easily discovered. In understanding Scripture one can not view the culture of the ancients by forcing twenty-first century issues upon it, even though sometimes there is a match. When this principle is understood, many of the apparent contradictions and paradoxes begin to make sense and major themes are discovered. When this is not understood, Scripture is distorted.

Before we begin the Gospels, the writer wants to again encourage the reader to remember that ancient writers were not overly concerned with exact historical details and chronology as modern historians are. Ancient writers wrote to teach and bring forth faith and transformation, to preserve a message, and they wrote mainly to express meaning not detail. Modern historians write more to show detail and chronology. Therefore in reading the Gospels look more for the underlying message, the theology, the themes, the vision of God, the virtues and values to emulate and the vices to ignore.

In reading the Gospels it is important to remember, contrary to popular opinion, the Gospel of Matthew was not the first one written, and the four Gospels were not the first books written in the New Testament. This is reserved for the Apostle Paul's writings. Paul wrote in the AD fifties and sixties whereas the Gospel of Mark was written in approximately AD 70. Matthew and Luke wrote around AD 80-85 and John wrote in the AD 90s. Thirty five years passed before the first gospel was written, and approximately twenty years pass before Paul wrote his first letter. All of this is the majority opinion of most scholars. A small minority of scholars disagree with the order and the date of their writing.

During that period of time, what Jesus said and did was mainly being passed on orally in narrative form. Many scholars believe since the people living in the time of Jesus lived in an oral society where writing was not the norm, the accounts of Jesus' birth, his parables, and his trial, crucifixion, and resurrection were probably passed on from community to community in some form of play acting. When it was finally put in writing, God inspired the writers in what to include, allowing each one to express it in the way they thought necessary, while preserving the truths necessary for humankind.

This book is designed to enable the reader to read through the Gospels or use it in group Bible studies. The books may be read in any order without having to read from front to back. Each gospel will be approached as though it is the only one included in the book. Because of the nature of the Synoptics, there will necessarily be some repetition. That is a good thing for the beginning reader. It will also be advantageous in that when reading an incident also reported in another gospel, the reader will not have to constantly be referring back to one of the other three gospels. This writer will begin with Mark because it is the shortest and earliest written, and consequently, the one that the other writers had when they wrote.

Before we begin it is important to be aware of the political, economic, and social conditions of the land where Jesus lived. Most of the people were very poor, in deep poverty and debt. All the power and wealth was concentrated in a small minority. The people were subject to three major groups of rulers with their competing political, economic, and taxing policies.

The Romans had overall control, for they had conquered the land as well as most of the known world. Their puppet kings were the Herod family who had descended from Esau, the twin brother of Jacob. A couple of thousand years before Esau had sold his birthright to Jacob who then became the father of the Israelites. Also with power and control was the Sanhedrin, consisting of priests (Sadducees) and scribes (Pharisees) both in competition with each other. They are part of the old theocracy having the political, economic, and religious power. The Herods and the Sanhedrin were not only in competition for local power but also with each other for power and favors from the Romans, and of course, with more power comes more wealth. All three power groupings used their taxing powers to pay for their building projects to please and honor the emperor, supply bread (food) and circus (entertainment) activities for the people keeping them placated and indebted to them, as well as increasing their own power, wealth, and lavish living.

Rome permitted the Herods and the Sanhedrin to have much power over local affairs but always subject to Roman approval. All three groups had a system of patronage, a network of systems and people working for them and subject to them that had economically exhausted the people. In order for the common people to pay their debts in this agrarian society, the people began to lose their land which made them tenant farmers or put them on the streets in the cities. This resulted in great poverty, hunger, and disease. Consequently, numerous and popular uprisings began to break out against these oppressive practices. It is within this environment that John the Baptizer appeared in the wilderness in Mark chapter one.

THE GOSPEL OF MARK

We begin with the book of Mark. The majority of scholars believe Mark is the first gospel written, even though Matthew is the first one listed in the New Testament. Mark is written at least thirty-five years after the death and resurrection of Christ. Many people are surprised by that, but in those times most people could not read and write. It is only after many of the apostles and eyewitnesses begin to die that a few of them realize that something needs to be written about this Jesus called the Christ.

The majority of scholars believe this gospel is written in approximately 70 AD; Matthew and Luke are written around 80-85 AD, and John is probably written in the AD 90s. A small minority of scholars disagree with the order and the date of their writing. Mark gives the basic structure of what Jesus does and teaches, and he puts an emphasis on making his audience think through the question of who they believe Jesus really is. Like the other gospels, we really do not know who the author is. The name of the author is not listed in the gospel. The name Mark is added some years after it was written.

Papias, a bishop who lived about sixty years after the book was written, wrote that Mark was Peter's interpreter. This possibly makes the book the Gospel of Peter written by Mark. The way it is written does seem to represent Peter's impetuous personality. It is thought Mark wrote it while he was in Rome. The Greek is very basic like it is written by someone whose Greek is a second language

Before we go through each gospel chapter by chapter, an introduction to each book is given highlighting the book's major characteristics. So let us begin with the basic characteristics of the Gospel of Mark.

*Many think it is Peter's gospel but Mark is the writer for him. Mark is probably John Mark, a cousin of Barnabas (see Acts 12:12, 15:37). He writes stressing the actions of Jesus, but gives many of the teachings of Jesus. It is the shortest gospel, and the thinking is that it is written to the Romans who are more action oriented than they are culturally oriented.

*It could have been written during the persecutions of Nero, the Roman emperor, because suffering is a huge theme. It is said that at one time Rome was lit up at night by the martyrs burning on stakes as a result of Nero's persecution of Christians. If this is true, then the date for the writing could be AD 64-68. Throughout the writing emotions such as fear, anger, amazement, and stunned are expressed. Mark warns continually that a serious Christian must be willing to accept suffering, even death by standing with and for Jesus and what he teaches.

*Mark records the miracles and actions of Jesus. These are mainly to exhibit that the kingdom of God has now broken in upon the kingdoms of the world. The Father sends his Son, the Anointed One, the Messiah, to be the King of the kingdom, which is to challenge the virtues, values, and visions of the

world's kingdoms. God's created world has many dimensions, which includes the material and spiritual. A miracle can be defined as anything not having a reasonable explanation in the visible world. In a sense it is an extraordinary event that goes beyond ordinary experience, but in reality it is God working in and through another dimension of the world he created. Done through Jesus and the Spirit, miracles demonstrate God's power over evil and teach that the kingdom of God is breaking into the world through his Son. Romans 14:17 will define the kingdom as a time of righteousness (justice) and peace and joy in the Holy Spirit. Horsley (2003, 75) says that the kingdom of God is the dominant theme in Mark.

*The words "immediately," "at once," or "then" are used eight times in the first chapter and about forty times in Mark's book. The whole book moves with precision and action which is how the Romans fight their wars, and construct the roads in their empire. Get to the point and get it done is their motto. They are a very practical and goal oriented people.

*In the four Gospels the word "gospel" (good news) appears twelve times while eight of the twelve are in Mark's gospel. The good news is that the kingdom has come. Christ has come. Christ has risen. Christ will come again. The good news is that sins are forgiven. The Jews at the time of Jesus would first understand the forgiveness of sins in the context of the nation. Jews believed the nation was punished and sent into exile in 722 BC, and then in 586 BC because of the sins of the nation. Now they believe they are occupied by the Romans for the same reason. They wait for the time God will forgive the nation again, return control of their land to them, and get rid of the hated

Romans. This is what the gospel or good news means to most Jews at the time of Jesus. Most of the people did not understand it as personal forgiveness of sins, for they received that with the sacrifices at the temple through their priests.

*Jesus is portrayed as the *eschatological* fulfillment of *apocalyptic* literature. He is the Son of Man coming in an everlasting kingdom described in Daniel 7:13-14. The Messiah has come. The last age has begun. The eschatological (end time) eternal kingdom has broken into the earth and will grow like a mustard seed. The final kingdom of God (reign of God) has begun, and its consummation or completion will be when he comes at the end of time. This is good news (gospel). Now we live between the times, the beginning of the end and the end of what has begun. By grace we know God's forgiveness, but it is not yet perfected and finalized. Already victory over Satan and death is ours; yet we will still die. Already we live in the Spirit; yet we still live in a world where Satan attacks. Already we are justified and sanctified and not condemned; yet we face a final judgment, a final justification and final sanctification based upon one's ongoing relationship with Jesus and God's grace.

*We are God's people called to live in his good future and final kingdom that has begun now. We do this by making him and his love, compassion, mercy, justice, and peace, present to all. God's people are now his presence in the world. They are called to continue the work and mission of Jesus by allowing him, through the power of the Holy Spirit, to live his life in them and through them as they wait for him to return and set up the final eternal kingdom. The Father now rules the world through his Son and those who truly represent the Son.

*The kingdom is not wealth or power, and it is not the prosperity gospel for this world. The kingdom is not about political domination and economic exploitation by the elite who expect to be served by the masses or by the church that would like to force its beliefs on everyone. The church is to stay out of power politics, but it must challenge power politics to represent those who Christ chose to represent. The kingdom of God is a counter-culture seeking not only individual transformation but the transformation of the world's structures, including its political, economic, and social structures, to the virtues, values, and vision of God. It is not a political system, but it still involves things that are political. The kingdom is about serving the masses, the common people, and standing with those who have no power and wealth just as Israel and Judah were supposed to do in the Old Testament but failed to do. Therefore, the kingdom is about renewal of both individuals and the world. Mark stresses Jesus as a prophet of the kingdom of God, and that the kingdom is about both judgment and renewal now and at the end time.

*The kingdom calls all people including the elites to humble themselves and follow him. The kingdom of God is about sacrifice and service for the well being of others and suffering for the vision and values of God. Jesus came preaching the kingdom, and Rom 14:17-19 says, the kingdom of God is not food and drink but righteousness (justice) and peace and joy in the Holy Spirit. The one who thus serves Christ is acceptable to God and has human approval. Let us then pursue what makes for peace and for mutual up-building. The kingdom is to be the light that worldly kingdoms are to follow. A system of politics and economics is not described, but the kingdom has much to say about politics and economics and serving the common good of all. God is Lord of all life both individual and public. He never separates himself from concern for the daily life people live.

*Mark emphasizes that no one understands Jesus, even his disciples, until after the crucifixion and resurrection, simply because his concept of the kingdom and theirs are not the same. Therefore things are to be kept secret (the Messianic Secret) until after the resurrection, and then his disciples will understand. Now, they will just follow by faith and learn from him. Jesus will do miracles, and then tell people not to tell anyone because, at this point, they will not understand the real purpose of the miracles. Too many will only come to him just to be healed, and then the real purpose of his coming, which is to teach a small group and plant seeds of the kingdom in the towns, will be hindered.

*Mark makes it plain that one can not really understand Jesus until they realize that being chosen by God means that they are chosen to suffer. They are chosen to suffer as they stand for his virtues, values, and his vision of the kingdom in a broken world that has eyes but will not see and ears that do not want to hear. Jesus will be put to death by the authorities who control the power and wealth because his concept of the kingdom is a threat to their values and the way they organize and control their nation. He told people if they do not eliminate their agenda of violence against the Romans that Rome will destroy Jerusalem and their temple. As Jesus suffers for these ideas, so will his real disciples. Only when one sees the world from his eyes and begins to think as he thinks will they understand and become his serious disciples. Later we will see that Jesus will die for both historical and theological reasons.

*One of the first things to notice is that there is no account of the nativity or birth of Jesus. What matters most to the action oriented Romans is what you are doing with your life now, and who you are now. Therefore Mark immediately gets into the meaning and purpose of his message.

Mark begins chapter 1:1 saying, The beginning of the good news (gospel) of Jesus Christ, the Son of God. (There is no doubt who Mark believes Jesus to be. He uses the Christ, Messiah, and Son of God interchangeably.) Verses 2-4 say, As it is written in the prophet Isaiah (40:3), "See I am sending my messenger ahead of you, who will prepare your way; the voice of one crying out in the wilderness: 'Prepare the way of the Lord, make his paths straight.' " John the baptizer appeared in the wilderness, proclaiming a baptism of repentance for the forgiveness of sin. (Dunn (2003, 360) says it was a baptism that brings to expression the repentance seeking the forgiveness of sin. This will not be finalized until the cross, see Mt 26:28, Mk 14:24, Heb 9:22.)

This John is not the writer of the Gospel of John; they are two different people. John is not claiming that his baptism forgives sin; it is to prepare a people for the one to come, who will initiate the new age, the new covenant in his blood, and in the process forgive the sin of the nation and then individuals. There are many at the time who think the one to come will be the Messiah or even God himself (Ezek 34:15-16, Zeph 3:16-17, Pss 2:6-9, 110:1-7, Isa 40:10-11). They are expecting that the one to come will restore Israel (Lk 24:21). This means the nation will be forgiven, redeemed, set free from exile, and set free from the Romans. It is a time when the Father will become the king of the world through his Messiah. John is just preparing a people for the one to come.

The coming of John is from Isaiah chapter 40. The reader is encouraged to read that chapter before reading on. The way of the Lord in context is the way that leads the nation out of exile and the execution of God's plan. Many Jews believe that as long as the nation is controlled by a foreign power, and as long as the people are not living as God commands both as individuals and as a nation, God is punishing them with a religious exile, and the Messiah will not come (Neh 9:36). Thus one reason for Mark's gospel is to show the way that leads the nation out of exile, even though Israel is in their own land, so they can become the true people of God and complete the mission God gave them. In reference to exile see Wright (1999, 268-279).

The people of the time are looking for the Messiah or even God himself to come and set them free. The way of return from exile is the way of Jesus and the kingdom he came to preach. At the cross Jesus takes the exile and all sin upon himself, and through the resurrection a new Exodus is established. The cross and resurrection will mean more than this, but it means this also.

The call from God is a call of repentance. The first call to repent is to the nation to begin the journey of return to God by entering the kingdom of God. It is about a new way of being Israel, as well as a new way of being for individuals. Mark claims that Jesus is the new Israel bringing God's kingdom to birth. The Jews following Christ are the remnant being called out from the old Israel to make up the new Israel of God. God is calling a people to complete the mission he gave his people long ago. The people of the old covenant had been called to be a beacon of light to all nations, but they ignored this call. In fact they made it very difficult for Gentiles to hear the message and call of God.

Verses 5-6 inform us that people from all over Judea came to be baptized in the river Jordan as they confessed their sins. (Baptize is a

Greek word that means immersion.) John was clothed with camel's hair, a leather belt around his waist, and he ate locusts and wild honey. (John comes in the tradition of Elijah the prophet and all the prophets of old, calling the nation and its leaders to repentance as he calls individuals to become God's remnant.)

Mark records that John the Baptist is the one foretold by the prophet Malachi. In Mark 9:9-13 Jesus tells his disciples that John is Elijah to come. John fulfills the prophecy of Malachi 3:1 that says, I am sending my messenger to prepare the way before me, and the Lord whom you seek will suddenly come to his temple. This implies that the Lord has left his temple. Jesus believes that he is the presence of God and called to be the new temple of God. Later 1 Peter 2:4-5 says, Come to him, a living stone, though rejected by mortals yet chosen and precious in God's sight, and like living stones, let yourselves be built into a spiritual house, to be a holy priesthood, to offer spiritual sacrifices acceptable to God through Jesus Christ. This becomes the new temple of God. The temple for God's presence is now the body of believers where the Holy Spirit resides. Because of this, when the church gathers God is in his holy temple.

Verses 7-8 say, He (John the Baptist) proclaimed, "The one who is more powerful than I is coming after me; I am not worthy to stoop down and untie the thong of his sandals. I have baptized you in water; but he will baptize you with the Holy Spirit."

This does not mean that Jesus and his followers will not baptize in water, but the Holy Spirit will be attached to the baptism of Jesus (see Acts 2:1-13, Acts 2:38, Titus 3:5, 1 Peter 3:20, 1 Jn 5:6-12). The water is the outward symbol while the Spirit works inwardly and even sometimes outwardly. Even so, both water and Spirit work together as symbols and are more than bare signs. By one Spirit we are baptized into one body . . . and we are all made to drink of one Spirit (1Cor 12:13). There is one Spirit coming from the Father and through Jesus who immerses in the Spirit and works in the way he wills. The Spirit is not controlled by humans, for sometimes the Spirit comes without water. God can do as he wills, but normally Spirit and water are together.

In verse 9 Jesus comes from Nazareth of Galilee and is baptized by John. (One reason he is baptized is to serve as an example to his followers and to show that eventually the Holy Spirit will be attached to those baptized with Christ's baptism.) For as verses 10-11 say, as he was coming out of the water, he saw the heavens torn apart and the Spirit descending like a dove upon him. And a voice came from heaven, "You are my Son, the Beloved; with you I am well pleased."

The message is that God tears open his created order and comes into it through his Son and the Holy Spirit in order to upset the status quo. Jesus is many things, but the reader will see one thing he is not in his society is a conservative. As defined by the dictionary a conservative opposes any changes to the established order, especially in political, social and economic issues. One can also add religious issues. Liberal is defined by the dictionary as one who is generous, broad-minded, tolerant, favoring reform in all areas, tending toward democracy and personal, progressive freedom. There is no doubt where Jesus fits into his culture and society. By his teaching he will turn Judea upside down and disturb the authorities, this will eventually cause them to put him to death.

The incident at his baptism is looked upon as a fulfillment of prophecy from a combination of Psalm 2:7, "You are my son, today I have begotten you," and Isaiah 42:1, "Here is my servant, whom I uphold, my chosen, in whom my soul delights; I have put my spirit upon him; he will bring forth justice to the nations." Justice in Scripture is primarily a reference to social justice. Here we see that through baptism, the Holy Spirit, the Son of God, and God the Father are together being made present on the earth. Here we have Father, Son, and Holy Spirit in unity and working together as one. So much for those who say the Trinity is not in the Bible. The Father is anointing the Son with the Holy Spirit for the mission he gave him, a mission that will end by both Rome and his own nation opposing him. Also see Mt 3:13-17, Lk 3:21-23, and Jn 1:29-34.

This is the beginning of Jesus' public ministry, and he, like us, will have need of the Holy Spirit. Verses 12-13 say, And the Spirit immediately drove him (Jesus) out into the wilderness. He was in the wilderness forty days, tempted by Satan; and he was with wild beasts; and the angels waited on him.

After a moving religious experience, the wilderness or desert representing great temptations, is sure to come. Religious life is a series of ups and downs, both mountain top and deep valley experiences. The desert, or a place apart from the crowd, is where one meditates with the help of the Spirit to prepare for God's calling in the world. We must remember that God has a purpose for each person, and the Holy Spirit is the believer's helper as Satan attempts to interfere.

Verses 14-15 say, Now after John was arrested, Jesus came to Galilee, proclaiming the good news of God, and saying, "The time is fulfilled, and the kingdom of God has come near, repent, and believe in the good news."

Repent means to be sorry for your sins and change your ways. The call is for individuals to repent of their sins and become the remnant that will be part of the kingdom, the new Israel of God. The call for the nation is to repent of its worship of many gods and its unjust national and social agendas to escape the curse of Deuteronomy chapters 28-30. A part of the call to repentance to the nation is for the militant nationalists to put away their agenda of violence against Rome and accept Jesus' agenda of peace and reconciliation. He will inform them that if they refuse, Rome will be the curse that comes and will destroy their nation, Jerusalem, and their temple.

The Bible does not separate the individual from the nation as many do today when Scripture is interpreted, but it keeps them together because they basically interact together. The nation is to set the example for the people to follow. Israel's sins of idol worship, violence, oppression, and social injustice were the reasons it was sent into exile to Assyria in 722 BC and later to Babylonia in 586 BC. The same pattern is now reoccurring. We will see that as God previously used Assyria and Babylon to judge Israel and Judah for their ungodly example and unjust structures as foretold in Deuteronomy 27-30, he will use Rome against Judah and Jerusalem for the same reason.

The call of John the Baptist and later Jesus for the nation and individuals to repent of sin without going to the temple to offer up animal sacrifices for their sin is a new and strange message to the people. The call for the nation to repent is normal, for that was always the call of the Old Testament prophets, first to the nation, and then to individuals. But the call of John and Jesus for the nation and individuals to repent of sin without use of the temple sacrifices is a new thing. Both John and later Jesus bypass the temple sacrifices with their call for repentance and baptism. This will eventually get them into trouble with the leaders of the nation and the temple, and for Jesus will be one of the major factors in his death.

The message of forgiveness of sin, at this point, is primarily understood by the Jews to mean that the nation's sin is about to be forgiven and liberation from the Romans will soon follow because God is returning to Israel, and the new age of reconciliation, peace with God and each other, and justice is about to begin. John is simply preparing a people for what is to follow, which is the beginning of the new age with the kingdom of God breaking into the world. This will cause great concern to the current leaders both of the Romans and the Jews.

The breaking in of the kingdom is one of the messages of the baptism of Jesus. Jesus will embody the presence of God, and wherever Jesus is made present the kingdom is present. The time of renewal, the *eschatological* end time kingdom, is breaking into the current world through Jesus as he begins to establish God's eternal end time (called eschatological) kingdom. The kingdom is just breaking in and will not be completed until the time of final judgment. Jesus will introduce and model a new way of being Israel. God is now going to rule the world through his Son and the followers of his Son, who make Jesus and his teachings present to the world. Of course, the current leaders of Israel's theocracy are not interested in any new kingdom, or a new way of being Israel. They will see Jesus as a traitor, unpatriotic, and a destroyer of Israel's traditions.

Verses 16-20 say, As Jesus passed along the Sea of Galilee he saw Simon and his brother Andrew casting a net into the sea—for they were fishermen. And Jesus said to them, "Follow me and I will make you fish for people." And immediately they left their nets and followed him. As he went a little farther, he saw James son of Zebedee and his brother John who were in their boats mending nets. Immediately he called them; and they left their father Zebedee in the boat with the hired men, and followed him. (This writer doubts if the fathers of the sons are really excited about this, for the fishing business is difficult and hard work. Now their sons are leaving to wander the countryside with this so-called vagabond.)

Verses 21-22 say, They went to Capernaum; and when the sabbath came he entered the synagogue and taught. They were astounded at his teaching, for he taught them as one having authority, and not as the scribes.

In Jewish life there is the *Mishna*, which is the oral Torah or the traditions that are put along side the written Torah. At this time it was not written. The Mishna consists of the teachings and commentaries of the rabbis down through the years that are used to interpret and explain the Torah. It was not written until the third century. Three hundred years later the *Gemara* will be a commentary on the Mishna and together it will make up the *Talmud*. At the time of Jesus many of these traditions became even more important than the written Torah. The Mishna is what the scribes quote from in order to support their teachings and traditions. *Midrash* is the word used for commentary on Scripture.

When Jesus teaches, he does not quote the Mishna as the other rabbis or scribes do. He teaches as though he has the authority from God to teach, to explain, and even reinterpret the Scriptures. He gives new and deeper meaning to Scripture and to the valid traditions that explain and adapt Scripture. At other times he rejects traditional teaching from the scribes and religious leaders and even rejects some Scriptures, especially those pertaining to the Sabbath laws, and the purity and dietary laws, making them invalid.

He tells them he is the fulfillment of the law. He teaches as having authority over Torah. This is why they say that he teaches as one having authority, and not as the scribes. Because he challenges the symbols of Torah and temple while challenging the Sabbath laws, purity laws and the food laws, he will be in deep trouble with the authorities. Jesus will become the new Torah and the new temple of God, and they ask him who gives him that authority.

In verses 23-27 Jesus heals a man with an unclean spirit in their synagogue. In verses 24-26 the man cries out, "What have you to do with us, Jesus of Nazareth? Have you come to destroy us? I know who you are, the Holy One of God." But Jesus rebuked him saying, "Be silent, and come out of him!"

It is interesting to note that the unclean spirit recognizes who Jesus is, and that he came to destroy them. The battle of Jesus with evil is both cosmic and within history. Evil has been cosmically defeated, and Jesus is in the process of making all things new. But it will not be completed until he comes again renewing the heaven and earth making heaven and earth a new creation. Jesus will later say, if it is by the Spirit of God that I cast out demons, then the kingdom of God has come to you (Mt 12:28). The kingdom has begun to make its mark on this world.

Verses 27-28 say, They were amazed, and they kept on asking one another, "What is this? A new teaching—with authority? He commands even the unclean spirits, and they obey him." At once his fame begins to spread around the surrounding region of Galilee. (The exorcisms and miracles he performs are the fulfillment that he is the Messiah, God's special Son sent to begin the new age. God's Son and Messiah fit together even though some of the people of that time had a difficult time putting them together.)

In verses 29-31 Jesus heals Simon's (Peter's) mother-in-law of a fever. Notice Peter is married. Many readers are surprised to learn that in the Roman Catholic Church for priests not to marry is simply a church discipline (rule) and could change in the future. In fact there are some priests who are married as they changed their ordained standing from a former religion to become Roman Catholic.

Verses 32-34 say, they brought to him all who were sick or possessed with demons. And the whole city was gathered around the door. And he cured many who were sick with various diseases, and cast out many demons; and he would not permit the demons to speak, because they knew him. In verses 35-40 he goes to a deserted place to pray, and verses 37-39 say, When they found him, they said to him, "Everyone is searching for you." He answered, "Let us go on to the neighboring towns, so that I may proclaim the message there also; for that is what I came out to do." And he went throughout Galilee, proclaiming the message in their synagogues and casting out demons.

The message he is proclaiming is about the coming of the kingdom, that a new age is beginning, that the exile is over, forgiveness of sins is now, as is the beginning of the new covenant, and God is returning to his people. In a sense the message is given in a subversive way as we will see when we read some of his parables and the way he taught. This is necessary in order to protect himself from the authorities and give him time to teach his disciples and prepare them to continue his plan, which is also why he is always on the move.

In verses 40-45 he heals a leper but tells him not to tell anyone. But in his excitement the leper tells people and soon Jesus could not go into a town openly. Verse 45 says, Jesus could no longer go into a town openly, but stayed out in the country; and people came to him from every quarter.

This explains why Jesus tells people not to say anything. He does not want people coming to him only to be healed physically, for that would take all his time. Another reason to back off the crowds at this point is because the people are expecting a political Messiah, one who will get rid of the dreaded Romans who control their land. Therefore, Jesus needs time to educate his disciples that this idea is not his concept of the kingdom. Jesus needs time to help his small group of disciples begin to understand who he really is and about the new kingdom he came to inaugurate. At this moment they do not really know who he is and what his real purpose is, even though they are attracted to his message. At this point the only ones knowing who Jesus really is are the demons and unclean spirits.

⚬

Chapter 2:1-2 says, When he returned to Capernaum (located on the Sea of Galilee) after some days, it was reported that he was at home. So many gathered around that there was no longer room for them, not even in front of the door; and he was speaking the word to them. In (3-4) four people carried a paralyzed man to him by removing the roof, and after having dug through it, they let down the mat on which the paralytic lay. (Houses have flat roofs made of mud mixed with straw, and outside stairways led to the roofs, so they dug through the roof.)

Verse 5 says, When Jesus saw their faith, he said to the paralytic, "Son your sins are forgiven." The scribes were sitting there in (6-7) questioning in their hearts. "Why does this fellow speak in this way? It is blasphemy! Who can forgive sins but God alone." (That is Jesus' point. The charge of blasphemy will later be one of the charges used against him to recommend that he be put to death.)

Verses 8-12 say, At once Jesus perceived in his spirit that they were discussing these questions, and he said to them, "Why do you raise such questions in your hearts? Which is easier to say to the paralytic, 'Your sins are forgiven,' or to say 'Stand up and take your mat and walk'? (Of course, it is easier to say your sins are forgiven.) But so that you may know that the Son of Man has authority on earth to forgive sins"—he said to the paralytic—"I say to you, stand up, take your mat and go home." And he stood up, and immediately took the mat and went out before all of them; so that they were all amazed and glorified God saying, "We have never seen anything like this!"

Jesus shows he has the power to heal both physically and spiritually. Also, the insinuation here is that when one is freed of the guilt and burden of sin, it is easier to get rid of physical problems. Only God has the authority to forgive sin, and according to the

Torah it is only done through the sacrifices at the temple. Jesus, by healing physically, is showing them that he is sent by the Father to forgive sin. He is showing them that he is God and will be the new temple of God, and the new Torah of God taking the place of the old temple in Jerusalem and the old Torah. Jesus will now become a threat to the powerful leaders of the temple whose power and wealth depend on that system. It is important to note that the temple was also the main banking system for the nation.

In verse 10 Jesus calls himself the *Son of Man*. It is the first time he is referred to by that name. Jesus is referring to himself as the one mentioned by the prophet Daniel. Daniel 7:13-14 says, "I saw one like a human being (also translated Son of Man) coming with the clouds of heaven. And he came to the Ancient One (God the Father) and was presented before him. To him was given dominion and glory and kingship, that all peoples, nations, and languages should serve him. His dominion is an everlasting dominion that shall not pass away, and his kingship is one that shall never be destroyed."

Jesus is saying that the kingdom of God is breaking in through him, the Son of Man, who is to reign with the Father as stated by Daniel and Ps 110:1. Jesus by calling himself the Son of Man is identifying himself as the one of whom Daniel is speaking. According to Mark, Jesus says the Son of Man has authority and power on earth to forgive sins (2:10). He is lord {*sic*} of the sabbath (2:28). The Son of Man must suffer, die, and rise again (8:31, 9:31, 10:33). And he says the Son of Man will reign in glory (8:38, 13:26, 14:62). With the resurrection, the Father will confirm Jesus as the Son of Man in Dan 7:13-14.

In the meantime this is not what Jews including the disciples think will happen when the Messiah comes. They are looking for a real king with political power to defeat the Romans, eliminate them from their land, and rebuild the temple on the order of

Ezekiel's plan in Ezek 40-48. Their literal way of interpreting Old Testament prophecy causes them to misunderstand prophecy. This is something modern day fundamentalists have not reckoned with.

In verses 13-14 Jesus went out beside the sea. He saw Levi son of Alphaeus (Matthew) sitting at the tax booth, and he said to him, "Follow me." And he got up and followed him.

The gospel writers, Mark, Luke, and John, call Matthew by the name of Levi. This may possibly be because he was a Levite who became discouraged with religion, and then became a tax collector. The Jews detest the tax collectors because most of them are Jews either working for the despised Roman government or working for Herod. The family of Levi, one of the twelve tribes of Israel, produced the priests and the helpers of the priests. Aaron, the bother of Moses, and his descendants become the priests. The rest of the Levites in the Old Testament were called by God to be the helpers of the priests in the temple.

Many of the tax collectors are unscrupulous not only because they work for the enemy but because of their personal greed and how they cheat their fellow Jews. The Romans do not pay the tax collector. His money comes from how much is left after giving the Roman government the amount requested from each tax payer. There is no limit on what these tax collectors can charge above and beyond what the Roman government demands, and that amount is their take.

While Jesus is at Levi's house eating dinner with many tax collectors, the scribes in (16) ask his disciples, "Why does he eat with tax collectors and sinners?" (It is very important for Jews not to eat with Gentiles in order to show that they have separated themselves from the unclean pagans, especially the Romans. Unfortunately, it is this attitude that keeps them from being a light to the nations as God called them to be.) When Jesus hears what they are saying, in (17) he says to them, "Those who are well have no need of a physician, but those who are sick; I have come to call not the righteous but sinners."

Jesus is not impressed with how they distort the original purpose of the purity laws. Jesus is saying only those who recognize their sin can receive forgiveness and healing. The arrogant righteous do not think they have any sin, and if they do, they believe their sins are so small in comparison to others that they are not an issue. Many of the Pharisees define righteousness as being ritually correct, being what they call ritually clean. They are extremely scrupulous with all the different rituals and food laws making it a key element in their way of life. They do not believe they have any reason to go to Jesus to become clean. After all, they have the temple sacrificial system and the Day of Atonement for anything related to forgiveness.

Jesus disagrees with their definition of righteousness, which is another reason they believe Jesus is dangerous and out to destroy their traditions and way of life. Jesus teaches that purity is not a matter of doing all the externals correctly; it is a matter of having a transformed and purified heart, and then relating to others with love, mercy, and compassion in the way of justice and peace, treating others as they would want to be treated.

The performance principle associated with the ritual works of the Old Testament laws and the law of separation deciding who is pure and impure is being transformed by Jesus. He expresses this through his concept of table fellowship with those the Pharisees called sinners. Feasting with these followers serves as a symbol of the coming messianic banquet and who will be with him at that time. The Pharisees could not fathom a man from God eating with such sinners and in the process being made unclean and unfit for worship.

In verses 18-20 John's disciples and the Pharisees are fasting, but the disciples of Jesus are not fasting, so they want to know why.

(Each Monday and Thursday Jews are to fast.) In (19) Jesus said, "The wedding guests can not fast while the bridegroom is with them, can they? As long as they have the bridegroom with them they can not fast. The days will come when the bridegroom will be taken away from them, and then they will fast on that day. "

Zech 8:19 promised that fasts will turn into feasts when God restores the people. Jesus is saying the time is now. He calls himself a bridegroom for he calls all to join him in a personal relationship. These verses are saying that while the presence of God is here through Jesus, there is no reason to fast each Monday and Thursday as the tradition defines the ritual of fasting. Fasting represents repentance for sin, but they are now in the presence of Jesus who forgives sin, so there is no need for sorrow; it is celebration time.

In verses 21-22 Jesus says, "No one sews a piece of unshrunk cloth on an old cloak; otherwise the patch pulls away from it, the new from the old, and a worse tear is made. And no one puts new wine into old wineskins; otherwise, the wine will burst the skins, and the wine is lost, and so are the skins; but one puts new wine into fresh wineskins."

Jesus is indicating that the hearts of the leaders of the Pharisees have become rigid, like old wineskins; they need new hearts. The new wine of the Spirit needs to be poured into new hearts, and when it enters, the old hearts will burst. By the power of the Spirit, Jesus is putting new life into what has become a dead, old law. He is saying the conventional religion of the Pharisees and the status quo of the nation are being ruptured like old wineskins. The old law is being transformed into the new law. Old hearts are being transformed into new hearts. Jesus is initiating new transformations.

In verses 23-24 Jesus is going through a grain field with his disciples on the sabbath, and his disciples began to pluck the grain to eat it. The Pharisees said to him, "Look, why are they doing what is not lawful on the sabbath?"

The Pharisees are religious leaders who interpret Scripture by the letter of the law. They added and continue to add so many petty rules, regulations, and restrictions to everything, especially the Sabbath laws, that the primary purpose of the laws is being lost. They make the law a heavy burden. They even make all the purity laws performed by the priests in the temple necessary for the common people; they are to practice them in their daily lives. Eating the grain is not the problem, but plucking it is considered work, so according to the Pharisees, they are in violation of working on the Sabbath.

In verse 25 Jesus reminds the Pharisees of a time when David was extremely hungry, but there was no food. He went to the high priest who had no food except the bread of the Presence, which was not lawful for anyone to eat but the priest. The priest gave it to David to eat because of his hunger (1Sam 21:4-6). Then in verse 27 Jesus said, "The sabbath was made for humankind, and not humankind for the sabbath; so the Son of Man is lord {*sic*} even of the sabbath."

Jesus is saying compassion for human need takes precedence over religious laws, and as the Lord of the Sabbath he has the authority to give new meaning to the Old Testament Sabbath law. Without compassion, God's people deny a key virtue his people are called to express. Jesus lived compassion, and the early church was a community of compassion and healing. Because the political and religious leadership lack compassion, one can see why the authorities begin to get upset with Jesus. They tell their people to stay away from his influence, for he is out to destroy their way of life.

Jesus is reinterpreting their traditions. He is claiming to be the authority over the Torah, Sabbath, and the system in operation at the temple. Jesus will claim to be the new Torah (word of God) and the new temple (presence of God where forgiveness of sins takes place). Old things are being made new, and old symbols are being replaced, and this puts Jesus on the wrong side opposed to the leadership.

In chapter 3:1-2 Jesus enters the synagogue where there is a man with a withered hand. They watch him to see whether he would cure him on the sabbath, so that they might accuse him. In verse 4 Jesus said, "Is it lawful to do good or to do harm on the sabbath, to save life or to kill?" But they were silent. He looked around at them with anger; he was grieved at their hardness of heart and said to the man, "Stretch out your hand." He stretched it out, and his hand was restored.

People's hard hearts are a constant theme because they are not open to having the presuppositions and preconceived notions behind their thinking changed. Isaiah (6:9-10) said that their eyes and ears would be closed, for they do not want to accept anything different. Their interest is always to maintain the status quo. Verse 6 says, The Pharisees went out and immediately conspired with the Herodians against him, how to destroy him.

The Herodians are those who back King Herod's political system. Herod is accepted by the Roman government and was made their puppet king. This makes them the main enemies of the Pharisees and the Sadducees who in Israel's theocracy are the rightful religious and political leaders. But Jesus now becomes a bigger enemy by challenging the religious and political system of the Jews by what he is teaching the people, so they come together to destroy him.

Thus we have religion and politics combining to defeat Jesus, who is challenging their actions by his teachings and thus their power base. It is important to remember that the system of government of the Jews is a theocracy. The rulers are both the religious and political leaders also making many of the economic and social decisions for the Jews.

In verses 7-10 Jesus departs to the Sea of Galilee. Because of his compassion for the suffering masses of people, he heals so many hurting people that the crowds barely allow him to move around. Verses 11-12 say, Whenever the unclean spirits saw him, they fell down before him and shouted, "You are the Son of God!" (Son of God is also used by the Jews at the time to refer to the Messiah.) But he sternly ordered them not to make him known. (At this point only the evil spirits recognize who he is, but he does not want their witness, for who knows when evil is telling the truth. Another reason is his concern for the time he needs to teach his disciples before the authorities, who are very jealous of possible rivals, end his time on earth.)

Verses 13-19 say, He went up the mountain and called to him those whom he wanted, and they came to him. And he appointed twelve, whom he also named apostles, to be with him, and to be sent out to proclaim the message, and to have authority to cast out demons. So he appointed the twelve: Simon (to whom he gave the name Peter); James, son of Zebedee and John the brother of James (to whom he gave the name Boanerges, that is, Sons of Thunder); and Andrew and Philip, and Bartholomew (identified with Nathaniel in John), and Matthew, and Thomas, and James son of Alphaeus, and Thaddaeus (identified with Judas son of James in Luke), and Simon the Cananaean, and Judas Iscariot, who betrayed him.

The existence of twelve is symbolizing that Jesus is bringing about the reconstitution of Israel. There had not been twelve tribes since the Assyrian invasion in 722 BC. Jesus is creating the new Israel of God for the new age. Even though Jesus is creating the new, he always is rooted in the old. One immediately notices there are no females appointed. Some churches believe Scripture does not permit women to have leading positions in the church. Others believe no women are appointed because of the social customs and cultural mores of the time. But like the slavery issue and the law saying no interest on money could be charged, customs can change as society changes.

At that time sending women out by themselves would be a safety issue as well as the fact that at that time to send a man and woman out together was unthinkable. Others say that once the church is planted, things are able to change. Later the New Testament does seem to verify a few women in leadership positions, but this is denied by some churches. This writer encourages the readers to go to their individual churches to understand its position and reasoning behind this issue.

Verses 20-21 tell us the crowds are so huge that he can not even eat. His family goes to restrain him, for people are saying that he has lost his mind. The scribes from Jerusalem in verse 22 say, "He has Beelzebul, (a pagan god identified with Satan), and by the ruler of demons he casts out demons." (Their position about him is beginning to harden.) In verses 23-27 Jesus says, "How can Satan cast out Satan? If a kingdom is divided against itself, that kingdom can not stand. And if a house is divided against itself, that house will not be able to stand. And if Satan has risen up against himself and is divided, he can not stand, but his end has come. But no one can enter a strong man's house and plunder his property without first tying up the strong man: then indeed the house can be plundered.

Here he points out how ridiculous their thinking is, and he tells them Satan has met his match. The kingdom of God is breaking into the world through the only one who can finalize the defeat of evil, and evil is in the process of being defeated.

Verses 28-30 continue, "Truly I tell you, people will be forgiven for their sins and whatever blasphemies they utter, but whoever blasphemes against the Holy Spirit can never have forgiveness, but is guilty of an eternal sin—for they have said, He has an unclean spirit."

The eternal sin they are guilty of is rejecting Jesus and the eschatological kingdom that Jesus with the power of the Holy Spirit is establishing. Jesus links himself with the Holy Spirit as one. The eternal sin is attributing to Satan what is the work of the Holy Spirit, and thus rejecting the Holy Spirit that the Father and Son will send to all people after his resurrection. It is the Holy Spirit that will continue the work of Jesus in the world making firm the kingdom and the forgiveness of sin (see Jn 14:26, Acts 2:38, Rev 1:5-6). If they reject Jesus now, they will still have an opportunity to enter the kingdom later. But if they reject the Holy Spirit that Jesus sends after he rises from the dead, they will eternally eliminate themselves from the kingdom.

In verses 31-35 his mother and his brothers come to see him, and the crowd informs him. Jesus replies in 33-35, "Who are my mother and my brothers?" And looking at those who sat around him, he said, "Here are my mother and my brothers! Whoever does the will of God is my brother and sister and mother."

Jesus is not being disrespectful. He is just stating the fact that there is a divine family that is part of the kingdom, and it is important to be part of that family. Being part of that family is even more valuable than one's genetic family. He is informing them that one becomes a member of that family by doing the will of God. Doing the will of God is being a disciple of Jesus, and this involves following the teachings of Jesus and making his priorities their priority. How is it that we moderns can say we believe in Jesus but give very little attention to his will and his priorities? Do the high percentage of Americans who say they are followers of Jesus listen to and read enough Scripture to even know his will and his priorities?

∽◯∾

Chapter 4:1-2 says, again he began to teach beside the sea. Such a very large crowd gathered around him that he got into a boat on the sea and sat there, while the whole crowd was beside the sea on the land. He began to teach them many things in parables, and in his teaching he said to them: "Listen! A sower went out to sow." In verses 3-9 he mentions that the sower sows seed on a path, but the birds eat them up. Other seed falls on rocky ground where it does not have much soil. When the sun scorches the ground, it has no root and withers away. Other seed falls on thorns, and the thorns choke it, and it yields no grain. Other seed falls on good soil and brings forth grain yielding thirty, sixty, and a hundred fold. And he said, "Let anyone with ears to hear listen!"

The twelve asked Jesus about the parables, and in (11-13) he said, "To you has been given the secret of the kingdom of God, but for those outside, everything comes in parables; in order that 'they may indeed look, but not perceive, and may indeed listen, but not understand; so that they may not turn again and be forgiven.'" And he said to them, "Do you not understand this parable? Then how will you understand all the parables?"

The writer's point is that when people are not open to understanding things from another angle, and when they will not allow their preconceived assumptions to be challenged, they are not going to hear and understand what Jesus is saying. Because parables are like puzzles that take time to comprehend, they slow down the leaders from harassing him. The parables function like the coded insider language of *apocalyptic* literature. Only those who have a committed faith are able to understand quickly. The others are not going to understand, and when they try, they will misunderstand. The point made throughout the Gospels is that unless one is born from above, and immersed in the Holy Spirit, and open to a new way of looking at and understanding things, they are not going to truly understand the things of God (1 Cor 2:6-16). He is even challenging his own people to open their minds even more.

In verses 14-20 Jesus explains the parable to the twelve. He says, "The sower sows the word. These are the ones on the path where the word is sown: when they hear, Satan immediately comes and takes away the word that is sown in them. And these are the ones sown on the rocky ground: when they hear the word, they immediately receive it with joy. But they have no root, and endure only for awhile; then, when trouble or persecution arises on account of the word, immediately they fall away. And others are sown among the thorns: these are the ones who hear the word, but the cares of the world, and the lure of wealth, and the desire for other things come in and choke the word, and it yields nothing. And these are the ones sown on good soil: they hear the word and accept it and bear fruit, thirty and sixty and a hundredfold."

This is reality throughout time for those who hear God's word taught and preached. Mark is challenging all readers to ask themselves what kind of influence God's word has on them. Or what kind of influence does Jesus have on them. He is giving people a mirror to locate where they are on the path of spiritual maturity. According to verse 11 this is also related to how the kingdom of God is breaking in upon the world.

The authority of God is exercised through his word. Jesus is the Word above all words that is to be listened to. The Spirit works through Jesus the Word and now through the Bible, and especially for Christians through the New Testament preached and taught by the church. The responsibility for this is the church, through which the word and the kingdom are to be made present in the world. This is God's purpose for the church and the world. One can read more fully about God's purpose for the world and his people who represent him in Genesis 1-2 and 12, Isaiah 40-55, Matthew 5-7, Romans 6 and 8, I Corinthians 15, Ephesians 1, Colossians 3 and Revelation 21-22.

In verses 24-25 Jesus says, "Pay attention to what you hear; the measure you give will be the measure you get, and still more will be given you. For to those who have, more will be given; and from those who have nothing, even what they have will be taken away." (This is in the context of one's hearing, accepting, and understanding God's word and allowing God's presence to live in them and through them.)

Then in verses 26-30 the result is the fruit of the kingdom of God. The idea is that if good seed like the word and the kingdom of God is sown in good soil, God will bring the increase in the same way seed sown by a farmer is brought to harvest. In other words spiritual growth and the spread of the kingdom of God is a continual gradual process that is finally harvested in spiritual maturity and the advance of the kingdom. The seed sprouts and grows until it is ripe, and then it is harvested or brought to fruition.

In a first century Jewish world context Jesus is using this narrative in the context of his kingdom message. The seed that comes to fruition and grows is a metaphor for the remnant, the true Israel, the people of the new covenant that have come from the old covenant. At the heart of the story is Jesus showing that the time foretold by the prophets of old is now beginning. Israel's God is restoring his people, but much of the seed will go to waste and remain in exile being eaten by the birds (Satan and his gang). Those of the old covenant are rejecting Jesus' message. Judgment, mercy, and new creation are taking place, which is always central with apocalyptic literature. As in most apocalyptic literature the message is subversive in order to keep it from the leaders in power who will not appreciate the message and who would violently oppose the messenger.

In verses 30-32 the kingdom of God is compared to a mustard seed. When sown in the ground, it is the smallest of seeds, yet when sown it grows up and becomes the greatest of all shrubs and puts forth large branches, so that the birds of the air can make nests in its shade.

Jesus is telling them that Christianity and the church, and consequently the kingdom will have a small beginning but will grow into a world wide force. The kingdom of God is not the church, but the kingdom of God is made manifest through the word spoken in and through the church. One might even possibly say that the kingdom of God is the church living according to the teachings of Jesus, minus its sin.

Verses 33-34 say, With many such parables he spoke to them as they were able to hear it; but he did not speak to them except in parables, but he explained everything in private to his disciples. (As they were able to hear, means at their rate of understanding. Their comprehension advanced according to their openness to hear and their attitude, or as the parable implies, the fertility of their soil.)

Jesus adapts his teaching to his audience. He teaches against the hypocrisy and impure motives of the religious leaders who follow him around in order to accuse him and get rid of him. When they leave, he always explains in more detail and answers the questions of his followers but always according to their ability to understand. Mark is trying to get us to understand that at that time those he taught were not capable of understanding completely who he was. This will not come without more teaching and until they experience the crucifixion and resurrection. At this point what they are looking for in a Messiah and the new kingdom is not what God has in mind. So Jesus has to go step by step teaching them with patience preparing them to be able to advance in their thinking and understanding.

Mark is saying to his listeners and readers, do not be upset if you do not understand everything right now. Do not let your current weakness or difficulty understanding overcome you. The question is: Are you trying to understand? How open are you to new ideas, or are you just wanting to accept what you can fit into what you already believe? How much effort are you putting into really grasping the message? Are you growing in understanding and wisdom?

In verses 35-41 a storm blows up while Jesus is asleep and the disciples are in a boat going across to the other side. Verses 38-40 say, they woke him up and said to him, "Teacher, do you not care that we are perishing?" He woke up and rebuked the wind, and said to the sea, "Peace! Be still!" Then the wind ceased, and there was a dead calm. He said to them, "Why are you afraid? Have you still no faith?" And they were filled with great awe and said to one another, "Who then is this, that even the wind and sea obey him?" (Mark is saying two things: first, Jesus even has power over nature just like the Father; therefore he is God. See the Psalms especially 8, 74, 78, 89, and 106. Second, Jesus will bring calm and peace to those who have faith and trust in him.)

If the reader reads this same basic incident in Mt 8:23-27, Lk 8:22-25, and Jn 6:16-21, it will be possible to see the process of passing along orally from one village to another the things Jesus said and did. The basic message stays the same but the details are adjusted usually for the audience or the theological purposes of the writer, who finally puts the narrative in writing. Dunn (2003, 205-210) documents a man named Kenneth Bailey who lived more than thirty years in a Middle Eastern village whose culture was completely oral. Bailey describes how narratives are passed along stressing how the basic theme is always the same but flexibility in exact details is adjusted to the different audiences. Bailey's experience can be seen in Scripture with the following narratives.

To examine this issue in more detail compare the following narratives: the Syrophoenician woman (Mk 7:24-30, Mt 15:21-28); the healing of the possessed boy (Mk 9:14-27, Mt 17:14-18, Lk 9:37-44); the dispute about greatness (Mk 9:33-37, Mt 18:1-5, Lk 9:46-48); and the widow's mite (Mk 12:41-44, Lk 21:1-4); the healing of a Roman soldier in (Mt 8:5-13, Jn 4:46-54).

After comparing the written versions it is obvious that the information from the Scripture writers comes from different oral performances that had been passed on in a culture, as Bailey describes, where few can read or write. Bailey describes this as *informal, controlled oral tradition.* This idea is also very obvious in the three conversion accounts of the Apostle Paul in Acts 9:1-22, 22:1-21, 26:9-23. When one examines the inspired Scriptures carefully, the fundamentalist belief that every word is God's exact word, and the way the narratives are described is historically accurate in all the details, must be put to rest. We must remember that God's inspired word is both human and divine. God works through humans in what is culturally appropriate to them as he relays his God inspired truths to his people.

Chapter 5:1-2 says, They came to the other side of the sea, to the country of the Geresenes. And when he stepped out of the boat, immediately a man out of the tombs with an unclean spirit met him. The man is described as being beyond control, who howls, constantly bruises himself, and can not be restrained. When he sees Jesus he bows before him and in (7) he shouts at the top of his voice, "What have you to do with me, Jesus, Son of the Most High God? I adjure you by God, do not torment me."

When Jesus asks him his name in (9) he replies, "My name is Legion, for we are many." In (10-13) Jesus casts out the unclean spirits. The unclean spirits in (12) beg him, "Send us into the swine; let us enter them." So he gave them permission. And the unclean spirits came out and entered the swine; and the herd, numbering about two thousand, rushed down the steep bank into the sea, and were drowned in the sea.

Mark always highlights the battle between Jesus and the demons who at this point are the only ones to recognize who he really is. The freedom that Mark always expresses is the freedom that sets individuals free from the control of sin and Satan. Thus Jesus in this incident frees the man from the demons, and allows the demons to go into unclean pigs. The controlling story is the authority Jesus has over evil. Later Jesus will say, "If I by the finger of God cast out demons, then the kingdom of God has come upon you." It is obvious that the kingdom Jesus is talking about is not to begin at the end of time; it is beginning now with his presence.

It is important for the reader to understand that when Scripture mentions freedom, it is not primarily the freedom defined by those living in a democratic capitalist type of environment. Many today are attempting to make that definition the same as the Scripture's definition, but if we are going to stay true to Scripture, then it must be said it is a misrepresentation of the concept of New Testament freedom, and an attempt by some to co-opt the meaning of the word for their own purposes. This writer does believe freedom is a God-given value, but it is important to understand that Jesus lived under a brutal dictatorship and in a culture that accepted slavery, but he did not mention anything about either of those particular issues.

Some people are concerned with Jesus destroying the pigs, but it seems Jesus is doing this to attract attention to a higher concern. In Jewish food laws, pigs are unclean animals, Jesus allows that which is unclean to enter into the unclean. He eliminates them from entering people by sending them into the unclean pigs. There are those who believe the pigs are probably owned by Jews living in this Gentile region. If they are Jews, they should not be earning a living by making themselves unclean working with pigs and selling unclean meat for people to eat. He reveals their hypocrisy to symbolize the hypocrisy of the leaders of the Pharisees, who he says do not practice what they teach. Later Jesus tells people to do what the Pharisees say but not what they do.

Others believe that Jesus is simply going into pagan territory to be surrounded by everything that from a serious Jewish point of view is opposed to God's teachings. The demons identify themselves as "legion." The Roman soldiers are part of what are called legions. The driving of the pigs into the sea may be symbolic of the fact that Roman control over the land will eventually end. The exorcism is then saying that Jesus is fighting a battle to oppose those things that oppose God and his people. But Rome is not the real enemy. Satan and his demons are deceiving the people into thinking the enemy is Rome when the real enemy is sin, Satan and his followers. The real enemy is symbolized in the death of the pigs. Jesus is saying that he has authority over that enemy. For Jesus to say for all to hear that Rome is controlled by sin and Satan would only cause him deep trouble. Therefore he uses the cryptic form of apocalyptic to get his message to those who have ears to hear.

Although this story appears to have its roots in something that happened historically, some scholars believe it is a parable developed from something that had a historical basis involving a man with a demon and a herd of pigs near him. Then it was passed along orally until Mark writes about it in his gospel. In verses 14-17 when the people learn what happened, they come out to Jesus and see the man, who had the demon, sitting there in his right mind, and they ask Jesus to leave.

Therefore, another point Jesus is making is that sometimes people are more concerned with material things and animals than with a man being mentally or physically healed. They are more concerned with their worldly kingdom than the kingdom of God breaking into the world signified by the miracles of Jesus. One may be tempted to see their concern especially when the pigs were their livelihood, but Jesus' point may be that he and the kingdom are even more important than their profits, or even the way they make their living. To get across his point, Jesus often uses hyperbole centered on parables developed from incidents that have some historical basis.

Then in verses 18-20 the man healed from the demons begs to go with Jesus, but Jesus refuses and says, "Go home to your friends, and tell them how much the Lord has done for you, and what mercy he has shown you." And he went away and began to proclaim in the Decapolis how much Jesus had done for him; and everyone was amazed. (If the man healed is a Gentile and the pig owners Jews, Jesus is saying that the Gentiles are open to being healed physically and spiritually, but most of his own people are rejecting him and have no concern about what he is teaching or doing.)

When Jesus told the man not to go with him but to go home and tell people how much the Lord has done for him, perhaps, Jesus is also teaching that everyone is not called to a far away mission field. Taking the message and living it in the midst of one's family and the situation where one is located is the mission field for most people. Decapolis is basically Gentile territory, so Jesus is keeping him in the area to plant seeds in preparation for planting future churches after his death and resurrection.

Is this story actual history, a parable, or a legend? We do know that it circulated orally for quite awhile as most of these writings did. This writer believes it probably is a type of parable that was based on something that actually happened historically. What that something was will never be discovered, and since a detailed history is not the purpose of these writings, it is not an issue. Since we will never be able to know for sure, the goal is not to argue whether or not it is word for word actual history but to discover the inspired truth contained within the story. This is the value this writer has gleaned from the books by Marcus Borg as listed in the bibliography. The purpose of inspired Scripture is theology, spiritual development, character development, and creating a type of catechism for people to understand who Jesus is, that God works in history, and to remember the things Jesus taught.

Verse 21 says, When Jesus had crossed again in the boat to the other side, a great crowd gathered around him; and he was by the sea. In verses 22-25 a synagogue leader named Jairus asks Jesus to heal his little daughter, who was near death. On the way to the house where they live, he heals a woman who had been suffering from hemorrhages for twelve years. Verse 26 says, she had endured much under many physicians, and had spent all she had; and she was no better, but rather grew worse. In (27-28) she touches Jesus' clothes, and (29) says, Immediately her hemorrhage (bleeding) stopped; and she felt in her body that she was healed of her disease.

A woman with a blood flow under the old law is considered unclean, and the unclean as well as those they touch are not permitted to be in the presence of God. In (30) Jesus aware that power had gone from him, says, "Who touched my clothes?" Verses 33-34 say, In fear the woman fell down before him and told him the truth. He said to her, "Daughter, your faith has made you well; go in peace, and be healed of your disease." (Under the new law the unclean and sinners will now be able to come into the presence of God for healing, and being declared clean will no longer be the responsibility of the priests at the temple. The priests see this as their power struggle with Jesus.)

Verses 35-40 say, While he was still speaking, some people came from the leader's house (Jairus) to say, "Your daughter is dead. Why trouble the teacher any further?" Jesus said to the leader of the synagogue, "Do not fear, only believe." He allowed no one to follow him except Peter, James, and John, the brother of James. When they came to the house of the leader of the synagogue, he saw a commotion, people weeping and wailing loudly. When he entered he said to them, "Why do you make a commotion and weep? The child is not dead but sleeping." And they laughed at him.

In verse 40 he puts the people outside and takes the child's father and mother with him and Peter, John, and James, and in verses 41-42 he says, "Talitha cum," which means "Little girl, get up!" And immediately the girl got up and began to walk about (she was twelve years of age). At this they were overcome with amazement. He strictly ordered them that no one should know this, and told them to give her something to eat. (This would show that he did not raise up a ghost or her spirit.)

To the Jews of that time the raising of all the dead will be a sign that the new age is breaking in (see Ezek 37:1-15). Although this is not the raising of all the dead, it is a sign that Ezekiel's prophecy is beginning or near. It is a sign that God is returning to Israel, the spiritual exile is over, and the nation's sins will be forgiven. For many it is a sign that God will set them free from the hated Romans and banish them from their land. It will be a time that glory will return to Israel and Judah as it had been in the time of David. It will be the time of the new age, the new covenant.

Jesus orders that for the moment no one should be informed about what he did. At this point Jesus does not want a major confrontation with the religious leaders, and he does not want crowds following him just for miracles of healing. His purpose now is to prepare a small group of Jews to understand by listening to his words and watching his actions. Then they will be prepared to carry on his message, after they all contemplate the meaning of his crucifixion and resurrection.

Chapter 6:1-3 says, He left that place and came to his hometown, and his disciples followed him. On the sabbath he began to teach in the synagogue, and many who heard him were astounded. They said, "Where did this man get all this? What is this wisdom that has been given to him? What deeds of power are being done by his hands! Is not this the carpenter, the son of Mary and brother of James and Joses and Judas and Simon, and are not his sisters here with us?" And they took offense at him.

Joseph is not mentioned. Possibly he has been dead for a long time, although Matthew and Luke do mention him in their birth stories, and he is mentioned in the trip to the Jerusalem temple when Jesus was twelve years old. The Roman Catholic Church believes Mary remained a virgin because her physical body was special in that she carried and gave birth to Jesus, God's unique Son. Therefore, according to them, these brothers and sisters are children by a former marriage of Joseph, and is normal in that part of the world. Relatives often live in an extended family compound and are called brothers and sisters. Most Protestant churches believe he did have real brothers and sisters because, even though Mary carried Jesus in pregnancy, she was a human and expected to have a normal sex life.

This writer does not believe Christians should allow these things to divide the churches, and whatever position one takes, it is *adiaphora,* meaning indifferent as far as church unity is concerned. The issue has nothing to do with the way a person lives or salvation.

THE GOSPEL OF MARK

Let us be tolerant of the various theories the different churches may have. All churches have their different traditions. These things do not need to be issues of unity.

In verses 4-7 Jesus says to them, "Prophets are not without honor, except in their hometown, and among their own kin, and in their own house." And he could do no deeds of power there, except that he laid his hands on a few sick people and cured them. And he was amazed at their unbelief. Then he went about among the villages teaching. He called the twelve and began to send them out two by two, and gave them authority over the unclean spirits. (They are going to go out with the same message and power of Jesus to heal and cast out demons.)

Verses 8-13 say, He ordered them to take nothing for their journey except a staff (walking stick); no bread, no bag, no money in their belts; but to wear sandals, and not to put on two tunics. He said to them, "Wherever you enter a house, stay there until you leave the place. If any place will not welcome you and they refuse to hear you, as you leave, shake off the dust that is on your feet as a testimony against them." (This is a cultural expression meaning they are to leave and those rejecting them will bear the consequences of their decision.) Verses 12-13 say, So they went out and proclaimed that all should repent. They cast out many demons, and anointed with oil many who were sick and cured them. (They are gathering believers for the kingdom, the restored Israel, the new Israel of God.)

In verses 14-18 King Herod heard about Jesus and what he was doing and thinks it is John raised from the dead. This King Herod is Herod Antipas, the son of Herod the Great and now the tetrarch of Galilee. He had previously jailed John the Baptist and allowed his wife to have John put to death. She had formerly been the wife of Herod's half brother, Philip, and John told them their relationship was not lawful. Mark inserts here the story of how John was murdered.

Verses 19-29 tell that story. Herodias had a grudge against John, and wanted to kill him. But she could not, for Herod feared John, knowing he was a righteous and holy man, and he protected him. When he heard him he was greatly perplexed; and yet he liked to listen to him. (Herod was intrigued but too proud to repent.)

Verses 21-23 say, An opportunity for Herodias came on Herod's birthday. He gave a party, and his daughter danced, and it pleased everyone. He offered to give her anything she wanted, even half of his kingdom. So she asked her mother, and in (24-28) she said, the head of John the baptizer. Immediately she rushed back to the king and requested, "I want you to give me at once the head of John the Baptist on a platter."

The king was deeply grieved; yet out of regard for his oaths and for his guests, he did not want to refuse her. Immediately the king sent a soldier of the guard with orders to bring John's head. He went and beheaded him in the prison, brought his head on a platter, and gave it to the girl. Then the girl gave it to her mother. Verse 29 says, When his disciples heard about it, they came and took his body, and laid it in a tomb.

Mark constantly points out that those who stand with Christ and his teachings will suffer persecution. This is especially true when the stand is against those in the political economic establishment. Mark is also setting the story for what will happen to Jesus.

In verses 30-44 the apostles return to tell Jesus all they had done and taught. Jesus in (31) said, "Come away to a deserted place all by yourselves and rest awhile." For many were coming and going, and they had no leisure even to eat. But the people saw where they were going and hurried to get there. Verse 34 says, As he went ashore, he saw a great crowd; and he had compassion for them, because they were like sheep without a shepherd; and he began to teach them many things.

Compassion is a key word in describing Jesus. Borg (1987, 129-131) describes it as the ethos of the movement. He says that Judaism spoke primarily of the holiness of God while Jesus primarily spoke of the love and compassion of God. Borg describes it as the politics of compassion. Christians believe this is a key word in describing anyone calling themselves a disciple of Christ, for compassion is very closely associated with love. A person or church without compassion is not part of the movement Christ began.

Verses 35-36 say, When it grew late, his disciples came to him and said, "This is a deserted place, and the hour is now very late; send them away so that they may go into the surrounding country and villages and buy something for themselves to eat." Jesus in (37) said, "You give them something to eat." They were puzzled, but Jesus asked them how many loaves they had. In (38) they said, Five, and two fish. Then in (39) he orders them to get all the people to sit down in groups on the green grass. Verses 40-44 say, So they sat down in groups of hundreds and fifties. Taking the five loaves and two fish, he looked up to heaven, and blessed and broke the loaves, and gave them to his disciples to set before the people; and he divided the two fish among them all. And all ate and were filled; and they took up twelve baskets full of broken pieces and of the fish. Those who had eaten the loaves were five thousand men.

Women and children are not counted in ancient cultures. This is the only miracle that all four Gospels replicate, which makes it one deserving special attention. This chapter is pointing out some very important things about Jesus and his mission. First, he is compassionate as verse 34 states. What he does next, as stated in this chapter, is teach, heal the physically ill, and make sure the hungry are fed.

The question all need to ask is: Are these three main activities of today's churches? How about the reader's church? Are they emphasizing the teaching of God's word? Are they emphasizing the need for the hungry to be fed, and are they doing anything about it? Are they emphasizing the need for people to have healing, to have health care, and are they doing anything about it? Millions in this country and throughout the world do not have the food they need, and millions in our own country do not have the health care they need.

The way to begin answering that question centers on where the money is spent. Jim Wallis in his books (see bibliography) strongly believes that the budget of churches and our government is a moral issue. Government is included, for that is the money of the people also, and institutions are also responsible to God. All of creation being responsible to God is clearly understood in both testaments with the teaching of the prophets and Jesus. It is also why Borg in describing Jesus talks about the politics of compassion. Those who attempt to ignore compassion, or make it apply to individuals only are captured by their current culture of individualism. Making what is popular in current culture fit with the teachings of Jesus is not the way to understand Jesus or his teachings.

Most Americans believe much of their hard earned tax money goes for compassion such as welfare, but if the recent federal budget is examined, a March 2011 Washington Post article states that a person earning $50,000 per year has only $43 of the year's $6,834 federal taxes going for welfare and social services. Spending for compassion is not what is busting the federal budget.

Verses 47-52 contain another story about the disciples on the Sea of Galilee in a storm. As they see him walking by on the water, they think he is a ghost. They cry out to him. Jesus in (50-51) says, "Take heart, it is I; do not be afraid." Then he got into the boat with them, and the wind ceased. (The writer is saying that Jesus like the Father has control over nature; therefore he is God (Ps 8, 89). Mark is also saying that Jesus can calm the storms in your life, but without him you will sink or live in fear.) Verses 51-52 say, they (the disciples) were utterly astounded, for they did not understand about the loaves, but their hearts were hardened. (Mark emphasizes the disciples being slow to understand.)

Verses 53-56 say, When they crossed over, they came to the land at Gennesaret and moored the boat. When they got out of the boat, people at once recognized him, and rushed about that whole region and began to bring the sick on mats to wherever they heard he was. And wherever he went, into villages or cities or farms, they laid the sick in the marketplaces, and begged him that they might touch even the fringe of his cloak; and all who touched it were healed. (From this example and others in the book of Acts will develop the cult of the relics and the reports of associated miracles greatly aiding the later conversion of Europe.)

In chapter 7:1-3 we are told that the Pharisees and scribes notice that some of the disciples are eating with defiled hands; they did not wash them ceremonially. This was a tradition of the elders (not in the Old Testament Scriptures) to purify the people in case they touch a sinner or anything unclean. So in verse 5 they asked Jesus, "Why do your disciples not live according to the tradition of the elders, but eat with defiled hands?"

Scribes are religious leaders, lay people who are specialists in the intricacies of the law, and most are Pharisees. They are among the few able to write well. They are very involved in keeping the temple regulations for purity and ritual observance and extending them into the life of the home, especially when eating. The purpose is to make all of life a religious experience. They believe the oral law is as important as the written law, which means they recognize the importance of tradition and interpretation. They believe in a physical resurrection, as well as angels and spirits. In these beliefs they are opposed by the Sadducees who are the priests primarily in the temple. The Pharisees are the leaders of many of the synagogues dispersed throughout the land.

The New Testament in a sense conveys that the Pharisees seem to be more concerned with the external things that make them look religious than they are with the condition of hearts. They add many of their own rules and regulations to God's laws and try to force the people to follow them in the name of religion. They attempt to put a fence around the law by surrounding the original law with many other laws so that the original law will never be broken. This often pulls them away from the spirit of the original meaning and purpose of the law and leads to a distortion of the law and an overemphasis on the externals in religion. (All Pharisees were not this way, but obviously many of the leaders who opposed Jesus most vigorously portrayed these traits.)

Verses 6-13 say, He (Jesus) said to them, "Isaiah prophesied rightly about you hypocrites, as it is written, 'This people honor me with their lips, but their hearts are far from me; in vain do they worship me, teaching human precepts as doctrines.' You abandon the commandment of God and hold to human tradition." Then he said to them, "You have a fine way of rejecting the commandment of God in order to keep your tradition! For Moses said, 'Honor your father and mother'; and, 'Whoever speaks evil of father or mother must surely die.' But you say that if anyone tells father or mother, 'Whatever support you might have had from me is Corban' (that is, an offering to God)—then you no longer permit doing anything for a father or mother, thus making void the word of God through your tradition that you have handed on. And you do many things like this." (Jesus is referring to some of the leaders of the Pharisees who make an offering in the temple to excuse themselves from caring for their aged parents.)

This is not an indictment against tradition but a certain kind of tradition. Every church has tradition, even those churches who think they are just believing and following the Bible. But when tradition is used to ignore a person in need, or reject or get around a plain teaching of God's word as the example in (10-12), then it is wrong. When this happens verse 13 indicates, one makes void or eliminates the word of God through their traditions.

In verses 14-23 Jesus not only eliminates tradition that goes against a plain teaching of Scripture, but he will eliminate some practices that were Old Testament Scripture. As the Messiah, the Son of God, sent by the Father to reveal the new covenant, he has an authority humans do not have. The reader must remember that at this point there is no written New Testament. The Old Testament is their Bible. For example, in the following verses, Jesus eliminates the Old Testament food laws. By doing this, he is saying that he has the authority of God. That is one reason why the people say that he speaks with authority not as the Pharisees do. He is beginning to teach that he will be the new Torah, the new word of God. The religious leaders will want him put to death for blasphemy, being unpatriotic to their tradition, their way of life, and their culture.

Jesus said in verses 14-15 "Listen to me, all of you, and understand: there is nothing outside a person that by going in can defile, but the things that come out are what defile." His disciples had a difficult time understanding what he was saying so in (18-19) he said, "Do you not see that whatever goes into a person from outside can not defile, since it enters not the heart but the stomach, and goes out into the sewer?" (Thus he declares all foods clean, eliminating the kosher food laws such as those of Leviticus 11.)

In verses 20-23 he says, "It is what comes out of a person that defiles. For it is from within, from the human heart, that evil intentions come: fornication, theft, murder, adultery, avarice, wickedness, deceit, licentiousness, envy, slander, pride, folly. All these evil things come from within, and they defile a person." The primary concern of Jesus is the transformation of hearts, attitudes, dispositions, motivations, and way of thinking.

Torah law, called *halakhah,* can regulate certain behaviors and create a minimum for obedience to the law, but it can not make one go beyond the law to a higher level, and the law can not change or touch the heart, which is the creator of attitudes, dispositions, and motivations. The form of Jesus' teaching, called *haggadah,* is by story, and emphasizes character development and the spirit of the law.

Verses 24-26 say, From there he set out and went away to the region of Tyre. He entered a house and did not want anyone to know he was there. Yet he could not escape notice, but a woman whose little daughter had an unclean spirit immediately heard about him, and she came and bowed down at his feet. Now the woman was a Gentile, of Syrophoenician origin (from the area of modern day Syria and Lebanon). She begged him to cast the demon out of her daughter. He said to her, "Let the children be fed first, for it is not fair to take the children's food and throw it to the dogs." (Mark is making it clear that Jesus is not rejecting the people from which he came; he is simply rejecting some of the ways their religion had developed and is transforming and renewing it.)

He is saying the children of Israel must be offered first the things of God. Even though that is true, it is surprising he said this to her, for he has already spoken to and healed non-Israelites. Possibly, he is simply testing her faith, or wanting to show his fellow Jews that the Gentiles in general will be the ones who will have faith in him, while most of his fellow Jews will reject him.

Her response in verse 28 is, "Sir, even the dogs under the table eat the children's crumbs." (She is recognizing the importance of the old covenant and the message it contains.) In 28-30 he said to her, For saying that, you may go—the demon has left your daughter. So she went home, found the child lying on the bed, and the demon gone.

He returns to the Sea of Galilee in the region of Decapolis. Verses 32-36 say, they brought to him a deaf man who had an impediment in his speech; and they begged him to lay his hand on him. He took him aside in private, away from the crowd, and put his fingers into his ears, and he spat and touched his tongue. Then looking up to heaven he sighed and said to him, "Ephphatha," that is, "Be opened." And immediately his ears were opened, his tongue released, and he spoke plainly. Then Jesus ordered them to tell no one; but the more he ordered them, the more zealously they proclaimed it. Verse 37 says, they were astounded beyond measure, saying, "He has done everything well; he even makes the deaf to hear and the mute to speak."

One can not blame the people for their amazement and excitement. Mark is saying this was all foretold by Isaiah as a sign of the new age (see Isa 29:18, 35:5-6). In addition to this being a physical miracle, this writer believes Mark is saying that Jesus opens the ears to hear both physically and spiritually. Jesus gives his people a new way of hearing. There is a way of hearing that the world hears, but those truly born of God and transformed hear things in a new and different way.

❧❧❧

In chapter 8:1-10 there is another miraculous feeding, a reminder of the wandering in the wilderness after the Exodus, and a messianic sign. As Moses fed the people in the wilderness, so does Jesus. This time it is in Gentile territory. Again, in (2-3) he tells them, "I have compassion for the crowd because they have been with me now for three days and have nothing to eat." His disciples in (4) reply, "How can one feed these people with bread here in the desert?"

Verses 5-9 say, He asked them, "How many loaves do you have?" They said, "Seven." Then he ordered the crowd to sit down on the ground; and he took the seven loaves, and after giving thanks he broke them and gave them to his disciples to distribute; and they distributed them to the crowd. They had also a few small fish, and after blessing them, he ordered that these too should be distributed. They ate and were filled; and they took up the broken pieces left over, seven baskets full. Now there were about four thousand people. And he sent them away. And immediately he got into the boat with his disciples and went to the district of Dalmanutha.

The incomprehension of the disciples, when they ask him how he could feed them in the desert, is difficult to understand since he has just fed the five thousand. Consequently, some scholars suggest that this was not a real feeding but was taking the Lord's Supper. This writer has difficulty with that explanation simply because there is nothing in context to suggest that was the case. Has the reader ever seen fish used in the Eucharist?

Some say that the story of a miraculous feeding circulated orally for a long time, and eventually the result is two stories. Others say there are two miraculous feedings, but the disciples are slow to understand. Still others say that maybe these feedings happened with mostly two different sets of disciples. What is important is the teaching that Jesus feeds people because of his compassion. Since the purpose of the Gospels is not exact historical detail but the message and the theology, there is no reason to squabble over the exact historical detail.

Verses 11-13 say, The Pharisees came and began to argue with him, asking him for a sign from heaven, to test him. (They want a verification of his divine authority.) And he sighed deeply in his spirit and said, "Why does this generation ask for a sign? Truly I tell you, no sign will be given to this generation." (Matthew 16:4 adds, except the sign of Jonah.) And he left them, and getting into the boat again, he went across to the other side. (How many signs do they need? Some people never have enough proof. If one does not have eyes to see or ears to hear, it does not matter how many signs there are.)

Verses 14-15 say, Now the disciples had forgotten to bring any bread; and they had only one loaf with them in the boat. And he cautioned them, saying, "Watch out—beware of the yeast of the Pharisees and the yeast of Herod." (The yeast of the Pharisees is their hypocrisy, their religious teaching and contrary actions, and the action of some who became part of the revolutionary movement to overthrow the Romans by any means including violence; the yeast of Herod or the Herodians is their worldliness.)

Becoming aware of it, Jesus in (17-21) said, "Why are you talking about having no bread? Do you still not perceive or understand? Are your hearts hardened? Do you have eyes and fail to see? Do you have ears and fail to hear? And do you not remember? When I broke the five loaves for the five thousand, how many baskets full of broken pieces did you collect?" And they said to him, "Twelve." And the seven for the four thousand, how many baskets full of broken pieces did you collect?" And they said to him, "Seven." Then he said to them, "Do you not yet understand?"

Notice how often the disciples fail to understand in Mark. Isaiah 6:9-10 referring to outsiders not understanding, is now applied to the disciples of Jesus. In Mark no one really understands what Jesus' kingdom is all about until after the crucifixion and resurrection because everyone's concept of the Messiah to come is different from the purpose and call of Jesus. The harsh questions to the disciples are immediately followed by the healing of a blind man in two stages which symbolizes the movement of the disciples understanding from blindness in understanding to a state of fuzzy understanding, and then complete understanding.

Verses 22-25 say, They came to Bethsaida. Some people brought a blind man to Jesus and begged him to touch him. He took the blind man by the hand and led him out of the village; and when he had put saliva on his eyes and laid his hands on him, he asked him, "Can you see anything?" And the man looked up and said, "I can see people, but they look like trees, walking." Then Jesus laid his hands on his eyes again; and he looked intently and his sight was restored, and he saw everything clearly. (Jesus could have healed the man with one touch, but Mark tells this story to symbolize the development of the disciples understanding of Jesus and his purposes.)

Jesus and his disciples go to Caesarea Philippi which is a pagan stronghold for the nature god Pan. And in (27-30) Jesus asked, "Who do people say that I am?" And they answered him, "John the Baptist; and others, Elijah; and still others, one of the prophets." He asked them, "But who do you say I am?" Peter answered him, "You are the Messiah." And he sternly ordered them not to tell anyone about him.

Peter is the first to get the answer right, but Peter still has the wrong concept of what the Messiah is going to do. He and the others need more teaching and understanding before they truly understand the nature of the kingdom he is inaugurating. Jesus begins this deeper explanation in verses 31-32 when he says, "the Son of Man must undergo great suffering, and be rejected by the elders (wealthy laymen), the chief priests (religious leaders, mainly Sadducees), and the scribes (mainly educated Pharisees), and be killed, and after three days rise again." He said all this quite openly. And Peter took him aside and began to rebuke him.

This is too much for Peter, for it does not fit with his concept of what the Messiah is supposed to do. Peter as well as most of the people are looking for a Messiah who will conquer the hated Romans who now control their land, and then throw them out of their promised land and set up a political kingdom like the glory days of David and Solomon. Peter and the rest of the twelve are planning to take power by being in Jesus' cabinet ruling with him. It is important to remember the Jews are under a brutal Roman dictatorship at this time and have very little freedom. Jesus in verse 33 rebuked Peter saying, "Get behind me Satan! For you are setting your mind not on divine things but on human things."

Peter is looking at things not from God's point of view but from the human point of view of how it will benefit him and his group, and even his country. They do not want a suffering Messiah; they want a glorious one on this earth, one that benefits them and their nation, one that will free them from the Romans.

This writer believes that many people today view things similar to Peter. There are those today who believe their nation is God's choice as Israel was in the past. There are those who believe their particular political party should rule, for their party is the party of God. Instead of trying to understand the situation from God's point of view through the teachings and actions of Jesus, they misinterpret some of his teachings, sometimes knowingly and sometimes unknowingly, to fit it into their particular ideology to get approval from the people to gain power. In the meantime they often ignore whatever does not fit into their way of thinking.

It must be noted that no nation, no institution, no human political party is the party of God; consequently they all are accountable to God. Throughout the history of Israel, the prophets and Jesus called all rulers and their followers to be accountable to God. This was contrary to everywhere else in the ancient world. In the Old Testament God chose a nation, but in the New Testament

God chooses a church to which all nations are to come. The church is also accountable. The message is that all humans and their institutions have sin and need purified, for everything is God's creation and accountable to him even government.

The teachings of Jesus not only have individual implications but also have political, economic, and social implications. No organized political system is described in the New Testament, but the kingdom has broken into God's created world, and its virtues, values, and vision are to impact all people, all nations, and all institutions. This kingdom will not be in completion until the final coming of Jesus, but the measuring stick is the kingdom that Jesus models and is now breaking into the world. Jesus is upset with Peter because his thinking is the thinking of humans not God.

In western society there has been a split between theology and politics that has dominated western society for over two hundred years. This thinking is not based on the thinking of Jesus. This way of thinking developed hundreds of years ago during the Age of the Enlightenment. The goal was to eliminate religion from the public square. Of course, the main reason for this human thinking was to allow the captains of industry and government leaders the freedom to do what they wanted politically, economically, and socially, without religion interfering or questioning them.

Jesus sets the pattern for true Christian discipleship in verses 34-38. He says, "If any want to become my followers, let them deny themselves and take up their cross and follow me. (Then in the following he explains what that means.) For those who want to save their life will lose it, and those who lose their life for my sake, and for the sake of the gospel will save it. For what will it profit them to gain the whole world and forfeit their life? Indeed, what can they give in return for their life? Those who are ashamed of me and of my words in this adulterous and sinful generation, of them the Son of Man will also be ashamed when he comes in the glory of his Father with the holy angels."

This is saying that if one truly wants to be a disciple of Christ, one must renounce their human thinking and think like Jesus. This is the message to Peter. They are to renounce their selfishness and a self-centered life that puts self or even nation first, and die to the thinking (conventional wisdom) and ways of the world, and let Christ's view of the world and his word be in control. As Romans 12:1-2 states, it is a renewal of the mind. Two ways are presented; life in the kingdom of God, that is a life in the Spirit of Christ Jesus, or life in the conventional wisdom of the world. Matthew 6:33 says, "Strive first for the kingdom of God and his righteousness," . . . and Phil 2:4 says, "Let each of you look not to your own interests but to the interests of others."

Radical monotheism is the choice: Jesus or the gods of this world. It is Jesus and his teachings, or the gods of one's creation. All nations tend to create their own religion, which historians have labeled "civil religion", which becomes a state religion masked in Christianity or Islam, or whatever is the prevalent religion of the area; usually it becomes a type of nationalism that leads to militarism. Individuals are notorious for creating their own gods, which are too numerous to list. That should not be for the people of God. The people of Christ need to be willing to be disciplined by the story of Jesus and to read it over against themselves and not read it in a self-serving defense of their personal or political interests but in the interests of the one who has established his kingdom.

Jesus will later say one can not have two masters. Pleasures, success, profits, materialism, consumerism, capitalism, sex, nation, and self are just a few of the modern gods. There are even some in America today who are in danger of making their nation and its political and economic system their god. Patriotism is good as are pleasure, success, sex, and profits, but when these things become primary in one's beliefs and action, while making the teachings of Christ second, or on par with them, which is an impossibility, then one is guilty of making the things of the world first in importance and Jesus and the kingdom second.

The Apostle Paul in Phil 3:20 said, "But our citizenship is in heaven, and it is from there that we are expecting a Savior, the Lord Jesus Christ." This means that the primary purpose of God's people is to serve as a colonial outpost for the kingdom Jesus established. Our secondary citizenship is the country in which we make our home. This is Jesus' message to Peter.

The path to transformation begins with a decision of priorities. Thus if we and the church claim to be disciples of Christ and claim to represent his interests, we must make his interests and his priorities ours, and that includes the political, economic, and social implications of his teachings. This is Jesus message to Peter.

The message to the church is that it is not to be involved itself in power politics, but it is to challenge power politics, not to gain power, but to see that power works for what Christ stood for. God is Lord of all, not just our so-called spiritual life. That is the implication of the kingdom breaking into the real world. One must stand with God's word, and be willing to stand with and for the things he stood for, as well as take the side of those with whom Jesus sided. In the process of doing so, when suffering (mental or physical) comes, one must be willing to suffer as Jesus did.

The religion of Christ is not to be a pie in the sky religion. It is not about a separation of the spiritual from the physical and material. It is not a separation of the inward and outward. It is not a religion about worldly success. It is not a religion of psychotherapy. It is not a feel-good religion. It is not about being entertained by the worship and religion of churches. It is not a personal salvation only religion.

For the followers of Christ it is living in this difficult world making the kingdom of God present by allowing Christ to live in them and through them, and in the process being willing to suffer for the things he suffered. It is about transformation, individual renewal, community renewal, and renewal of the world. It is not about political control nor is it about any political or economic system, even though his teachings have political and economic ramifications. It is about being an ambassador for Christ (2 Cor 5:20), influencing all for the kingdom of God. This is Jesus' message to Peter. Jesus said pray this way, Your kingdom come, your will be done on earth as it is in heaven. That means now, in the present.

The kingdom is breaking into the world. It is the Father's way of ruling the world through his Son and those responding to the call of his Son. The people of Jesus throughout time are to carry his message and actions forward until he comes again at the end of time to complete his task. Mark wants the church and individuals who call themselves Christians to ask themselves where they are in attitude and actions as serious disciples of Jesus. Christians need to ask themselves not only why did he die, but also why did he live. He did not live only to die.

The mission he gives each follower is the key to understanding the issue, and the mission is about transformation and renewal of self and the world in which we live. This is done by keeping attached to Jesus through the Spirit, allowing the Spirit to do his work in and through each follower. At some time the day of the Lord will come like a thief, and then the heavens will pass away with a loud noise, and the elements will melt with fire, and the earth and everything that is done on it will be disclosed.

The kingdom is breaking into the world. The kingdom will be brought to its completion with a new heaven and a new earth when Jesus comes again. Meanwhile, Jesus, the Lord of all his creation, has called his people to be his eyes, ears, mouth, hands, and feet until he returns. The mission of the kingdom is much more than individual salvation, and it is not personal political power or any kind of power the people of the world love and strive to obtain. This is what Jesus is in the process of getting Peter to understand. Individuals and creation itself (the world and its institutions) are groaning in labor pains and yearn to be set free from its bondage (Rom 8:19-23).

This writer believes the incarnation, the life of Christ, is as important as the crucifixion and resurrection. The choice is not one as opposed to the other. They must be integrated. The meaning of Jesus life for his people is every bit as important as is the meaning of his death.

In chapter 9:1 Jesus said, "Truly I tell you, there are some standing here who will not taste death until they see that the kingdom of God has come with power."

Jesus is talking about the end time kingdom that soon would be breaking in upon the world through him in their time. The end is coming forward into the world through Jesus. This is called the *eschatological* kingdom. It is the hope Israel is waiting for. Jesus is not primarily talking about the end of the world. He is talking about the end-time kingdom beginning to break into the world now through him, and then growing like a mustard seed influencing everything in its path. He is talking about the new age, and the people of God becoming the new Israel through the kingdom he is establishing with its virtues and values and vision for the world.

This kingdom is what he came to preach (Lk 4:43). It is being modeled by him and guided by those who will become his disciples, who will continue to plant seeds of the kingdom in the local communities. Seeing the kingdom coming in power may be a reference to Acts chapter 2 with the coming of the Spirit sent by Jesus into the church on the day of Pentecost.

It is important to remember that God so loved the world . . . He loved the world he created not just the individuals he created. Jesus was modeling that kingdom in word and deed and calling disciples to be a part of it. In 1:15 Jesus said, "The time is fulfilled, and the kingdom of God has come near; repent, and believe in the good news." When the church is planted, it will have the same mission Jesus had. Its purpose is much more than saving souls; it is to gather and prepare people to be kingdom people so that God's will be done on earth as it is in heaven. It will never be done perfectly until Christ comes again, but where Christ and his teachings are made present the kingdom is being made present.

After he told them that some of them would see the kingdom come with power, six days later Jesus is transfigured (supernaturally transformed) on a mountain. Peter, James, and John are there and see him transfigured. Verses 3-4 say, his clothes became dazzling white, such as no one on earth could bleach them. And there appeared to them Elijah with Moses, who were talking with Jesus. (Peter being excited wants to equally honor all three.) Verses 7-8 say, Then a cloud overshadowed them, and from the cloud there came a voice, "This is my Son, the Beloved, listen to him!" Suddenly when they looked around, they saw no one with them any more, but only Jesus. (The divinity of Jesus is revealed on this mountain to these three disciples. Why this is not revealed to the others is a mystery. Were these three ready for advanced learning more than the others?)

Moses represents the Old Testament law, and Elijah represents the Old Testament prophets. Even though they are important and necessary to stay in touch with, Mark is saying Jesus also a law-giver and prophet is more than a prophet and law-giver. He is to supersede them. The old law and the prophets were to lead to Jesus, and Jesus as prophet, priest, and king will continue the law-giving and prophetic tradition. There is continuity with the old as Jesus leads the old Israel to the new Israel. Mark makes it plain that Jesus is greater than Moses and Elijah. Now the Old Testament teachings will be understood and interpreted through the words and works of Jesus. Jesus is the fulfillment of the law and prophets. The time of promise has led to the age of fulfillment. The new age and the new Israel are beginning.

The New Testament book of Hebrews 1:1-3 says, Long ago God spoke to our ancestors in many and various ways by the prophets, but in these last days he has spoken to us by a Son, whom he appointed heir of all things, through whom he also created the worlds. He is the reflection of God's glory and the exact imprint of God's very being, and he sustains all things by his powerful word.

The word of Christ is the word that has priority. It is through Jesus actions and his words that the Old Testament and even the rest of the New Testament are to be interpreted and understood. It is called the law of the Spirit of life in Christ Jesus (Rom 8:2). Yes, even the rest of the New Testament letters are to be understood through Christ, for most of them are primarily an attempt to apply Jesus' teachings while correcting local issues in certain cultural situations.

We can learn much through all the writings, but we must not forget that all things are fulfilled in and through Jesus. This does not eliminate the Old Testament or other New Testament writings; they are still very important and inspired writings. The New Testament writings are on a higher level than the Old, and the teachings and actions of Jesus are higher than even the rest of the New Testament. Everything needs to be in its proper perspective. Colossians 1:16-17 says, All things have been created through him and for him. He himself is before all things, and in him all things hold together. It is a sad situation that only forty-five percent of Americans polled can even name the four Gospels.

Verses 9-10 say, As they were coming down the mountain, he ordered them to tell no one about what they had seen, until after the Son of Man had risen from the dead. So they kept the matter to themselves, questioning what this rising from the dead could mean. (Mark continually indicates that without the cross and resurrection, the real Jesus can not be known nor his words really understood.)

When they asked him in (11-13) "Why did the scribes say Elijah must come first?" (The question relates to the prophecy of Malachi in 4:5.) He said to them, "Elijah is indeed coming first to restore all things. How then is it written about the Son of Man that he has to go through many sufferings and be treated with contempt? But I tell you that Elijah has come, and they did to him whatever they pleased, as it is written about him." (His reference is to John the Baptist. This should warn us about taking any prophecy too literally.)

In verses 14-18 they come to a place where there is an argument and much commotion. The disciples can not heal a man's son, who from childhood had a spirit that threw him on the ground. Jesus responded in (19) saying, "You faithless generation, how much longer must I be among you? How much longer must I put up with you? Bring him to me." The father of the son in (22) said to Jesus, "if you are able to do anything, have pity on us and help us." In verses 23-24 Jesus said to him, "If you are able!—All things can be done for the one who believes." Immediately the father cried out, "I believe; help my unbelief!" (The statement of this father is something all Christians need to reflect upon for their own spiritual development.)

In verses 25-27 Jesus rebukes the unclean spirit and heals the boy. In verses 28-29 the disciples asked Jesus, "Why could we not cast it out?" He said to them, "This kind can come out only through prayer." (This is in contrast to their argumentative attitude as in verse 14. Christians and the churches need to be more about prayer than arguing with one another. This will bring many more believers than arguing and debating.)

In verses 30-32 they pass through Galilee, but Jesus does not want the masses of people to know it because he is trying to teach his disciples. In (31-32) he said to them, "The Son of Man is to be betrayed into human hands, and they will kill him, and three days after being killed, he will rise again." But they did not understand what he was saying and were afraid to ask him.

Characteristically, Mark continues to present the side of the disciples that indicates they are afraid and do not understand. At this point they still can not accept that there is not going to be earthly success. It is like people today who believe if they accept Christ into their lives they will always have earthly happiness, even material success and windfalls of money. They usually come up with this by taking Old Testament verses out of context. Although happiness is a concern of Jesus, worldly happiness and success are not his primary concern.

In verses 33-34 in a house in Capernaum the disciples argue about who is the greatest among them. In (35) Jesus says to them, "Whoever wants to be first must be last of all and servant of all." Then in (36-37) he took a little child and said to them, "Whoever welcomes one such child in my name welcomes me, and whoever welcomes me welcomes not me but the one who sent me."

Children represent the lowest possible status in the superiority/inferiority power structure. They represent the powerless in the world's power structure whose worth is only in being human and loved by their relatives. They represent total trust, for their only hope is in trusting their parents. Jesus' point is that his disciples are to trust and act as children and the powerless do and to use any power they have for the benefit of those with the greatest need. Jesus is always teaching the reverse of the world's wisdom and its superiority/ inferiority system. He often talks about the last being first and the great being humbled as he reverses the thinking of the values of this world and turns them upside down. He challenges the deepest, thoughts, feelings, and identity of people.

The radical teachings and actions of Jesus disturb us because they challenge the status quo, our complacent self-understanding, and how our culture has imprinted us. It seems that many people would prefer that Jesus' message co-exist with the dominate ways of our culture in order to pick and choose what benefits one the most in different situations. Christ strongly opposes that type of thinking.

In verses 38-39 the disciples are upset for demons are being cast out in the name of Jesus by those who are not followers, but Jesus in (40-41) said, "Whoever is not against us is for us. For truly I tell you, whoever gives you a cup of water to drink because you bear the name of Christ will by no means lose the reward."

He seems to be saying those who are not Christians but act like Christ will not lose their reward. Later he will say that those who are not for us are against us, which is the exact opposite of here (Mt 12:30). Compare with Luke 9:50. The difference is the context. There are those who do not really know and understand Christ, but do as he did like those in this context. But there are those who do not know and understand Christ because they have rejected him, which is the other context. Context makes the difference in what Jesus says at different times. That is why pulling Scripture out of context distorts and misrepresents Scripture.

In verses 42-48 Jesus warns them about hell which will be for those who cause others to stumble. He warns them about hell if they allow hands, feet, or eyes to cause themselves to stumble. He says, "If any of you put a stumbling block before one of these little ones who believe in me, it would be better for you if a great millstone were hung around your neck and you were thrown into the sea." (This is about the Christian's responsibility to be an example for other believers including their own children. The greatest mission field for most is their family. If the example is rejected, it is not the one giving the good example that is responsible.)

He continues, "If your hand causes you to stumble, cut it off; it is better for you to enter life maimed than to have two hands and go to hell, to the unquenchable fire. And if your foot causes you to stumble, cut it off; it is better for you to enter life lame than to have two feet and to be thrown into hell. And if your eye causes you to stumble, tear it out; it is better for you to enter the kingdom of God with one eye than to have two eyes and be thrown into hell, where their worm never dies, and the fire is never quenched." (Of course, this is not to be taken literally. Jesus often uses hyperbole in his teaching. As he teaches elsewhere the most important thing is a transformed heart, for it is from the heart that good and bad fruit originate. What good is it to tear out eyes, if the heart is not transformed?)

Verses 49-50 say, "For everyone will be salted with fire. Salt is good; but if salt has lost its saltiness, how can you season it? Have salt in yourselves, and be at peace with one another."

He is saying everyone is going to be judged, so judge yourself and make sure you are reconciled with each other, and do not become like salt that loses its preservative power, meaning its purpose. Jesus later calls his people to be peacemakers, making peace where there is strife and being at peace whenever possible with everyone (Rom 12:18-21). One of the New Testament's major themes is about reconciliation meaning peace with God and peace with each other.

There are scholars who say in historical context this message of trust in Jesus and his way is first a message to those in Israel who are advocating the overthrow of Rome by violence, and if they do not change their agenda for his agenda, Rome will come and destroy their nation, the city of Jerusalem, and the temple. Because the leaders and others do not pay attention to him, this very thing will happen in AD 70. Second it is a message of principle for everyone throughout time.

Chapter 10 continues on discipleship. In 10:1-2 crowds gather around Jesus, and while he is teaching them, Pharisees come to test him, and they ask, "Is it lawful for a man to divorce his wife?" Jesus reminds them in (3-5) that Moses did allow divorce, but in (5-9) Jesus says, "Because of the hardness of hearts, he wrote this commandment for you. But from the beginning of creation, 'God made them male and female.' 'For this reason a man shall leave his father and mother and be joined to his wife, and the two shall become one flesh.' So they are no longer two, but one flesh. Therefore what God has joined together, let no one separate." Later in the house in (11-12) he tells the disciples, "Whoever divorces his wife and marries another commits adultery against her; and if she divorces her husband and marries another, she commits adultery."

Up to this point only a woman could commit adultery because she was thought to be the property of a man. Jesus changes this thinking and puts the woman on the same level as the man. Jesus is saying that remarriage after a divorce by either a man or a woman is the sin of adultery. This is a passage of Scripture we moderns tend to ignore. The point that must be emphasized is that remarriage is not the sin that can not be forgiven. Instead of ignoring this teaching, possibly the focus needs to be on the mercy and grace of the forgiveness Jesus offers, and then begin again anew. There are those who believe Roman Catholics and some fundamentalist Christians are not flexible enough saying remarriage is not acceptable, while many mainline Christians are too flexible as they basically ignore the teaching. To others both groups seem to ignore the spirit of the law, either by ignoring the teaching or making a rigid law from it.

War is not taught in New Testament Scripture, but most Christians believe there is such a thing as a just war to protect and defend against oppressors. Can we also say there can be such a thing as a just divorce to protect against abuse and other forms of oppression? Or should both be rejected? Did Jesus mention remarriage as adultery in order to make it a timeless ethic, or is it to teach an attitude about marriage that God wants his people to have, even as he knows imperfect people will fall short of his ideal? This writer does not have all the answers, but believes these things should be discussed by leaders of the churches and among churches.

Verse 13 says, People were bringing little children to him in order that he might touch them, and the disciples spoke sternly to them. Jesus saw this in (14-15) and said to them, "Let the little children come to me; do not stop them; for it is to such as these that the kingdom of God belongs. Truly I tell you, whoever does not receive the kingdom of God as a little child will not enter it." And he took them up in his arms, laid his hands on them and blessed them.

Jesus is saying as small children depend and trust completely in their parents, so his disciples are to depend and trust totally and completely on the teachings and actions of Jesus. This teaching really is not to be used as a proof text for or against infant baptism or even about laying hands on them; the primary teaching is about developing an attitude about belief and trust in him, his actions, and his teachings.

In verses 17-19 a man came to him and said, "Good teacher what must I do to inherit eternal life?" (Actually he is asking what he is to do to share in the age to come, to be among those vindicated when God acts decisively and becomes king.) Jesus says to him, "Why do you call me good? No one is good but God alone." (Jesus is asking the man if he understands the true meaning of good, and if he recognizes that Jesus is God with the authority to answer his question.) Then Jesus said, "You know the commandments: 'You shall not murder; You shall not commit adultery; You shall not steal; You shall not bear false witness; You shall not defraud (not listed in the ten commandments but probably used in place of not coveting); Honor your father and mother.' "

It is interesting that Jesus does not mention he is to have no other gods than the one God (YHWH) and that he is not to worship idols. He saves these commandments until the end. The man in verse 20 says, "Teacher I have kept all these from my youth." Jesus in verse 21 says, "You lack one thing; go, sell what you own, and give the money to the poor, and you will have treasure in heaven; then come, follow me."

Jesus is testing where his real commitment lies, and if he is willing to do what Jesus tells him to do. Jesus is helping him to see that he has an idol in his life that has replaced God. He is also pointing out his lack of love for those whom God loves, the disadvantaged, those of society, who are not the wealthy and powerful. Jesus is showing him that he is in disobedience to the summary and heart of the commandments, which is to love God with all your heart and your neighbor as yourself. He is teaching that one's life is either governed by possessions, the things of the world, or the things of God. This man is discovering his life is governed by his idol of wealth. Is this teaching of Jesus meant to be a timeless ethic where one is to sell all to be a follower of Jesus? It may be for some, but we will see that everyone is not called to this. But all are called to respond to the spirit of this law.

Verse 22 says, When he heard this, he was shocked and went

away grieving, for he had many possessions. (The point of this story is in verses 23-25.) Jesus said, "How hard it will be for those who have wealth to enter the kingdom of God!" And the disciples were perplexed at these words. (Many people in those times as ours are also perplexed and believe that people are wealthy because God is rewarding them. Of course, that is not true; many people are wealthy for other reasons, and not all of them are good reasons.)

But Jesus said to them again, "Children, how hard it is to enter the kingdom of God! It is easier for a camel to go through the eye of a needle than for someone who is rich to enter the kingdom of God." Verse 26 says, the disciples were astounded and said, "Then who can be saved?" Jesus looked at them and said, "For mortals it is impossible, but not for God; for God all things are possible."

Jesus is saying humans can not save themselves or enter into the kingdom through their wealth or anything they do. Entering the kingdom and salvation comes for those who trust God and follow the ways of his Son. Following the ways of the Son can not earn one the kingdom, but by not following his ways one can miss out on it. One can not be part of the kingdom if one does not attempt to follow the agenda of Jesus. One is not saved by works, but one is not saved without works. Peter in 2 Peter 10-11 says, "Therefore, brothers and sisters, be all the more eager to confirm your call and election, for if you do this, you will never stumble. For in this way, entry into the eternal kingdom of our Lord and Savior Jesus Christ will be richly provided for you." God's people must confirm their part of the covenant by their obedience.

Dunn (2003, 338-339) calls it *covenantal nomism*. It is maintaining one's status in the covenant agreement that God has made with his people and depending on trust and God's grace. It is the followers confirming their part of the covenant. This is done by allowing the Father and the Son to bear their fruit in and through the believer (Jn

15). God says throughout that I will be your God and you will be my people. Being on the side of those in need and being a help to them is a primary agenda of God throughout the Old Testament and Jesus in the New Testament. One can not avoid that and be in the kingdom (see Mt 25:31-46, Lk 16:19-31, James 2:14-26).

That is why Jesus challenges this man to sell all he has and give it to the poor. Jesus, like the prophets before him, sees many of those in need as victims of the policies and actions of people with wealth and power. Yes, victims! Jesus never says blessed are the wealthy and powerful. In Scripture the wealthy and powerful are always challenged to use their wealth and influence for the common good, and they are always warned about judgment if they do not do so. Elsewhere he calls the rich, fools (Lk 12:20).

This would be a good message to all of us comfortable people in today's churches, but this writer does not remember hearing it in a sermon (homily) very often, if at all. Jesus is saying that the rich will have a hard time entering, and one can not enter the kingdom of God without standing with or showing concern for those who do not have wealth and power (Mt 25:31-46, Lk 16:19-31). According to both the Old and New Testaments those who only concern themselves with their own wealth and power, showing no concern for the health and welfare of those who are disadvantaged, will be the ones disadvantaged in the end.

He is not telling everyone to sell everything and give it to the poor as a timeless ethic. Later Zacchaeus will only give half of what he has, and the women who followed Jesus gave to him what they could as did those giving to the Apostle Paul's collection for the poor in Jerusalem. This particular rich man is told to sell everything to humble him and point out to him that he is a sinner who needs to repent because his life is being governed by idolatry, which is his self concern and his wealth. He is also saying mortals can not save themselves, even if they give their wealth to others, but God saves those whose hearts are in the right place.

In verses 28-31 Peter reminds Jesus they left everything to follow him, and Jesus tells him that they would receive eternal life in the age to come. "But many who are first will be last, and the last will be first." (Jesus is saying that those who are nothing in the eyes of this world may be everything in the kingdom, the eternal age, and those who are everything in this age may be zero in the age to come. In the kingdom of God the positions of insider and outsider are reversed. It seems to this writer that Scriptures such as this tend to be ignored by too many of us in comfortable America.)

In verses 32-34 Mark states they were amazed and afraid. Jesus again pulls the twelve aside and says, "See, we are going up to Jerusalem, and the Son of Man will be handed over to the chief priests and the scribes, and they will condemn him to death; then they will hand him over to the Gentiles; they will mock him, and spit upon him, and flog him, and kill him; and after three days he will rise again." (This is the third time he attempts to tell them about what is going to happen to him.)

They ignore him, and in verses 35-40 James and John, the sons of Zebedee ask Jesus to let them sit with him in power when he comes into his glory, but they really do not know what they are asking. In Mt 20:20-28 it is the mother who comes to Jesus asking for James and John. The question for the literalists and those who believe nothing is in error in the Bible is: Who asked Jesus? Was it the mother or the sons? Because, like Peter, they think it is going to be a real political kingdom on this earth with Jesus as the ruler and the twelve as his ruling cabinet, they really do not hear what he is saying. Even when he tells them exactly what is going to happen to him, they can not accept it. When his crucifixion finally occurs, they will all be in shock, and then surprised when they see him raised from the dead.

Verse 41 informs us that when the other ten found out what James and John had done, they were upset. (A power struggle related to the values of this world is in progress.) In verses 42-44 Jesus again upturns the superiority-inferiority relationship scale by calling them and saying to them, "You know that among the Gentiles those whom they recognize as their rulers lord it over them, and their great ones are tyrants over them. But it is not so among you; but whoever wishes to become great among you must be your servant, and whoever wishes to be first among you must be slave of all. For the Son of Man came not to be served but to serve, and to give his life a ransom for many." (The original word in the Greek is slave.)

Ransom means to be set free. Individuals are set free from sin, and the nation is to be set free from its sin in order to end their punishment; then the new Israel can reign in service to all, including the Gentiles. Thus they become a light to the nations, a city set upon a hill. Jesus is saying that true divine power is in serving each other, especially those in need. Followers of Christ are to serve their fellow humans and take his mission into the world. This is the meaning of losing self and becoming a slave to Christ. Again, Jesus turns the thinking of the world upside down. Jesus is always reversing the thinking of the world.

The vision and virtues and values of God's kingdom are most often the reverse of the world's vision and its virtues and values. It seems to this writer that too many Christians seem to live the world's values instead of the kingdom's values. Too many seek political power and human power for their own interests instead of using divine power in the service of others and promoting the common good. Possibly, that is the reason there seems to be little respect for those who call themselves Christian politicians and even for those in power in the churches.

In verses 46-47 as they came to Jericho, Bartimaeus son of Timaeus, a blind beggar, begins to shout and say, "Jesus, Son of David, have mercy on me!" (Here he addresses him as Son of David which is referring to him as the Messiah, the King of the Jews, which is a dangerous thing to do politically.) In verses 48-49 Many sternly ordered him to be quiet, but he cried out even more loudly, Son of David have mercy on me!" Jesus stood still and said, "Call him here." Verses 50-52 say, So throwing off his cloak, he sprang up and came to Jesus. Jesus said to him, "What do you want me to do for you?" The blind man said to him, "My teacher, let me see again." Jesus said to him, "Go; your faith has made you well." Immediately he regained his sight and followed him on the way.

Jesus first enables him to see physically, and then because he calls him my teacher and follows Jesus, he sees spiritually. Mark's gospel is about seeing who Jesus really is and seeing what being a follower of Jesus really means. Mark is challenging all readers to have their sight transformed and to see with new eyes.

Chapter 11:1-3 says, when they were approaching Jerusalem, at Bethphage and Bethany, near the Mount of Olives, he sent two of his disciples and said to them, "Go into the village ahead of you, and immediately as you enter it, you will find tied there a colt that has never been ridden; untie it and bring it. If anyone says to you 'Why are you doing this?' just say this, 'The Lord needs it and will send it back here immediately.' " Verse 7 says, Then they brought the colt to Jesus and threw their cloaks on it; and he sat on it.

This is a reference to Zechariah 9:9. The day is Palm Sunday, the Sunday beginning the week that leads to his crucifixion. Jesus is not entering Jerusalem on a war horse but on the colt of a donkey, an animal symbolizing peace and used by the common working man.

Verses 8-9 say, Many people spread their cloaks on the road, and others spread leafy branches that they had cut in the fields. Then those who went ahead and those who followed were shouting "Hosanna! Blessed is the one who comes in the name of the Lord! Blessed is the coming kingdom of our ancestor David! Hosanna in the highest heaven!"

With this statement the people are addressing him as the king they are expecting to come to throw out the hated Romans who control their land. This action of the crowd is a concern for both the Jewish and Roman political authorities, for there always seem to be riots in Jerusalem at this time of the year. The Passover is the time that people think God will step in and save the nation. The word Hosanna that the people are using means save us now. To the majority this meant save us from the hated Romans.

Jesus enters Jerusalem, goes to the temple, and then he goes to Bethany with the twelve. The following day verses 12-14 say, they approached a fig tree, but there were no figs, and Jesus said to it, "May no one ever eat fruit from you again." (The cursing of the fig tree and the following incident involving the temple are interwoven and meant to be interpreted together as each interprets the other.)

Verses 15-17 say, Then they came to Jerusalem. And he entered the temple and began to drive out those who were selling and those who were buying in the temple, and he overturned the tables of the money changers and the seats of those who sold doves; and he would not allow anyone to carry anything through the temple. He was teaching and saying, "Is it not written, 'My house shall be called a house of prayer for all nations'? But you have made it a den of robbers." (This is quoted from Jer 7:11.)

Too often this is portrayed as an emotional display of anger by Jesus, but that is not true. The incident needs to be understood within the symbolic actions of the prophetic tradition of Israel by referring to prophets like Isaiah, Jeremiah, Ezekiel, and Hosea then his actions become nothing more than enlivened symbolic actions prophesying the temple's destruction as well as the reason for its future destruction. This is an example of the more the Old Testament is read and understood, the more one is able to understand the New Testament. This is important for a number of reasons, one is that among other things Jesus is also a prophet.

The temple has become a place where people are fleeced in the name of religion. People coming from distant lands to worship at the temple are being charged outrageous prices to exchange their money and to buy the animals to sacrifice as their worship. This is done in the Court of the Gentiles, the only place in the temple Gentiles have an opportunity to pray. The temple leaders backed by the Sanhedrin have become corrupt oppressors who have institutionalized greed and the oppression of its own people.

Keep in mind the temple is the main banking center for the leaders of the nation who are economically exploiting the people through their system of taxation and their interest policies, then confiscating their homes, land, animals, and crops when they could not pay their taxes and debts. The people are then made tenant farmers and slaves, while the high priests and Romans enrich themselves.

Jesus by these symbolic actions does what the prophet Jeremiah did before him. It is a way of criticizing their greed and oppression toward their fellow Jews. Jesus is using his actions in this way, and he is warning the temple leaders, the nation, and the resistance movement bent on a violent overthrow of Rome, that if they do not change their ways both Jerusalem and the temple will be destroyed just as it was in the past.

The temple has become like the barren fig tree, no longer producing fruit. Many of the disadvantaged in the land see the temple and its leaders as all that is taking advantage of them. They see the leaders as a rich, corrupt aristocracy in cahoots with the Romans taking their lands, overtaxing them, and keeping the masses indebted to them. God's light has dimmed through Israel's systemic injustice. See note on the peasants and the economy at the end of the section called More Interpretation Issues. Later when the nationalistic rebels attack the temple, the first thing they do is destroy all the tax records. The temple then will become the center of the revolution against Rome.

Jesus during his time on earth, like Jeremiah, warns the rebels to give up their violent resistance movement, for it will end in the destruction of the temple and the city. But like their forefathers they reject him. The end result will turn out to be the same as in the time of Jeremiah. The temple and the city will be totally destroyed. But this will not happen for at least twenty-five more years. God gives them ample time to repent of their agenda and take on the agenda of Jesus, but they refuse.

In verses 18-19 the chief priests and the scribes (the professional interpreters of Jewish law from the Sanhedrin) keep looking for a way to kill him; for they are afraid of him, because the whole crowd is spellbound by his teaching. When evening comes, Jesus and his disciples leave the city.

If the reader looks back historically, it is important to understand that the authorities were not trying to kill Jesus because he loved everyone and desired to atone for the sin of the world. Later this will become the theological reason for the Father allowing it to happen, but it is not the actual historical reason.

The Sanhedrin consists of seventy religious and political leaders of Israel also in charge of the temple. Some are the elders, who are landowners and very wealthy. The majority are the priests who are the Sadducees that work closely with the Romans in order to keep their power positions and the wealth that goes with it. The priests are among the wealthiest people in Israel. They oppose the religious thinking of the Pharisees. Unlike the Pharisees the Sadducees do not believe in a physical resurrection, angels or spirits, and only accept the first five books of the Old Testament. In the Sanhedrin, a minority are the Pharisees, who are the scribes.

A sizeable number of the Pharisees in the land are encouragers of the resistance movement. They want Jesus out of the way because he is not an observant Jew and is opposing their traditions, especially their Sabbath, dietary, and purity laws (Leviticus 11-15).

Another group, though not part of the Sanhedrin, are the Zealots, who lead the resistance movement. It is thought most of them originally were Pharisees. They want him gone because he is not a loyal, flag waving patriot. Jesus condemns their attitude and warns them to repent, to change their violent agenda for the kingdom's agenda. All these leaders of the nation want to get rid of him.

In the morning verses 20-21 say, as they passed by they saw the fig tree withered away to its roots. Then Peter remembered and said to him, "Rabbi, look! The fig tree you cursed has withered." (When putting together the incident of the fig tree with the temple, Jesus is saying the temple will soon be like the fig tree; there will no longer be any value or purpose for it.)

In verses 22-24 Jesus answered them, "Have faith in God. Truly I tell you, if you say to this mountain, 'Be taken up and thrown into the sea,' and if you do not doubt in your heart, but believe that what you say will come to pass, it will be done for you (an obvious hyperbole on the power of faith). So I tell you whatever you ask for in prayer, believe that you have received it, and it will be yours."

This is in the context of the kingdom of God bearing fruit and the listener or reader bearing fruit for the kingdom, and the temple not bearing fruit. The fig tree and the temple are bearing bad fruit or no fruit for God. So he is saying pray to bear good fruit for God and the kingdom, and it will happen. Horsley (2003, 93) notes that the temple is on Mt Zion. He believes that in Jesus saying with faith the mountain shall be thrown into the sea that Jesus is also saying because the people are so oppressed by the corrupt leadership in control of the Sanhedrin and the temple, the people's prayers for relief from their oppression will be answered.

Then Jesus says in verse 25, "Whenever you stand praying, forgive, if you have anything against anyone; so that your Father in heaven may also forgive you your trespasses." (This is stated in Mt 6:15 as, but if you do not forgive others, neither will your Father in heaven forgive your trespasses. The custom in Jewish prayer is to stand.) In verses 27-33 the chief priests, scribes, and elders (lay leaders of wealth and power) asked him, "By what authority are you doing these things? Who gave you this authority to do them?"

They want to know who gives him the authority to challenge their business practices in the temple and ignore their traditions. Jesus is doing just as Jeremiah had done approximately six hundred years before. They both went to the temple to symbolize its future destruction. They both called the religious and political authorities to repentance for their oppression and militant nationalism and both were rejected. At first the Sanhedrin was not militant, but later they join the revolt. Consequently, both times God allows the temple and the city to be destroyed.

Answering their question Jesus said to them, "I will ask you one question; answer me, and I will tell you by what authority I do these things. Did the baptism of John come from heaven, or was it of human origin? Answer me." They argued with one another, "If we say, 'From heaven,' he will say, 'Why then did you not believe him?' But shall we say, 'Of human origin'?"—they were afraid of the crowd, for all regarded John as truly a prophet. (Jesus answers their question with a question that puts them in a bind.) So they answered Jesus, "We do not know." And Jesus said to them, "Neither will I tell you by whose authority I am doing these things." (The reader must remember that in the historical context of the time John's message to repent is first applied to the nation's system of governance, which includes all aspects of life.)

If Jesus says his authority is from God, they will ask him to prove it or charge him with blasphemy. So to expose their real motives he counters their question with a question. Previously, it was noted they plotted to kill him. The problem, as they see it, is that he is a rebel and false prophet. He is undermining their political and religious authority and challenging the nation's business practices. His opposition to the temple authorities controlled by the Sanhedrin is one of the main reasons they will conspire with the Romans to kill him.

Chapter 12:1 says, Then he began to speak to them in parables. Parables are narrative stories illustrating things familiar in order to challenge one's thinking. Their literary style is often apocalyptic with hidden messages and subversive stories. The purpose of parables is to break open old world views and create new ones while disguising it to some extent from the authorities.

The core of many of the parables is about the return of God to Israel to judge, redeem, renew, and restore her. Most of them deal with the kingdom with the goal of re-working and re-appropriating the worldview of the nation and applying it to new times. The parables fit well into the prophetic background from which Jesus came. They compel individuals to discover truth for themselves. The message is usually only understood by those willing to listen and look at things in a different light, or as Jesus says those who have eyes to see and ears to hear.

In the following parable, which is an extension of Isa 5:1-7, this writer will add in parentheses who is being symbolized, then the parable will be self explanatory. Verses 2-9 say, "A man (God) planted a vineyard, (his people, the nation) put a fence around it, dug a pit for the wine press, and built a watchtower; then he leased it to tenants (his people, especially the leaders who were in charge) and went to another country (heaven). When the season came, he sent a slave (prophet) to the tenants to collect from them his share of the produce of the vineyard. (The produce he was seeking centered on Godly virtues and values.) But they seized him, and beat him, and sent him away empty handed. And again he sent another slave (prophet) to them; this one they beat over the head and insulted. Then he sent another and that one they killed. And so it was with many others; some they beat, and others they killed. He had still one other, a beloved son (Jesus).

"Finally he sent him to them saying, 'They will respect my son.' But those tenants said to one another, 'This is the heir; come, let us kill him, and the inheritance will be ours.' So they seized him, killed him, and threw him out of the vineyard. (Jesus exposes the plot of the leaders to kill him.) What then will the owner (God) of the vineyard do? He will come and destroy the tenants and give the vineyard to others."

The priestly aristocracy who controlled the temple and the money system and confiscated the people's homes, land, crops, and animals, because they could not pay their taxes and interest debt, are being told in this parable that they are going to lose what they have. They will be upset with Jesus over teachings like this and will conspire against him.

Later the temple and the city of Jerusalem are destroyed, the old covenant is fulfilled and the new covenant emerges. Jesus then establishes a community (the church) to which all people from all nations are invited. In this parable Jesus is subverting Israel's world view with a new twist. The leaders of the people of God have become the enemy of God by opposing God's message just as they had in the time of the Old Testament prophets. At that time God sent Assyria (722 BC), and then later Babylon (586 BC) to punish his people by sending them into exile.

Soon he is going to send Rome with the same purpose. This time a new Israel will be formed from the remnant Jesus is gathering. God always saves a remnant, and it is always just a remnant, for the majority of people never seem to be serious about his teachings, even though they accept them in name only. (Later Jesus will express the same idea with those he calls when he says, many are called but few are chosen, Mt 22:14.)

Verses 10-12 continue, "Have you not read the scripture: 'The stone that the builders rejected (Jesus) has become the cornerstone; (of the new Israel and new covenant) this was the Lord's doing, and it is amazing in our eyes'?" When they realized that he had told this parable against them, they wanted to arrest him, but they feared the crowd. So they left him and went away.

In verses 13-17 the Pharisees and Herodians attempt to trap him. They said in (14) "Teacher, we know that you are sincere, and show deference to no one; for you do not regard people with partiality, but teach the way of God in accordance with truth." (They said this because Jesus spent his time teaching and helping the average people and people with no means. He did not bow to and favor the people of wealth and power like they did.) Then in (14) they asked him their trick question in order to trap him. "Is it lawful to pay taxes to the emperor, or not?"

If he says no, they will tell the governing authorities that he is telling people to evade their taxes. If he says pay the tax, he will upset the people and the religious leaders who hate the Romans and their occupation of their country with their unjust taxes. The purpose of the question is to put him in a bind where he will have to choose one or the other which will make one of the groups angry.

Jesus in verse 15 says, "Why are you putting me to the test? Bring me a denarius (coin) and let me see it." In (16-17) they brought one and he points to the image of the emperor and says, "Give to the emperor the things that are the emperor's, and to God the things that are God's." And they were amazed at him.

There are some who think that when Jesus says give to the emperor what he deserves, he is saying, that he deserves nothing. But this writer believes that when he points to the image of the emperor, he is saying the governing leaders have a certain right to taxes to govern the land. But he is also saying because all people are made in the image of God they are to give to God for the purposes of God. Thus Jesus thwarts their goal of making him choose one over the other.

In verses 18-23 the Sadducees, who do not believe in the resurrection, attempt to stump Jesus with a question about a woman who had seven husbands who had died. So in (23) they ask, whose wife will she be? For the seven had married her. Jesus said to them, "Is not this the reason you are wrong, that you know neither the scriptures nor the power of God? For when they rise from the dead, they neither marry nor are given in marriage, but are like angels in heaven. And as for the dead being raised, have you not read in the book of Moses, in the story about the bush, how God said to him, 'I am the God of Abraham, the God of Isaac, and the God of Jacob'? He is not the God of the dead, but of the living; you are quite wrong."

Jesus is not saying that loved ones will not know each other. But he is saying that in heaven there will no longer be new marriages or giving birth to children, so there is no need for sexual activity. There will also be perfect love, and all will know each other in a perfected, intimate, non-sexual eternal happiness. Because all sin will be eliminated, something we have never experienced, this future perfected eternal life is beyond our total comprehension.

In verse 28 a scribe asks him, "Which commandment is the first of all?" In (29-31) Jesus answered, "The first is, 'Hear O Israel: The Lord our God, the Lord is one; you shall love the Lord your God with all your heart, and with all your soul, and with all your mind, and with all your strength.' The second one is this, 'You shall love your neighbor as yourself.' There is no other commandment greater than these." (Another way to put the latter is to do to others as you would have them do to you.)

This is the essence of all the Old Testament and New Testament laws or at least that to which they are to lead. As the world moves forward the laws that are created in different situations and contexts are to be of this spirit. What is lasting are not the situational laws. What is lasting is the Old Testament story of God working his plan. What lasts are God's virtues, values, vision and the spirit of the law of life in Christ Jesus as well as always doing the most loving thing. Many of the laws that can be defined as the letter of the law develop and change as time moves on. If the reader understands this concept, one will be able to better interpret both the Old and the New. This will help eliminate many interpretation problems.

The scribe agrees with Jesus' answer in (32-33) and states, this is much more important than all whole burnt offerings and sacrifices (Old Testament worship). When Jesus saw that he answered wisely, he said to him, "You are not far from the kingdom of God." After that no one dared to ask him any questions.

Verses 35-37 say, While Jesus was teaching in the temple, he said, "How can the scribes say that the Messiah is the Son of David? David himself, by the Holy Spirit, declared, 'The Lord said to my

Lord, "Sit at my right hand, until I put your enemies under your feet." ' David himself calls him Lord; so how can he be his son?" And the large crowd was listening to him with delight.

The religious leaders do not understand that the Messiah will be far more than a human descendant of David, even God himself in human form. Jesus quotes Ps 110:1 to show that David considered the Messiah to be his Lord, and not just his Son, and that the Messiah would sit in power with the Father which relates to Dan 7:13-14.

In verses 38-40 Jesus said, "Beware of the scribes who like to walk around in long robes, and be greeted with respect in the market places, and to have the best seats in the synagogues and places of honor at banquets! They devour widows' houses and for the sake of appearance say long prayers. They will receive the greater condemnation." (Most of the scribes are Pharisees. Jesus strongly opposes hypocrisy, especially of the religious who use their position to gain social acceptance and favors, and then use their position to take advantage.)

Verses 41-44 say, He sat down opposite the treasury, and watched the crowd putting money into the treasury. Many rich people put in large sums. A poor widow came and put in two small copper coins, which are worth a penny. Then he called his disciples and said to them, "Truly I tell you, this poor widow has put in more than all those who are contributing to the treasury. For all of them contributed out of their abundance; but she out of her poverty has put in everything she had, all she had to live on."

Are we not all humbled by this teaching? Jesus looks at giving differently than most of us, who are impressed with the sum the giver gives. But Jesus is impressed with the heart and spirit behind the giver. God wants our life and possessions to be dedicated to his glory, even though he does not expect all of it to be put into the church treasury. But it seems to this writer that the more we have, the more we want for our own benefit.

Chapter 13:1-2 says, As he came out of the temple, one of his disciples said to him, "Look, Teacher, what large stones and what large buildings!" Then Jesus asked him, "Do you see these great buildings? Not one stone will be left here upon another; all will be thrown down." (Jesus is foretelling the total destruction of the temple and even the city of Jerusalem.)

Verses 3-6 say, When he was sitting on the Mount of Olives opposite the temple, Peter, James, John, and Andrew asked him privately, "Tell us when this will be, and what will be the sign that all these things will be accomplished?" (The reference is to the temple and the destruction of the city.) Then Jesus began to say to them, "Beware that no one leads you astray. Many will come in my name and say, 'I am he!' and they will lead many astray.

Verse 7 says, "When you hear of wars and rumors of wars, do not be alarmed; this must take place, but the end is still to come." (The end will not be even when you hear of wars and rumors of war. The end is still in reference to the temple and Jerusalem in the time of Jesus and his disciples.) Jesus in (8) continues, "For nation will rise against nation, and kingdom against kingdom; there will be earthquakes in various places; there will be famines." This is but the beginning of the birth pangs. (This whole chapter is using apocalyptic language, which is symbolic language used by Hebrew writers throughout their history to express times of judgment and great change.)

Notice it is just the beginning of the end of the temple and its sacrificial system where the Jews had worshiped and had their sins forgiven for at least one thousand years. The birth pangs signal the imminence of judgment and the establishment of the new age, which Jesus announced at the beginning of his ministry, when he preached, the kingdom of God (reign of God) has come near. The kingdom is a new age where worship and forgiveness of sin are without the temple and without God's presence in the Most Holy Place in the temple.

The kingdom is breaking in through the presence of Jesus; it is a new age where God's presence will be experienced, first in Jesus and then through his real followers. But this new kingdom and new presence will make a new impact in the world only after a time of the disciples giving testimony to Jesus' teachings and after the temple in Jerusalem is destroyed. What follows is what will happen in that 35-40 year time span. He tells them what will happen when they spread the message of Jesus and the kingdom.

In verses 9-10 he continues, "As for yourselves, beware, for they will hand you over to councils; and you will be beaten in synagogues; and you will stand before governors and kings because of me, as a testimony to them. And the good news must be proclaimed to all nations." (The reference is to his particular disciples and all nations in their known world. When we read the book of Acts, which follows the Gospels, we will see that this happens between the time of Jesus crucifixion and resurrection in 33 AD and the destruction of the temple and the city of Jerusalem by the Romans in AD 70.)

Verses 11-13 continue, "When they bring you to trial and hand you over, do not worry beforehand about what you are to say; but say whatever is given you at the time, for it is not you who speak, but the Holy Spirit. Brother will betray brother to death, and a father his child, and children will rise against parents and have them put to death; and you will be hated by all because of my name. But the one who endures to the end will be saved." (This is first applied to the disciples to whom Jesus is now speaking.)

The endurance that leads to salvation is later to be appropriated by all who follow, but this message is directed to his current disciples and is about a new age, a new covenant breaking into the world. Salvation initially comes by grace through faith and in the end it is also by grace through faith, if one endures. It must be emphasized that endurance is necessary for salvation. The idea that once you are saved, (justification by faith) you are always saved is a biblical truth only if one remains a disciple of Jesus and endures (sanctification). After the sanctification process, which is based on one's relationship with Jesus and the working of the Holy Spirit, then in the end one is then saved by grace through faith (justification by faith). The Scriptures call the gift an inheritance. With any inheritance one must stay in the family to receive it. Rarely is an inheritance given to one who has rejected the family.

Second, Mark's gospel emphasizes that Jesus' disciples will suffer persecution. Third, this context is the period between the ministry of Jesus in AD 33 and the coming of Jesus in power by sending the Spirit upon his disciples on the day of Pentecost (Acts 2), and the destruction of the temple and the city of Jerusalem in AD 70. That does not mean these same things will not happen to followers after the destruction of the temple and later, but our world today is not the primary context of this chapter.

Jesus continues giving instructions to his disciples in verses 14-20 mentioning a desolating sacrilege set up where it should not be and suffering to come with instructions to flee the city when it occurs. This is a reference to the Romans and paganism taking the place of the temple when it is destroyed. And in verses 21-22 he says, "And if anyone says to you at that time, 'Look here is the Messiah!' or 'Look! There he is!'—do not believe it. False messiahs and false prophets will appear and produce signs and omens, to lead astray, if possible, the elect. (He is telling them that his final return with a final judgment will not be at that time, but there is going to be a judgment on the current city and temple.) Then in verse 23 he says, But be alert; I have already told you everything."

Jesus is telling his disciples to be aware of false messiahs bringing a different message. Jesus is reminding them that long ago when the prophet Jeremiah preached the destruction of the temple that would come through Babylon, if they did not repent from their economic oppression and militant nationalism, this is what happened. He is telling them that history is going to repeat itself. Unfortunately then as now, people do not pay much attention to history.

In the following some believe the writer jumps to the end of this known world, while others do not think so. The writer knows that the disciples think the destruction of the temple and the city of Jerusalem will be the end of the world, but Mark, writing after that destruction, knew it was not. It may be possible that Mark is indicating that like the destruction of Jerusalem and the temple it will also be similar for Christians throughout history and especially during the end of times, the end of this known world. It does seem the ideas behind the prophets repeat themselves.

Verses 24-25 are apocalyptic and used in the Old Testament in reference to God making a major judgment on his people, but out of it creating something new. Jesus says, "But in those days after that suffering, (when the Romans attack) the sun will be darkened, and the moon will not give its light, and the stars will be falling from heaven, and the powers in the heavens will be shaken." (This is the apocalyptic language and not to be taken literally. When used in the Old Testament, this cosmic activity symbolized that a great upheaval or time of judgment and redemption was about to occur, as well as political and social change.)

Attached to this apocalyptic in verses 26-27 he adds, "Then they will see the 'Son of Man coming in the clouds' with great power and glory. Then he will send out the angels, and gather his elect from the four winds, from the ends of the earth to the ends of heaven." Wright says that the word parousia often rendered as 'coming' actually means 'presence.' What matters is the presence of Jesus made known, his judgment, not a literal coming.

To understand the New Testament it is truly important to have a grasp of the Old Testament. To not have that background is to lose the context, continuity, and background of God's plan. God making his presence known is often symbolized in Scripture with him appearing in a cloud. Is Mark now jumping to the end of time, or is he applying all this to the time of Jesus and the beginning of the church?

NT Wright (1996, 339-66) understands these verses as apocalyptic and metaphorical making a theological statement about a current event. Clouds in Scripture represent God's presence, so this is saying people will see that the Father will vindicate Jesus, not only at the resurrection but when Rome destroys the city and temple in AD 70, the very thing he foretold.

This metaphor represents Jesus coming to Jerusalem as the vindicated rightful king taking the place of Torah and temple making official the establishment of the church and the new covenant. Then sending out from Jerusalem the angels to gather the elect is the real beginning of the harvest, meaning the real missionary expansion of Christianity. Angels can also be translated as messengers. It has nothing to do with the ending of the world in space and time. In fact most prophecy in the Old Testament is basically a reference to the end of an old age, the present evil age, and the beginning of the new age and the new covenant. It is about covenant, judgment, and new beginnings, which was the constant theme of the Old Testament prophets.

Here Jesus is retelling and reworking the great story found in the prophets such as Zechariah 14, Micah 7:2-10, Isaiah 40-55, Jeremiah 7, Ezekiel 34-37, Daniel 7, 9, 12, Hosea 11:1-9 and many others. There we have examples of Jesus using the story line from the prophetic tradition and reconstructing and retelling it to focus on what is happening in his context. What God had done in the past, he will at last do again, even more gloriously.

There will no longer be exile for Israel, God will return to his people and be king, the temple will be rebuilt, the new covenant will begin, the time of great renewal will be here. Jesus is saying all this is happening through him. He is the Messiah, the chosen of God, the word of God, the new temple where sins are now forgiven, and when the Romans destroy Jerusalem and the temple, he and his prophecy will be fulfilled. In the cross Jesus takes the exile and the reason for exile (sin) upon himself, and through the resurrection the new exodus from this world of captivity to sin begins.

Wright's point is Jesus constantly warned the nationalist resistance movement to give up their agenda of getting rid of Rome through violent action, and if not, God would act against them. This is part of the meaning of the word repentance, for both the nation and individuals are included in the call to repent. Because neither the nationalist resistance movement stopped their violence, nor did the Jewish leaders and the temple authorities change their unjust and oppressive ways, the nation is punished once again for the same reasons they were punished by God that culminated in the Assyrian (722 BC) and Babylonian (586 BC) exiles. Rome is called by God to punish his people for the same reasons as he previously did with the Assyrians and the Babylonians.

After the fall of the temple and the end of the sacrificial system, Christianity will begin to really make its mark and expand. History always seems to repeat itself. Since this is so, will it happen again with his church that has become soft and comfortable, refusing to be prophetic against itself, the unjust ways of the world, and even its own society?

Verses 28-29 are basically saying that when the signs appear he is near, at the gates. The Greek can be translated "it" is near instead of "he". If the translation is "it", the reference is to Rome's destruction. If the translation is "he", then the reference could be to Christ's judgment on the people at that time or as some believe his final coming and judgment. Possibly there is a good reason the word chosen can be translated two ways, but verse 30 tells us the reference is to this generation. Even if the reference is to that generation most of the signs appear over and over throughout the ages. For example there are always earthquakes, famines, wars and rumors of wars; suffering by Christians, and there are always those saying the Messiah is coming soon. It is Wright's belief that the translation should be "it."

In verses 30-31 Jesus says, "Truly I tell you, this generation will not pass away until all these things have taken place. Heaven and earth will pass away, but my words will not pass away. (All that he is speaking of will occur in that generation. Heaven and earth may pass away, which is an apocalyptic metaphor, but his word will always stand. It is possible that this generation could have reference to this age, the last age, the age we have been in since the establishment of the new covenant making the message applicable to both those times and time at the end.) Verses 32-33 say, "But that day or hour no one knows, neither the angels in heaven, nor the Son, but only the Father. Beware, keep alert; for you do not know when the time will come."

It is interesting that some modern day fundamentalist preachers apply all of this to the end of the world. They create all kinds of charts out of current events indicating they know when Jesus is coming to end the world. Actually this has been going on for almost two thousand years using the current events of the time. When the end does not come, they just keep adjusting to whatever is happening in world events to show that the time is now. This author finds their statements incredible, especially when Jesus himself said he did not even know when it would all take place.

Let us expand somewhat on the idea that this generation will not pass away until *all* these things have taken place. Often, when the Bible talks of this generation, the reference is to this evil generation. Since in Scripture all generations are evil; therefore, the application of these verses possibly may be applied to both the time of the destruction of the temple and Jerusalem, but also the end of this world as we know it. This would make the prophecy a double or multiple fulfillment. Therefore the signs that occur in all generations are simply to remind people to be alert and prepared for the coming of Jesus as well as judgment and renewal. The idea is to be prepared at all times for his coming. But the primary application in the context of this chapter is that the temple and Jerusalem will be destroyed in that generation as Jesus said it would.

If most of this chapter is to be applied to the breaking in of the kingdom of God, the kingdom broke into the world with Jesus' life, and is confirmed after Jesus rises from the dead and goes to the right hand of the Father, and then comes in power by sending the Holy Spirit upon the disciples. This occurs on the day of Pentecost, and one can read about that miraculous in breaking of the Holy Spirit in Acts chapter two. The day of Pentecost is the reference to Jesus coming in power for all to see. On the day of Pentecost the church officially begins with the Holy Spirit falling upon it and being planted within it. The mission of the church is to spread the message about Jesus and his kingdom. Later with the destruction of the temple and Jerusalem, the prophecy of Jesus is fulfilled, and the age of the church is cleared to make its impact. According to Wright it now all fits together.

There are various interpretations, and as the reader can see when one interprets some of the verses in this chapter, it can be quite difficult. Sometimes the end of the known world seems to be integrated with the end of the temple and destruction of Jerusalem. Even so, the main theme is not that difficult. The Day of the Lord (however that is interpreted) is sure to come, so be prepared.

The question scholars debate is the question about the nature of the language. Is this language, known as apocalyptic language, to be interpreted as totally metaphorical language used in reference to the in-breaking of the kingdom and the destruction of Jerusalem and the temple, where none of it has any reference to the second coming of Jesus, the end of the known world, and the last judgment? Or can this prophecy possibly be seen as a double fulfillment of Scripture, which is also applicable to the end of the known world? Prophecy seems to be reworked over and over throughout time. Understanding prophetic prophecy is no easy task. Be wary of those who say it is an easy task, and all one has to do is listen to them.

In chapter 14 two days before the Passover the chief priests (Sadducees) and the scribes (mainly Pharisees) are looking for a way to arrest Jesus and have him killed. He has become too much of a threat to their power base. Keep in mind that in a theocracy the religious leaders are not only the leaders of religion but they are also Israel's political, economic, social, and cultural leaders. Other than the temple incident or when the authorities came after him to question him, it does not seem that he was constantly confronting the authorities. But the content of his teaching was apparently reaching them and upsetting them, for they knew if he continued to gather followers their actions and positions of power would be questioned and in great jeopardy.

While at Bethany in the house of Simon the leper, a woman

pours expensive ointment on him. Some of his disciples object saying that the money should be given to the poor. In verse 6 Jesus said, "Let her alone; why do you trouble her? She has performed a good service for me. For you always have the poor with you, and you can show kindness to them whenever you wish; but you will not always have me. She has done what she could; she has anointed my body beforehand for burial. Truly I tell you, wherever the good news is proclaimed in the whole world, what she has done will be told in remembrance of her."

To use this verse that says, you always have the poor with you, as an excuse to not give to the poor as some have done in our society today is a misuse of Scripture, especially when the concept of economic justice and having compassion for those in need are practically on every page. It is interesting the loopholes the selfish and the greedy use to ignore the common good of all and to keep their money and possessions only for themselves and their own interests.

As Jesus in Mt 19:24, Mk 10:25, and Lk 18:25 indicates, it is easier for a camel to go through the eye of a needle than for someone who is rich to enter the kingdom of God. In both testaments God's people are commanded not only to help the disadvantaged but to represent them to those in power. Allen Verhey (2002, 410-11) says, in using this verse from Deut 15:11, Jesus is reiterating the ancient judgment against the politics of Israel that it had forgotten the covenant and reminded those who heard him of the old command to "open your hands to the poor and needy neighbor in your land."

In verses 10-11 Judas Iscariot goes to the chief priests to betray him, and they promise him money to do so. (Many have wondered why Judas did this. No one knows the real answer, but the Gospel of John says, he was greedy, and even robbed the treasury. The Gospel of John says Judas was a thief who stole from the common purse, see Jn 12:4-6.)

Some scholars suggest he is trying to force Jesus into declaring the political kingdom he thinks Jesus is going to establish in order to put them all into power. As the treasurer he is looking forward to the power he will have and the money to which he will have access. The betrayal of Judas is part of God's sovereign plan, but it is still Judas' choice. One way to look at it is that God moved Judas into that position because he knew the choice he would make.

In verses 12-16 on the first day of Unleavened Bread, when the Passover lamb is sacrificed, he sends his disciples (Peter and John) to a certain man who would show them the upper room where they would prepare the Passover meal. In verses 17-21 while they were eating the meal, he tells them that one of them will betray him, and they were distressed. Jesus said, "woe to that one by whom the Son of Man is betrayed! It would have been better for that one to not have been born."

Verses 22-26 say, While they were eating, he took a loaf of bread, and after blessing it he broke it, gave it to them, and said, "Take; this is my body." Then he took a cup, and after giving thanks he gave it to them, and all of them drank from it. He said to them, "This is my blood of the covenant, which is poured out for many. Truly I tell you, I will never again drink of the fruit of the vine until that day when I drink it new in the kingdom of God." When they had sung the hymn, they went out to the Mount of Olives.

The hymn is one of those from Psalms 115-118; they are traditionally the Passover hymns. Jesus transforms and gives new meaning to the Passover meal. Christians call it the Eucharist or Holy Communion, and it replaces the Passover. The Passover is the time to remember the story of the Exodus, the return from exile. Jesus fuses this story together with the Lord's Supper, the story of his life, his coming death and resurrection, a new covenant, which will be a new freedom, the new exodus, one that frees from sin, with a new way of forgiveness of sins. The symbols are changing. The Passover meal is changed to the Eucharist, which includes the forgiveness of sins, and Jesus replaces the temple for that very purpose. In a sense the two symbols of temple and Eucharist interpret each other.

In verses 27-31 Jesus tells them that they will all desert him. He quotes the prophecy of Zechariah (13:7) that says, "I will strike the shepherd, and the sheep will be scattered." Peter denies that he will desert him, but Jesus says, "Truly I tell you, this day, this very night, before the cock crows twice, you will deny me three times. Peter as well as the others said, "Even though I must die with you, I will not deny you."

In verses 32-42 they go to Gethsemane (a garden on the Mount of Olives, east of the city, across the Kidron Valley). He takes Peter, James, and John and goes to pray; he told the others to wait for them. Jesus became agitated and in (34-36) says to them, "I am deeply grieved, even to death; remain here, and keep awake." And going a little farther, he threw himself on the ground and prayed that, if it were possible, the hour might pass from him. He said, "Abba, Father, for you all things are possible; remove this cup from me; yet not what I want, but what you want." (Here Jesus expresses his humanity.)

He returns and finds them sleeping, and in (37-38) he said to Peter, "Simon, are you asleep? Keep awake and pray that you may not come into the time of trial; the spirit indeed is willing, but the flesh is weak." This happens two more times, and in (41-42) he says, "Are you still sleeping and taking your rest? Enough! The hour has come; the Son of Man is betrayed into the hands of sinners. Get up, let us be going. See, my betrayer is at hand." (Can all of us identify with the spirit is willing, but the flesh is weak?)

Verses 43-46 say, Immediately, while he was still speaking,

Judas, one of the twelve, arrived; and with him there was a crowd with swords and clubs, from the chief priests, the scribes, and the elders. (Notice it is the leadership, representing the Sanhedrin, that is coming after him.) Now the betrayer had given them a sign, "The one I will kiss is the man; arrest him and lead him away under guard." So when he came, he went up to him at once and said, "Rabbi!" and kissed him. Then they laid hands on him and arrested him. As this happened verse 47 says, one of those who stood near drew his sword and struck the slave of the high priest, cutting off his ear. (Jn 18:10 tells us the slave's name is Malchus, and Lk 22:51 states that Jesus heals his ear and told Peter, "No more of this!")

Verses 48-49 say, Jesus said to them, "Have you come out with swords and clubs to arrest me as though I were a bandit? Day after day I was with you in the temple teaching, and you did not arrest me. But let the scriptures be fulfilled." Verses 50-52 say, All of them (his disciples) deserted him and fled. A certain young man was following him, wearing nothing but a linen cloth. They caught hold of him, but he left the linen cloth and ran off naked. (Tradition says this is John Mark, the writer of this gospel. This incident is not mentioned in any other gospel.)

Verses 53-59 inform us that they take Jesus to the Sanhedrin, the supreme ruling body of the Jews, while Peter follows into the courtyard and warmed himself by the fire. The leaders want to put him to death, so they get many to testify against him, but there is no agreement. In verse 58 some say, "We heard him say, 'I will deliver this temple that is made with hands, and in three days I will build another, not made with hands.' " (Jesus will be the new temple, and those who are born of him and who worship him will be built upon him, the stone, which becomes the new spiritual house.)

In verses 60-62 the high priest asked Jesus, "Have you no answer? What is it they testify against you?" But he was silent and did not answer. Again the high priest asked him, "Are you the Messiah, the Son of the Blessed One?" Jesus said "I am; and 'you will see the Son of Man seated at the right hand of the Power' and 'coming with the clouds of heaven.' "

First of all when Jesus says, I am, he is saying that he is the one prophesied about in Ps 110:1 and Dan 7:13-14. Second, when he says to the high priest that he will see the Son of Man seated at the right hand of the Power and coming with the clouds of heaven, this does not happen unless as NT Wright said, coming on the clouds of heaven is a metaphor. As previously mentioned Wright believes Jesus is speaking metaphorically to mean that the high priest and his generation will be alive, and Jesus will be vindicated when God makes his presence known, by using the Romans to destroy Jerusalem and the temple in 70 AD.

When the high priest heard Jesus answer in (63-64) he said, "Why do we still need witnesses? You have heard his blasphemy! What is your decision?" All of them condemned him as deserving death. (The high priest knows what Dan 7:13-14 and Ps 110:1 are referring to and is the reason he charges Jesus with blasphemy. Blasphemy carries a death penalty under Jewish law. This indicates both a theological and a historical reason for his death.) In (65) some began to spit on him, to blindfold him, and to strike him, "Prophesy!" The guards also took him and beat him.

According to Mark one of the reasons Jesus is condemned to death is because he is saying he is the Messiah, the one Daniel wrote about. Daniel said that the Son of Man would be given the kingship of an eternal kingdom. So the historical reasons for Jesus being put to death are both political and theological. They believe their positions of power are being threatened. Neither they nor the Romans are interested in a regime change. They are threatened by any talk of a new king replacing them in the only type of kingdom they can imagine and understand.

Dunn (2003, 786) says, in the final analysis, Jesus is executed because he has become too much of a thorn in the side of the religious-political establishment. So they find a way to charge him with blasphemy. Later, another theological reason for the death of Jesus will be for the sins of humankind. This will be elaborated on in detail later in John's gospel and by the Apostle Paul when the crucifixion and resurrection make its full impact, but that is not the immediate historical reason.

The Jewish leaders need permission to put him to death by the Romans, and the Romans permit it. Death will be by crucifixion. It is interesting to note that according to Griffith-Jones (2000, 37) and Borg and Wright (1999, 88-89) only revolutionaries charged with treason, and run away or defiant slaves are put to death by crucifixion. Jesus was a revolutionary in his thinking, but he was not a militant revolutionary, even though he will be charged with that crime.

In verses 67-68 one of the servant-girls of the high priest sees Peter in the courtyard and said, "You were with Jesus, the man from Nazareth." But he denied it saying, "I do not know or understand what you are talking about." And he went out into the forecourt. Then the cock crowed. In (69-70) the servant-girl begins to say to bystanders, "This man is one of them." But again he denied it. Then after a little while the bystanders again said to Peter, "Certainly you are one of them; for you are a Galilean." Verses 71-72 say, But he began to curse, and he swore an oath, "I do not know this man you are talking about." At that moment the cock crowed for the second time. Then Peter remembered that Jesus had said to him, "Before the cock crows twice, you will deny me three times." And he broke down and wept. (Peter, being human and under extreme pressure, like most of us many times in our lives, deny Christ by our words and actions.)

⌒∽⊙∾⌒

Chapter 15:1 says, As soon as it was morning, the chief priests held a consultation with the elders and scribes and the whole council (the Sanhedrin). They bound Jesus, led him away, and handed him over to Pilate.

The council is dominated by the priests who are Sadducees in control of all temple activity. The Sanhedrin is the highest ruling body for the Jews. Rome gave the Jews much authority to rule in local issues. This is primarily done through the Sanhedrin, who rules in both religious and political matters. The Herods were primarily puppet kings for the Romans, but by this time they were replaced in Judea by the Roman procurator (governor) Pilate, but a son of Herod remained a puppet king in Galilee. The high priest is the president of the Sanhedrin. In addition to the aristocratic Sadducees, who work closely with the Romans, there are also some Pharisees, who are the scribes, and the elders. Those who make up the Sanhedrin are the wealthiest and most powerful people of Judea making all the religious, political, social, and economic decisions.

Pilate is the Roman military governor. Later these people are called procurators or prefects. Because of the Roman occupation, the Romans have to approve any capital punishment. The Jews want Jesus to die crucified because they believe he is a curse from God (see Deuteronomy 21:23). They do not want anyone to think he is blessed.

In verses 2-5 Pilate asked him, "Are you the King of the Jews?" He answered him, "You say so." Then the chief priests accused him of many things. Pilate asked him again, "Have you no answer? See how many charges they bring against you." But Jesus made no further reply, so that Pilate was amazed.

Verses 6-8 say, Now at the festival he used to release a prisoner for them, anyone for whom they asked. Now a man called Barabbas was in prison with the rebels who had committed murder during the insurrection. So the crowd came and began to ask Pilate to do for them according to the custom. In (9-10) Pilate asks the crowd, "Do you want me to release for you the King of the Jews?" For he realized it was out of jealously that the chief priests had handed him over. But the chief priests stirred up the crowd to have him release Barabbas for them instead. (Notice it is primarily the leaders who are behind this.)

In verses 12-15 Pilate asks, "Then what do you wish me to do with the man you call the King of the Jews?" They shouted back, "Crucify him!" Pilate asked, "Why, what evil has he done?" But they shouted all the more, "Crucify him!" So Pilate wishing to satisfy the crowd, released Barabbas to them; and after flogging Jesus, he handed him over to be crucified.

The soldiers led him into the governor's headquarters and verses 16-20 say, And they clothed him in a purple cloak; and after twisting some thorns into a crown, they put it on him. And they began saluting him. "Hail, King of the Jews!" They struck his head with a reed, spat upon him, and knelt down in homage to him. After mocking him they stripped him of the purple cloak and put his own clothes on him. Then they led him out to crucify him.

Jesus will be put to death by the political leadership of the Romans in cooperation with the religious and political leadership of the Jews. It is important to understand all Jews were not involved, but it is primarily the leadership of the Jews that stir up the emotions of that particular crowd at that time. It is the same idea with the Crusades and the Holocaust. All Christians are not accountable for the wrong done during the Crusades and the Holocaust; it was certain Christians of the time. Therefore it has been wrong to blame all Jews for the death of Christ. In 1 Corinthians 2:8 we are informed that it was the rulers of that age that put him to death. It must be added that it was not all the rulers, but certain rulers of that age had Jesus put to death. There should be no reason to stereotype anyone.

Verses 21-24 say, They compelled a passer-by, who was coming in from the country, to carry his cross; it was Simon of Cyrene (N Africa-Libya), the father of Alexander and Rufus (Rom 16:13). Then they brought Jesus to the place called Golgotha. (Golgotha means the place of a skull; it is located outside the city, for putting one to death inside the city is against the law.) And they offered him wine mixed with myrrh (a fragrant bitter tasting herb); but he did not take it. And they crucified him, and divided his clothes among them, casting lots to decide which each should take.

Verses 25-32 say, It was nine o'clock in the morning when they crucified him. The inscription of the charge against him read, "The King of the Jews." (Rome is saying he is a revolutionary, and he is put to death for treason.) And with him they crucified two bandits, one on his right and one on his left. Verse 9 says, Those who passed by derided him, shaking their heads and saying, "Aha! You who would destroy the temple and build it in three days, save yourself, and come down from the cross." In the same way the chief priests, along with the scribes were also mocking him among themselves and saying, "He saved others; he can not save himself. Let the Messiah, the King of Israel, come down from the cross now, so that we may see and believe." Those who were crucified with him also taunted him. It is important to note that he was put to death for the crime of being an insurrectionary. Horsley (2003, 131), Griffith-Jones (2000, 37), Wright and Borg (1999, 88-89) all state that under Roman law only revolutionaries and run away slaves were to be crucified.

Verses 33-34 say, When it was noon darkness came over the whole land until three in the afternoon. (This is apocalyptic language for a time of judgment.) At three o'clock Jesus cried out with a loud voice, "Eloi, Eloi lema sabachthani?" which means, "My God, my God, why have you forsaken me?"

At this point God takes his presence away from Jesus so that Jesus can experience the weight of the world's sins upon him. At the cross Jesus is bearing the world's sins and will bury all sin in his blood, both individual and institutional sin, both past, present and future.

Verses 35-39 say, When some of the bystanders hear it, they say, "Listen, he is calling for Elijah." And someone ran, filled a sponge with sour wine, put it on a stick, and gave it to him to drink saying, "Wait, let us see if Elijah will come to take him down." Then Jesus gave a loud cry and breathed his last. And the curtain of the temple was torn in two, from top to bottom. Now when the centurion, who stood facing him, saw that in this way he breathed his last, he said, "Truly this man was God's Son." (This is also translated, a son of god!)

The curtain in the Old Testament kept everyone away from the presence of God except the high priest, who entered one day each year, the Day of Atonement. Being torn in two symbolizes that God's presence is now available to all who come to him.

Verses 40-41 say, There were also women looking from a distance. Among them were Mary Magdalene, and Mary the mother of James the younger and of Joses, and Salome. (Salome is the wife of Clopas, see Lk 24:18.) They used to follow him and provided for him when he was in Galilee; and there were many other women, who had come up with him to Jerusalem. (This is abnormal since women in this culture are very protected and not given much freedom to roam. The writer may be saying that a new day for women is beginning.)

In verses 42-45 Joseph of Arimathea, a respected member of the Sanhedrin, asks Pilate for the body, and when he learns that he is dead, he grants the body to Joseph. Verses 46-47 say, Then Joseph brought a linen cloth, and taking down the body, wrapped it in the linen cloth, and laid it in a tomb that had been hewn out of the rock. He then rolled a stone against the door of the tomb. Mary Magdalene and Mary the mother of Joses saw where the body was laid.

Why was Jesus put to death? Wright (1996, 551-552) sums up the reasons as follows. The leaders saw him as a false prophet leading Israel astray. They saw his temple action as a blow against the central symbols not only of national life but also of God's presence with his people. He was proclaiming a new kingdom with himself as the Messiah-king thus opening himself to be charged with serious revolutionary activity. They saw him as a dangerous political nuisance, a seditious trouble-maker, a false prophet, a traitor, and a blasphemer. He had an opportunity to deny the charges but did not. Jesus came as did the prophets of old leveling the same charges against Israel that those prophets leveled. As they put the prophets to death, they would do the same to him.

In chapter 16:1-4 Mary Magdalene, Mary the mother of James, and Salome bought spices to anoint him, and early on the first day of the week, when the sun had risen, they went to the tomb. When they got there, they saw the stone to the tomb was rolled away. Verses 5-8 say, As they entered the tomb, they saw a young man, dressed in a white robe, sitting on the right side; and they were alarmed. But he said to them, "Do not be alarmed; you are looking for Jesus of Nazareth, who was crucified. He has been raised; he is not here. Look there is the place they laid him. But go, tell his disciples and Peter that he is going ahead of you to Galilee; there you will see him; just as he told you." So they went and fled from the tomb, for terror and amazement had seized them; and they said nothing to anyone, for they were afraid.

Mark wants to show that everyone was surprised by the resurrection, for no one was expecting it. Nowhere was a resurrection of the Messiah prophesied. At his death the disciples feel defeated and depressed. Mark wants everyone to understand they all had the wrong idea of the Messiah, his kingdom, and what he would do. The women were in shock, for they were not expecting a resurrection. First of all, they all thought Jesus had come as the Messiah to cast out the hated Romans. Their idea of a kingdom was an earthly political kingdom, but now their leader had been put to death, so they were sulking in their defeat. Second, making his first appearance to a woman, was an extremely strange maneuver, since in those times a woman's witness was not even accepted in a court of law.

With the announcement that Jesus had been raised from the dead and that he would meet them in Galilee, some of the ancient manuscripts bring the book to a close at the end of verse 8. Many believe Mark ends his gospel here. They believe by his ending he is summoning his readers, then and now, to supply their own ending by taking up their cross and completing the message with their own lives. Others do not agree.

One ending adds, And all that had been commanded them they told briefly to those around Peter. And afterward Jesus himself sent out through them, from east to west, the sacred and imperishable proclamation of eternal salvation. (This shorter ending is missing from the earliest Greek manuscripts.)

Other ancient manuscripts add the following verses 9-20, which is the traditional closing of Mark. This is also missing from the earliest, most reliable Greek manuscripts. These verses say, Now after he rose early on the first day of the week, he appeared first to Mary Magdalene, from whom he had cast out seven demons. She went out and told those who had been with him, while they were mourning and weeping. But when they heard that he was alive and had been seen by her, they would not believe it.

After this he appears in another form to two of them, as they are walking into the country (Lk 24:13-35). And they go back and tell the rest, but the disciples do not believe them. Later he appears to the eleven as they are sitting at the table; and he upbraids them for their lack of faith and stubbornness, because they did not believe those who saw him after he had risen. And he said to them, "Go into all the world and proclaim the good news to the whole creation. The one who believes and is baptized will be saved; but the one who does not believe will be condemned. And these signs will accompany those who believe: by using my name they will cast out demons; they will speak in new tongues; they will pick up snakes in their hands, and if they drink any deadly thing, it will not hurt them; they will lay their hands on the sick, and they will recover."

One example of a snake bite not bringing death is Paul in Acts 28:1-6. These miraculous signs will be for those disciples in that era, and when the book of Acts is read, the reader will see all these things are accomplished as confirmation that what is written is true. This writer would not suggest for any Christian today to handle snakes and drink poison to test God. (See Mt 10:1, Acts 3:7-8, 28:1-10.)

Verses 19-20 say, So then the Lord Jesus, after he had spoken to them, was taken up into heaven and sat down at the right hand of God. And they went out and proclaimed the good news everywhere, while the Lord worked with them and confirmed the message by the signs that accompanied it.

Confirming who he is and his message is the purpose of the signs. Once the message is confirmed and written as the Scriptures, there is no longer a need for the signs. That does not mean there will not be any more signs (miracles), but if his people need more signs as some Pharisees and Sadducees said they needed to believe, then his people are no better than the Pharisees and Sadducees. Jesus tells his people the sign that remains is the resurrection and the sending of the Holy Spirit. Hebrews 11:6 says, without faith it is impossible to please God. Later in Jn 20:29 Jesus tells Thomas, Blessed are those who have not seen and yet have come to believe. There were only three times in Scripture God immersed the earth in numerous miracles. They were during (1) the time of Moses (2) the time of Elijah and Elisha (3) the time of Jesus. At other times God works in the manner he wills.

Mark's gospel is rooted in history but is primarily a type of catechism, a book of theology, to be meditated upon for understanding and spiritual development. It is the message that is inspired, and not every detail of history. No where does Scripture say every detail of history must be exact in order for the Bible to be inspired. That is a philosophical theory developed by fundamentalists a couple hundred years ago. It is written in the form of an ancient Greek biography, but it is Mark's testimony to tell people who Jesus is, and to help them remember the story of Jesus and his teachings. It is to encourage all who are faint of heart, like the disciples, to keep struggling on the road to deeper faith. The message contained in Mark is what remains important for all.

In chapter 9:23-24 Jesus said, "All things can be done for the one who believes." When the man heard that he cried out, "I believe; help my unbelief!" Mark is saying, remember how the first disciples struggled, so keep on struggling as they did. Remember Mark is writing during a major persecution of Christians in the city of Rome. So Mark is reminding them that nobody said it was going to be easy; keep on the path, endure, Christ will calm the storm, for there is more fruit to bear through his people. Make the kingdom of God present wherever you are, and carry on his mission of transformation and renewal. Be the eyes, ears, hands, and feet of Christ until he comes to complete his mission, making all things new. As an old clergyman once said, God has more light and truth to break forth from his holy word.

The message they take out is: Christ has died. He has taken the exile upon himself. Sin has been forgiven. Christ has risen. He is the new creation, the new Exodus from sin's captivity for the new people of God. The new covenant has begun. Christ will come again. He will come to restore all of creation creating a new heaven and new earth. The kingdom of God has begun.

The reader will see after reading the other gospels that the trial, crucifixion, and resurrection accounts differ in some of their details. The reader will find differences in which women were at the tomb, who else was there, how many were there, who was the first to whom Jesus appeared, where the appearances occurred, among other things. The resurrection accounts as well as the birth, life, trial and crucifixion accounts are not meant to be detailed historical accounts, but they all agree on the primary events. It is the message that is important, and it is the message that is inspired of God.

Even though rooted in history to show these things truly happened, these writings are inspired theological reflections and testimonies of faith, mainly gathered by Mark from different remembered oral accounts passed around by different communities over a period of thirty-five to forty years. All agree that Jesus' life is real, and that he really did rise from the dead. They are to inform and remind God's people who God is, who we are as God's creations, how we are to relate to God, to ourselves, to other humans God created, to God's created earth, and to remind his people about the mission he gives them, the mission of life in him and the kingdom. In the process it should be remembered that Scripture is both divine and human, but it is all God inspired.

The following is a practical exercise to help the reader see differences and to understand that these writings are not meant to be history as people today write history, even though they are historical in the ancient sense. God gave the human writers freedom as he inspired them in their time to present what happened from their different points of view. In the meantime God's basic truths are preserved.

Make a chart comparing the four accounts of the women coming to the tomb using the following Scriptures: Mt 28:1-10, Mk 16:1-8, Lk 24:1-11, Jn 20:1-8. Then answer the following questions.

1. Who goes to the tomb and how many?
2. At what time of the day do they go?
3. What reasons, if any, are given?
4. What do they see when they arrive?
5. When do they meet and precisely where?
6. How many do they meet?
7. What are they told about the risen Jesus?
8. What is their response, and do they comply with instructions?
9. Who sees the risen Jesus first? To the above Scriptures add I Cor 15:1-8.
10. If you were an historian what difficulties would you encounter in attempting to write about the empty tomb incident?

Luke Timothy Johnson (1996, 107-11) mentions numerous

differences. He states that the narrative sequence between John and the Synoptics is very different. In John the ministry of Jesus is one year and mainly in Judea. In the Synoptics Jesus ministers for three years mainly in Galilee. In John Jesus cleanses the temple at the beginning of his ministry, but in the Synoptics he does it at the end. In John Jesus dies on the day of preparation for the Passover, but in the Synoptics he dies on the day of Passover. In John Jesus has followers with him at the cross, but in the Synoptics he is by himself. In John the empty tomb story involves Peter and John. In the Synoptics it is a group of women at the empty tomb. In John Jesus works no exorcisms. Instead he does seven signs. In the Synoptics Jesus' exorcisms are connected to the proclamation of the kingdom. John repeats none of the parables that are all through the Synoptics. In John the controversies with opponents often lead to long discourses, but in the Synoptics the controversies are short with brief pronouncements made. These are just a few of the differences. More on this later.

If the four Gospel accounts are fiction, as some scholars believe, made up to convince people Jesus is both the Messiah and God, this writer believes some of the numerous, minor, and conflicting details would certainly have been smoothed over, but they are left standing. They are left standing because they are no issue for the people of the time. They had no bearing on their understanding of how history is written or its underlying meaning. For the writers there is no doubt in the truths that Jesus taught, what Jesus did, and the fact that Jesus rose from the dead. Because of that, thousands were willing to be martyred for him and the kingdom he came to establish, and the church was established. The truth is: Christ has lived. Christ has died. Christ has risen. Christ will come again.

THE GOSPEL OF MATTHEW

The majority of scholars believe Matthew was written between 80-85 AD either in the Holy Land or Antioch, Syria. The most popular choice is in Antioch in AD 85. A small minority of scholars disagree. Like Mark it is written in Greek, even though Matthew writes primarily to a Jewish audience. Some scholars believe Matthew wrote much of it and his disciples finished it, but other scholars are not so sure. Like the other gospels, we really do not know who the author is. The book does not tell us. Matthew's name was eventually added to it, for there was a long standing tradition saying that he was the one who wrote the gospel.

It is basically agreed that the writer uses at least three sources. He had a copy of Mark's gospel, a lost sayings source that scholars label as the "Q" source, and his own sources that scholars label as the "M" source. The sources most likely would be both written and oral sources, probably mostly oral. These thoughts are based on many years of analyzing the four Gospels, but it is still *speculative theology*, for there are a minority of scholars who disagree.

The Gospel of Matthew has some of the following characteristics.

*Matthew's genealogy links Jesus with Abraham, the father of the Jews, to show that Jesus is the fulfillment of God's promise to Abraham that a nation coming from him will bless the world. Jesus is also linked with King David who is promised an everlasting kingdom through one of his descendants. Matthew wants to show that Jesus is the legitimate heir to the royal house of David. In the first verse he calls Jesus the Son of David, and Son of God, and then he says he will be called Emmanuel meaning God is with us. He writes to show that the presence of Jesus is also the presence of God.

*The virgin birth is mentioned linking Jesus to the prophet Isaiah's statement that a young woman (Hebrew Scriptures) or virgin (the Greek Septuagint) would conceive (see Isa 7:14). Matthew wants to show that Jesus is the Messiah who has instituted a new kingdom. He uses the word kingdom so often that some call it the gospel of the kingdom. Matthew's emphasis is showing that the story of the Old Testament is coming to its climax and fulfillment with the establishment of a new kingdom and a new king, God himself. A new age with a new covenant, a new Torah, and a new temple is beginning. Jesus institutes the new covenant, and he is the new Torah and new temple of God. The old covenant of promise yields to the new covenant of fulfillment.

*Matthew apparently is also called Levi. Some believe he is probably a former Levite, who is from a family of priests or those who aided the priests in the temple. Apparently he had rejected his former religion and had become a tax collector. Matthew has Jesus teaching a higher righteousness, the fulfillment of the law. Jesus brings the Torah (the law or teachings) to its ultimate intention or purpose. The Torah with its letter of the law approach, which was necessary for ordering society, could only set a minimum law. The law could not address the condition of a person's heart, the humane impulses that lay beneath the law, and it could not inspire most to go beyond the law to a higher righteousness. This is what Jesus is able to do with his emphasis on a transformed heart and the law of the Spirit of life in Christ Jesus.

*The heart of this higher righteousness is found in the Sermon on the Mount with the Beatitudes of true happiness as its beginning. The Sermon on the Mount expresses the core virtues, values and vision of the kingdom. It is God's ultimate vision for humankind. Jesus comes to show us the deeper spirit and attitude behind the rules and regulations of the law in order to inspire our imagination as to how we can most thoroughly love God and our neighbor as ourselves. The new law or higher righteousness is about a transformation of the heart. Both Jeremiah (31:31-33) and Ezekiel (36:26-27) said that God would give them a new heart and put his law and spirit within them and that he would give them a new covenant. Matthew shows how Jesus comes to purify hearts, intentions, attitudes, motivations, and dispositions. Jesus is the fulfillment of the law of Moses, the Prophets, and the Psalms and the model of the new law.

*Matthew is a manual of the teachings of the kingdom. The Beatitudes and the Sermon on the Mount are the center of those teachings. Jesus as the teacher is the emphasis while Mark's gospel emphasizes his actions, even though it gives many of his teachings. There are many parables in the Gospel of Matthew as Jesus attempts to uproot the conventional way of thinking in order to move his people in a different direction. It is important to understand that the thrust is on a radical new way of seeing things, a new way of thinking, acting, and living–one that is different from the conventional thinking of the past. And it is much different from the conventional thinking of the world that is more concerned with self-identity and security of possessions. The words and actions of Jesus model the kingdom's new way of thinking, acting, and living.

*One reason the Father sends the Son to his people is to teach and demonstrate why one is created, what being truly human means, and how life in the kingdom is to be ordered. He is sent to be the people's mentor to model the way for both individuals and nations.

*Matthew gathers the major teaching Scriptures into 5 major sections. This is done to convey that the teachings of Jesus fulfill the books of Moses, called the Pentateuch. The Pentateuch centers on the first 5 books of the Old Testament. The rest of the Old Testament expands those central teachings. Keep in mind that the Hebrew Scriptures are the Scriptures for the first Christians who are Jews. He is simply explaining, reworking, reinterpreting, and taking those Scriptures to their highest level for the new and last age, the age of the Spirit which is now beginning.

*Matthew quotes the Old Testament 61 times. He says often, "This was done to fulfill what was spoken by the Lord through the prophets." To understand Jesus and what he is doing, it is imperative to understand the Old Testament prophets and the environment in which they prophesied. Without that background one is going to misunderstand and misinterpret many of his words and actions. This writer will clarify some of those teachings as we move on.

*After the birth of Jesus, Matthew has the holy family going into Egypt to escape Herod who wants to put Jesus to death. Remember Pharaoh in Egypt tried to put Moses to death also. Now God will call the family of Jesus out of Egypt as he called Israel out of exile from Egypt under Moses. The old Israel was disobedient in the desert after being set free from Egyptian exile. Jesus becoming the new Israel will be obedient to the Father's commands reversing Israel's wrongdoing. Writing to Jews Matthew is saying Jesus is the new Moses and more; he is the Messiah, God's Son called to again bring his people out of exile from the evil of sin. The people of the time thought Rome was the evil because they were the foreign conquerors, but Jesus will teach that the real evil is sin, and that includes the sin of God's people. The people of God had become their own problem.

*Matthew uses the term kingdom of heaven instead of kingdom of God, for Jews will not say the word God (*YHWH* in Hebrew). They use the Hebrew word for Lord, *Adonai*, which is printed in the Old Testament Scripture as LORD. Jesus is king of a new kind of kingdom, one that is different from the kings and kingdoms of the world. The kings and their assistants lord it over the people and demand service, but Jesus teaches that greatness in his kingdom comes through humbleness, service and peacemaking.

*The Greisbach Hypothesis says that Matthew's gospel was written first. It is a very small minority of scholars who agree with this theory. They believe Matthew was written before Mark, primarily to Jews in order to prove that Jesus is the Messiah. There is another extremely small group that believes the Gospel of John was written first, but the vast majority believe Mark was written first. Who wrote these Gospels, when, how, and who they wrote them to is *speculative theology*.

*Jesus is more than a teacher and prophet, but he is both. He is also called prophet, priest, king, Son of God, Savior, and Messiah. He is always challenging his listeners toward a new way of thinking, acting, and a new vision of life. He is a true liberal, a progressive opposed to the accepted thinking and ways of doing things. Surprise and challenge are characteristics of his approach. In opposition to greed, hatred, violence, and oppression of those who do not have power and wealth, he teaches love, peace, compassion, and social justice.

*Jesus opposes a religion accommodated to the conventional wisdom of the times. He opposes the religion of current culture, sometimes called civil religion, which legitimates the dominant thinking of the current society. He opposes the temple and its leadership because they control the religion, politics, and economics that are oppressing the people. Both the Old Testament prophets and Jesus indict the ruling elites of power, wealth, and religion who are responsible for the oppression of the people and the direction the nation is moving. This trend has at least a thousand year history. The ruling elites through history say they believe in God, but their real trust is in their wealth, power, violence, the military, and the religious and political order they establish. As the prophets of old were put to death for challenging these things, Jesus will be put to death also.

*Infidelity to God and an absence of compassion in the life of a society means the collapse and destruction of its social world, and in this world prophets do not usually change the thinking of or defeat the powers that be. War, oppression, injustice, and the institutionalization of greed brought on by leaders who control through their power and wealth are some of the major actions responsible for the greatest sources of human suffering in history. It is no different today. But God cares about what happens in people's lives, so he sends the prophets to teach and challenge the people. Jesus teaches there are two ways to choose from; one is broad, the way of the conventional wisdom of the time. The other is narrow, one of transformation, a change of heart brought by the Spirit of God. Jesus initiates and stresses the kingdom of God that is beginning to break into the world through him. In Lk 4:43 Jesus informed his disciples it is that which he came to preach. The kingdom of God is about judgment and renewal both now and at the end when he comes to perfect all things.

*Matthew indicates the basic thrust of the culture one lives in is always to a great extent in conflict with the Father and his Son because of sin. The way of Jesus dies to self as a center of concern; it also dies to the world and its way of thinking. It dies to the self concern of the world, its security, and its identity, and accepts the agenda of Jesus. The way of Jesus and his kingdom is always challenging the thinking of the world. When it no longer challenges the thinking of the world and its structures, it has been brought into captivity by its culture. Until the reader understands that, Jesus and his teachings will not really be understood or applied.

Matthew chapter 1:1 says, An account of the genealogy of Jesus the Messiah, the son of David, the son of Abraham. Verses 2-16 list some of the people in the genealogy, which is divided into three groups of the perfect number seven. The groups are divided by the most important events in Israel's history. The purpose is not to give a complete list of all descendants; it is to show that God is at work in history. Jesus the Messiah is traced back to David, the greatest king, from whom the Messiah is to come, and to Abraham the father of the Jews. The Messiah will establish a kingdom that will last forever.

The first of three divisions ends at verse 6. Four women are included. They are Tamar, Rahab, Ruth, and Bathsheeba the wife of Uriah. All four are Gentiles, and at least three of them and probably all four had irregular sexual unions by New Testament standards. They as women were not granted the privilege of being educated in the things of God, and at least two of them were foreigners. They are to symbolize that through Jesus all the barriers to equality and access to God are broken down.

The second division (1:7-11) traces the genealogy through the Davidic kings. The third division (1:12-16) contains mostly unknown names leading to Jacob the father of Joseph. This latter group is to indicate the kind of people Jesus will spend his time with on earth, the poor, the nobodies of the world, and those without power and wealth. The reader will see this as we move through the Gospels. Jesus rarely went to the rich and powerful, and when he did, it was to call them to follow him in serving those who had little or nothing.

Verse 16 informs us that Matthew is tracing his genealogy through Joseph, the husband of Mary, because the Jews trace their genealogies through the male side. Matthew is primarily writing to the Jews. Verse 17 says, So all the generations from Abraham to David are fourteen generations; and David to the deportation to Babylon, fourteen generations; and from the deportation to Babylon to the Messiah, fourteen generations. (Fourteen is the sum of the numerical value of the three letters in the name of David in Hebrew (DWD). All Hebrew letters are assigned a numerical value. Abraham, David, the deportation to Babylon, and the coming of the Messiah are the major events in Hebrew history, so the genealogy is summed up through them. Its purpose is not to list every name for historical purposes.)

Verses 18-21 begin to describe the birth of Jesus. Now the birth of Jesus the Messiah took place in this way. When his mother Mary was engaged to Joseph, but before they lived together, she was found to be with child from the Holy Spirit. Her husband Joseph, being a righteous man and unwilling to expose her to public disgrace, planned to dismiss her quietly. But just when he resolved to do this, an angel of the Lord appeared to him in a dream and said, "Joseph, son of David, do not be afraid to take Mary as your wife, for the child conceived in her is from the Holy Spirit. She will bear a son, and you are to name him Jesus, for he will save his people from their sins. (In the Hebrew Scriptures the Spirit is the source of creation and life.)

The name Jesus is the Greek form of the Hebrew Joshua and means, he saves. His mother Mary is with child while engaged to Joseph. Mary was probably approximately thirteen years old, which was the normal age for girls to marry. Joseph plans to dismiss her quietly because he knows he is not responsible for the pregnancy, and for a woman to be with child before marriage is grounds for divorce. In those days engaged couples could stay engaged for up to a year, and it is only broken by divorce. Joseph decides to divorce her quietly because her crime under Jewish law is adultery, which includes a death penalty. Joseph is called a righteous man, meaning he is a man of God, a man of faith, compassion, mercy, and grace, always doing what is best for others. He lived the faith, worshiped God, and used the temple sacrificial system for the forgiveness of sins.

Verses 22-23 say, All this took place to fulfill what had been spoken by the Lord through the prophet (Isa 7:14) "Look the virgin shall conceive and bear a son, and they shall name him Emmanuel," which means, "God is with us."

The Hebrew Bible uses the word young woman instead of virgin. This is not surprising for a young unmarried woman is to be a virgin, and if not, can be put to death by stoning. But the Septuagint, the Greek Bible, uses the word virgin. This is the Bible that Matthew and the early Christians used. Matthew uses the word virgin to express the fact that the birth of Jesus is miraculous and his origin and nature is of God.

Even though the birth is miraculous and of God, could Jesus be fully human without the cooperation of Joseph is the question many ask. If she were not a virgin, and Joseph was involved in the birth of Jesus, could it not still be miraculous in that God is behind the whole process bringing about his plan through the cooperation of two humans? Must the birth be a virgin birth? These are the questions scholars discuss.

Verses 24-25 say, When Joseph awoke from sleep, he did as the angel of the Lord commanded him; he took her as his wife, but had no marital relations with her until she had borne a son; and he named him Jesus. (This indicates the birth was without the help of Joseph and that his humanity comes solely through Mary.)

Protestants believe the word *until* shows that Mary was not a perpetual virgin. Catholics say the word, until, does not prove or disprove the idea because it was simply used to show the virgin birth of Jesus, that Joseph was not involved. Catholics believe she remained a virgin because she gave birth to the Son of God and no one else was to be born of her. This author wonders if any of these mental gymnastics by both Protestants and Catholics need to be a point of contention in bringing about acceptance of each other and unity between the two groups. Has it contributed to anyone having a transformed heart and living life as Christ has called his people to live? Why not allow each group to believe its point of view without that being something that divides us? Neither point of view can be proven by Scripture or history.

The virgin birth has been debated down through the centuries. Some say if the Bible says it was a virgin birth, then it was, and if you do not believe that, then you do not believe the Bible. That is the basic fundamentalist answer, but since this writer is not a fundamentalist, he can not accept that approach. The non-fundamentalist approach is that it should not be something that divides the churches because there are different ways to understand God's inspired word. Some scholars believe it is a literary device to state something that history can not prove one way or the other, even as it is professing the mystery that somehow Jesus is the Messiah and divine Son who was sent from the Father. He is God's chosen one. But if denying the virgin birth is to say Jesus was human only, just like the rest of humanity as some scholars do, then one is denying what the rest of Scripture is pointing toward.

Some even say that the birth accounts are theological meditations or reflections on the birth of Jesus, for it can not be historically described. Even so, this does not mean that it is not in some sense real history. One could also say that if the Father could create the world, he could also send his divine-human Son into the world through a virgin birth. If one is not denying that Jesus is God's unique Son, and if they are saying the Father sent his divine-human Son as the Messiah into the world, then the different approaches can be acceptable.

Are these different opinions really worth dividing over? Do those things have anything to do with living and standing for the things Jesus stood for in this broken world? But it seems for some those things become the litmus test for who is a true believer. To some Christians these things are more important than standing for the message of the kingdom, even more important than having one's mind transformed by Jesus' teachings, and more important than living the life he calls his people to live.

Chapter 2 says, In the time of King Herod, after Jesus was born in Bethlehem of Judea, wise men from the East came to Jerusalem, asking, "Where is the child who has been born king of the Jews? For we have observed his star at its rising, and have come to pay him homage (worship)." (Herod has been in power since 36 BC. Jesus being called the King of the Jews is the sign that the kingdom, the new age is about to begin, and this disturbs Herod. Herod probably does not believe this, but he knows the people believe it.)

Scholars believe these wise men were of the priestly cast of Persia (Iran) from a religion called Zoroastrianism. The Greek word for wise men is *magi*. Actually we do not know where they are from or what religion, if any. Notice it does not say there were three of them, and it does not say they were kings. All of this thinking comes from tradition passed down through the years. The star seen confirms the ancient belief that when a great king or great religious sage is born, a star rises in the sky that can be identified by star gazers or astrologers. Matthew draws upon the Old Testament story of Balaam who prophesied that a star (king) shall come from Jacob (see Numbers 24:17). The light of a star is mentioned symbolizing that he shall be the light of the world.

Verses 3-4 tell us that Herod is frightened by the thought of a new king and calls the chief priests and scribes of the Jews to inquire where the Messiah is to be born. Verse 5 says, They told him, "In Bethlehem of Judea; for so it has been written by the prophet: 'And you, Bethlehem, in the land of Judah, are by no means least among the rulers of Judah; for from you shall come a ruler who is to shepherd my people Israel.' "

The belief that the new king of the Jews would be born in Bethlehem is a quote from Micah 5:2. David, the greatest king of the Jews, had been born and anointed king in Bethlehem, and Ezekiel in chapter 34 had prophesied that God himself would come into the earth and shepherd his people.

In verses 7-9 Herod secretly calls for the wise men, and then sends them to Bethlehem and tells them to return to inform him where the child is located, so he can go worship him. (Of course that is not his motive. His purpose is to kill anyone who may be a threat to him, which he had previously done to those in his own family. He had even killed his wife and at least two of his sons. The Roman emperor said he would rather be Herod's pig than a family member. It is interesting to note that those in power attempt to put Jesus to death at both the beginning of his life and at the end of his life.)

Verses 10-11 say, When the star stopped over the place the child was, they were overwhelmed with joy. On entering the house they saw the child with Mary his mother; and they knelt down and paid him homage. (In Matthew they are in a house thought to be Joseph's house; they are not in a stable. In fact Matthew does not mention coming from Nazareth. Matthew seems to be saying they had a home in Bethlehem. There will be more on some of the differences between Matthew and Luke's birth accounts later.) Then, opening their treasure chests, they offered him gifts of gold (appropriate for a king and to be used to escape to Egypt to flee from Herod), frankincense (used in worship), and myrrh (used for both anointing and embalming). (The gifts appear to be symbolic.) Verse 12 says, And having been warned in a dream not to return to Herod, they left for their own country by another road.

These wise men are the first Gentiles to worship Jesus. These verses are used in the church calendar for Epiphany, which is twelve days after Christmas. Many Christians celebrate three kings day and/or the baptism of Jesus on this day. Some of the Orthodox Church celebrate Christmas on this day. The passage echoes Isaiah 60:6 where people come on camels bearing gifts of gold and incense. Because they brought gold a tradition developed that the men were kings. Because there were three gifts, tradition developed the idea that there were three men.

In verses 13-16 Joseph is warned by an angel in a dream to go to Egypt because Herod wants to kill Jesus. So Joseph and Mary go to Egypt, and they remain there until Herod's death. This was to fulfill what had been spoken by the Lord through the prophet (Hosea 11:1), "Out of Egypt I have called my son." When Herod saw that he had been tricked by the wise men, he was infuriated, and he sent and killed all the children in and around Bethlehem who were two years old and under, according to the time he had learned from the wise men.

Matthew is paralleling Herod and the story of Jesus with the story of Pharaoh and Moses. For Matthew Jesus is the new Moses, the new law giver. As the Egyptian Pharaoh wanted to kill all the new born males, including Moses, Herod will kill all the young boys of Bethlehem in an attempt to kill Jesus, for he is not interested in a new king taking his position. As Moses was saved from death, Jesus was saved from death. As Moses delivered the people from Egyptian exile and slavery, Jesus will also deliver the people from slavery as he comes out of Egypt to deliver a remnant from exile. This deliverance from exile will be a new Exodus and the establishment of the new Israel of God that will be more complete by including Gentiles. The old Exodus resulted in Israel being freed from slavery. This new Exodus will result in humans being freed from the slavery of evil and sin.

Herod wants to make sure this so-called new born king is eliminated. Because Herod kills two year olds, this may indicate that the visit of the wise men to the house of Joseph and Mary happens much later than his birth. Then the story of the holy family being in a house and chased into Egypt because of Herod may be an account of what occurred as many as two years after his birth. Thus chapter one tells of Joseph's experience with an angel and the virgin birth without Matthew mentioning that he came from Nazareth and being born in a manger, while chapter two mentions the incident with Herod two years later. If this is correct, a number of the differences between Matthew and Luke can be eliminated. But it also eliminates the coming of the wise men as a Christmas story. Sorry about bursting anyone's bubble.

In reference to the deaths of these children, which would not be a huge number because Bethlehem was very small at this time, Matthew in (17-18) quotes Jeremiah as prophesying these murders. Jeremiah 31:15 says, "A voice was heard in Ramah, wailing and loud lamentation, Rachel weeping for her children; she refused to be consoled, because they are no more." Matthew makes this a double fulfillment of prophecy. The original reference of the verse was to the exile of the northern tribes to Assyria (721-722 BC) because of their sin and oppression. Rachel was the wife of Jacob who died in childbirth and was buried in Ramah near Bethlehem.

In verses 19-21 an angel appears to Joseph in a dream and tells them to return to their land because Herod is dead. He is warned in a dream to go to Galilee to a town called Nazareth. (Archelaus, one of Herod's sons, has taken Herod's place in Judea; he is as evil and cruel as his father. He will soon be removed, and Rome will send a governor to rule Judea. Later this governor is called a procurator.) Matthew says that living in Nazareth was foretold by the prophets. In verse 23 his quote is, "He will be called a Nazorean."

This can not be found in the Old Testament. But the word Nazorean may be referring to the Hebrew word for *Branch* which sounds like Nazareth. In the Old Testament Branch is a word that means the Messiah. Still it is difficult to see how Matthew could use this as a prophecy about Jesus making his home in Nazareth of Galilee other than to demonstrate that these events are the climax and fulfillment to the Old Testament story. Matthew's thrust is to show that the old covenant of promise is merging into the new covenant of fulfillment.

When Herod dies the Romans divide his kingdom among his three sons. Archelaus is given Judea, Samaria, and Idumea (Edom). The Herod family are Edomites whose descendants go back to Esau. Philip is given the areas north and east of the Sea of Galilee (Decapolis). Herod Antipas is given Galilee and Perea (east of the Jordan). Antipas will figure in the life and death of Jesus as well as executing John the Baptist.

The question that has been asked throughout the years is: Are the birth stories that are found only in Matthew and Luke history? First, there is no way to find proof for them one way or another. Second, even though one finds history in the Bible, the Bible is not meant to be a detailed, scientific history book. Is there history in the accounts? The answer is yes. Can the history be verified? The answer is no. Most ancient history can not be proven. To the question of it being possible that Mary could have related the birth stories, again, the answer is yes.

There are some problems with a yes answer. One is related to the nature and differences of the infancy accounts, if there are real differences. Also, questionable are some of the responses of the family made by Mary and those called his brothers, and the incident at the temple when Jesus was twelve; these will be discussed later. This writer wants to stress that the inspired message is what is important not the historical details left to the human writers who God used to convey his inspired message.

Hill (2004) and Brown (1993) point out similarities and differences of the infancy accounts, if they are both infancy accounts. There are some major differences. Most scholars agree that the stories are not a twenty-first century type of history. They believe they are more like inspired theological reflections or meditations drawn from the Hebrew Scriptures, and they were developed after the resurrection to show why Jesus was born, and that he is the Messiah, the Son of God. Against charges that he was illegitimate, it is explained that his birth is from God from a mother who was blessed and holy.

The idea that the birth narratives are developed after the resurrection does not mean that there is no real history involved, and does not mean that he is not the Messiah, God's unique Son, and does not mean that the Scriptures are not inspired. The details could be the result of theological development around an historic core as they were passed on in an oral society.

The idea that every word in Scripture must be exact history and science to be inspired is a fundamentalist belief that developed not from Scripture but from a philosophy about Scripture. This philosophy only developed within the last three hundred years as a response to the Age of Enlightenment's attack on religious doctrine and Scripture. It was the leaders of the Enlightenment's effort to get the teachings of Jesus and the prophets out of the way of what the politicians and the captains of industry wanted to accomplish for themselves in politics, economic, and social structures. The movement led to an attack on Scripture that weakened people's belief and trust in the Bible. The purpose of the fundamentalist to save the Bible was very noble. But in the long run their danger is making the Bible their idol. To some it became their god, forgetting that the Bible is both human and divine, and its purpose is to witness to God.

Some of the similarities of the infancy narratives are the following. Both parents are named Mary and Joseph with Davidic descent. Both stories include an angelic annunciation, conception through the Holy Spirit, the intended naming of Jesus, and his designated role as Savior. Both stories place the birth in Bethlehem during the reign of Herod the Great, and point out that he was raised in Nazareth.

Some of the differences are the following. Matthew's genealogy differs considerably from Luke's. Matthew traces Joseph's lineage back to Abraham; Luke goes back through Adam. Matthew traces through kings from David, while Luke seems to trace through Nathan the prophet listed as a son of David. Jesus will be both king and prophet. Matthew focuses more on Joseph; Luke pays more attention to Mary. Matthew has Jesus born in a house in Bethlehem, not while engaged, but after they had been married. After a visit from the magi, they flee to Egypt to protect the child's life, and then they settle in Nazareth. In Luke the engaged couple has to travel from Nazareth to Bethlehem for a census. Here Jesus is born and laid in a manger. Then after a visit from shepherds, the family goes not to Egypt but to Nazareth.

The writers probably did not get all their information from Mary. And no, God did not drop the Scriptures into the writers' laps. It seems the writers drew from a variety of sources both oral and written, but mostly from the Hebrew Scriptures. Prophetic verses from Micah, Isaiah, Hosea, and Jeremiah are linked with his birth. Again, the purpose of the Bible is not scientific history. It serves more like an inspired catechism, and a book of theology to stress religious truths. But that does not mean there is no history. Yes, Jesus is the Messiah, God's Son. In this story we discover that the birth of Jesus is an extraordinary, divine event, one that had long been anticipated. Jesus is the new shepherd king from the lineage of David, who supersedes Moses and is the Savior of God's people. The virginal conception, the message from an angel, and the prophecies serve to convey the clear message that this birth is from God.

Chapter 3:1-3 says, In those days John the Baptist appeared in the wilderness of Judea, proclaiming, "Repent, for the kingdom of heaven has come near." This is the one of whom the prophet Isaiah spoke when he said, "The voice of one crying in the wilderness: 'Prepare the way of the Lord, make his paths straight.' " (Matthew uses kingdom of heaven instead of kingdom of God because he is writing to Jews who do not pronounce the word God.)

The Old Testament quote is from Isaiah 40:1-3, which begins by saying that Jerusalem has served her term, and her penalty is paid. She has received from the Lord's hand double for her sins. Then verse 3 follows with John's announcement of a voice calling in the wilderness. Verses 10-11 of Isaiah 40 say, See, the Lord God comes with all his might, and his arm rules for him, and his recompense before him. He will feed his flock like a shepherd; he will gather the lambs in his arms, and carry them in his bosom, and gently lead the mother sheep. Verses 29-31 say, He gives power to the faint, and strengthens the powerless. Even youths will faint and be weary, and the young will fall exhausted; but those who wait for the Lord shall renew their strength, they shall mount up with wings like eagles, they shall run and not be weary, they shall walk and not faint. (John the Baptist through Matthew is saying all this is occurring now as prophesied.)

Matthew will refer to Old Testament fulfillment sixty-one

times to show that what is happening is in continuity with Jewish tradition and is congruent with the expectations of Israel's prophets for the eschatological restoration of Israel. For example, Thielman (2005, 85-86) states that Jesus' birth in Bethlehem shows that he is the Davidic king who Micah promised would bring security and peace to Israel. Herod's slaughter of the infants in Bethlehem sets the stage for the restoration of Israel that Jeremiah promised (31:15). Jesus decision to settle in Galilee shows that he fulfills Isaiah's expectation for a Wonderful Counselor who would reign on David's throne. He is the suffering servant described in Isaiah chapter 53. He is the Messiah king expected by Zechariah (11:4-13). The old covenant of promise is becoming the new covenant of fulfillment.

The restoration of Israel is in progress. Salvation is coming. The first application of salvation that makes sense to the Jews at the time is salvation for the nation, the inauguration of the age to come. The people of the time consider themselves still in exile and being punished by God for their sins. That is why they are occupied by the hated Romans. The resistance group threatens violence to get rid of the Romans, and many support them, including many Pharisees. John and Jesus call them to repent from that agenda and take on the way of the coming kingdom about which Jesus will teach. So the message is first to the nation.

In the meantime the individuals who will be the remnant from the old covenant made with the nation of Israel are to repent and be prepared for a new way of being Israel, a new way of thinking and living life. Individual repentance is always in relationship to the covenant initiated by God with a group of people. The people of the time would first understand the message of repentance in relation to the nation who is still suffering exile for her national sins (Neh 9:36-37). They would first understand the meaning of repentance in relationship to the blessings and curses of the covenant stated in Deuteronomy chapters 27-30. Individual repentance is related to the covenant God made with the nation. Without the nation repenting, a new covenant with a new group must be initiated.

Verses 4-5 inform us that John wore clothing made of camel's hair with a leather belt around his waist, and his food was locusts and wild honey. (He dresses like Elijah who the people thought would come announcing the Messiah. Jesus will later say that John is the Elijah to come.) People from all around are coming to him, and (6-7) say, they were baptized by him in the river Jordan, confessing their sins. But when he saw many Pharisees and Sadducees coming for baptism, he said to them, "You brood of vipers! Who warned you to flee from the wrath to come?" (John was not known for his diplomacy. Can you imagine a religious leader today reacting like John?)

The Pharisees are mostly scribes that rigorously apply the Jewish law and traditions to everything and everybody. The Sadducees are the priests in leadership positions at the temple and the *Sanhedrin*, the ruling body working closely with the Romans. The wrath to come is first a reference to the destruction of Jerusalem and the temple that Jesus will foretell because of their violent actions toward Rome. Most of them at the time do not think God will again bring wrath upon the nation.

In verses 8-12 John says, "Bear fruit worthy of repentance. Do not presume to say to yourselves, 'We have Abraham (the father of the Jews) as our ancestor'; for I tell you, God is able from these stones to raise up children to Abraham. Even now the ax is lying at the root of the trees; every tree therefore that does not bear good fruit is cut down and thrown into the fire. (Here fire represents the wrath to come.) I baptize you with water for repentance, but one who is more powerful than I is coming after me; I am not worthy to carry his sandals. He will baptize you with the Holy Spirit and fire.

His winnowing fork is in his hand, and he will clear his threshing floor and will gather his wheat in his granary; but the chaff he will burn with unquenchable fire."

John's baptism is only for repentance that leads to the forgiveness of sin that will come with the outpouring of Jesus blood in 26:28. But remember at this point this forgiveness is not just for individuals. It is first for the nation of Israel. Its people are being told that they must repent of their sins toward their fellow Israelites and their violent approach toward Rome, or their judgment will come through the Romans. Rome will destroy them and history shows they would be scattered for centuries. Israel called to repent by the prophets or be judged by God is not new. It is the theme of all the Old Testament prophets. Being judged for not repenting is not new either. God sent Assyria in 722 BC and Babylon in 586 BC to conquer them and send them into exile.

In Scripture baptism by fire can be used in several different ways. Its first use will be for the nation. As stated, if it does not repent, God will use the Romans to destroy their city and their temple, which he does in AD 70. For individuals fire can be the wrath of God meaning hell fire. Also, through the fire of suffering a remnant is purified for the new covenant and the new age, the age of the Spirit and the kingdom of God.

On the other hand those individuals who do not repent and receive the Spirit will be judged by fire. What sometimes makes things difficult is that the language used is often *apocalyptic*, which is metaphorical language used to express the theology of a current event in cryptic form. This language is most often used for judgment and renewal in both the world in which people continue to live as well as eternally. Apocalyptic language is often used with *eschatology*, meaning the in-breaking into the current world of end time events called the kingdom. Luke (4:43) will state the purpose of Jesus coming into the world is to preach the kingdom. God's kingdom is about to break into the world. As the reader goes through the Gospels this will become more clear.

For Christians, baptism by the Holy Spirit is the beginning not the end of salvation; it gives one the Spirit that cleanses sin and brings the forgiveness of sins upon repentance. Acts 2:38 says, Repent, and be baptized every one of you in the name of Jesus Christ so that your sins may be forgiven; and you will receive the gift of the Holy Spirit. Then the baptism with fire can be seen as first a reference to the nation, and then eternal judgment for individuals who reject Christ. Some scholars see the Holy Spirit and fire as synonymous, and the effect of this baptism as both purification and destruction.

Most people of the time do not understand all the implications behind where John is leading them because the nation's sin and individual sin are only forgiven in the temple through the temple sacrificial system. John is circumventing the temple. This teaching by John and later Jesus will lead to conflict with the temple authorities. They will challenge that authority and the sacrificial system of the temple. At this point John's baptism is only leading to what the baptism of Jesus will signify.

In verses 13-17 Jesus comes to John for water baptism, not because he needed the forgiveness of sins, but as (15) says, to "fulfill all righteousness."

One definition of righteousness means right conduct in accord with God's will. Many scholars believe that in this situation to fulfill all righteousness means to submit to the plan of God for the salvation of both the nation and the human race, and this is his anointing by God. It is to show that for the nation the law is fulfilled through Jesus, and a new way forward is beginning. The new covenant and the new age are about to begin.

Verse 16 says, And when Jesus had been baptized, just as he came up from the water, suddenly the heavens were opened to him and he saw the Spirit of God descending like a dove and alighting on him. And a voice from heaven said, "This is my Son, the beloved, with whom I am well pleased." (In this verse the Trinity is expressed.)

This is considered a fulfillment of prophecy taken from Ps 2:6-7 and Isa 41:1-4. This begins the ministry of Jesus. God the Father with the Holy Spirit witnesses to the truth that Jesus is his Son and is anointed by the Father for his mission. Ignatius, an early church father, said in Jesus baptism the water is sanctified and purified for all of us.

In addition to fulfilling all righteousness Jesus points the way forward by allowing himself to be baptized as an example for all who are to become his followers. He also receives the Holy Spirit from the Father at his baptism. The Holy Spirit will strengthen him, guide him, and release power through him. When Jesus comes to be baptized by John verse 14 says, John would have prevented him, saying, "I need to be baptized by you, and do you come to me?"

It is important for Jesus to be baptized as an example to his followers but also to receive the Holy Spirit to help him against Satan who constantly will go after him as we will see in the next chapter. It is this Spirit that will be given to his followers as they are baptized to also strengthen them, guide them, and work in them and through them. Also see comments in Mk 1:9-11 and Lk 3:21-23, and Jn 1:29-34.

Chapter 4:1-2 says, Then Jesus was led by the Spirit into the wilderness to be tempted by the devil. He fasted forty days and forty nights (like Moses and Elijah), and afterwards he was famished. In the following Satan tempts Jesus to get him to be a prophet, priest, and king for Satan and his purposes. Verses 3-4 say, The tempter

came and said to him, "If you are the Son of God, command these stones to become loaves of bread." But he answered, "It is written, 'One does not live by bread alone, but by every word that comes from the mouth of God.' "

Satan is reminding Jesus that Moses and Elijah miraculously created food for the people. Jesus quotes Deut 8:3 refusing to use his power for Satan's benefit. Satan tempts Jesus to do miracles to get people to follow him. Give the people all the food and material things they want, and then they will follow you. Satan knows if Jesus gets people to follow him for the wrong reasons, Satan can more easily distort Christianity.

Verses 5-7 say, Then the devil took him to the holy city and placed him on the pinnacle of the temple, saying to him, "If you are the Son of God, throw yourself down; for it is written, 'He will command his angels concerning you,' and 'On their hands they will bear you up, so that you will not dash your foot against a stone.' " (Even the devil quotes Scripture quoting Ps 91:11-12.) Jesus said to him, "Again it is written, 'Do not put the Lord your God to the test.' "

Jesus quotes Deut 6:16 and refuses to test God the Father by demanding an extraordinary show of power at the temple that will give more control to what Satan already has over the temple. Such control will be discussed in more detail later. As we will see Satan already has some control of the temple because religion is being used by the leaders for wrong purposes. Satan wants Jesus to cement his control for him. But Jesus will later defeat and overthrow Satan and the temple. Satan is saying do extraordinary miracles in the name of religion at the temple to excite the people to follow you. Jesus rejects this sensational approach to his form of religion.

The first two temptations involve bread and circuses, which are still used by today's Christian charlatans to hook people into a totally material and sensational form of Christianity. An example today is the so-called prosperity gospel, which says if you truly trust Jesus, he will make you materially prosperous. These charlatans take Old Testament Scripture out of context to dupe the people, and it seems to work very well on those uneducated in Scripture. Daily in America people receive through the internet a passage from Scripture and a note to pass it on, then wait for a huge windfall of money that God is sure to send to bless you.

Jesus will control the future of the temple, but it will be for the purposes of God the Father. Jerusalem and the temple will be destroyed, and Jesus will become the new high priest of God as well as the new temple to which God's people are added. Later 1 Peter 2:4-5 says, Come to him, a living stone though rejected by mortals yet chosen and precious in God's sight, and like living stones, let yourselves be built into a spiritual house, to be a holy priesthood, to offer spiritual sacrifices acceptable to God through Jesus Christ.

Verses 8-11 say, Again the devil took him to a very high mountain and showed him all the kingdoms of the world and their splendor; and he said to him, "All these things I will give you, if you fall down and worship me." Satan wants Jesus to be the king of the world for his purposes. Jesus said, "Away with you, Satan! For it is written, 'Worship the Lord your God and serve only him.' "

Jesus refuses to worship Satan or the things of the world in order to become Satan's king, and he quotes Deut 6:13. Later Matthew in 16:26 will say, what will it profit them if they gain the whole world but forfeit their life? Jesus will become a king, but it will be the king of God the Father's kingdom not Satan's. Life and politics are not disowned but liberated from the hold of the demoniac.

The kingdom Jesus establishes will consist of using religion to serve others instead of using religion to serve self. Instead of Satan's system of domination using political oppression, economic exploitation, and making it all legitimate by co-opting religion for selfish interests, economics, politics, and religion will be used for the common good of all. See Wink, *Naming the Powers, Unmasking the Powers,* and *Engaging the Powers.* Verse 11 says, Then the devil left him, and suddenly angels came and waited on him.

The victory over Satan begins here. The present age is ruled by Satan, but in these temptations Jesus is showing that he defeats and overcomes Satan, and he can help his followers do the same. In the process Jesus will become the reinterpretation and personification of the new Israel. He will become the new Torah, the new word of God, the new wisdom of God and the new temple of God, the living stone of the new spiritual house, and the king of the new kingdom of God.

Where Israel fails by yielding to the devil, Jesus succeeds. Israel failed by testing God, worshiping other gods, and demanding extraordinary miracles from God. Jesus reverses Israel's lack of faith and is totally obedient to God the Father and becomes the living stone of the new spiritual house called the new Israel. Jesus is reconstituting the new Israel around himself. All this will lead to the current Jewish authorities, who are in Satan's grip, desiring to put him to death. Also see Lk 4:1-13, and Mk 1:12-13.

Verses 12-16 say, Now when Jesus heard that John (the Baptist) had been arrested, he withdrew to Galilee. He left Nazareth and made his home in Capernaum by the sea (a fishing, farming, and trading village), in the territory of Zebulun and Naphtali, so that what had been spoken through the prophet Isaiah (9:1-2) might be fulfilled. "Land of Zebulun, the land of Naphtali, on the road by the sea, across the Jordan, Galilee of the Gentiles——the people who sat in darkness have seen a great light, and for those who sat in the region and shadow of death light has dawned."

The rest of that quotation in context of Isaiah 9:6-7 says, For a child has been born for us, a son given to us; authority rests upon his shoulders; and he is named Wonderful Counselor, Mighty God, Everlasting Father, Prince of Peace. His authority shall grow continually, and there shall be endless peace for the throne of David and his kingdom. He will establish and uphold it with justice and with righteousness from this time onward and forevermore. The zeal of the Lord of hosts will do this.

The land of these two tribes was the first to be devastated during the Assyrian invasion of Israel as expressed in the Old Testament. Healing will now come to them as Jesus comes to live in their land. Verse 17 says, From that time Jesus began to proclaim, "Repent for the kingdom of heaven has come near."

The kingdom is being made present and embodied in Jesus. He is the king of a new kingdom breaking in upon the earth. That is what he came to announce. The story of Israel is coming to its climax and fulfillment. With him and his kingdom comes a new way of thinking, a new way of seeing things, and a new way of doing things. Jesus will make present the new kingdom and will be the kingdom's model. It will not be of this world, but it will be in this world. Both the people of the nation and the nation are called to repent of their actions and take on the way Jesus teaches and models. The corporate sin and social injustice of the nation and its institutions are a major issue in biblical thinking. See any of the Old Testament prophets, especially Amos. Also see Jesus' opening statement in Lk 4:18-19.

Most Americans believe that if individuals do what is right the nation will automatically be just, but the Jews of the Old Testament taught it the other way around; they understood the meaning and power of corporate sin. They believed that in an imperfect society the nation, its leadership and institutions, are called to set the example, and then the individuals will follow. Too many Americans, because they focus so strongly on individualism, do not understand the devastating nature of corporate sin, which is one of the major reasons this country is moving in the direction it is moving, destroying the middle class in the process.

The Jews in Jesus time understand corporate sin; consequently, they understand that they are still in exile and occupied by a foreign nation because God is still punishing them for the nation's sins. They are looking for the fulfillment of what Daniel and many of the other prophets had foretold, the one that is to come to set the nation free. They are going to be set free but in a way different from what they thought.

In verses 18-22 Jesus begins the process and calls his first four disciples. They are all fishermen at the Sea of Galilee. They are Simon, who is called Peter, and his brother Andrew. Jesus in (19) said, "Follow me and I will make you fish for people." Then he saw James and John, sons of Zebedee, who were mending their nets. He called them and (22) says, Immediately they left the boat and their father, and followed him.

Strangely Peter and Andrew's father is not mentioned while the father of James and John is. This writer doubts if Zebedee is very excited about James and John leaving him. Fishing the Sea of Galilee is tough business, and he needs all the hands he can get to make the business function. Often Jesus forces upon people a difficult decision in regards to becoming a serious follower. He challenges people to decide if they are willing to exchange an old way of life for a new one, even exchange something they believe is necessary for what Jesus knows is necessary. He challenges people to decide if they are open to thinking and seeing things in a way different from the world's norm. He challenges people to decide if they are ready to take on a new set of virtues and values and a new vision about what is really important. This is true for all his followers even though he does not call everyone to leave their current profession.

Verses 23-25 inform us that Jesus goes through Galilee teaching in synagogues, proclaiming the good news of the kingdom, curing sickness, disease, pain, and casting out demons, and great crowds follow him. (The good news of the kingdom is being made concrete through the merciful and compassionate healings of Jesus. These are the signs from Isaiah chapters 29, 32, 35, 42 and 43 that he is the Messiah of the in-breaking of God's kingdom.)

The following three chapters are called the Sermon on the Mount. This is the way Jesus thinks, lives, and acts. It is the way of life and attitude that Jesus asks his people to follow. It is the way of the kingdom. It is the manual for the kingdom for both the nation and its people, and especially to the resistance movement with its plan of violence to overthrow the Romans. It will be a mistake to read these chapters and make timeless laws out of every statement and to say they are unbreakable to the letter and are to be followed in the manner that Old Testament laws were followed.

What is important in the teachings of Jesus is character formation and the values, the virtues, the vision, the attitude, disposition, and motivation or intention behind what appear to be new laws. Christians are under the new law of the Spirit not the old law of the letter that has served its purpose; it is the spirit of life in Christ Jesus (Rom 7:6, 8:2). That does not mean the law is thrown out; it is taken to a higher level. That will be explained later. In the meantime it is important to understand that Jesus is the new Torah, the new law, who brings to us the highest and deepest meaning of the old law as well as the authority to reinterpret it. God is moving forward into the new age and the new covenant.

Later during the transfiguration (Matt 17:1-9) Jesus, Moses, and Elijah are together, and God says this is my Son listen to him. In the book of Hebrews 1:1-2 the writer says that long ago God spoke to our ancestors in many and various ways, but in these last days he has spoken to us by the Son. With those thoughts as background, let us look at the heart of the teachings of the kingdom.

Chapter 5:1-3 says, When Jesus saw the crowds, he went up to the mountain; and after he sat down, his disciples came to him. Then he began to speak, and taught them, saying: "Blessed (happy or fortunate) are the poor in spirit, for theirs is the kingdom of heaven."

These are the *Beatitudes* all starting with the word blessed. More than anything else they are virtues, values, attitudes and dispositions to develop character, not laws to blindly follow. Again, the first application of this message is the challenge to Israel to be the nation God called it to be, a city upon the hill, a light to the world. The second application is for individuals to be what God has created and called them to be in order to be fully human, different from the animals.

Moses received his commandments from God on a mountain; so Matthew has Jesus on a mountain. It is upon mountains that many of the revelations from God originated throughout the history of the Jews, and do not forget that Jesus is a Jew. The Gospel of Luke has Jesus saying, "Blessed are the poor." But he does not add poor in spirit as Matthew does. Luke emphasizes material poverty, for that is who Jesus spends his time with, but Matthew seems to emphasize spiritual poverty, meaning those who recognize they are not filled with the Spirit of God like they should be.

Matthew expands the teaching to apply it to anyone willing to accept the spirit of the teaching. On the other hand Luke is very much ordered to the social justice of economics. It is not abnormal for Jesus to alter his emphasis according to who he was teaching as all good teachers must do. When Matthew and Luke finally put some things in writing, Matthew will emphasize one aspect while

Luke emphasizes another. It must be remembered that in an oral society Jesus said these things many times to different people. Jesus adapts the spirit and essence of his teachings over and over until the writer finally writes it as he perceived it for his particular situation. By not understanding this, the Bible becomes very rigid.

Matthew wants to extend blessedness to all nations and all people who realize their need for God. Jesus is not just for the poor materially whose condition makes them depend upon God because he is their only hope. He is for anyone who realizes they need to depend on God. Matthew is saying, because a poor person has no other hope than to trust and depend on God, blessed are those who trust and depend on God like many poor people must. Blessed are those who are on the way, but realize they are not yet what God wants them to be. Again, this is for both individuals and nations who want to represent his kingdom. Those who do, are the poor in spirit for Matthew.

Verse 4 says, "Blessed are those who mourn, for they will be comforted."

Jesus is saying that the compassionate are blessed and comforted by God. He is talking about those who weep with those who weep, and those who mourn for sin and evil that hurts and destroys people. They mourn for their own sin as well as others, for they realize what sin does to both individuals and nations. A time of no more mourning will come for God's people; they will eventually be comforted.

Verse 5 says, "Blessed are the meek, for they will inherit the earth."

The meek are the gentle, the non-violent, and those who do not have to have their way in everything. They work with and for others, are patient, kind, gentle, respectful, and not arrogant. They live in harmony with others, are not envious, or boastful, and are willing to give others credit (1 Cor 13:4-7). They even outdo one another in showing honor (Rom 12:10). They do not seek vengeance but overcome evil with good. Again, this attitude is for both individuals and nations. The earth they inherit is the new heaven and new earth which is now beginning to break in upon the earth and will come to its final eternal state when Jesus comes in glory. Jesus is not saying, blessed are the spineless who are not willing to stand for something.

Verse 6 says, "Blessed are those who hunger and thirst for righteousness, for they will be filled."

Righteousness means the ways of God found in his word and actions. It is not the way of man or the way of nations that oppose God. When Jesus tells people to pray and to ask and it will be given, this is mainly what he is referring to. Ask for the righteousness of God, the forgiveness of sin, and the fruits and gifts of the Spirit, and you will be filled.

Verse 7 says, "Blessed are the merciful, for they will receive mercy."

Mercy and compassion go together. Jesus' life is a life of compassion and mercy. On every page of the Gospels his compassion is displayed. He sees the masses of people victimized by the structures of religion and politics led by the people of power and wealth whose hearts are hard. Never once do we see him blaming the common people and using the clichés about them that are most often uttered by the people of comfort, wealth, and power, who have very little or no compassion. These people like to pick out the characteristics of a small minority, and then transfer them on to everyone and everything they oppose in order to justify themselves. Jesus never did this. Jesus teaches that if one shows love, compassion and mercy to others, especially those who are struggling, God will show love and be compassionate and merciful to them. Later Jesus even says, I desire mercy rather than sacrifice, meaning worship. He desires both, but his point is mercy has the priority.

Verse 8 says, "Blessed are the pure in heart, for they will see God."

The pure in heart keep their hearts cleansed of sin and filled with the things of God. The kingdom of God is for the pure in heart not the hardened heart. Since the world's thinking is led by hardened hearts, the kingdom stresses a heart filled with the Spirit of God, and a way of life different from the way of the world. God in reference to the new covenant through the prophet Jeremiah said, I will put my law within them, and I will write it on their hearts; and I will be their God, and they shall be my people (31:33). This will not happen to those who do not open their hearts to let the Spirit work.

Verse 9 says, "Blessed are the peacemakers, for they will be called children of God."

Jesus is primarily talking about peacemakers not peace believers. He is talking about those who try to bring peace to relationships both individually and nations world wide. He did not say, blessed are the war makers no matter what their excuse may be. How can the church of Christ support war in the name of Christ? The church, if it is going to be loyal to Christ first and its country second, has to be the last to accept the war its government declares, and the first to call that government to look for ways to bring it to a close. That is the prophetic call of Christ's church. Pacifism is not the new law, but peace is the spirit of the law. Unfortunately, too many Christians and too many of their churches are too quick to agree to war. An example is making their nation first and Christ second in our government's call to war in Iraq. Be aware of the propaganda that urges war first without a just cause, and then labels unpatriotic those who urge peacemaking and caution as the way to go. Jesus said, you can not have two masters. If the people of Christ are going to follow him, then his priorities need to be their priorities.

Christ calls his followers to first be loyal to him and then loyalty to whatever cause one may have.

Verses 10-11 say, "Blessed are those who are persecuted for righteousness sake, for theirs is the kingdom of heaven. Blessed are you when people revile you and persecute you and utter all kinds of evil against you falsely on my account. Rejoice and be glad, for your reward is great in heaven, for in the same way they persecuted the prophets who were before you."

Jesus is encouraging his people to stand with and for his vision, and for the virtues, values and principles behind his teachings, knowing that when they compete in opposition to the world's values, some form of mental or physical persecution will come. It is impossible to completely understand Jesus, his teachings, and his demand upon his followers without knowledge and understanding of the Old Testament prophets. Jesus is more than a prophet, but he comes from the tradition of the Old Testament prophets. In this writer's opinion that is one of the main reasons too many Christians and their churches have little or no understanding of what the kingdom that is breaking into the world is all about. That is the reason this writer's first book is called *Reading and Understanding the Old Testament* (see bibliography).

Verses 13-16 give the reason for his followers to reflect Christ and his kingdom in their lives. Jesus says, "You are the salt of the earth; but if salt has lost its taste, how can its saltiness be restored? It is no longer good for anything, but is thrown out and trampled under foot."

Salt preserves flavor. When it no longer has its preservative quality, or loses its taste, it is useless. Jesus is saying if you do not preserve my vision, my virtues and values, and the attitude behind them, then you as an individual and as a nation are of no value to me. You are useless to the kingdom. The nation of Israel was warned over and over that if it did not exchange its agenda for his agenda, it would be destroyed. If they do not exchange their words and actions for his words and actions the kingdom can not make its impact upon the society. Should it be any different for the time in which we live?

Verses 15-16 say, "You are the light of the world. A city built on a hill cannot be hid. No one after lighting a lamp puts it under the bushel basket, but on the lampstand, and it gives light to all in the house. In the same way, let your light shine before others, so that they may see your good works and give glory to your Father in heaven." (This is humankind's purpose according to Jesus: Be a beacon of light in this dark world for him, his kingdom, his vision, his virtues, his values, and his attitude. In this way, individuals, nations, and churches glorify God.)

Verses 17-20 say, "Do not think I have come to abolish the law or the prophets, I have come not to abolish but to fulfill. (Matthew quotes the Old Testament sixty-one times to demonstrate that Jesus fulfilled the law.) For truly I tell you, until heaven and earth pass away, not one letter, not one stroke of a letter, will pass from the law until all is accomplished. Therefore, whoever breaks one of the least of these commandments, and teaches others to do the same, will be called least in the kingdom of heaven. For I tell you, unless your righteousness exceeds that of the scribes and Pharisees, you will never enter the kingdom of heaven." (He is not encouraging a lawless society. A system of law is necessary for order in a society and too keep the hard hearted under control, but he is saying laws can only bring about a minimum ethic.)

The higher righteousness is not religious ritual but to love God with all your power, heart, mind, and soul, and your neighbor as yourself. Love demands justice, but justice demands love. Jesus comes to fulfill the story that began with Abraham, to bring it to its climax, to fulfill the law that began with Moses, and to show its deeper meaning, to show its highest intention, to stress its themes, its vision, virtues, and values. The law and the prophets are not being abolished, but the deeper meaning brought to light. The Old Testament will now be understood through and in the light of Christ, who is the full and completed Torah and the deepest understanding of God's wisdom. Ethics will now be done by way of remembering Jesus' words, actions, and his Spirit, not by a total system of timeless hard and fast rules and laws.

Doing what is right can not be reduced to outward acts, a set formula, a law that emphasizes the minimum of what can be done to please God, and does not transform the heart. To take literally that one can not break even the least of the commandments misses what he is saying. He will eliminate many of them himself; for example he will eliminate the purity laws, the food laws, and the laws of worship with their ritual.

According to NT Wright (2005, 52-59, 121-141) Jesus brings the story of Scripture to its climax. Jesus is the new Israel formed by Scripture bringing the kingdom to birth not just for Israel but for the whole world. The entire story beginning with Genesis is coming to fruition. It will continue through the New Testament and the church age until the end of that age. Israel failed in God's mission to take God's light to the nations. The authoritative word of God in the Old Testament is now embodied in Jesus and is to be brought to the world. There is both continuity with the old as well as discontinuity.

Wright discusses living Scripture serving its purpose with the Mosaic law in a multilayered manner but now brought to its climax. We no longer live in the time of creation, the Fall, the time of Israel, or even the time of Christ. We now live in the last age called the church age, the new covenant, the age of the Spirit. God's plan moves in stages. Christians must be loyal and rooted to the past as well as being open to God's plan and the age we are in and the one that is coming. Jesus as found in the New Testament is the core and foundation for the new age, but the new is still rooted in the old. All Scripture is culturally conditioned, but many of the virtues, values, principles, and themes behind the rules and regulations are still valuable but must be applied in new ways to different situations.

In the following there will be six antitheses in which the words of the Old Testament (You have heard) are replaced by what Jesus says (But I say to you). The antitheses illustrate a few examples of how Jesus came to fulfill the law, taking it to its deepest intention and in the process reinterpreting it. Verses 21-22 say, "You have heard that it was said to those of ancient times, 'you shall not murder'; and 'whoever murders shall be liable to judgment.' But I say to you that if you are angry with a brother or sister, you will be liable to judgment; and if you insult a brother or sister, you will be liable to the council; and if you say, 'you fool,' you will be liable to the hell of fire."

Christ is turning the way people think upside down. He goes inward to the heart and mind where thinking and emotions originate in order to get at the root disposition beneath the actions. He is demonstrating that inside a person is where intentions, sin, evil, and goodness originate. The first application of this teaching is to those wanting to overthrow Rome by violence. He is saying to them, if you keep agitating the Romans, the city is going to become like the continual fire of Gehenna, which was the garbage dump outside the city. As usual the spirit of the teachings of Jesus has many applications, but seeking the original application is important.

So verses 23-24 say, "So when you are offering your gift at the altar, if you remember that your brother or sister has something against you, leave your gift there before the altar and go; first be reconciled to your brother or sister, and then come and offer your gift." (Jesus is saying to be reconciled and at peace with other humans as much as possible is one's first order of business, and then go worship. Jesus will say, I desire mercy rather than sacrifice, meaning worship. Jesus is setting priorities straight. He seems to be saying that reconciliation with your fellow humans as much as possible is necessary for your worship to be acceptable.)

Along this same line of reconciliation, verses 25-26 say, "Come to terms quickly with your accuser while you are on the way to court with him, or your accuser may hand you over to the judge, and the judge to the guard, and you will be thrown into prison. Truly I tell you, you will never get out until you have paid the last penny."

He is telling his people to do what they can to bring reconciliation. If they are in the wrong then make it right. Others say this was Jesus' message to those plotting violence against Rome, and his attempt to get them to act toward Rome in a different manner and warning them of the consequence, if they do not. It is a message to the nation to settle its accounts quickly, to get its house in order, to take seriously the message of the kingdom before they are judged.

Verse 27 says, "You have heard that it was said, 'You shall not commit adultery.' But I say to you everyone who looks at a woman with lust has already committed adultery with her in his heart." (Again, he goes to the root of the action. The message is get lust under control so that it never gets to the next stage.) In verses 27-30 he tells them, "If your right eye causes you to sin, tear it out and throw it away; it is better for you to lose one of its members than for your whole body to be thrown into hell." Then he says the same about the right hand. (Jesus uses hyperbole, an overstatement, as he often does, to jolt them into thinking about the message he is trying to get them to understand. If one takes all this literally, we would have a lot more blind people and those with artificial limbs walking around.)

In verses 31-32 Jesus basically eliminates remarriage. He says, "anyone who divorces his wife, except on the ground of unchastity (pornea), causes her to commit adultery; and whoever marries a divorced woman commits adultery."

Much has been written about the meaning of the word, *pornea*. There are many interpretations. Protestants and Catholics do not agree, and Protestants do not agree with each other. Some Protestants believe that pornea means fornication, so divorce and remarriage is acceptable, if fornication is involved. Catholics refer back to Leviticus 18 stating, if there are marriages with blood relatives, they can be separated. Others believe it means any kind of unlawful sex as stated in Leviticus 18. This writer will simply state that if one takes this teaching of Jesus literally all groups are in violation, along with many individuals, no matter how many reasons or excuses they offer.

This writer believes in the New Testament it is important to look at the spirit of the law (2 Cor 3:6). The spirit of the law tells us that Jesus does not approve of divorce for his followers. In Malachi 2:16 God says, I hate divorce. The spirit of the law recognizes the imperfection of humans, and that divorce will happen. Jesus does not want divorce, but it will happen as does the sin of gossip, jealously, fornication, war, and many others. Separation or even divorce may or may not be an individual's personal sin. But according to this teaching remarriage is a sin. But is this the sin that can not be forgiven, and thus anyone who divorces and remarries is going to be in hell? This writer does not think so. God is a merciful, forgiving God. According to Scripture, the only sin that is not forgiven is blasphemy against the Holy Spirit.

Even though in God's good future the kingdom does not include divorce, in this age of imperfection, where the kingdom is breaking into this world at different places at different rates, are there legitimate times for divorce and remarriage? Matthew, Luke, and Paul all handle the question of divorce somewhat differently. There is a realization that we are still living in the time of hard hearts, even as the kingdom is breaking in. If we can have a just war, is it also possible to have a just divorce? What about a just remarriage?

This writer believes that the God of mercy, grace, and compassion can forgive any sin including remarriage, but it is apparent that God wants his people to have an attitude that rejects divorce and remarriage. The sin that can not be forgiven is unrepentant sin. No matter how much a divorced and remarried person blames the other person, or does not accept any responsibility for the divorce, if they have remarried, this general teaching is that they have sinned, and sin must be forgiven. If there is no repentance, then it is a sin that can not be forgiven. This is not popular thinking, but it does appear to this writer to be what Jesus is teaching. Also see Mk 10:2-12 and Lk 16:18. This writer encourages the readers to go to their particular church to hear its point of view.

Jesus continues in verses 33-37. "Again, you have heard that it was said to those of ancient times, 'You shall not swear falsely, but carry out the vows you have made to the Lord.' But I say to you, do not swear at all, either by heaven, for it is the throne of God, or by the earth, for it is his footstool, or by Jerusalem, for it is the city of the great king. And do not swear by your head, for you cannot make one hair white or black. Let your word be 'Yes, Yes' or 'No, No' anything more than this is from the evil one." (Not to swear at all is a statement of hyperbole.)

This may be in reference to certain personal religious vows and everyday speech taken in a haphazard manner in every day life and not those made in a courtroom or those of solemn religious importance. Even Jesus (Mt 26:63) had to swear by an oath in the courtroom and the Apostle Paul to a church (2 Cor 1:23, Gal

1:20). The teaching here is to be honest and straightforward in one's speech, then others will not have to make one swear an oath before one is believed. If a civil law demands an oath, then abide by it, but do not swear oaths in your personal relationships.

Verses 38-42 say, "You have heard that it was said, 'An eye for an eye and a tooth for a tooth.' But I say to you, Do not resist an evil doer. But if anyone strikes you on the right cheek, turn the other also; and if anyone wants to sue you and take your coat give your cloak as well; and if anyone forces you to go one mile, go also the second mile. Give to everyone who begs from you, and do not refuse anyone who wants to borrow."

Again, these are not laws that are timeless ethics to blindly adhere to, so look to the values or spirit behind them and the situation in which they are said. Each of these teachings challenges instinctive human behavior. The first one attempts to intervene in the cycle of revenge and violence to bring about peace and reconciliation. The Old Testament law brought revenge in families that continued forever. The second and third teachings are to encourage people to go out of their way, not to be argumentative, but to bring about change for the better in relationships.

In these two incidents it is possible the teachings are meant to embarrass the Roman aggressors as it points out that they are taking unfair advantage. It may also be teaching that followers of Christ are to be unselfish, generous people. The last teaching is also about generosity encouraging the disciples to help people in need. If one looks at these teachings as law, the point will be missed. Look for the spirit behind the law. Horsley (2003, 119) says that by giving both coat and cloak the person would be standing naked which would embarrass whoever was demanding the clothes.

To follow these teachings in a legalist fashion is not the purpose of these particular teachings, for the results may not be best for all involved. Common sense is called for. For example, letting oneself be pounded into the ground may not be best for the individual being pounded, or the one doing the pounding. The teaching is avoid violence and revenge. Giving to everyone who begs from you or wanting to borrow from you may not be best for those involved. The teaching to follow is: What is most helpful, what is best for those involved, what is the most loving thing to do in this circumstance? God loves us, but giving us everything we want is not always the best thing to do for us. It is the same when we relate to others.

It is also possible that these teachings are meant for the resistance movement, especially do not resist evil, and not to seek revenge but to go the second mile. Jesus does not want them to agitate the Romans, for he knows it would end in their destruction. In fact it is believed that the purpose of this Sermon on the Mount is not only the new way for the kingdom, but is also an agenda to change the attitude for all those plotting against the Romans. Ghandi learned from the Sermon on the Mount, and India was changed. (See the movie Ghandi.) As far as not resisting evil, the opposite is said in another context in 1 Thess 5:22 where it says abstain from every form of evil. Again interpreting Scripture properly must involve the contexts of the Scriptures.

Verses 43-47 say, "You have heard that it was said, 'You shall love your neighbor and hate your enemy.' (That was not the teaching of the Jews, but it was the way some acted, see Ps 139:19-22.) But I say to you, Love your enemies and pray for those who persecute you, so that you may be children of your Father in heaven; for he makes his sun rise on the evil and on the good, and sends rain on the righteous and the unrighteous. For if you love those who love you, what reward do you have? Do not even the tax collectors do the same? And if you greet only your brothers and sisters, what more are you doing than others? Do not the Gentiles do the same?

Be perfect therefore, as your heavenly Father is perfect." Again, the first application of these teachings is thought to be that Jesus is teaching how to respond to the Romans to avoid being crushed.

To be asked to love your enemies is upturning the way the world thinks, acts, and defines love. Jesus is not asking people to feel love; he is asking them to act in a certain way toward all people. Love is defined in 1 Cor 13:4-7. Love is patient; love is kind; love is not envious or boastful or arrogant or rude. It does not insist on its own way; it is not irritable or resentful; it does not rejoice in wrongdoing, but rejoices in the truth. It bears all things, believes all things, hopes all things, endures all things. Jesus is not saying that with love justice is eliminated. Love does demand justice, but justice demands love There needs to be a balance with a definite leaning toward love.

Love is also defined by the actions of Jesus and finally by giving up his life for the well being of others. The question asked in (46) is what are you doing that is different from what the people of the world are doing. When Jesus says be perfect as your heavenly Father is perfect, he is saying, in your relationship with your fellow humans have the attitude of perfect love, mercy, compassion, and peace as your Father in heaven does. He is saying do to others as you would have them do to you.

Chapter 6:1-2 says, "Beware of practicing your piety before others in order to be seen by them; for then you have no reward from your Father in heaven. So whenever you give alms, do not sound a trumpet before you, as the hypocrites do in the synagogues and in the streets, so they may be praised by others. Truly I tell you they have received their reward." In verses 3-4 he tells them to give alms in secret, and then God will reward them. (That simply means

give alms without sounding your own horn for everyone to see.) In verses 5-6 Jesus presents the same idea in reference to praying. He tells them to pray in secret not like the hypocrites do who pray to get people's praise.

These verses are in the context of hypocrisy. These are not laws to follow to the letter. These are not timeless laws where one can never give money that is seen in church or in public, or one can never pray in public. The spirit of the law is for followers to examine the reason, or their motivation for giving and praying.

Verses 7-9 say, "When you are praying, do not heap up empty phrases as the Gentiles do (the pagans); for they think they will be heard because of their many words (their babbling or long winded prayers). Do not be like them, for your Father knows what you need before you ask him."

In verses 9-10 Jesus says, "Pray in this way: Our Father in heaven, hallowed be your name." (This addresses and recognizes that God is holy and of a higher state than humans.) "Your kingdom come. Your will be done, on earth as it is in heaven." (The prayer is for God's ways and his kingdom of love, peace, justice, compassion, and mercy to break in upon the earth more fully. The prayer is for God's will to be on earth like it is in heaven. Millions pray this prayer daily, but do they understand what it means and do they apply it in their daily decision making?) Verse 11 says, "Give us this day our daily bread." (This is a prayer that basic spiritual and material needs, not wants, be met. Jesus is the bread from heaven who feeds people both spiritually and materially.)

Verse 12 says, "And forgive us our debts as we also have forgiven our debtors." (Debts are another Jewish way of saying sins. Because forgiveness is given to another, one can then receive forgiveness from God for one's own sins. Some scholars believe the reference is to literal debts which enslaved many of the common people and brought about the loss of their property leaving them in destitute poverty.) Verse 13 says, "And do not bring us to the time of trial, but rescue us from the evil one." (Do not let Satan tempt us beyond more than we can handle, and protect us from Satan and all evil.)

Verses 14-15 say, "For if you forgive others their trespasses, your heavenly Father will also forgive you, but if you do not forgive others, neither will your heavenly Father forgive your trespasses." In verses 16-18 Jesus gives the same message about fasting as he did for giving alms and prayer. They are not to do it for show as the hypocrites but to do it without seeking praise.

Verses 19-24 say, "Do not store up for yourselves treasures on earth, where moth and rust consume and where thieves break in and steal, but store up for yourselves treasures in heaven, where neither moth nor rust consumes and where thieves do not break in and steal. For where your treasure is, there your heart will be also." (This appears to be a major problem in the world, including for many Christians.)

Verse 22 says, "The eye is the lamp of the body." So, if your eye is healthy, your whole body will be full of light; but if your eye is unhealthy, your whole body will be full of darkness. If then the light in you is darkness, how great is the darkness. (He is saying whatever anyone sets their sights on is what will fill their hearts.) In verse 24 Jesus says, "No one can serve two masters; for a slave will either hate the one and love the other, or be devoted to the one and despise the other. You can not serve God and wealth."

Anything served more importantly than the things of God becomes one's idol. Americans need to begin to look closely at what America's witness is to the world. Is it commercialism, consumerism, profits, greed, guns, war, violence, and drugs? Specialists in world affairs say America has armed the world, which makes up the majority of what we call foreign aid. In the federal budget only .4

of 1 per cent of American aid goes to foreign economic help. (See the note on the federal budget, and how much of your tax money goes to helping the poor in America on page seventy.) Specialists also say that America's drug habit is what keeps the drug trade moving. Are these things taking the place of the teachings of Jesus as what motivates us as a nation? Consumerism, commercialism, greed, and profits seem to become the goals of business and the big corporations. They all talk about service, but the only thing that really seems to matter to most of them is the bottom line and pleasing the stockholders. Since they are outsourcing the jobs, supplying jobs to Americans to feed their families certainly is not their goal. When the world looks at America, do they see a nation of God and a nation of a people following the ways of God? Many Americans think so and justify themselves by singing God Bless America. Are these the things that lead to God blessing America?

In verses 25-30 Jesus teaches on overcoming worry. He says, "Therefore I tell you, do not worry about your life, what you will eat or what you will drink, or about your body, what you will wear. Is not life more than food, and the body more than clothing? Look at the birds of the air; they neither sow nor reap nor gather into barns, and yet your heavenly Father feeds them. Are you not of more value than they? And can any of you by worrying add a single hour to your span of life? And why do you worry about clothing? Consider the lilies of the field, how they grow, they neither toil nor spin, yet I tell you, even Solomon in all his glory was not clothed like one of these. But if God so clothes the grass of the field, which is alive today and tomorrow is thrown into the oven, will he not much more clothe you—you of little faith?

Verses 31-34 say, "Therefore do not worry saying, 'What will we eat?' or 'What will we drink?' or 'What will we wear?' For it is the Gentiles who strive for these things; and indeed your heavenly Father knows that you need all these things. But strive first for the kingdom of God and his righteousness, and all these things will be given to you as well. So do not worry about tomorrow, for tomorrow will bring worries of its own. Today's trouble is enough for today." Is striving first for the kingdom of God and his righteousness the primary purpose for our nation and the individuals living in this nation?

This as well as most of the Sermon on the Mount are not about the letter of the law but are about character development and creating attitudes, dispositions, intentions, and motivations. It is about how to most fully love God and neighbor as self. It is about trust and dependence on God and his ways. As we go through the Gospels, Jesus often uses hyperbolic metaphors to challenge imaginations and to draw his people toward a deeper conversion. Too often the conversion of the followers of Jesus ends because they get overcome with the things of the world; consequently, deeper growth is hindered. See the parable of the sower in 13:3-23. Actually, spiritual growth is like physical growth; it is either exercised in order to grow or it decreases.

In these verses (25-34) the spirit of the law is not saying there is never anything to be concerned about, or nothing to plan for, he is simply teaching his followers not to be overly concerned for the material things of life, and do not spend your days deep in worry. He is saying do not spend all your effort on things that may not matter. He is saying organize your life around my teachings and my ways, be responsible, and trust me, and then things in the long run will work out. Unfortunately, the literalists, those who interpret Scripture by the letter of the law, usually miss the real message.

Chapter 7:1 is another example of the literalist misunderstanding the biblical message when no judging at all is permitted. The verse

says, "Do not judge, so that you may not be judged." (Soon in this chapter the reader will see that the follower is to judge, so what does not to judge mean? The statement is made in the context of hypocritical judging and in the context of a rash, fault-finding disposition, which nitpicks and condemns without fair examination.)

Verses 2-5 say, "For with the judgment you make you will be judged, and the measure you give will be the measure you get. Why do you see the speck in your neighbor's eye, but do not notice the log in your own eye? Or how can you say to your neighbor, 'Let me take the speck out of your eye,' while the log is in your own eye? You hypocrite, first take the log out of your own eye, and then you will see clearly to take the speck out of your neighbor's eye." (Once that is understood and done, one can make fair and just judgments.)

In the very next verse judgment must be made between who is a dog and who is a swine. Verse 6 says, "Do not give what is holy to dogs; and do not throw your pearls before swine, or they will trample them underfoot and turn and maul you." (Jesus is saying not to force God's message upon those who despise you and refuse to hear it. Use your time wisely and spend it on those who may want to hear God's message.)

Verses 7-8 say, "Ask, and it will be given you; search and you will find; knock and the door will be opened for you. For everyone who asks receives, and everyone who searches finds, and for everyone who knocks, the door will be opened. Is there anyone among you who, if your child asks for bread, will give a stone? Or if the child asks for a fish, will give a snake? If you then, who are evil, know how to give good gifts to your children, how much more will your Father in heaven give good things to those who ask him." (This statement seems to be in the context of receiving those things that are holy like the gifts and fruits of the Holy Spirit. This is also to encourage trust and to put your dependence on God and the power of prayer.)

Verse 12 says, "In everything do to others as you would have them do to you; for this is the law and the prophets." (If individuals, institutions, and nations would follow this teaching, it would be a great world.)

The sermon ends with a series of contrasts regarding the decision for or against God. Verses 13-14 say, "Enter through the narrow gate; for the gate is wide and the road is easy that leads to destruction, and there are many who take it. For the gate is narrow and the road is hard that leads to life, and there are few who find it."

When Matthew says that few find the way to life, he is first talking about finding true life by letting the kingdom that is breaking into the world rule their lives. Too often the match between the kingdom's values and those people who claim to be followers of Christ do not always match very well, especially when their attitude, thinking, and works are compared to the teachings of Jesus. Too often his followers are not finding the abundant life Jesus talks about either in this life or the life to come.

Verses 15-20 say, "Beware of false prophets, who come to you in sheep's clothing but inwardly are ravenous wolves. You will know them by their fruits. Are grapes gathered from thorns, or figs from thistles? In the same way, every good tree bears good fruit, but the bad tree bears bad fruit. A good tree can not bear bad fruit, nor can a bad tree bear good fruit. Every tree that does not bear good fruit is cut down and thrown into a fire. Thus you will know them by their fruits." (To know them by their fruits one must be able to make judgments between good and bad fruit.)

Verses 21-23 say, "Not everyone who says to me, Lord, Lord, will enter the kingdom of heaven, but only the one who does the will of my Father in heaven." (Doing God's will is essential for entering the kingdom. Those who say all one must do is believe is true, only if believing includes letting God do his will through you. When one allows God to do his will through you, one is confirming the covenant God has made between him and his people. When one does not do God's will, one has left the covenant.)

"On that day many will say to me, 'Lord, Lord, did we not prophesy in your name, and cast out demons in your name, and do many deeds of power in your name?' Then I will declare to them, 'I never knew you; go away from me, you evil doers.' " (The first application is to the religious leaders who believe in Jesus name, who do great acts of power in his name, but as verse 21 says, they are not obedient to following God's will. They are evil doers.)

Verses 24-27 say, "Everyone then who hears these words of mine and acts on them (something many of the religious and political leaders of the time are not doing) will be like a wise man who built his house on a rock. The rain fell, the floods came, and the winds blew and beat on that house, but it did not fall, because it had been founded on rock. And everyone who hears these words of mine and does not act on them will be like a foolish man who built his house on sand. The rain fell, and the floods came, and the winds blew and beat against that house, and it fell—and great was its fall."

Matthew is giving his audience and readers a choice. They can build their life on Jesus and his word and find life, or they can build it upon anything else and find darkness and death. The heart of Jerusalem is the temple built upon a rock. Religious life is centered on the temple. The sacrificial system is where sin is forgiven, and it is the headquarters for the theocracy, the religious and political leadership of the Jews. Jesus is now teaching that the real house on the rock will be his followers, who will be built into the new temple of Jesus and his words, and that is the true rock.

Jesus is in the process of endangering himself with the religious and political authorities. He is undercutting the two main institutions of Judaism. He is claiming to be the new Torah, God's word, and the new temple, the place where sins are forgiven and in which the new Israel will be built. All this is going to eventually lead to the leaders putting him to death.

Verses 28-29 say, Now when Jesus had finished saying these things, the crowds were astounded at his teaching, for he taught them as one having authority, and not as their scribes. (Jesus did not quote the authorities or tradition; he spoke on his own authority like he is God or sent from God. He even reinterprets some of the Scriptures and eliminates others destroying their traditions, which is another reason the Jewish leaders want to get rid of him.)

In chapter 8:1-4 Jesus comes off the mountain and great crowds follow him. A leper comes before him saying, "Lord, if you choose, you can make me clean." Jesus said, "I do choose. Be made clean!" Immediately his leprosy was cleansed. Then Jesus said to him, "See that you say nothing to anyone; but go, show yourself to the priest, and offer the gift that Moses commanded, as a testimony to them. (This disease excludes the person from associating with others. So the leper seeks not only freedom from the disease but freedom to rejoin the Jewish community, Lev 14.)

Jesus enters Capernaum and in (5-10) a centurion (probably a Roman soldier in command of 50-100 men) says to him, "Lord, my servant is lying at home paralyzed, in terrible distress." And he said to him, "I will come and cure him." The Centurion answered, "Lord, I am not worthy to have you come under my roof; but only speak the word, and my servant will be healed. For I also am a man under authority, with soldiers under me; and I say to one, 'Go,' and he goes, and to another, 'Come,' and he comes, and to my slave, 'Do this,' and the slave does it."

When Jesus heard him, he was amazed and said to those who

followed him, "Truly I tell you, in no one in Israel have I found such faith." Verses 11-13 say, "I tell you, many will come from east and west and will eat with Abraham and Isaac and Jacob in the kingdom of heaven, while the heirs of the kingdom will be thrown into the outer darkness, where there will be weeping and gnashing of teeth." (That is quite a strong statement.) And to the centurion Jesus said, "Go; let it be done for you according to your faith." And the servant was healed at that hour. (Luke 7:1-10 and John 4:46-53 describe the details somewhat differently.)

The Jews think the nation will be saved when God comes, but the fact is when God comes, he is going to judge the nation. This is called an *eschatological reversal*. Because the nation and its leaders are corrupt and reject the kingdom, they will be judged when God uses the Romans to destroy Jerusalem and the temple. This is not the first time the nation of God waited for him to judge their enemies, but instead he judged his own people for their sin.

In verses 14-17 Jesus heals Peter's mother-in-law and that evening he heals many others who were possessed with demons and cures all who were sick. Verse 17 says, This was to fulfill what had been spoken through the prophet Isaiah (53:4), "He took our infirmities and bore our diseases." (Matthew is saying this is the one we have been expecting; this is the Messiah.) With great crowds upon him he gives orders to go to the other side where a scribe says to him in (19) "Teacher, I will follow you wherever you go." And Jesus said to him, "Foxes have holes, and birds of the air have nests; but the Son of Man has nowhere to lay his head."

He is saying under these circumstances do you really want to follow me? Jesus challenges a man who is probably, at the moment, emotionally moved to follow him. He challenges him to use his reason and think through what he is saying. He is telling him that life as his follower will not be one of prosperity and ease. Unfortunately, the opposite message is given by numerous Christians and their churches in comfortable, prosperous America in these times. The response of Jesus, who makes prospective followers count the cost of following him, is not like many churches today, who will do practically anything to get more members, including using emotions to get a decision.

Another of his disciples said to him, "Lord, first let me go bury my father." But Jesus said to him, "Follow me, and let the dead bury their own dead."

Some say the man is making an excuse not to commit to him saying wait until my father dies, and then I will come and follow you. Others say the father is spiritually dead, so he is saying to let the spiritually dead bury the spiritually dead. He is not telling people to ignore their family responsibilities, but he is telling people that he is not going to accept their excuses for not making a commitment to him. In Jewish law a proper burial is a most important responsibility, but Jesus teaches, possibly through hyperbole, that following him is even more important.

In verses 23-24 Jesus gets into a boat and is asleep when a windstorm causes the waves to go into the boat. The disciples wake him in (25-27) saying, "Lord, save us! We are perishing." And he said to them, "Why are you afraid, you of little faith?" Jesus then calmed the sea, and they were amazed and said, "What sort of man is this, that even the winds and the sea obey him?" (Matthew is saying that Jesus is God, for in Genesis 1 and the Psalms only God has power over nature, for it is God's creation.)

In verses 28-34 two demoniacs from the tombs met him. In (29) they shout, "What have you to do with us, Son of God? Have you come here to torment us before the time?" (The demoniacs recognize him for who he is.) Jesus then cast them into the swine, and they ran over a steep bank and perished in the water. The whole town came and begged him to leave. (Some think this is a parable like story to show the power of Jesus as God's Son over demons and all evil. If it is not a parable it is strange that Jesus destroys the livelihood of a group of people. See the more complete explanation and different details of the story in Mark 5:1-20.)

In chapter 9 Jesus crosses the sea and comes to his own town (Capernaum). Some people are carrying a paralyzed man on a bed. In verses 2-6 Jesus said to him, "Take heart, son; your sins are forgiven." The scribes said to themselves, "This man is blaspheming." (They are saying that he is claiming to be God.) But Jesus perceiving their thoughts said, "Why do you think evil in your thoughts? For which is easier, to say, 'Your sins are forgiven,' or to say, 'Stand up and walk'? But so that you may know that the Son of Man has authority on earth to forgive sins"—he then said to the paralytic—"Stand up, take your bed and go to your home." In (8) the crowds are filled with awe and they glorify God. (Jesus heals the man physically to show he has the authority and power to forgive sin. In the process he bypasses the temple's sacrificial system, which is unheard of in those times, and by doing that, he upsets the Jewish authorities.)

Verse 9 says, As Jesus was walking along, he saw a man called Matthew sitting at the tax booth; and he said to him, "Follow me." And he got up and followed him. (Mark and Luke call him Levi, probably because he was a former Levite. Levites were from either priestly families or those who help the priests in the temple.) In (10-11) many tax collectors and sinners sat with him at dinner. The Pharisees said to his disciples, "Why does your teacher eat with tax collectors and sinners?"

Those Jews who are collecting taxes for the Romans are considered by other Jews to be the scum of the earth. The Romans did not pay them for collecting taxes. They make their money by charging way beyond what they are to collect. Many of them take great advantage of the people and in the process become quite wealthy. The system has continued throughout history, but not just in the tax collecting business.

The sinners in this context are the tax collectors, and those who do not follow all the ritual laws of the Pharisees. The Pharisees never eat at the same table with those who do not follow to the letter their ritual laws, especially their purity and food laws, for violating their food laws makes one impure. The Pharisees have taken their purity and dietary laws to the extreme, making themselves an exclusive club, shutting themselves off to Gentiles, those to whom they are to be God's witness.

Verses 12-13 say, When he (Jesus) heard this, he said, "Those who are well have no need of a physician, but those who are sick. Go and learn what this means, 'I desire mercy not sacrifice.' For I have come to call not the righteous but sinners."

The word righteous and its derivatives are used numerous ways in Scripture. Here Jesus is saying that those who think they have no sin, do not see a need for Jesus; only those who know they have sinned know their need for him. Jesus is also saying he prefers compassion first, and then sacrifice (proper ritual and worship). He is not saying he does not want their worship, but compassion and mercy have priority. In the process we will see that Jesus will determine what is and is not proper worship. God will no longer be worshiped through the temple but through him. So here he is forgiving sin and in the process making new rules about worship, which continue to undercut the law and the temple authorities. It is no wonder that the authorities feel he is undermining them and destroying their traditions and want to get rid of him.

In verses 14-17 the disciples of John the Baptist came to Jesus asking why his disciples do not fast. He told them as long as he is with them there is no reason to fast. (He is telling them that through him the presence of God is in their midst, so it is a time to celebrate. After he leaves then they can fast. Zechariah 8:19 mentions fasting because Israel is still in exile. Fasting becomes a feast when God forgives sin and restores his people.) Then Jesus said, "No one sews a piece of unshrunk cloth on an old cloak, for the patch pulls away from the cloak, and a worse tear is made. Neither is new wine put into old wineskins; otherwise the skins burst, and the wine is spilled, and the skins destroyed; but new wine is put into fresh wineskins, and so both are preserved.

Jesus is talking about the new covenant with a new way of thinking in the coming new age compared to the old traditions of the Pharisees. The new ways can not be contained in the old structures, for when they are stretched they tear. A new structure is needed, a new way of thinking, a new covenant that can be adapted and appropriated by all people, and one that does not focus on the minimum way to please God but on the maximum way.

Verses 18-38 are about the power of faith and include numerous healings. A leader of a synagogue whose daughter just died asks Jesus to lay his hand on her so she would live. Jesus is impressed with the man's faith and raises her.

Being raised from the dead is a sign to some Jews that the new age may be breaking in (see Ezek 37:1-14). The Jews believe that when the new age comes, everyone will be raised from the dead. So this may be a sign that the time is near. The resurrection of Jesus will be the Father's confirmation that the new age has come into the world. Colossian 1:15 calls him the firstborn of all creation, meaning because of him all who are his, will be raised up with him.

On the way a woman who had been suffering from hemorrhages for twelve years thought if she could touch the hem of his cloak, she would be healed. Verse 22 says, Jesus turned and seeing her he said, "Take heart daughter; your faith has made you well." (Mark 5:21-43 has more detail on these particular incidents.)

Verse 27 says, As Jesus went on from there, two blind men followed him, crying loudly, "Have mercy on us, Son of David!" Jesus impressed with their faith heals them. In (32-34) after they had gone away a mute demoniac was brought to Jesus. Jesus cast the demon out and the man began to speak. The crowds were amazed and said, "Never has anything like this been seen in Israel." (For those with eyes to see and ears to hear, these are signs from passages like Isaiah 29:18-19, 35:5-10, 42:6-8, 43:8 that the new age is breaking into the world.) But the Pharisees said, "By the ruler of the demons he casts out the demons." (The Pharisees want to get rid of him; he is too much of a threat to them, so they attribute his healing to evil and Satan.)

Verse 35 says, Then Jesus went about all the cities and villages, teaching in their synagogues, and proclaiming the good news of the kingdom, and curing every disease and sickness.

The number one message of Jesus is the importance of the kingdom breaking into the world and the necessity of becoming a part of it (Lk 4:43). His next action of importance is not what one must do to be saved eternally, for that is part of the first but his compassion for people such as their physical health and having food to eat. One wonders why the kingdom breaking into the world and care of people's health no longer seem to be a priority with many of his churches. Has much of modern day Christianity revived the ancient heresy of *Docetic Gnosticism* where being saved has become separated from the physical and material world? When this is the teaching, the physical world and physical needs are no longer important.

Verses 36-38 say, When he saw the crowds, he had compassion for them, because they were harassed and helpless, like sheep without a shepherd. (They are harassed religiously, politically, economically, and socially by leadership that was concerned only with their own selfish wealth and power.) Then he said to his disciples, "The harvest is plentiful, but the laborers are few; therefore ask the Lord of the harvest to send out laborers into his harvest." (Harvesting is in reference to the kingdom that is coming into the world. Making it apply only to souls being saved only deals with one part of the message.)

The gospel message is not only entry into the kingdom but inviting people to join Christ in making the kingdom present in this world. Somehow this message has become distorted into a message of believe and be saved and ignore the world, or the other extreme of changing the world without him. Both approaches misrepresent Scripture. Personal renewal and the beginning of salvation is part of the message but so is the beginning of renewing the world. Both of these are begun by Jesus and will be completed when he comes to make all things new, which includes a new heaven and new earth.

In chapter 10 Jesus summons his twelve disciples and gives them authority over unclean spirits, to cast them out, and to cure every disease and every sickness. Verses 2-4 say, These are the names of the twelve apostles: first, Simon, also known as Peter, and his brother Andrew; James son of Zebedee, and his brother John; Philip and Bartholomew; Thomas and Matthew the tax collector; James son of Alphaeus, and Thaddaeus; Simon the Cananaean, and Judas Iscariot, the one who betrayed him.

In verses 5-15 the twelve are sent only to the lost sheep of Israel. The task of the apostles is to go to the Jews. It will later be the task of the Apostle Paul and others to go to the Gentiles. They are to proclaim the good news that the kingdom of heaven has come near.

They are to cure the sick, raise the dead, cleanse the lepers, and cast out demons. They are not to take any payments or to have any money with them. They are to depend on the people to feed them. They are to find out who is worthy and stay with them until they leave. They are not to jump from one place to another. They are to welcome those who welcome them and let their peace be upon them.

Jesus is not making laws that must always be followed, but within his instructions to the twelve are principles to guide his future disciples. Most important is always do only whatever gives a good name to the movement and never be like the world in its desire for importance, power, and wealth.

Then verse 14 says, If anyone will not welcome you or listen to your words, shake off the dust from your feet as you leave that house or town. (This is a cultural tradition, a type of prophetic object lesson, to display that the consequences of the people's decisions are now upon them.) Verse 15 says, truly I tell you, it will be more tolerable for the land of Sodom and Gomorrah on the day of judgment than for that town. (The day of judgment is a reference to the towns in the nation of Israel that reject Jesus and the kingdom. The day of judgment for them will first be the destruction of the nation, Jerusalem, and its temple by the Romans.)

In verse 16 Jesus says, "See, I am sending you out like sheep into the midst of wolves; so be wise as serpents and innocent as doves." In the rest of the chapter he tells the twelve what will happen to them when they go out proclaiming the good news. Verses 17-23 inform us that they are going to be flogged in the synagogues and dragged before governors and kings. They are told not to worry about what to say, for the Spirit of the Father will speak through them. Families will be split over him and betray each other even sometimes putting each other to death.

In verses 22-23 Jesus says, " and you will be hated by all because of my name. But the one who endures to the end will be saved. When they persecute you in one town, flee to the next; for truly I tell you, you will not have gone through all the towns of Israel before the Son of Man comes."

This is apocalyptic language used as a reference to the presence of the Son of Man coming, when at the right hand of the Father he will send his Spirit. Then with the destruction in AD 70 his prophesy about the city, the nation, and temple will be fulfilled. The Son of Man coming is always about judgment and renewal. Son of Man coming in these verses is that judgment will be on Judea. Often the judgment is now or soon and not necessarily at the end times, even though judgment will also be at the end of the world.

Since Matthew is writing approximately fifty years after the death of Christ sometime in the 80s, he is looking back and referring to Jesus who came in the power of his kingdom as stated in Mt 16:28, Mk 9:1, and Lk 9:27. Thus he is showing the people that the prophecy made by Jesus has been fulfilled. According to Matthew the coming of Christ in the power of his kingdom began at his death, resurrection, and his rising to be at the right hand of God, and then his sending of the Holy Spirit in power on the day of Pentecost as written in Acts chapter 2, and finally the judgment of the nation in AD 70.

In verses 24-25 Jesus tells them that if they malign him and call him Beelzebul (a demon) how much more will they malign his followers. In 27-31 Jesus tells them to proclaim from the housetops and (28) says, Do not fear those who kill the body but can not kill the soul; rather fear him who can destroy both soul and body in hell. Are not two sparrows sold for a penny? Yet not one of them will fall to the ground apart from your Father. And even the hairs of your head are all counted. So do not be afraid; you are of more value than many sparrows.

The people that Matthew is writing to are obviously going through the suffering Jesus said his followers would experience. Matthew is encouraging them to continue by telling them that God is aware of what is happening with his people and will work all things according to his purpose. The kingdom will grow like a mustard seed, but the disciples of Jesus must complete the mission he gave them.

In verses 32-33 Jesus says, "Everyone therefore who acknowledges me before others, I also will acknowledge before my Father in heaven; but whoever denies me before others, I also will deny before my Father in heaven." (Matthew's message is for those to whom he is writing but also for all Christians throughout time. Christians affirm Christ or deny him not only in their everyday words but also in their everyday attitudes and actions. For followers of Christ each day is a new day to affirm Christ or deny him.)

Verse 34 continues, "Do not think I have come to bring peace on earth; I have not come to bring peace, but a sword. For I have come to set a man against his father and a daughter against her mother . . . and one's foes will be members of one's household." (This is about the seriousness of being a true follower. The choice to follow Christ in a serious manner often involves family conflict. All of this will be experienced by the disciples of Jesus in the book of Acts.)

The concept of peace must be understood in the light of the principle of complementarity as explained in the section of this book titled, "More Interpretation Issues." Context is most important. In one context he came to bring peace on earth, but in this context he says, do not think I have come to bring peace on earth. The explanation is that on the one hand he did come to bring peace but on the other hand he did not. The context or situation makes the difference.

Verses 37-39 continue, "Whoever loves father or mother more than me is not worthy of me; and whoever loves son or daughter more than me is not worthy of me; and whoever does not take up the cross and follow me is not worthy of me. Those who find their life will lose it, and those who lose their life for my sake will find it." (The message is that Jesus and the kingdom's vision, virtues, and values are to be their priority and not to let anyone, including family members, keep them from following this agenda.)

Whatever one loves more than one loves God and his vision becomes a person's idol, and that includes one's family, especially if one's family is discouraging one from being a dedicated follower. For Christians to pick up one's cross is to die to self and the world, and live as servants to others and the common good, just as Christ did. This is the way one finds real meaning and purpose in life. To pick up the cross is to live for Christ and his interests. To not do so is to lose the purpose for which one is created. Picking up the cross is to be accomplished through everyday living as well as one's politics. God did not create us to live for ourselves and our purposes only, but to first live for him and his purposes. It is not necessary to become a world wide missionary or clergy; it can be accomplished through everyday living in the situation God has given.

Verse 40 continues, "Whoever welcomes you (his disciples) welcomes me, and whoever welcomes me welcomes the one who sent me." Then he states in (41-42) that whoever welcomes them as prophets, and welcomes them as his righteous followers, and gives a cup of cold water to those who are his, will receive their reward. (These verses are best explained in the context of Mt 25:31-46 and Lk 16:19-31 and others like them practically on every page of Scripture.)

∽◦∾

Chapter 11:1 says, Now when Jesus had finished instructing the twelve disciples, he went on from them to teach and proclaim his message in their cities. (Herod Antipas had imprisoned John the

Baptist because John accused Antipas and his wife of being in an illegal marriage.) John sends word to Jesus by his disciples in (2) asking, "Are you the one who is to come, or are we to wait for another?" In (4-6) Jesus answers, "Go and tell John what you hear and see: the blind receive their sight, the lame walk, the lepers are cleansed, the deaf hear, the dead are raised, and the poor have good news brought to them. And blessed be anyone who takes no offense at me."

As previously noted, this is a reference to Scriptures like Isaiah 35 to show that the new age is beginning. After a period of the nation suffering, God is returning to Israel. Israel will be set free from its theological exile. Her sins will be forgiven. The new Israel will then be the light to the nations, a city upon the hill to usher in the beginning of the age of justice (meaning social justice) and peace. This is the purpose of the kingdom that is now breaking into the world through the presence of Jesus and his followers.

Reading second temple writings as well as Ezra 9 and Nehemiah 9, even though the Jews had returned to their land from the Babylonian exile, the Jews in the land still believe they are in exile because they are occupied by a foreign power. Wright (1999, 268-269) discusses in detail this concept of exile. They look forward to the time they will be set free. They will be set free but not in the way they expect. The signs Jesus is performing are signs from the Old Testament that indicate the new age is dawning.

John is confused probably because he expects Jesus to preach a message of fiery judgment just as he did. The answer Jesus gives from Isaiah pictures the time of the new age marked by the deeds Jesus is doing. John is also warned not to disbelieve because his expectations of Jesus are not what he thinks. Jesus changes the emphasis of John's message from judgment to grace, even though he does not eliminate the judgment aspect but presents it in a different manner. Love is not without justice, but justice is not to be without love.

John represents the old law, the letter of the law, and non-bending laws, rules, and regulations. Jesus represents the new law, the spirit of the law being applied in different situations, emphasizing character formation, transformation of the heart, attitudes, dispositions, motivations, virtues, and values and not timeless codes to which everything is to be reduced for all time. That does not mean living in a world where hearts are still hardened that life can be without laws. Laws are still important in a broken world. But it does mean the more the kingdom breaks into the world the more ways of thinking and the ways of doing things change from a minimum law to a maximum of always doing the most loving thing.

Verses 7-8 say, As they went away, Jesus began to speak to the crowds about John: "What did you go out into the wilderness to look at? A reed shaken by the wind? (In other words were you expecting someone without strong convictions, someone who bends with every drift of wind?) What then did you go out to see? Someone dressed in soft robes? Look, those who wear soft robes are in royal palaces. (He is asking if they expected someone just dressed for show parroting what government leaders and their important supporters want the people to hear.)

Verses 9-10 continue, "What then did you go out to see? A prophet? Yes I tell you more than a prophet. This is the one about whom it is written, 'See I am sending my messenger ahead of you, who will prepare your way before you.' " (This is a reference to Malachi 3:1 where the prophet foretells of one who will prepare the way for the king of the new kingdom. John will be the last of the Old Testament prophets.)

In verse 11 Jesus continues, "Truly I tell you, among those born of women no one has arisen greater than John the Baptist; yet the least in the kingdom of heaven is greater than he." (John's greatness is in announcing that the kingdom is near and preparing the way for Jesus. But to be in the kingdom, when it is established is greater. Jesus is expressing the idea that the new covenant is greater than the old because it is the in-breaking of God's final kingdom.)

Then in (12) Jesus says to his disciples, "From the days of John the Baptist until now the kingdom of heaven has suffered violence, and the violent take it by force." (John is put to death before the kingdom is officially established, and Jesus is saying his opposition is trying to kill him, and will try to kill them, his disciples, in order keep power. He also may be referring to the resistance party advocating violence against the Romans.) Then in verses 13-14 Jesus says, "For all the prophets and the law prophesied until John came; and if you are willing to accept it, he is Elijah who is to come. Let anyone with ears listen."

This is prophecy fulfilled. Hundreds of years before, Malachi 4:5 said, "I will send you the prophet Elijah before the great and terrible day of the LORD comes." The literalists missed this because they are waiting for the real Elijah to return from the dead. This should be a lesson for the interpretation of biblical prophecy and the use of metaphorical language. The great and terrible day he mentions is not always meant to be the end of the world, even though it usually has reference to a time of judgment and great change. Here the reference is to the transformation of the old into the new kingdom and the destruction of Jerusalem and the temple. To the Jews this is like an end of the world experience.

In verses 16-19 Jesus continues, "But to what will I compare this generation? It is like children sitting in the marketplaces and calling to one another, 'We played the flute for you, and you did not dance; we wailed, and you did not mourn.' For John came neither eating and drinking, and they say, 'He has a demon'; the Son of Man came eating and drinking, and they say, 'Look a glutton and drunkard, a friend of tax collectors and sinners!' Yet wisdom is vindicated by her deeds."

(Wisdom is being vindicated by the actions of John and Jesus.)

The people are rejecting John because he is too conservative, and they reject Jesus because he is too liberal. Jesus' point is they use any excuse to reject the new age, the kingdom of God, for its values and vision are not their values and vision. They are not looking for God's truth or the common good but looking only to get the thinking and policies established that benefits them the most. Does the reader believe things have changed in our times?

In verses 20-24 Jesus reproaches the cities where he had done great deeds of power because they did not repent. He tells Chorazin, Bethsaida, and Capernaum that on the day of judgment it will be more tolerable for Tyre, Sidon, and Sodom. (Not only will individuals be judged for their words and actions but so will cities, nations, and institutions. Nations and institutions are judged for their words and actions usually during this world as were Tyre, Sidon, and Sodom. The cities mentioned will suffer, as most cities in Judea will, in the war with Rome from 66-70 AD.)

Verses 25-26 say, At that time Jesus said, "I thank you, Lord of heaven and earth, because you have hidden these things from the wise and the intelligent and have revealed them to infants (new believers); yes Father, for such was your gracious will."

God did not really hide things. They are there for all to see, but they are not seen because of people's hard hearts. As it is seen throughout the Scriptures, God is sovereign. He can stop anything he wants, but he allows free choice. Because of the sovereignty of God, the biblical writers attribute to the will of God almost everything that happens. This style of writing makes everything appear that God is pulling strings and just toying with humans, but God is not up there playing with humans like they are puppets on a string. If one does not take into consideration the Hebrew literary style, then that is the conclusion people come to and misinterpret as the old definition of predestination did. This concept is explained in detail with the example of God hardening Pharaoh's heart in the book of the Exodus in this author's book on the Old Testament as listed in the bibliography.

His true will is for all to come to the knowledge of the truth (1 Tim 2:4-5, Jn 6:37), but he never takes away free choice. Jesus reveals the Father. Those able to understand are those who humble themselves, are open to new light, and are willing to change their thinking and actions. Others are too arrogant and hard hearted to want to understand (Isa 6:6-13). Even though his will is for all, he does have a preferential option for the poor, the disadvantaged, the oppressed and non-educated because most of them are more open to learn from him than the people of position and comfort.

In verse 27 Jesus says, "All things have been handed over to me by my Father; and no one knows the Son except the Father, and no one knows the Father except the Son and anyone to whom the Son chooses to reveal him." (He chose to go to the poor, disadvantaged, and oppressed, but all are welcome. Jesus claims a special relationship to the Father, who has chosen the Son to reveal himself to the world. Those who listen and respond to God's grace become God's chosen.)

In verses 28-30 Jesus says, "Come to me all you that are weary and are carrying heavy burdens, and I will give you rest. Take my yoke upon you, and learn from me; for I am gentle and humble in heart; and you will find rest for your souls. For my yoke is easy and my burden is light."

Compared to all the external laws, rules, and regulations the Pharisees laid upon the people, the yoke and burden of Jesus is, in one sense, light. The Pharisees took many of the laws and rituals made for the priests and put many of them upon the common people. They also built a fence around the original law through their traditions by adding many more regulations to make sure the people would not violate any of the original external laws. The law became a heavy burden, too much for the people, as they drowned in rules and regulations with every move they made. They lost their freedom and the flexibility to respond to the spirit of the law. Their intention was good, but their methodology was flawed.

All genuine searchers of wisdom are invited to come to God's wisdom which is being revealed in Jesus. All who are weary and carrying heavy burdens are invited to come to Jesus. Compared to the Pharisees, being a follower of Jesus is rest for the soul, for the burden is light. This will be explained in more detail in chapter 23.

In chapter 12:1-8 Jesus and his disciples pluck grain from a field and eat it on the Sabbath, and the Pharisees charge them with working on the Sabbath, a violation of the law. Plucking the grain on the Sabbath is defined as working; eating it is not the problem. This is an example of distorting the original intent of the law and making the law a burden. Jesus reminds them of the incident of David when he was hungry, and the priest gave him the bread of the Presence, which only the priests were permitted to eat.

In verse 5 Jesus asks, " Or have you not read in the law that on the sabbath the priests in the temple break the sabbath and yet are guiltless? I tell you something greater than the temple is here. But if you had known what this means, 'I desire mercy and not sacrifice,' you would not have condemned the guiltless. For the Son of Man is Lord of the sabbath." (Jesus is telling them that he is greater than the Sabbath and need takes precedence over religious law. He is also saying that he has the authority to redefine the Sabbath and its laws.)

In verses 9-14 he enters a synagogue, and a man was there with a withered hand, and they ask him, "Is it lawful to heal on the sabbath?"

so that they might accuse him. He said to them, "Suppose one of you has only one sheep and it falls into a pit on the sabbath; will you not lay hold of it and lift it out? How much more valuable is a human being than a sheep! So it is lawful to do good on the sabbath." Then he says to the man, "Stretch out your hand." He stretched it out, and it was restored, as sound as the other. But the Pharisees went out and conspired against him, how to destroy him.

Many people ask why he did not wait until another day to heal the man, thus staying away from controversy. But his purpose was not to shy away from controversy, but to challenge wrong thinking. The tradition of man-made religious laws they developed had become more important than helping a person in need. His point is that needs are to have priority over any law. This is an important message for all time.

The leaders in the end will put him to death for teachings like this because they will see him as a threat to their nation and its cultural tradition. This, along with the fact that he is discouraging them from fighting against the Romans who occupy their land is exhibiting to many that he is not being loyal to the nation. They do not see him as an observant Jew nor a loyal flag waving patriot supportive of the leaders of the nation. Therefore in their eyes he deserves death. Verses 15-16 say, When Jesus became aware of this, he departed. Many crowds followed him, and he cured all of them, and he ordered them not to make him known.

Verses 17-21 say, This was to fulfill what had been spoken through the prophet Isaiah (42:1-4). "Here is my servant, whom I have chosen, my beloved, with whom my soul is well pleased. I will put my spirit upon him, and he will proclaim justice to the Gentiles. He will not wrangle or cry aloud, nor will anyone hear his voice in the streets. He will not break a bruised reed or quench a smoldering wick until he brings justice to victory. And in his name the Gentiles will hope."

He knows the authorities will try to find him in order to gather more evidence against him. The people are not yet prepared to understand him and his mission, and at this point he does not want crowds following him. They have the wrong idea of what his kingdom consists, and he has not had enough time to educate those who will become his leaders. Crowds are following him so much that he has very little time to prepare his disciples about the real meaning of the kingdom and the message he wants to go into the whole world. Therefore he tells them, for the moment, not to make him known.

In verses 22-24 he cures a man with a demon who is blind and mute. The crowds are amazed and say, "Can this be the Son of David?" (The Son of David is to be the Messiah.) But the Pharisees say, "It is only by Beezebul, the ruler of the demons, that this fellow casts out demons." Verses 25-28 say, He knew what they were thinking and said to them, "Every kingdom divided against itself is laid waste, and no city or house divided against itself will stand. If Satan casts out Satan, he is divided against himself, how then will his kingdom stand? If I cast out demons by Beelzebul, by whom do your own exorcists cast them out? Therefore they will be your judges. But if it is by the spirit of God that I cast out demons, then the kingdom of God has come upon you."

His message is that the kingdom of God is beginning. Light will begin to dispel darkness and renew the world. The kingdom breaking in upon the earth is beginning to overcome evil. Apparently there are Jewish exorcists who also cast out demons. He points out the absurdity of the charge by saying if I am casting out demons through Satan, then your exorcists are working with Satan also. Jesus does not deny that Jewish exorcists can cast out demons.

Jesus continues by saying "Or how can one enter a strong man's house and plunder his property, without first tying up the strong man? Then indeed the house can be plundered." (Jesus is saying that it is foolish to think he and the demons are working together while he is establishing the kingdom of God. Then he tells them that he is tying up Satan and plundering his kingdom; that is what his casting out sin and demons and healing people physically expresses.) In verse 30 Jesus says, "Whoever is not with me is against me, and whoever does not gather with me scatters."

Elsewhere he said (Mk 9:40), "Whoever is not against us is for us." Again, the key is context. Here it is said in reference to the Pharisees who oppose him and scatter his disciples. In Mark those involved are not opposing him. It must be said over and over in interpreting Scripture the key is context. Because too many people pull Scripture out of context for their own ideological purposes, the Scriptures become distorted.

Verses 31-32 continue, "Therefore I tell you, people will be forgiven for every sin and blasphemy, but blasphemy against the Spirit will not be forgiven. Whoever speaks a word against the Son of Man will be forgiven, but whoever speaks against the Holy Spirit will not be forgiven, either in this age or the age to come.

Blasphemy against the Spirit is attributing to Satan what is the work of God through the Spirit, and thus rejecting God and his work, which is what these Pharisees and scribes are doing. We must understand that not all Pharisees and scribes are guilty; many were beginning to follow him. If one rejects Jesus now, it will not be too late, but when the Spirit comes that Jesus sends after he has risen, and one still rejects the Spirit, then it will be too late.

Verse 33 says, "Either make the tree good, and its fruit good; or make the tree bad, and its fruit bad; for the tree is known by its fruits. (Recognize that the fruit and tree are alike. The idea is that a good person does good, and a bad person does bad. His point is that his casting out demons, and the casting out demons by their own exorcists are all good works by good people; it is not the work of Satan.)

Then in (34-37) he continues, "You brood of vipers! How can you speak good things when you are evil? For out of the abundance of the heart the mouth speaks. The good person brings good things out of a good treasure, and an evil person brings evil things out of an evil treasure. I tell you on the day of judgment you will have to give an account for every careless word you utter; for by your words you will be justified, and by your words you will be condemned."

The question then, is one justified by faith, or justified by words and actions? Scripture includes all of them. The best way to answer is to refer the reader to the principle of complementarity explained in the section titled, "More Interpretation Issues." One is not justified by works and not justified without works. But the works that justify are the works God does through his people and then accounts those works to them (Phil 2:12-13, Augustine, Epistle 194.5.29).

Verse 38 says, Then some of the scribes and Pharisees said to him, "Teacher we wish to see a sign from you." (Because they refuse to accept his casting out demons as a sign from God, they want to see something more spectacular as proof.) Verses 39-40 say, But he answered them, "An evil and adulterous generation asks for a sign, but no sign will be given to it except the sign of the prophet Jonah. (The word adulterous was used by Old Testament prophets to describe Israel's turning away from God and following after idols.) For just as Jonah was three days and three nights in the belly of the sea monster, so for three days and three nights the Son of Man will be in the heart of the earth." (His sign will be the crucifixion and resurrection.)

Verses 41-42 say, "The people of Nineveh will rise up at the judgment with this generation and condemn it, because they repented at the proclamation of Jonah, and see, something greater than Jonah is here! The queen of the South will rise up at the judgment with this generation and condemn it, because she came from the ends of the earth to listen to the wisdom of Solomon, and see, something greater than Solomon is here."

The people of Nineveh and the queen of the South were Gentiles who recognized their need and responded. He is saying the Messiah, God's Son, is here and you refuse to recognize your need as well as the need of the nation. You refuse to repent of your sin and accept the one the Father sent.

Then in verses 43-45 Jesus says, "When the unclean spirit has gone out of a person, it wanders through waterless regions looking for a resting place, but it finds none. Then it says, 'I will return to my house from which I came.' When it comes, it finds it empty, swept, and put in order. Then it goes and brings along seven other spirits more evil than itself, and they enter and live there; and the last state of that person is worse than the first. So will it also be with this evil generation."

He is saying that even though evil is expelled from a person, the Holy Spirit is not put in its place. Therefore, there is no protection from evil, and when it returns, the evil is far worse than its former state. As far as the nation of Israel is concerned, the ministry of Jesus has broken the hold of Satan over Israel. But if the nation does not accept the kingdom of God now breaking in, then the state of the nation will be worse than it was. He also may be reminding them that God's people were exiled into Assyria, and then later Babylonia. Each time they were warned that if the nation did not repent they would be punished, but each time they rejected the prophets, and each time God punished them. Jesus is saying the same thing is happening again; the nation does not seem to learn from it. Things only get worse. The same principle applies to the church and nations today.

Verses 46-50 say, While he was still speaking to the crowds, his mother and his brothers were standing outside, wanting to speak to him. Someone told him, "Look, your mother and your brothers are standing outside, wanting to speak to you." But to the one who had told him this, Jesus replied, "Who is my mother, and who are my brothers!" And pointing to the disciples, he said, "Here are my mother and my brothers! For whoever does the will of my Father in heaven is my brother and sister and mother."

He is not showing disrespect for his family, but he is pointing out that those who obey God are the real divine family of Jesus. Being part of the divine family as God's adopted children is even more important than one's genetic family. He teaches this because he knows that his teaching will divide families. He is also telling them that if Israel is going to continue as God's special people, the nation needs to allow the kingdom to permeate it and be the city on the hill and light to the nations they are called to be.

In chapter 13 Jesus sits beside the sea. The crowds are so great on the beach that he has to get in a boat. Verses 3-9 say, And he told them many things in parables, saying: "Listen! A sower went out to sow. And as he sowed, some seeds fell on the path, and the birds came and ate them up. Other seeds fell on rocky ground, where they did not have much soil, and they sprang up quickly, since they had no depth of soil. But when the sun rose, they were scorched; and since they had no root, they withered away. Other seeds fell among thorns, and the thorns grew up and choked them. Other seeds fell on good soil and brought forth grain, some hundred fold, some sixty, some thirty. Let anyone with ears listen!" (Most parables have something to do with the kingdom that Jesus is introducing.)

In verses 10-17 his disciples ask him why he speaks in parables.

He answers by quoting Isaiah 6:9-10 which in verse 13 is summarized by basically saying that most people really do not want to see, or hear, or understand. They have their minds made up and are not looking to repent or learn anything new. He tells his disciples that they have been given to know the secrets of the kingdom, but to those others it has not been given. Verse 12 says, "For to those who have, more will be given, and they will have an abundance; but from those who have nothing, even what they have will be taken away." (He is saying those who are seeking wisdom and understanding will get it and more, but those who are not seeking will even lose what they have. It can be compared to the physical exercise of one's muscles. If you do not use them, you lose them.)

Jesus then explains the parable of the sower, a parable about both hearing and understanding God's word but also about the in-breaking of the kingdom of God. Verses 18-23 say, "Hear then the parable of the sower. When anyone hears the word of the kingdom and does not understand it, the evil one comes and snatches away what is sown in the heart; this is what was sown on the path. As for what was sown on the rocky ground, this is the one who hears the word and immediately receives it with joy; yet such a person has no root, but endures only for awhile, and when trouble or persecution arises on account of the word, that person immediately falls away. As for what was sown among thorns, this is the one who hears the word, but the cares of the world and the lure of wealth choke the word, and it yields nothing. But as for what was sown on good soil, this is the one who hears the word and understands it, who indeed bears fruit and yields, in one case a hundredfold, in another sixty, and in another thirty." (Matthew writes this in order to get his hearers and readers to evaluate which ground fits them. It is also to show how the kingdom is breaking into the world.)

Verses 24-30 say, He put before them another parable: "The

kingdom of heaven may be compared to someone who sowed good seed in the field; but while everybody was asleep, an enemy came and sowed weeds among the wheat, and then went away. So when the plants came up and bore grain, then the weeds appeared as well. And the slaves of the householder came and said to him, 'Master did you not sow good seed in your field? Where, then, did these weeds come from?' He answered, 'An enemy has done this.' The slaves said to him, 'Then do you want us to go and gather them?' But he replied, 'No; for in gathering the weeds you would uproot the wheat along with them. Let both of them grow together until the harvest; and at harvest time I will tell the reapers, Collect the weeds first and bind them in bundles to be burned, but gather the wheat into my barn.' "

As God sows good seed, Satan sows evil seed. Harvest time is judgment time, which can be applied to both the judgment God is going to bring upon Jerusalem and Judea as well as the end-time judgment when Jesus comes to complete his mission and turn the kingdom over to the Father (1 Cor 15:20-28). Jesus is saying that both true believers and false believers will be together claiming to be part of the kingdom, so let it be. He is telling his disciples to follow his teachings but not to do the sifting, for he will take care of that work. God will do the sifting at the appropriate time.

Verses 31-35 say, He put before them another parable: "The kingdom of heaven (God) is like a mustard seed that someone took and sowed in his field; it is the smallest of all the seeds, but when it is grown it is the greatest of shrubs and becomes a tree, so that the birds of the air come and make nests in its branches."

God's kingdom is not necessarily the church; the church is to proclaim the kingdom and bear witness to it. We might say the church is making present in word and works the kingdom, when it is not acting in the way of sin. When the words and actions of Jesus are being made as a witness, the kingdom is being made present. God's kingdom will start small, but it will have such great growth that many will make their home within it. He is referring to the kingdom breaking in now, and then its completion when Jesus comes to bring it to his intended final state.

He told them another parable: "The kingdom of heaven (God) is like yeast that a woman took and mixed in with three measures of flour until all of it was leavened." (As yeast makes the bread grow, the kingdom will grow likewise.) Jesus told the crowds all these things in parables; without a parable he told them nothing. (This is a hyperbole that says he often used parables.) "This was to fulfill what had been spoken through the prophet: I will open my mouth to speak in parables; I will proclaim what has been hidden from the foundation of the world." (The quote is actually from Ps 78:2 and ascribed to Asaph the seer of 2 Chron 29:30.)

Verses 36-44 say, Then he left the crowds and went into the house. And his disciples approached him saying, "Explain to us the parable of the weeds of the field." He answered, "The one who sows the good seed is the Son of Man; the field is the world, and the good seed are the children of the kingdom; the weeds are the children of the evil one, and the enemy who sowed them is the devil; the harvest is at the end of the age, and the reapers are angels. Just as the weeds are collected and burned up with fire, so will it be at the end of the age. The Son of Man will send his angels, and they will collect out of his kingdom all causes of sin and all evil doers, and they will throw them into the furnace of fire, where there will be weeping and gnashing of teeth. Then the righteous will shine like the sun in the kingdom of the Father. Let anyone with ears listen!" (Many modern people do not like to hear these Scriptures and even deny their validity, but it is clear they teach that God is both a God of love and a God of wrath and is true to his covenant.)

The following parables liken the kingdom to a great treasure worth risking all one has. Verses 44-45 say, "The kingdom of heaven is like treasure in a field, which someone found and hid; then in joy he goes and sells all that he has and buys that field. Again, the kingdom of heaven is like a merchant in search of fine pearls; on finding one pearl of great value, he went and sold all that he had and bought it."

Parables often use hyperbole to get their point across. The idea behind these parables is that the one who understands the value of the kingdom makes the kingdom first in priority and gives up whatever is necessary to obtain it and proclaim it. The kingdom is abundant life and eternal life, breaking into the earth now, renewing and transforming both individuals and the world, until Jesus comes in his final glory in final judgment, and then making all things new in a new heaven and new earth. Jesus is the Lord of all life both spiritual and the material.

Jesus in verses 47-50 says, "Again the kingdom of heaven is like a net that was thrown into the sea and caught fish of every kind; when it was full, they drew it ashore, sat down, and put the good into baskets but threw out the bad. So it will be at the end of the age. The angels will come out and separate the evil from the righteous and throw them into the furnace of fire, where there will be weeping and gnashing of teeth." Apparently there are some who think they belong in the kingdom but in the end will not be there. They will be thrown out of the everlasting kingdom.

In verses 51-54 Jesus asks, "Have you understood all this?" They answered, "Yes." And he said to them, "Therefore every scribe who has been trained for the kingdom of heaven is like the master of the household who brings out of his treasure what is new and what is old." When Jesus had finished these parables, he left that place.

(His point is that both the Old Testament and what he is saying are of value in the kingdom. But everything is now understood in the light of the words and actions of the master who is Jesus.)

In verses 54-56 he comes to his hometown and begins to teach the people in their synagogues. The people are astounded and say, "Where did this man get this wisdom and these deeds of power? Is this not the carpenter's son? Is not his mother called Mary? And are not his brothers James and Joseph and Simon, and Judas? And are not his sisters with us? Where then did this man get all this?" Verses 57-58 say, And they took offense at him. But Jesus said to them, "Prophets are not without honor except in their own country and in their own house." And he did not do many deeds of power there, because of their unbelief. (Most people who know a person as they are growing up usually have a difficult time accepting them as extraordinary when they become such. This is especially so in the area of religion.)

The sisters and brothers are thought to be real sisters and brothers by Protestants, but not so by Catholics. Both groups have explanations for their position. Protestants believe because Mary was human, therefore she had sexual relations with Joseph, which produced offspring. The Catholic position centers on the idea that because Mary carried the Son of God, she would carry no one else in her womb, and the children living with them were probably Joseph's from a former marriage.

In that culture where the extended family all lived together in compounds, it was normal to call them sisters and brothers. It would be interesting to know the real answer, but it will probably never be known on this side of the divide. There is no proof one way or the other. Therefore it is *adiaphora*, meaning not important enough to cause division. Even from the beginning, the churches did not agree on everything, only the essentials. But the church has always struggled on what those essentials are.

❦

In chapter 14:1-12 the story of John the Baptist and how he dies under Herod Antipas is told. Antipas is the son of Herod the Great. When the latter dies, his territory is divided among his three sons. Archelaus receives half the kingdom (Judea and Samaria), Antipas becomes the ruler of Galilee and Perea, and Philip becomes the ruler of the northern Transjordan. Because Antipas receives about one-fourth of the territory he is called a tetrarch.

Verses 3-5 say, Herod (Antipas) had arrested John, bound him, and put him in prison because of Herodious, his brother Philip's wife, because John had been telling him, "It is not lawful for you to have her." (His reason is based on Leviticus 18:16, 20:21. This Philip is not the ruler but another half brother.) Verse 5 says, Though Herod wanted to put him to death, he feared the crowd, because they regarded him as a prophet.

Verses 6-12 tell us that during Herod's birthday the daughter of Herodias dances before those invited to the party. Herod is pleased and promises her anything she wants. Prompted by her mother she asks for the head of John the Baptist on a platter. In this way John dies, and his disciples come for his body and bury him. (A more complete account is in Mark 6:14-29.) Since Antipas was the ruler of Galilee, verses 13-14 say, when Jesus heard this, he withdrew from there in a boat to a deserted place by himself. But when the crowds heard it, they followed him on foot from the towns. When he went ashore, he saw a great crowd; and he had compassion for them and cured their sick.

Everywhere Jesus goes he heals the sick. Because Jesus makes people's health a priority, it is difficult for this writer to understand how comfortable Christians with a good health care plan, either from their business or through the government Medicare program, including members of Congress, can not get behind agreeing to a health care plan for those who do not have one. Those opposing this do not have a problem with government spending billions of dollars of tax money for war, but they do not want government to spend tax money to heal people through a decent health plan, unless it is for their plan. Many seniors in Medicare want their plan but do not want others to have one. Members of Congress want their government controlled plan but do not want their constituents to have one. They call it socialism. The issue they say is socialism and that it costs too much. Well, if that is the issue, should they not give up their plan? A pure capitalist and free enterprise economy is something this country has never had, including now as we continue bail outs for banks and auto companies, and tax breaks and subsidies for the rich and also for wealthy companies like oil companies, General Electric, agribusiness and many others who pay no taxes and get millions back from tax breaks and subsidies. This country has always had a mixed economy. Our congressmen and women yelling socialism about health care issues for individuals when they have the very thing others need, is hypocrisy.

What makes this interesting is that Jesus never supported violence or war, but on practically every page of the Gospels he heals someone. Many people accept their government run Medicare health plan but want others to have a plan governed by the market. The problem centers on the fact that history shows a market for profit program has a priority for profits, not sick people. They favor market capitalism for others, but for themselves they are happy with what they call socialism. Compassion and caring about the health needs of people and caring for the common good are not liberal ideas; they are teachings of Jesus. Should not the nation's health needs of its people be a priority?

When Scripture is read, God's people need to constantly ask themselves how they think Jesus would act in today's world. How would he apply his thinking to our times? Jesus did not live under a democratic republic; he lived under a brutal dictatorship in a time of no hospitals as is known today, and no medical technology. Consequently, people died young. There was no possibility of him encouraging government to help cure people. But if he had been in an environment that offered that possibility, this writer is positive that he would do so, simply because his primary concern was for people not profits. His life centered on helping hurting people and encouraging others, who could, to do the same. Incidentally government is under God's jurisdiction and accountable to God just as individuals and nations are.

In verses 15-21 Jesus feeds the five thousand men, besides women and children. This miracle had such an impact that it is the only miracle of Jesus that is in all four Gospels. Verses 15-21 say, When it was evening, the disciples came to him and said, "This is a deserted place, and the hour is now late; send the crowds away so that they may go into the villages and buy food for themselves." Jesus said to them, "They need not go away; you give them something to eat." They replied, "We have nothing here but five loaves and two fish." And he said, "Bring them to me." Then he ordered the crowd to sit down on the grass. Taking the five loaves and two fish, he looked up to heaven, and blessed and broke the loaves, and gave them to his disciples, and the disciples gave them to the crowds. And all ate and were filled; and they took up what was left over of the broken pieces, twelve baskets full. And those who ate were about five thousand men, besides women and children.

Jesus does for his disciples what they can not do, but then orders them to do what they can do, which is to organize and distribute the food to the people. Since Jesus is concerned with feeding people and taking care of their needs, does not the reader think that serious Christians should promote everything possible that creates jobs so people can feed their families? And should not both government and business work together to do so? The job is too big for either to do it alone.

Again, it amazes this writer to see how many well fed Christians rebel against government creating jobs so people can feed their families. And then because of profits, they would rather have jobs sent overseas and food destroyed instead of being used here and world wide to feed the starving. Again market capitalism and profits seem to be first and doing what Jesus did is second instead of the other way around. What does the reader believe Jesus would say about such activity?

This writer has a difficult time with people's thinking when they want absolutely no government action, interference, or regulation, which then allows big corporations and big money almost total freedom to regulate people's lives and limit their freedom as to what is available to them. The result of this thinking is disastrous to middle and lower class America as the rich get richer and the poor get poorer in an environment of the survival of the fittest. Government is God's creation also and accountable to God for its actions. Individuals influence government, but government also influences individuals. The question is: Would Jesus approve the influence being asserted?

People on the right worry about government moving toward socialism, but people on the left need to begin to worry about the right moving toward an oligopoly, or plutocracy, and at the extreme even fascism where government and corporations work together to control and manipulate the people in order to benefit their own selfish interests. Corporations make more exorbitant profits to give more incredible bonuses, and then big money kicks back money to the politicians to run their campaigns to stay in office so they can continue to benefit each other. How does that benefit the common good?

Does the reader really believe that Jesus, whose option was for the poor, those who were not wealthy and powerful, would support that type of thinking? It seems to this writer that it is not a choice between government and/or corporate control, the need is for a balance between the two in order to benefit the common good. On practically every page of Scripture God's concern is with the needs of people and the common good. In America it seems that the concern is with profits first. Where is the line between acceptable profits and greed?

On September 11, 2002 three thousand people died, which is a real tragedy. The U.S. then attacked Iraq, who had nothing to do with it, with the blessing of many Christians and their churches. Many thousands have died both Americans and people of Iraq. In the meantime around the world from thirty to thirty-four thousand children die every day of starvation and preventable diseases (see Sider, 1997 and Wallis, 2005), and most Christians never mention it. Is this not also a tragedy? What does the reader think Jesus, the Lord of all life, would say if he were an American living in this country? Would he remain silent about such things?

This writer wonders where the voice of many of the churches is, especially local churches in things such as this? Have too many of the churches, in general, also become too wealthy and comfortable? There is no question about Jesus and the kingdom being counter-culture, favoring the struggling, as opposed to taking the side of the wealthy and powerful and their interests. The question is not about the right to a profit; the issue is greed. Jesus calls his people to pick up their cross, meaning to die to self and the world and its interests for the well being of others just as he did. Is there no longer an interest in the common good?

Unfortunately, the wealthy and powerful, and the people of comfort, and even the church often times co-opt the teachings of Scripture and twist them to their self interests. Of course, this is nothing new. Again, when Christians claim to be followers of Christ, then should they not make his interests and priorities their interests and priorities? His interests and priorities are plain to see, for they are practically on every page of the New Testament.

The path to transformation begins with a decision of priorities. Thus if we and the church claim to be disciples of Christ and claim to represent his interests, we must make his interests and his priorities ours, and that includes the political, economic, and social implications of his teachings. The church is not to be involved itself in power politics, but it is to challenge power politics, not to gain power, but to see that power works for what Christ stood for. God is Lord of all not just our so-called spiritual life. That is the implication of the kingdom breaking into the real world.

One must stand with God's word, and be willing to stand with and for the things he stood for, as well as take the side of those with whom Jesus sided. In the process of doing so, when suffering (mental or physical) comes, one must be willing to suffer as Jesus did.

After feeding the people in verses 22-25 he made the disciples get into the boat and go ahead to the other side, while he dismisses the crowds. Then he goes up the mountain by himself to pray. In the meantime the disciples on the sea, far from the land, are being battered by the wind and waves. Early in the morning Jesus comes walking toward them on the sea. But in (26-27) when the disciples see him, they are terrified saying, "It is a ghost!" But immediately Jesus spoke to them and said, "Take heart, it is I; do not be afraid."

Verses 28-33 say, Peter answered him, "Lord, if it is you, command me to come to you on the water." He said, "Come." So

Peter got out of the boat, started walking on the water, and came toward Jesus. But when he noticed the strong wind, he became frightened, and beginning to sink, he cried out, "Lord, save me!" Jesus immediately reached out his hand and caught him saying to him, "You of little faith, why did you doubt?" When they got into the boat, the wind ceased. And those in the boat worshiped him, saying, "Truly you are the Son of God."

There are those who make the boat represent the church as it struggles in the world. Jesus will save those in the church who worship him, even with their weak faith, as they struggle and are harassed by the world. But the main purpose of Matthew is to show those of weak faith that Jesus is God and deserving of worship, for in the Old Testament only God controls the waters of chaos (Gen 1:1-2, Pss 65:7-8, 89:9, 93:3-4, 107:29).

Verses 34-36 say, When they had crossed over, they came to land at Gennesaret (Gentile territory). After the people of that place recognized him, they sent word throughout the region and brought all who were sick to him, and begged him that they might touch even the fringe of his cloak; and all who touched it were healed.

Matthew's message to Christians is that Jesus spent his time on earth meeting the needs of people, healing, feeding, and serving them, for his life was one of losing self for the well being of others. His question to all of his followers is: What are they spending their time, money, and interests on?

Is that the message of America and its churches? What answers do their budgets give? Is it not time that we begin to line up the teachings of Jesus with our own thinking and actions as well as the thinking and actions of the churches and our nation? Where in Scripture does it say, me first, and the teachings of Christ second? Where in Scripture does it say, my church first, and the teachings of Jesus second? Where in Scripture does it say, my country first, and the teachings of Christ second? Where in Scripture does it say, me first and the common good second? Have we created our own idols?

✍ ✑

In chapter 15 the Pharisees and scribes came to Jesus from Jerusalem and said, "Why do your disciples break the tradition of the elders? For they do not wash their hands before they eat."

This is another example of the unwritten human laws that built up a body of tradition designed to ensure the observance of the written law by building a fence around the law. Thus they expect Jesus and his followers to observe these rules. The particular law of washing hands before eating has to do with a ceremonial washing that is to eliminate any ritual uncleanness and has nothing to do with real dirt, or anything in the Old Testament. These laws are also tied to the Leviticus dietary laws.

Jesus in (3-9) answered them, "And why do you break the commandment of God for the sake of your tradition? For God said, 'Honor your father and your mother,' and, 'Whoever speaks evil of father or mother must surely die.' But you say that whoever tells father and mother, 'Whatever support you might have had from me is given to God,' then that person need not honor the father. So, for the sake of your tradition, you make void the word of God."

The tradition of the Pharisees makes void the word of God by allowing a person to place money or property under sacred vow as a way of preventing the parents from having access to it, if they are in need. The tradition that claims to protect the law actually violates a sacred obligation of the law to take care of those in need, especially parents, by teaching contrary to the word of God. This is basically the same principle discussed in the last chapter. This is the kind of tradition Jesus opposes.

In verses 7-9 Jesus continues, "You hypocrites! Isaiah (29:13) prophesied rightly about you when he said: 'This people honors me with their lips, but their hearts are far from me; in vain do they worship me, teaching human precepts as doctrines.' " Then he called the crowd to him and said to them, "Listen and understand: it is not what goes into the mouth that defiles a person, but it is what comes out of the mouth that defiles."

Here he begins to eliminate all the clean and unclean food laws by teaching that his concern is what is morally clean or unclean. At the time this is a very radical and progressive statement, for it totally reinterprets the Old Testament law by teaching contrary to the law. Thus Jesus claims the authority to teach contrary to the law because he is the new Torah. Of course, this does not endear him to the authorities.

The disciples approach him and tell him that the Pharisees are offended, but in (13-14) he said, "Every plant that my heavenly Father has not planted will be uprooted. Let them alone, they are blind guides of the blind. And if one blind person guides another, both will fall into a pit." (The unfortunate part of this is that those who do not take the time to educate themselves, and those that can not distinguish fact from opinion from the leaders they follow will receive the same judgment as the one who has gathered the followers.)

Peter asks that the parable be explained to them, so in (16-20) he said, "Are you still without understanding? Do you not see that whatever goes into the mouth enters the stomach, and goes out into the sewer? But what comes out of the mouth proceeds from the heart, and this is what defiles. For out of the heart come evil intentions, murder, adultery, fornication, theft, false witness, slander. These are what defile a person, but to eat with unwashed hands does not defile." (Jesus comes to purify hearts for the kingdom, to soften hard hearts and fill them with his Spirit. Keep in mind that eating with unwashed hands is a reference to being ceremonially unclean and has nothing to do with real dirt.)

In verses 21-28 Jesus goes to Tyre and Sidon. (Today it is known as Lebanon; at the time it was Gentile territory.) A Canaanite woman in (22) starts shouting, "Have mercy on me Lord, Son of David; my daughter is tormented by a demon." But he did not answer her at all. And his disciples came and urged him, saying, "Send her away, for she keeps shouting after us." He answered, "I was sent only to the lost sheep of Israel." But she came and knelt before him saying, "Lord, help me." He said, "It is not fair to take the children's food and throw it to the dogs." She said, "Yes, Lord, but even the dogs eat the crumbs that fall from the master's table." Then Jesus answered her, "Woman great is your faith! Let it be done for you as you wish." And her daughter was healed instantly.

Some Jews do not think Gentiles are worthy of God. Jesus is teaching them differently through this Gentile woman who has faith in the one that God sent, while most of the Jews reject him. There are some who believe the Father sent this woman to Jesus to help him begin to see that he is sent for both Gentiles and Jews. Because he was both God and man, his humanness had to develop both physically and mentally. Others believe when he said he was sent only to the lost sheep of Israel, that means his purpose was to spend the brief time he had trying to convince a small group of the Father's overall plan, and then train a small group, and from that effort they would go to the Gentiles. Time is running out for Jesus, but this is a sign for them to understand that Gentiles are in his plan. They always have been included according to God's promise to Abraham in Gen 12:1-3, but the Jews ignored the Gentiles.

In verses 29-31 Jesus goes to a mountain near the Sea of Galilee, and great crowds come to him bringing people that are in need of healing, and he cures them. The crowd is amazed when they see the mute speaking, the maimed whole, the lame walking, and the blind seeing. And they praise the God of Israel. (These actions are to be signs of the Messiah, Isaiah 29, 35, 42, 43.)

In verses 32-34 Jesus has compassion for the crowd who was with him for three days with nothing to eat. The disciples said to him, "Where are we to get enough bread in the desert to feed so great a crowd?" Jesus asked them what they had and learned it was seven loaves and a few small fish. Verses 35-39 say, Then ordering the crowd to sit down on the ground, he took the seven loaves and the fish; and after giving thanks he broke them and gave them to the disciples, and the disciples gave them to the crowds. And all of them ate and were filled; and they took up the broken pieces left over, seven baskets full. Those who had eaten were four thousand men, besides women and children. After sending away the crowds, he got into the boat and went to the region of Magadan. (Over and over we see the compassion of Jesus in feeding and caring for the health of people. Should his people think and act otherwise?)

This along with the feeding of the five thousand indicates that Jesus most definitely impresses everyone by performing a miracle that feeds thousands. The question scholars debate is whether these are two separate miracles, or do the two passages represent independent accounts of one event that were first passed on orally, and then fifty or so years later written down. We do know that before the Gospels are written what Jesus does and says is mainly passed along orally for approximately 35-50 years. We will probable never know the answer for sure, but we do know it was remembered that he did miraculously feed the crowds.

❦

In chapter 16:1-4 the Pharisees and Sadducees come to test Jesus and ask for a sign. (He has already given them many signs, but because they do not want to accept him, they make themselves blind to what he does, Isa 6:9-13.) Jesus tells them that they can read the weather signs, but they can not read the signs of the times. In (4) he says, "An evil and adulterous generation asks for a sign, but no sign will be given it except the sign of Jonah." Then he left them and went away. (The sign is in reference to his resurrection. Jonah was three days and nights in the big fish, and then came out.)

In verses 5-12 the bread theme appears again. The disciples reached the other side, and they became aware that they had no bread when Jesus said to them, "Watch out, and beware of the yeast of the Pharisees and Sadducees." Jesus noted their little faith and reminded them of the feeding of the five thousand and the four thousand, not even counting women and children. Being aware of the yeast of the Pharisees and Sadducees is explained in verse 12 to mean beware of the teaching of the Pharisees and Sadducees.

Verses 13-18 say, Now when Jesus came into the district of Caesarea Philippi (It was located at the foot of Mt Hermon on the Jordan River. It was the seat of Pan, the Greek nature god.), he asked his disciples, "Who do people say that the Son of Man is?" And they said, "Some say John the Baptist, but others Elijah, and still others Jeremiah or one of the prophets." He said to them, "But who do you say that I am?" Simon Peter answered, "You are the Messiah, the Son of the living God." And Jesus answered him, "Blessed are you, Simon son of Jonah! For flesh and blood has not revealed this to you, but my Father in heaven. And I tell you, you are Peter, and on this rock I will build my church, and the gates of Hades will not prevail against it."

The Catholic Church teaches that Jesus is saying the church will be built upon Christ, and then Peter as the human leader of the church. Protestants believe Jesus is saying that the church is built upon Peter's statement that Jesus is the Messiah, the Son of the living God and has nothing to do with Peter's leadership throughout time.

It is difficult to know the answer. It is obvious that the church is built upon Christ as the Messiah and Son of God. And as we go through the rest of the Gospels as well as the book of Acts, we will see also that Peter is the designated leader, at least for that time era. What can be deduced from that is the area of conflict.

Verses 19-20 say, "I will give you the keys of the kingdom of heaven, and whatever you bind on earth will be bound in heaven, and whatever you loose on earth will be loosed in heaven." Then he sternly ordered the disciples not to tell anyone that he was the Messiah.

The Catholic Church believes this gives Peter and the Catholic Church teaching authority, and the power to forgive or not forgive sins, along with the power of excommunication. The Protestant Church rejects all this authority going to Peter. They say (18:18) gives this authority to all the leaders. Thus all clergy have the power to pronounce the forgiveness of sins and teach authoritatively. Is it possible that in some way both are correct? Only in western thinking must one be chosen over the other.

Verses 21-23 say, From that time on, Jesus began to show his disciples that he must go to Jerusalem and undergo great suffering at the hands of the elders and chief priests and scribes and be killed, and on the third day be raised. And Peter took him aside and began to rebuke him, saying, "God forbid it, Lord! This must never happen to you." But he turned and said to Peter, "Get behind me, Satan! You are a stumbling block to me; for you are setting your mind not on divine things but on human things."

Peter as well as the rest envision earthly glory not suffering, for they see themselves throwing out the Romans who control their land, and then becoming the leaders in a new earthly kingdom. Jesus is telling them it is not going to happen that way, and they are thinking like humans not as God thinks. Peter and the others were much like many Christians today who think the reason for Christ and Christianity is to benefit themselves in today's world. He then explains what they need to understand.

Verses 24-26 say, Then Jesus told his disciples, "If any want to become my followers, let them deny themselves and take up their cross and follow me. For those who want to save their life will lose it, and those who lose their life for my sake will find it. For what will it profit them if they gain the whole world but forfeit their life? Or what will they give in return for their life?"

Jesus is calling his followers to die to the world's interests and self interest and live for the interests of Christ and the kingdom's interests. In this way they will find their reason for being, the reason for which they were created. Only in this way can real freedom and happiness be found. He is telling them that if they live for their own interests and the world's interest not only will they lose their reason for being, but they will lose real freedom. This is the freedom the Scriptures emphasize.

Verses 27-28 say, "For the Son of Man is to come with his angels in the glory of his father, and then he will pay everyone for what has been done. Truly I tell you, there are some standing here who will not taste death before they see the Son of Man coming in his kingdom."

This is a difficult series of verses to explain. The Son of Man is going to make judgments on what everyone has done, and the people living in that time are going to be alive when he comes in his kingdom. First of all, he will see if they fulfilled their covenant obligations, not to save themselves but to see if they are part of the covenant of his grace or not. Salvation is not by works but it is not without works.

Second, did Jesus think the end time was going to happen in that generation? Or are these simply two separate statements with the first a reference to the day of Pentecost in Acts chapter two when the kingdom officially begins with Christ risen and at the right hand of the Father? It is then that he comes in the Spirit by sending the Spirit upon his people. Then the judgment on Israel is for their rejection of his kingdom for their agenda of violence to rid the land of Rome. If this is what he is referring to, then it can make sense. If he is referring to the end of time when the kingdom on earth ends with the judgment, then he was mistaken telling some of them that they would be alive when he comes.

Is it possible that the ideas of what he said can be applied to both? We do know the kingdom was breaking into the world, but it will not be completed until the eternal age is established and judgment made. This whole time period is called the last age. The Son of Man coming in his kingdom is used with the Father confirming Christ in the resurrection, the coming of the Spirit to the church in Acts 2, and for his prophecy concerning judgment on Israel by the Romans in AD 70, (see Mk 13, Mt 24, Lk 21) as well as at an end time judgment.

NT Wright (1999, 80-119) understands these verses in Matthew as metaphorical. He says that the clouds in Scripture always represent God's presence, even judgment. Jesus coming in the clouds is a metaphor for saying the kingdom is now established and is free to advance. It also symbolizes that his prophecy about Jerusalem and the temple is fulfilled when Rome destroys the city and temple in AD 70.

Wright's point is that Jesus constantly warned the nationalist resistance movement to give up their agenda of getting rid of Rome through violent action, and if not, God would act against them. Because neither the militant nationalist resistance movement stopped their violence, nor did the Jewish leaders and the temple authorities change their unjust, oppressive ways, the nation is punished once again for the same reasons they were punished by God with the Assyrian and Babylonian exiles. So for Wright and a few others the application of these verses is a reference to the destruction of

Jerusalem and the temple. Eschatology an aspect of apocalyptic literature and its metaphorical language used in both testaments as well as in second temple literature is not easy to interpret.

Chapter 17:1-2 says, Six days later (after Peter's confession), Jesus took with him Peter and James and his brother John and led them up a high mountain, by themselves. And he was transfigured before them, and his face shown like the sun, and his clothes became dazzling white. (Transfiguration involves a spiritual experience of Jesus in his heavenly glory. Apparently, these three are the advanced learners, so Jesus is going to increase their understanding, for they are prepared to go to a higher level.)

Verses 3-4 say, Suddenly there appeared to them Moses and Elijah, talking with them. Then Peter said to Jesus, "Lord, it is good for us to be here; if you wish, I will make three dwellings here, one for you, one for Moses, and one for Elijah." (An interesting note is Matthew's effort throughout his gospel to show that Jesus is the new Moses. Here he has his face shining like the sun as Moses was when he came down from the mountain.)

Peter is so impressed that he wants to mark the spot by building three monuments one for the greatest lawgiver, one for the greatest prophet of Israel's history, and one for Jesus. In a sense Peter is saying that they are all to be listened to with equal value; all three performed basically the same miracles. Elijah even raised the dead (1 Kings 17:17-24). But the Father is going to interrupt him and disagree. Verses 5-8 say, While he was still speaking, suddenly a bright cloud overshadowed them, and from the cloud a voice said, "This is my Son, the Beloved; with him I am well pleased; listen to him!" When the disciples heard this, they fell to the ground and were overcome with fear. But Jesus came and touched them, saying,

"Get up and do not be afraid." And when they looked up, they saw no one except Jesus himself alone.

The message is that Jesus, the Son, has the Father's final revelation in which all the past and the future are to be related. As great as Moses was and as great as Elijah was they will now be further understood in relation to the words and acts of Jesus. Hebrews 1:1-2 says, Long ago God spoke to our ancestors in many and various ways by the prophets, but in these last days he has spoken to us by a Son, whom he appointed heir of all things, through whom he has also created the worlds. (This is another example of clouds appearing with the Father or the Son and a judgment being expressed.)

Jesus is God's final revelation. That does not mean there is no value in the old, and that does not mean as time goes on we will not be given any new insights. As time and circumstances change we will see new ways to apply God's final revelation, but there is no more revelation; there will only be illumination. There is always more truth and light to break forth from God's holy word.

Jesus is the norm for Christianity, which Scripture, tradition, reason, and one's experience is to be related and adjusted. Scripture is inspired of God and the resource of Christianity, but Jesus is the center and the norm that guides the Christian in thinking and understanding it. As time and circumstances change the Spirit illuminates believers on the meaning and application of God's living word (Jesus) and his written word (Scripture). This illumination becomes part of Christian tradition as the believer uses rational thinking and experience to apply Scripture and the words and acts of Jesus. Tradition is not bad as some Christians believe; it can be very beneficial. It is God's word applied. In fact Scripture in itself is a form of tradition. Tradition is generally only bad when it totally rejects or contradicts God's plain word, or it is forced into new circumstances where the sense of the Scripture is no longer appropriate.

The basic message of the transfiguration is Jesus is Lord, which is the meaning of verse 8, And they saw no one except Jesus himself alone. Verse 9 says, As they were coming down the mountain, Jesus ordered them, "Tell no one about the vision until after the Son of Man has been raised from the dead." The reasons for this are numerous. One is that people are not going to be able to understand the real significance of this experience until after the cross and resurrection. Another is that Jesus is going to be proclaimed Lord and King throughout the land. This will come into conflict with the Jewish leaders as well as the Roman emperor, who claims to be the only lord and king as well as the world's savior and source of peace.

Verses 10-13 say, the disciples asked him, "Why, then, do the scribes say that Elijah must come first?" He replied, "Elijah is indeed coming and will restore all things; but I tell you that Elijah has already come, and they did not recognize him, but they did to him whatever they pleased. So also is the Son of Man about to suffer at their hands." Then the disciples understood that he was speaking to them about John the Baptist (see 11:14). The Jews did not understand this prophecy concerning Elijah because they took Malachi 4:5 literally. Many modern day interpreters of the Bible misunderstand books like Daniel, Zechariah, Ezekiel and the book of Revelation because they force everything into a literal, fundamentalist mold to support their preconceived notions.

Verse 11 refers to restoring all things. The kingdom is about restoring Israel to be what God intended it to be and do, which was to be a blessing to the whole world. They had ignored this mission by turning in upon themselves and becoming oppressors of their own people.

In verses 14-21 a man was brought to him who had an epileptic son who often fell into fire or the water. Jesus' disciples had not been able to heal him. Jesus rebuked them saying, "You faithless and perverse generation, how much longer must I put up with you? Bring him here to me." The man knelt before Jesus and pleaded for mercy; Jesus rebuked the demon, and the boy was cured instantly. Later the disciples went to him privately and said, "Why could we not cast it out?" He said to them, "Because of your little faith. For truly I tell you, if you have faith the size of a mustard seed, you will say to this mountain, 'Move from here to there,' and it will move; and nothing will be impossible for you."

The point the writer is making, who is writing fifty years after the death of Jesus, is not that one will be able to literally move mountains (a hyperbole), but humankind and the church in the battle against evil are not achieving what they could because of their weak faith. They are succumbing too often to the perverse generation in which they live (Acts 2:40). The issue for most humans today is not the power to heal a sick person miraculously though that may happen. The real issue today is the battle with evil that produces a culturally sick society that eventually produces mentally and physically sick people. Progress and the real cure will come as the people of God push back evil by applying the words and actions of the kingdom.

Verses 22-23 say, As they were gathering in Galilee, Jesus said to them, "The Son of Man is going to be betrayed into human hands, and they will kill him, and on the third day he will be raised." And they were greatly distressed. (This is not the way they are planning things as you will see in the next chapter.) Verses 24-27 say, When they reached Capernaum, the collectors of the temple tax came to Peter and said, "Does your teacher not pay the temple tax?" He said, "Yes, he does. (The half-shekel is paid by Jewish males for the upkeep of the temple.)

When Jesus returned home he asked, "What do you think, Simon? From whom do the kings of the earth take toll or tribute?

From their children or from others?" When Peter said, "From others," Jesus said to him, "Then the children are free. However, so that we do not give offense to them, go to the sea and cast a hook; take the first fish that comes up; and when you open its mouth, you will find a coin; take that and give it to them for you and me."

Jesus is saying as God's Son he does not need to pay this tax, and they as children of the real king are free, but since they still are part of this world, they must pay their worldly obligations in order to avoid unnecessary problems.

In chapter 18:1-5 the disciples came to Jesus and asked, "Who is the greatest in the kingdom of heaven?" He called a child whom he put among them, and said, "Truly I tell you, unless you change and become like children, you will never enter the kingdom of heaven. Whoever becomes humble like this child is the greatest in the kingdom of heaven. Whoever welcomes one such child in my name welcomes me."

Humbleness not arrogance is a characteristic of greatness in God's eyes. This humbleness is further explained by describing the faith and trust of a child in his parents. The young child learns from his parents, and in the growing up process, their life and purposes become the child's also. This is how a child of God is to relate to Jesus.

Verse 3 says, "Truly I tell you, unless you change and become like children, you will never enter the kingdom of heaven." (For most people entering the kingdom at the age of accountability involves change, changing the way one thinks and acts in order to think and act like children of God. This is about attitude and disposition and being a model for the kingdom.) Romans 12:1-2 says, I appeal to you . . . present your bodies as a living sacrifice, holy and acceptable to God, which is your spiritual worship. Do not be conformed to this world, but be transformed by the renewing of your minds, so that you may discern what is the will of God—what is good and acceptable and perfect.

In verses 6-7 Jesus says, "If any of you put a stumbling block (something that hinders or destroys faith) before one of these little ones who believe in me (his disciples with childlike faith), it would be better for you if a great millstone were fashioned around your neck and you were drowned in the depth of the sea. Woe to the world because of stumbling blocks! In verses 8-9 he tells people to cut off their hands and feet, or pluck out their eyes, if they cause them to stumble, because it is better to be maimed than to be thrown into the hell of fire." (He does not mean for them to take this literally, for it is not the eyes, feet, or hands that cause them to sin but their heart. He is telling them to allow their heart to be transformed and eliminate whatever it is that causes one to go against his teachings and commit sin.)

In verses 10-14 he tells them not to despise any of his children, for in heaven their angels continually see the face of his Father. (Scripture teaches that each child of God has an angel in heaven. It is believed that a person's guardian angel represents them in heaven.) He tells them his children are like the sheep of a shepherd. If he has one hundred but one goes astray, that one lamb is worth searching for and finding. Verse 14 says, it is not the will of your Father in heaven that one of these little ones should be lost.

In verses 15-17 an order for church discipline is given. Jesus says, If a church member sins against you, go and point it out to the person when the two of you are alone. If you are not listened to, take two others with you so that everything is confirmed by two or three witnesses. If the member still refuses to listen, tell the church. If the person still does not listen, let the person be as a Gentile or tax collector.

In other words cast him from the church. In those days that threat had a major effect, for Christians were in such a minority, but in these times it is no issue; they just go to another church. But the principle is still valid. Church members need to solve their differences by bringing in church leaders to help. Of course, this writer does not know of many examples of that happening.

Then in verses 18-20 Jesus says, "Truly I tell you, whatever you bind on earth will be bound in heaven, and whatever you loose on earth will be loosed in heaven. Again, truly I tell you, if two of you agree on earth about anything you ask, it will be done for you by my Father in heaven. For where two or three are gathered in my name I am there among them." (The space is sacred where the people of God meet in the presence of Jesus. This is in context with the forgiveness of sin and reconciliation as the following parable in verses 21-35 indicate and connects with verses 15-20.)

The agreement of forgiveness, or not forgiving, by the community joined in prayer will be accepted by God as binding because God is joined to the community in a special way. These last verses are interpreted in various ways. The Roman Catholic Church believes this gives the priests power to pronounce the forgiveness of sins in the name of Christ. Some Protestants believe this gives authority to pastors during worship to pronounce and assure that sins are forgiven. Other Protestants believe that when two or three are together Christ is among them, and when they confess their sins to each other, Christ gives forgiveness. Other Protestants basically ignore this other than to say that one only needs to confess their sin to Christ.

Verses 21-22 say, Then Peter came and said to him, "Lord, if another member of the church sins against me, how often should I forgive? As many as seven times?" Jesus said to him, "Not seven times, but I tell you, seventy-seven times.

Jesus is saying that his people are to be known as grace filled, merciful, compassionate, and forgiving people who do not hold grudges, so they are always to be open to granting forgiveness. It should be noted that Jesus asks for repentance before forgiveness is granted as the following story teaches. On the other hand he died on the cross before we repented. In attempting to understand when to forgive a person who sins against another both teachings need to be held in tension by grace, mercy and justice. Love demands justice, but justice demands love.

In verses 23-31 Jesus continues the message of forgiveness. He tells them that the kingdom of heaven may be compared to a king who wished to settle accounts with his slaves. One of his slaves owed him an astronomical amount of money that was impossible to repay. The king ordered him to be sold with his family and all his possessions. But when the slave begged him to have patience with him, out of pity, the king released him and forgave him his debt.

Later that same slave refused to forgive a small debt that was owed him by a fellow slave. When his slave begged forgiveness, he grabbed him by the throat and had him thrown into prison. When his fellow slaves saw what happened, they reported all that had taken place to the king, who summoned the non-forgiving man and in (32-35) said, "You wicked slave! I forgave you all that debt because you pleaded with me. Should you not have had mercy on your fellow slave, as I had mercy on you?" And in anger his lord handed him over to be tortured until he would pay his entire debt. So my heavenly Father will also do to every one of you, if you do not forgive your brother or sister from your heart."

The king is Jesus who forgives all our sins. The slave is represented by those of us who receive abundant mercy, grace, and forgiveness of sins from Christ but in the process refuse to forgive our fellow humans of their sins toward us. The purpose of the story is to inform us that if we will not forgive sin and injustice done toward us, God will not forgive the sin and injustice we commit against God. As one goes through the Gospels it is easy to see that Jesus teaches ethics primarily by the way of story and character development.

Chapter 19 says, When Jesus had finished saying these things, he left Galilee and went to the region of Judea beyond the Jordan. Large crowds followed him, and he cured them there. Some Pharisees came to him, and to test him they asked, "Is it lawful for a man to divorce his wife for any cause?" He answered, "Have you not read that the one who made them at the beginning 'made them male and female,' and said, 'For this reason a man shall leave his father and mother and be joined to his wife, and the two shall become one flesh'? So they are no longer two, but one flesh. Therefore what God has joined together, let no one separate."

They said to him, "Why then did Moses command us to give a certificate of dismissal and to divorce her?" He said to them, "It was because you were so hard-hearted that Moses allowed you to divorce your wives, but from the beginning it was not so. And I say to you, whoever divorces his wife, except for unchastity, and marries another commits adultery." (Jesus claims the authority to reinterpret the Old Testament law.)

Whoever divorces his wife, except for unchastity, and then marries another commits adultery. Is this a statement of ideals or a command? This writer believes it is both but tempers that statement with the fact that Jesus can forgive all sin. Those who sin can be given new life. In fact those who are born of God are called each day to repent and be born of God more fully. Even so, because God is merciful and full of grace, that does not give one a license to deliberately sin.

Matthew does make an exception for unchastity. The Greek word used is *pornea,* usually defined as unlawful sexual activity. How one defines unchastity is the question that is controversial. Many Protestants claim it means fornication from the spouse who has committed adultery. Catholics interpret it to apply to Leviticus 18:6-23 for those already in illegal marriages. In the meantime Catholics have developed courts to declare certain marriages null and void (annulments) stating that a marriage was never really a marriage, which then permits a new marriage.

Jesus is saying that remarriage after a divorce is the sin of adultery. This is a passage of Scripture most moderns tend to ignore. The point that must be emphasized is that this is not the sin that can not be forgiven. Rather than ignoring this teaching, possibly the focus should be on the mercy and grace of the forgiveness Jesus offers, and then begin again anew. There are those who believe Roman Catholics and some fundamentalist Christians are not flexible enough, while many mainline Protestant Christians are too flexible. They believe that both groups seem to ignore the spirit of the law, either by ignoring the teaching or making a rigid law of it with no granting of forgiveness and/or not permitting a remarried person to have Eucharist. Again, the writer encourages each to go to their respective churches for further information.

Something to think about: War is not taught in the New Testament Scripture, but we believe there is such a thing as a just war to protect and defend against oppressors. Can we also say there can be such a thing as a just divorce and even a just remarriage to protect against abuse and other forms of oppression? Did Jesus say this in order to make it a timeless ethic, or is it to teach an attitude about marriage that God wants his people to have, even as he knows imperfect people will fall short of his ideal? This writer does not have all the answers. We do know that in the kingdom, there will be no divorce, and there will be no war. But we are still in the age of hard hearts, and the kingdom is breaking into this world at different places at different paces. We do know the attitude God wants his people to have about both war and divorce.

Verses 7-10 say, His disciples said to him, "If such is the case with a man and his wife, it is better not to marry." But he said to them, "Not everyone can accept this teaching, but only those to whom it is given. For there are eunuchs who have been so from birth, and there are eunuchs who have been made by others, and there are eunuchs who have made themselves eunuchs for the sake of the kingdom of heaven. Let anyone accept this who can."

Jesus is saying that not everyone must marry. There are provisions for non-marriage. The Catholic Church uses the latter part of the statement as a church rule forbidding priests to marry. Their reasoning is to follow the example of Jesus. There are a small number of priests who are married, but they are converts from another denomination. Since it is a church rule, it is a rule that can change. If one church decides to make it a rule for its clergy for the time being and another does not, so be it. This also is adiaphora, meaning not a major issue.

Verses 13-15 say, little children were being brought to him in order that he might lay his hands on them and pray. The disciples spoke sternly to those who brought them; but Jesus said, "Let the little children come to me, and do not stop them; for it is to such as these that the kingdom of heaven belongs." And he laid his hands on them and went on his way.

The child represents those without legal claims or rights, those who must receive everything as a gift. It is interesting to note he laid his hands on them; it does not say he baptized them. That does not mean infant baptism is not permitted, but it does not seem to be practiced by the very early church, although it soon became an acceptable church practice.

In verses 16-22 someone came to him and said, "Teacher, what good deed must I do to have eternal life?" (This can also be translated to be in the age to come, meaning to be in the eternal kingdom that is near and breaking in upon the earth.) And he said to him, "Why do you ask me about what is good? There is only one who is good. (He is asking him if he is recognizes that he is the good or only good one, which is God.) If you wish to enter into life, keep the commandments." He said to him, "Which ones?" "And Jesus said, You shall not murder; You shall not commit adultery; You shall not steal; You shall not bear false witness; Honor your father and mother; also, You shall love your neighbor as yourself." The young man said to him, "I have kept all these; what do I still lack?" Jesus said to him, "If you wish to be perfect, go sell your possessions, and give the money to the poor, and you will have treasure in heaven; then come follow me." When the young man heard this word, he went away grieving, for he had many possessions. (This command is one most literalists ignore, suddenly they become non-literalists.)

Notice in response to the question of what good deed he must do to have eternal life, the answer is not, believe on the Lord Jesus, and be saved as though all you have to do is believe something and do nothing else. James 2:19 says, even the demons believe. The first response of Jesus is to challenge him to see if he recognizes who Jesus was, thus giving Jesus the authority to answer the question. Then Jesus answers by listing some of the commandments. So he is asking the man, are you following my teachings?

When he answers, yes, Jesus really challenges this man where his weakness is, which is his wealth. He is telling him that his wealth is keeping him from following Jesus and his teachings. Jesus teaches that his followers are to lose self for the well being of others. They are to deny self. Too often one's own interests and desire for possessions and wealth get in the way. This is what is keeping this man from eternal life. A former student of this author once said that it seems Jesus is always "picking on" people with money. The student was correct, but Jesus does this to alert them to the fact that their souls are in danger.

This man has done no harm to his neighbor, but neither has he done him any good. It is like Luke's story of the rich man and Lazarus. He does not seem to answer the man's question other than to expose to the man the thing that is keeping him from dying to self and the things of the world. Notice that when Jesus lists commandments he does not list the beginning of the commandments stating that one shall have no other gods before him and not to worship idols. Jesus leads the man into seeing that his idol is keeping him from true life, and that he really has not been keeping the basic overall meaning of the commandments, which is to love God with all his heart and his neighbor as himself.

Verses 23-26 say, Then Jesus said to his disciples, "Truly, I tell you, it will be hard for a rich person to enter the kingdom of heaven. Again, I tell you, it is easier for a camel to go through the eye of a needle than for someone who is rich to enter the kingdom of God." When the disciples heard this, they were greatly astounded and said, "Then who can be saved?" But Jesus looked at them and said, "For mortals it is impossible, but for God all things are possible." (No one can save themselves, even with their wealth, but the Father and Son can live in and through anyone, including the rich, through the power of the Holy Spirit and make them a dispenser of blessings to anyone, especially to those in need.)

The disciples thought, as many do today, that those who are wealthy with great possessions are so because they are favored by God. Jesus is challenging that thinking, and he teaches them it has nothing to do with salvation. Mortals will not save themselves through their wealth. In fact mortals will not save themselves at all. Only God's children, rich or poor, who follow Christ's teachings as they allow him to live in them and through them, will be saved by his grace. This is the meaning of John 3:16-18, 36 and Phil 2:12-14 in context with Scripture.

In verses 27-30 Peter reminds Jesus that they have left everything to follow him. Jesus tells him that they will sit on the twelve thrones judging the tribes of Israel, and all who have left everything for him (or make the life of Jesus their life) will inherit life in the kingdom. Then in verse 30 Jesus says, "But many who are first will be last, and the last will be first." Jesus is always expressing reversals to conventional thinking.

To sit on the thrones judging Israel is a metaphorical reference to their responsibility of going to their fellow Jews calling them to repentance in order to bring them into the kingdom. The twelve apostles represent the restored Israel, an Israel that is forgiven, the new covenant, the new age. The nations and Jews who reject the twelve's message of repentance will be judged. He is also saying that those who are on top in this life will be in a reversed situation at the final judgment. Jesus always opts for the poor as opposed to the rich, even as he calls the rich to become like him, thus finding true life. Who are the rich today? Most of the people in the world earn no more than one hundred dollars a month and sixty-five percent of the world's people do not have enough food to eat. From that let the reader determine who the rich may be.

Chapter 20:1-16 tells us that the kingdom of heaven is like a landowner who went out early in the morning to hire laborers for his vineyard. He hired people for the same wage at different times of the day from early morning to late afternoon. When those hired

early, realized that everyone received the same wage, they grumbled. (The early hires are meant to symbolize the Jewish religious leaders.) The owner replied that he was doing no wrong, for everyone had agreed to the wage. He asked them if they were envious because of his generosity to everyone. Then in verse 16 he says, So the last shall be first, and the first will be last. (The things of God do not fit into the boxes we humans create.)

This story is about grace and the eternal kingdom that has already broken into the world but will not be in its final state until the end time judgment. The wage is the gift of grace as being part of the eternal kingdom that has broken into the world but will culminate in the new heaven and earth. The wage is not earned; it is a gift, for it is an honor just to be a part of the kingdom. Working in the kingdom is simply the way God's people confirm their part of the covenant. The covenant involves God saying, I will be your God, and you will be my people. It is a way to use the gifts and talents God gives his people for God's purposes. But the gift will not be dispensed if one is not working in the vineyard. This is always the dilemma.

The payment is not about how much work one does, or when one comes into the vineyard. But it is important to be in the vineyard working for the kingdom, for only those in the vineyard receive the gift. It is a type of inheritance, but if one rejects the Father and the family, one is not going to receive the inheritance. Theologically it is explained this way: The new covenant is instituted by the Father through the Son. Salvation is by grace through faith, also meaning justification is through faith. God gives all faith, but one must be open to faith, and then faith must be realized. God the justifier is also God the sanctifier.

Sanctification is part of the process. It means being made holy, which is a life long process. Being made holy is God working in his people and through his people for the purpose he created them. As one allows God to do his work in them and through them, God then accounts to the individual, nation, church, or institution their part of the covenant. This is how the covenant is confirmed. This is how the kingdom advances. In the end justification is by grace through faith as God's gift as the sanctification process is completed. John 3:17 says, Indeed, God did not send the Son into the world to condemn the world, but in order that the world might be saved through him. The word used is "world." This means God sent his Son to save and renew all creation, which includes individuals, nations and its institutions, and creation itself. God is Lord over all his creation, and all thing have been created through him and for him, and in him "all things" hold together (Col 1:15-20).

Entry into the vineyard is by God's grace and the final reward is by God's grace. Reward is about participating in God and God working through his followers, allowing God to make the kingdom present in the believer and through the believer (Phil 2:12-14). In this way the kingdom advances. Reward is also tied to the continual forgiveness of sin. Only by the grace of the blood of Jesus is there the reward of continual and final purification. This is the new purification law that takes the place of the temple and the Old Testament purity laws.

The theological sequence to the parable is found in teachings such as Romans 6:6-11. We know that our old self was crucified with him so that the body of sin might be destroyed, and we might no longer be enslaved to sin. For whoever has died is freed from sin. But if we have died with Christ, we believe that we will also live with him. We know that Christ, being raised from the dead, will never die again; death no longer has dominion over him. The death he died, he died to sin, once for all; but the life he lives, he lives to

God. So you also must consider yourselves dead to sin and alive to God in Christ Jesus, and Hebrews 9:22 adds, without the shedding of blood there is no forgiveness of sins. This is the essence of the parable in the context of Jesus and the kingdom. It is all about God. His people are his slaves, his instruments, his treasure in clay jars (2 Cor 4:1-12). (God's created people are either slaves to self or slaves to the God who created them.)

In verses 18-19 as Jesus and the twelve disciples were going up to Jerusalem, Jesus said, "See we are going up to Jerusalem, and the Son of Man will be handed over to the chief priests and scribes, and they will condemn him to death; then they will hand him over to the Gentiles to be mocked and flogged and crucified; and on the third day he will be raised." (The following is added to show that at this point no one understands what he is saying, not even his twelve.)

Verses 20-21 say, the mother of the sons of Zebedee came to him with her sons, and kneeling before him, she asked a favor of him. And he said to her, "What do you want?" She said to him, "Declare that these two sons of mine will sit, one at your right hand and one at your left, in your kingdom." (They still think he is going to take the seat of David with an earthly kingdom and throw out the hated Romans from their land. Incidentally, in Mark 10:35-50 the mother did not ask this question, the sons asked it.)

In verses 22-23 Jesus asks them if they are able to go through the suffering he is about to go through. They answer they are able, but obviously they do not understand. He tells them that they will suffer, but who will sit at his right and left will be determined by his Father. (This is an attempted power grab by the sons of Zebedee and their mother.) Verse 24 says when the ten heard it, they were angry with the two brothers.

In verses 25-28 Jesus gives them a lesson about power in the kingdom of God. He said, "You know that the rulers of the Gentiles lord it over them, and their great ones are tyrants over them. It will not be so among you; but whoever wishes to be great among you must be your servant, and whoever wishes to be first among you must be your slave; just as the Son of Man came not to be served but to serve, and to give his life a ransom for many."

Jesus reverses the idea of conventional power. Power in the kingdom is defined differently from power in the world. Throughout Scripture Jesus reverses the superiority-inferiority syndrome. Again this is the kingdom message meant for individuals, institutions, nations, and most importantly the church. Greatness is in serving your fellow humans in need.

In verses 29-34 after leaving Jericho two blind men say to him, "Have mercy on us, Lord, Son of David." (The men recognize him as the Messiah.) Jesus asked, "What do you want me to do for you?" They said, "Lord let our eyes be opened." Moved with compassion, Jesus touched their eyes. Immediately they regained their sight and followed him. (Scripture shows that Jesus heals both physically and spiritually. The question must continually be asked: Should the followers of the Lord of all life be concerned about one and not the other?)

Chapter 21 says, when they had come near Jerusalem and had reached Bethphage at the Mount of Olives, Jesus sent two disciples, saying to them, "Go into the village ahead of you, and immediately you will find a donkey tied, and a colt with her; untie them and bring them to me." Matthew quotes Zechariah 9:9 in verse 5 saying, "Tell the daughter of Zion, Look, your king is coming to you, humble, and mounted on a donkey, and on a colt, the foal of a donkey."

Jesus enters not on the horse of a military commander, but on the beasts of burden of a humble man. It is interesting that Matthew has Jesus sitting on two of the animals whereas the other gospel writers do not. He probably misunderstands Zechariah's quote of two animals when Zechariah was simply describing the type of donkey.

Verses 6-11 say, The disciples went and did as Jesus had directed them; they brought the donkey and the colt, and put their cloaks on them, and he sat on them. A very large crowd spread their cloaks on the road, and others cut branches from the trees and spread them on the road. The crowds that went ahead of him and that followed were shouting, "Hosanna to the son of David! Blessed is the one who comes in the name of the Lord! Hosanna in the highest heaven!"

Hosanna means save us. In context they are saying save us from the hated Romans, for that was their expectation for the Messiah. A few days later when they learn that is not his purpose, they turn against him and yell for him to be crucified. Verses 10-13 say, When he entered Jerusalem, the whole city was in a turmoil, asking, "Who is this?" The crowds were saying, "This is the prophet Jesus from Nazareth in Galilee." Then Jesus entered the temple and drove out all who were selling and buying in the temple, and he overturned the tables of the money changers and the seats of those who sold doves. He said to them, "It is written (Isa 56:7), 'My house shall be called a house of prayer'; but you are making it a den of robbers." (Jeremiah experienced the same things hundreds of years before, Jer 7:11.)

This is not an act of violence but a symbolic object lesson such as practiced by the Old Testament prophets. It is in protest of the over-commercialization of the temple. The temple authorities are taking advantage of pilgrims coming to worship where they have to buy animals to sacrifice in worship and to exchange their currency for the currency used in Jerusalem.

The temple has become a place where people are being fleeced in the name of religion. People coming from distant lands to worship at the temple are being charged outrageous prices to exchange their money and to buy the animals to sacrifice as part of their worship. The temple leaders have become corrupt oppressors, who have institutionalized greed and the oppression of their own people. The temple is the primary banking center for the nation, and the leaders in violation of the law have been charging extremely high interest rates. They taxed the people heavily, and then took their land, homes, and animals making them tenant farmers or slaves.

Jesus simply does what the prophet Jeremiah did before him; he criticizes their actions and warns them and the nation, and the resistance movement bent on militant nationalism and a violent overthrow of Rome that if they do not change their ways, both Jerusalem and the temple will be destroyed as it had been previously.

The temple has become like the barren fig tree, no longer producing fruit. Many of the disadvantaged in the land see the temple as everything that is taking advantage of them. They see the leaders as a rich corrupt aristocracy in cahoots with the Romans overtaxing them, taking their land from them, and keeping the masses indebted to them. Their light has dimmed through their systemic injustice. Later when the nationalistic rebels attack the temple, the first thing they do is destroy all the tax records. The temple then becomes the center of the revolution against Rome.

Jesus in his time on earth, like Jeremiah, warns the rebels to give up their violent resistance movement, for if not, it will end in the destruction of the temple and the city. But like their forefathers they reject this thinking. The end result will turn out to be the same as in the time of Jeremiah. The temple and the city will be totally destroyed. But this will not happen for at least twenty-five more years. The chief priests and the scribes, the professional interpreters of Jewish law from the Sanhedrin, keep looking for a way to kill Jesus, for they are afraid of him because the whole crowd is spellbound by his teaching. When evening comes, Jesus and his disciples leave the city.

The Sanhedrin consists of seventy religious and political leaders of Israel in charge of the temple and basically the nation. Most of the priests are the Sadducees. There are some Pharisees, many of them scribes. Others completing the Sanhedrin are the elders, who are the wealthy landowners. The majority are the priests who are working closely with the Romans in order to keep their power positions, for Rome had appointed them. All of them are among the wealthiest in Israel.

It seems a number of Pharisees join the resistance movement, wanting Jesus out of the way because he is not an observant Jew and is opposing their traditions. Also the Zealots, who lead the resistance movement, want him gone because he is not a loyal, flag waving patriot and opposes the goals of the nation. Jesus condemns their attitude and warns them to repent, to change their violent agenda for his kingdom's agenda. They refuse his request.

Verses 14-17 say, The blind and the lame came to him in the temple and he cured them. (Again, Jesus is concerned with healing the sick and hurting.) But when the chief priests and the scribes saw the amazing things that he did, and heard the children crying out in the temple, "Hosanna to the Son of David," they became angry and said to him, "Do you hear what these are saying?" Jesus said to them, "Yes; have you never read, Out of the mouths of infants and nursing babies you have prepared praise for yourself?" He left them, went out of the city to Bethany, and spent the night there.

Verses 18-22 say, In the morning, when he returned to the city, he was hungry. And seeing a fig tree by the side of the road, he went to it and found nothing at all on it but leaves. Then he said to it, "May no fruit ever come from you again!" And the fig tree withered at once. When the disciples saw it, they were amazed saying, "How did the fig tree wither at once?" Jesus answered them, "Truly I tell you, if you have faith and do not doubt, not only will you do what has been done to the fig tree, but even if you say to this mountain, 'Be lifted up and thrown down into the sea,' it will be done. Whatever you ask for in prayer with faith, you will receive." (Again, this is another hyperbolic statement.)

Jesus is pointing out that the fig tree like the holy city of Jerusalem and the temple no longer bear any fruit. Their lack of any fruit of righteousness is prefiguring the reason for the fall of the temple and Jerusalem. On the other hand he is telling them if they have faith in him and pray for a holy life, he will, through the Holy Spirit, bear the fruit of righteousness through them.

In verses 23-24 at the temple the chief priests and the elders of the people ask him by what authority he is doing these things, and who gives him the authority. He asks them if they think the baptism of John the Baptist came from heaven or if it is of human origin. They argued with one another, and in (25-27) say, "If we say 'From heaven,' he will say to us, 'Why then did you not believe him?' But if we say, 'Of human origin,' we are afraid of the crowd; for all regard John as a prophet." So they answered Jesus, "We do not know." And he said to them, "Neither will I tell you by what authority I am doing these things." (They are not open to learn the truth, so he will not fall into their traps.)

In verses 28-32 he tells them a parable. "What do you think? A man had two sons; he went to the first and said, 'Son, go and work in the vineyard today.' He answered, 'I will not'; but later he changed his mind and went. The father went to the second and said the same; and he answered, 'I go sir'; but he did not go. Which of the two did the will of his father?" They said, "The first." Jesus said to them, "Truly I tell you, the tax collectors and the prostitutes are going into the kingdom of God ahead of you. For John came to you in the way of righteousness and you did not believe him, but the tax collectors and the prostitutes believed him; and even after you saw it, you did not change your minds and believe him."

In the following parable this writer will add in parentheses who those mentioned represent. Verses 33-44 say, "Listen to another parable. There was a landowner (God) who planted a vineyard (Israel), put a fence around it, dug a wine press in it, and built a watchtower. Then he leased it to tenants (Jewish leaders) and went to another country (heaven). When the harvest time had come, he sent his slaves (prophets) to the tenants to collect his produce (fruits of righteousness). But the tenants seized his slaves and beat one, killed another, and stoned another. Again he sent other slaves, more than the first; and they treated them in the same way. Finally he sent his son (Jesus) to them, saying, 'They will respect my son.' But when the tenants saw the son, they said to themselves, 'This is the heir; come, let us kill him and get his inheritance.' So they seized him, threw him out of the vineyard, and killed him. Now when the owner of the vineyard comes, what will he do to those tenants?"

They said to him, "He will put those wretches to a miserable death, and lease the vineyard to other tenants (the church) who will give him the produce at the harvest time." Jesus said, to them, "Have you never read in the scriptures: 'the stone (Jesus) that the builders rejected has become the cornerstone, this was the Lord's doing, and it is amazing in our eyes'? Therefore I tell you, the kingdom of God will be taken away from you and given to a people that produce the fruits of the kingdom. The one who falls on this stone will be broken to pieces; and it will crush anyone on whom it falls." (This is a metaphor for rejecting Jesus.)

Verses 45-46 say, When the chief priests and the Pharisees heard his parables, they realized he was speaking about them. They wanted to arrest him, but they feared the crowds, because they regarded him as a prophet. (They have had it with his teachings and criticism of their religious traditions and their nation with its great city Jerusalem and its temple. Listening to what he said convinced them that his purpose was to destroy their religion and their nation.)

Chapter 22:1-12 says, Once more Jesus spoke to them in parables, saying: "The kingdom of heaven may be compared to a king who gave a wedding banquet for his son. He sent his slaves to call those who had been invited to the wedding banquet, but they would not come." (The wedding banquet is the eschatological [end time] banquet of God making his presence available now through the presence of Jesus and his kingdom, but will not be finalized until the judgment.) Again he sent other slaves, saying, 'Tell those who have been invited: Look I have prepared my dinner, my oxen and my fat calves have been slaughtered, and everything is ready; come to the wedding banquet.' But they made light of it and went away, one to his farm, another to his business, while the rest seized his slaves, mistreated them, and killed them. (They killed God's messengers, the apostles and those he sent out.)

"The king was enraged. He sent his troops, destroyed those murderers, and burned their city. (The Romans came and killed many in Jerusalem and destroyed the temple and the city in AD 70.) Then he said to his slaves, 'the wedding is ready, but those invited were not worthy. (Christ and his disciples first went to the nation of Israel, the people of the original covenant, then he sends his messengers into all the world.) Go therefore into the main streets, and invite everyone you find to the wedding banquet.' Those slaves went out into the streets and gathered all whom they found, both good and bad; so the wedding hall was filled with guests. But when the king came in to see the guests, he noticed a man there who was not wearing a wedding robe, and he said to him, 'Friend how did you get in here without a wedding robe?' And he was speechless."

God's messengers invited all to marry themselves to Jesus through the Spirit and be clothed in white representing the forgiveness of sins with a cleansed and transformed heart. This man tried to get into the feast without the Spirit, without marrying himself to the one the Father sent in his name, and without receiving forgiveness of sins and a new heart.

Verses 13-14 say, "Then the king said to the attendants, 'Bind him hand and foot, and throw him into the outer darkness, where there will be weeping and gnashing of teeth.' For many are called but few are chosen." (Few are chosen because most do not respond seriously to the call of repentance and discipleship in the kingdom; they do not stand for and live the ways of the kingdom. Apparently, the person thrown out thought he should have been included.)

Verses 15-17 say, Then the Pharisees went and plotted to entrap him in what he said. So they sent their disciples to him, along with the Herodians, saying, "Teacher, we know that you are sincere, and teach the way of God in accordance with truth, and show deference to no one; for you do not regard people with partiality. Tell us then, what do you think. Is it lawful to pay taxes to the emperor, or not?"

The Pharisees and Herodians are bitter enemies, but here they unite to trap Jesus in order to eventually get rid of him. They are trying to force him into a choice between paying the tax to the emperor or paying the temple tax, so they could tell the one he did not choose that Jesus is teaching others to ignore their responsibility to them.

But Jesus in (18) aware of their malice, said, "Why are you putting me to the test, you hypocrites? Show me the coin used for the tax." Then he pointed out the side of the coin with the emperor's head. In (21) he said to them, "Give therefore to the emperor the things that are the emperor's, and to God the things that are God's." When they heard this, they were amazed; and they left him and went away. (Many of the people believed that they were not free because they were forced to pay taxes to the Romans.)

One day this writer saw a Tea Party gathering with a clergyman carrying a sign saying, God does not like taxes. Apparently he had not yet discovered these verses. The freedom most Americans talk about is not the freedom Jesus promoted. Jesus' freedom is primarily about being set free from being controlled by such things as sin, selfishness, greed, or supporting only those things that benefit oneself and one's group. Although this writer does believe given the choice, Jesus would prefer to live in a free nation; he just never had that choice. On the other hand, he never says anything about living in his nation while under the control of the Romans.

The right to be free is important to Americans and those who live in America greatly appreciate it, but it is not the primary way freedom is used in Scripture. Jesus did not live in a free, democratic, capitalist society. The concepts of American democracy and capitalism had yet to be created. There were even many slaves in the time of Jesus, and he did not mention the issue. This writer does believe if Jesus lived in America he would promote the positive aspects of democracy and capitalism, but would also be critical of their negative aspects. But the fact is he never said anything about those ideas. And if they truly are God given ideas as stated in the Constitution, which this writer believes they are, even though it is difficult to prove it from Scripture, one wonders why he never mentions them, or what he is saying to everyone by not mentioning them. Possibly being a slave to Christ and what he taught as being most important is more important.

One day this writer watched on television one of our congressmen, who is opposed to taxes because of the freedom issue, state that those in Congress who oppose him need to come

READING AND UNDERSTANDING THE GOSPELS

to Jesus in order to get on the right side of the taxes and freedom issues. How incredible is that? This writer believes that God must get stomach pains listening to some of our congressmen.

The same day in verses 23-28 some Sadducees came to him, saying there is no resurrection; and they asked him a question, saying, "Teacher, Moses said, 'If a man dies childless, his brother shall marry the widow, and raise up children for his brother. The second did the same, so also the third, down to the seventh. Last of all the woman herself died. In the resurrection then, whose wife of the seven will she be? For all of them had married her." (In the Old Testament this is called a levirate marriage.)

In verses 29-33 Jesus answered them, "You are wrong, because you know neither the scriptures nor the power of God. For in the resurrection they neither marry nor are given in marriage, but are like angels in heaven. (This is not saying the married are separated.) And as for the resurrection of the dead, have you not read what was said to you by God, 'I am the God of Abraham, the God of Isaac, and the God of Jacob'? He is God not of the dead, but of the living." And when the crowd heard it, they were astonished at his teaching. (For those who will be in the final eternal state there is perfect love and no need to create offspring.)

Verses 34-40 say, When the Pharisees (who believe in a resurrection) heard that he had silenced the Sadducees, they gathered together, and one of them a lawyer, asked him a question to test him. "Teacher, which commandment in the law is the greatest?" He said to him, " 'You shall love the Lord your God with all your heart, and with all your soul, and with all your mind.' This is the greatest and first commandment. And a second is like it: 'You shall love your neighbor as yourself.' On these two commandments hang all the law and the prophets." (Jesus is saying everything the law and the prophets taught was geared toward loving God and neighbor.)

Verses 41-45 say, Now while the Pharisees were gathered together, Jesus asked them this question: "What do you think of the Messiah? Whose son is he?" They said to him, "The son of David." He said to them, "How is it then that David by the Spirit calls him Lord saying, 'The Lord said to my Lord, "Sit at my right hand, until I put your enemies under my feet" '? If David thus calls him Lord, how can he be his son?" (The first Lord refers to God; the second Lord refers to the Messiah. David is saying, God said to the Messiah who is the Lord, . . . Matthew is saying this Jesus is the son of David who is the Messiah.) No one was able to give him an answer, nor from that day did anyone dare ask him any more questions.

Chapter 23 verses 1-3 say, Then Jesus said to the crowds and to the disciples, "The scribes and the Pharisees sit on Moses' seat; therefore, do whatever they teach you and follow it; but do not do as they do, for they do not practice what they teach."

The scribes are religious leaders able to read and write, and they are learned in the Old Testament law. The Pharisees are a religious group who believe in angels, spirits, and the resurrection. They believe in the exact observance of the law, and they have built a fence around the law by developing all kinds of laws to make sure the original laws will not be broken. Many of the scribes are Pharisees, Jesus appears very harsh with the Pharisees, but he is this way only with the leadership and those who are extreme in their thinking and actions. Some believe he may have even had training under the Pharisees, but that can not be proven. Their purpose is noble, but their methodology is flawed. They impose the Old Testament priestly regulations on the lay people, which contrast with the easy yoke and light burden of Jesus. In religious terms today, many of the Pharisees would be called legalists. These people occupy the teaching chairs in the synagogues.

In verses 4-5 Jesus continues, "They tie up heavy burdens, hard to bear, and lay them on the shoulders of others; but they themselves are unable to lift a finger to move them. They do all their deeds to be seen by others; for they make their phylacteries broad and their fringes long." (The phylacteries from Deut 6:8 are Scriptures they place in small, leather boxes that they strap around their head, hands, and arms. The fringes are tassels worn at the four corners of their cloaks with a blue cord on them to remind them to do all the commandments the Lord commanded, Deut 22:12, Num 15:38-39.)

Verses 6-8 continue, "They love to have the place of honor at banquets and the best seats in the synagogues, and be greeted with respect in the marketplaces, and to have people call them rabbi. But you are not to be called rabbi (means teacher), for you have one teacher, and you are all students. And call no one your father on earth, for you have one Father—the one in heaven. Nor are you to be called instructors (master), for you have one instructor, the Messiah. The greatest among you will be your servant. All who exalt themselves will be humbled, and all who humble themselves will be exalted."

Not to call anyone teacher, instructor, or father is in one sense difficult to explain, for even the Apostle Paul calls himself father, (1 Cor 4:15) and we call our fathers, father and our teachers, teacher. So what is Jesus saying? It is either taken literally, and if so, most of us are in disobedience, or it is a hyperbolic statement to be taken in the spirit of the teaching. Is he simply saying not to use those terms in such a way that make those people a substitute for God? In other words do not make an idol of them. For as verse 9 says, "you have only one Father–the one in heaven." (He is the real authority to whom everyone is to submit.)

In verses 13-15 Jesus continues, "But woe to you, scribes and Pharisees, hypocrites! For you lock people out of the kingdom of heaven. For you do not go in yourselves, and when others are going in, you stop them. Woe to you, scribes and Pharisees, hypocrites! For you cross sea and land to make a single convert, and you make the new convert twice as much a child of hell as yourselves." (They are distorting the religion of the one God. We are experiencing some very strong language by Jesus. Obviously, hypocrites strongly stirred up his wrath.)

In verses 16-22 Jesus says, "Woe to you blind guides, who say, 'Whoever swears by the sanctuary is bound by nothing, but whoever swears by the gold of the sanctuary is bound by the oath.' You blind fools! For which is greater, the gold or the sanctuary that has made the gold sacred? And you say, 'Whoever swears by the altar is bound by nothing, but whoever swears by the gift that is on the altar is bound by the oath.' How blind you are! For which is greater, the gift or the altar that makes the gift sacred? So whoever swears by the altar, swears by it and by everything in it and by everything on it; and whoever swears by the sanctuary, swears by it and by the one who dwells in it; and whoever swears by heaven, swears by the throne of God and by the one who is seated on it." (How does this teaching compare to 5:33-37 that says, "Do not swear at all . . . Let your word be 'Yes, Yes' or 'No, No'; anything more than this comes from the evil one.")

It seems that judicial oaths, and oaths taken in the name of God on occasions of solemn religious importance are not included in this prohibition. Jesus takes an oath in his trial (Mt 26:63), and the Apostle Paul later will take an oath (2 Cor 1:23, Gal 1:20). On the other hand Jesus seems to be saying oaths in everyday conversation and the normal affairs of life are not necessary, so be a person of honesty so your word can be trusted. Not swearing at all is not meant to be a timeless ethic; it is about attitudes, dispositions, and purity of heart in the spirit of the law that Jesus desires. Laws can only produce a minimum ethic that easily leads to pride and self congratulations. Jesus goes to a higher righteousness, the spirit behind the law, which is be a person of honesty so your word is always trusted.

Jesus in verses 23-24 continues, "Woe to you, scribes and Pharisees, hypocrites! For you tithe mint, dill, and cumin, and have neglected the weightier matters of the law; justice and mercy and faith. It is these you ought to have practiced without neglecting the others. You blind guides! You strain out a gnat but swallow a camel!" (By only paying attention to the exactness of the law, they miss the spirit of the law, and in the process the intention of the law is distorted.)

They are more concerned with paying the temple tax, even on vegetables and spices, than they are with genuine faith, justice, and mercy. Jesus encourages them to go beyond what the minimum law demands and be meticulous in being humane in their relationships with others, the thing that really matters. If one reads the Old Testament prophets and the teachings of Jesus the word justice in Scripture usually refers to social and economic justice not justice in the courts, although such is included. He tells them that their overwhelming interest in trivia (the gnat) leads them to overlook the big things (the camel).

In verses 25-26 Jesus continues his straining out gnats and swallowing a camel metaphor, "Woe to you, scribes and Pharisees, hypocrites! For you clean the outside of the cup and of the plate, but inside they are full of greed and self-indulgence. You blind Pharisee! First clean the inside of the cup, so that the outside also may come clean."

Jesus is saying clean your heart from its greed, self indulgence, injustice, and oppression so your actions will not be phony and hypocritical. They are so obsessed with the externals that their religion too often lacks substance.

Verses 27-28 say, "Woe to you, scribes and Pharisees, hypocrites! For you are like whitewashed tombs, which on the outside look beautiful, but inside they are full of the bones of the dead and of all kinds of filth. So you also on the outside look righteous to others, but inside you are full of hypocrisy and lawlessness."

Their hearts are impure, so Jesus is making them look at their hearts in order for them to see their need for purification. He is showing them the need to change their concept of purity and adopt his idea of purity. We must keep in mind Matthew is writing and living in a time when Jews greatly increased their action of expelling Christian Jews from the synagogue, so these are difficult times between the two groups.

In verses 29-36 Jesus continues, "Woe to you, scribes and Pharisees, hypocrites! For you build the tombs of the prophets and decorate the graves of the righteous, and you say, 'If we had lived in the days of our ancestors, we would not have taken part with them in the shedding the blood of the prophets.' Thus you testify against yourselves that you are descendants of those who murdered the prophets. Fill up, then, the measure of your ancestors. You snakes, you brood of vipers! How can you escape being sentenced to hell?

Therefore I send you prophets, sages, and scribes, some of whom you will kill and crucify, and some you will flog in your synagogues and pursue from town to town, so that upon you may come all the righteous blood shed on earth, from the blood of righteous Abel to the blood of Zechariah son of Barachiah, whom you murdered between the sanctuary and the altar. Truly, I tell you, all this will come upon this generation." (We will read in Acts how this is fulfilled.)

In verses 37-39 Jesus continues, "Jerusalem, Jerusalem, the city that kills the prophets and stones those who are sent to it! How often have I desired to gather your children together as a hen gathers her brood under her wings, and you were not willing! See your house (temple) is left to you, desolate. For I tell you, you will not see me again until you say, 'Blessed is the one who comes in the name of the Lord.' "

Jesus is describing the city and temple authorities as murders of the prophets and opponents of the Messiah that refuse to repent. Jesus speaks as the Father's prophet unhappy over Israel's apostasy, foretelling Jerusalem's destruction, and as the Messiah being vindicated by coming in glory in his kingdom.

Chapter 24:1-2 says, As Jesus came out of the temple and was going away, his disciples came to point out to him the buildings of the temple. Then he asked them, "You see all these, do you not? Truly I tell you, not one stone will be left here upon another; all will be thrown down."

Jesus tells them the temple is going to be destroyed. The disciples do not believe that will ever happen, and if it did, the world would be at its end. Even so, there are some at the time who believe something of this nature will take place within history as the Old Testament prophets had prophesied. It happened previously when the Babylonians destroyed the first temple approximately six hundred years before. Again, there will be a time of suffering, then the nation's exile will come to an end, then God himself will come and set up his kingdom of justice and peace.

Verses 3-8 say, When he was sitting on the Mount of Olives, the disciples came to him privately, saying, "Tell us, when will this be, and what will be the sign of your coming and of the end of the age?" (Notice there are three questions, which they may mistakenly believe is one question. The end of the age is actually a reference to the end of the old age (covenant) and the beginning of the new (covenant) as prophesied by the prophets, Isa 55, Jer 31, and Ezek 36.)

Jesus answered them, "Beware that no one leads you astray. For many will come in my name, saying, 'I am the Messiah!' And they will lead many astray. And you will hear of wars and rumors of wars; see that you are not alarmed; for this must take place, but the end is not yet. For nation will rise against nation, and kingdom against kingdom, and there will be famines and earthquakes in various places; all this is but the beginning of birth pangs."

Note this is not the end but just the beginning. It is also important to note that this is a form of Jewish apocalyptic literature. The reader will notice that these very signs have appeared in every generation from the beginning of time and will continue to occur in every generation until the end of time.

Jesus in verses 9-13 continues, "Then they will hand you over to be tortured and will put you to death, and you will be hated by all nations because of my name. Then many will fall away, and they will betray one another and hate one another. And many false prophets will arise and lead many astray. And because of the increase in lawlessness, the love of many will grow cold. But the one who endures to the end will be saved." (Jesus tells his disciples that this will happen to them in their time, and later the book of Acts will verify this. Jesus tells them that when this does happen, they must endure to the end.)

Verse 14 says, "And this good news of the kingdom (the words and acts of Jesus) will be proclaimed throughout the world as a testimony to all nations; and then the end will come." (Some believe everything up to verse 14 pertains to the disciples in that generation, and he is talking about the end meaning the destruction of Jerusalem and the temple by the Romans. Since prophecy often tends to repeat itself, others believe these teachings can apply to both the destruction of Jerusalem and to the final judgment at the end of time.)

Verses 15-24 say, "So when you see the desolating sacrilege standing in the holy place, as was spoken by the prophet Daniel (9:27, 11:31), let the reader understand, then those in Judea must flee to the mountains; the one on the housetop must not go down to take what is in the house; the one in the field must not turn back to get a coat." (According to Josephus, in his writing of The Jewish War and Antiquities, this actually occurred. When the Romans began their attack, this was the sign for the Jews who had become Christians to escape the city.)

The desolating sacrilege or the Abomination of Desolation was first related to 167 BC. The Seleucid, King Antiochus Epiphanes IV, who defeated the Jews and butchered a pig on the temple altar, and then set up the Greek god Zeus is the first fulfillment of this prophecy. He even refused them the right to perform their Jewish rituals. Matthew is making it also a double fulfillment of prophecy as he applies it to AD 70 and the Roman destruction of the temple and pagans occupying the temple.

Jesus continues in verse 19 saying, "Woe to those who are pregnant and to those who are nursing infants in those days! Pray that your flight may not be in winter or on a sabbath. For at that time there will be great suffering, such as has not been since the beginning of the world until now, no and never will be. And if those days had not been cut short no one would be saved; (from the Roman destruction) but for the sake of the elect those days will be cut short. Then if anyone says to you, 'Look! Here is the Messiah!' or 'There he is!'—do not believe it. For false messiahs and false prophets will appear and produce great signs and omens, to lead astray, if possible, even the elect." (Jesus is still talking to the disciples of his generation.)

In verses 26-28 Jesus continues saying, "So if they say to you, 'Look! He is in the wilderness,' do not go out. If they say, 'Look! He is in the inner rooms,' do not believe it. For as the lightning comes from the east and flashes as far as the west, so will be the coming of the Son of Man. Wherever the corpse is, there the vultures will gather."

The Son of Man coming at the end of the space time universe will not be in the generation of Jesus' time, for when that occurs, everyone will know. This is simply referring to the destruction by Rome of the temple and Jerusalem, and the killing of Jews where the vultures will feed on all the dead bodies. All of this pertains to those living in the generation of Jesus. There were many false messiahs later claiming they were the returning Messiah. Most of them called for revolution against the Romans. Jesus is telling them they will not be he, for when he returns all will know without doubt. He is also telling them when the destruction of Rome and the temple happens, it will not be the end of the world.

These following verses 29-31 are typical of apocalyptic literature usually referring to a time of judgment and new creation. This type of literature is very symbolic presenting bizarre symbols, figures, and numbers to present God's unfolding plan. "Immediately after the suffering of those days the sun will be darkened, and the moon will not give its light; the stars will fall from heaven, and the powers of heaven will be shaken. Then the sign of the Son of Man will appear in heaven, and then all the tribes of the earth will mourn, and they will see the 'Son of Man coming on the clouds of heaven' with power and great glory. And he will send out his angels with a loud trumpet call, and they will gather his elect from the four winds, from one end of heaven to another."

The word "immediately" has presented a problem to scholars along with the Son of Man appearing. He had just said at that time he would not be appearing in person. He may be saying that after the suffering of those days meaning the whole Christian period of time, not just the time of the first apostles, then he will come immediately and gather the elect. But verse 34 says this generation will not pass away until all these things have taken place. Is he saying the suffering generation, which is throughout the Christian era, will not pass away until he comes the last time?

Or is this metaphorical language describing his presence and coming kingdom which officially begins on the day of Pentecost in Acts chapter 2, but will not come in its fullness until the last judgment is accomplished? Or did he really believe the end time was going to come in his generation? If the latter is the answer we can justify this error of his belief by going to verse 36 that has Jesus saying no one knows when that final day will be not even the Son, but only the Father. In other words while he is on this earth, his humanity does not know the answer to that question.

The interpretation presented by George Caird, NT Wright, and Marcus Borg among others is that this is apocalyptic language and pertains to that generation. NT Wright (1996, 339-366) understands these verses as apocalyptic and metaphorical. They are making a theological statement about current events. Clouds in Scripture represent God's presence, even judgment, so this is saying people will see that the Father will vindicate Jesus, not only at the resurrection but when Rome destroys the city and temple in AD 70, the very thing he foretold.

The coming in clouds symbolizes and represents Jesus, the Son of Man, coming to Jerusalem making his presence known as the vindicated rightful king as stated in Dan 7:12-14. Then sending out the angels to gather the elect is the real beginning of the harvest, meaning the real expansion of Christianity. It has nothing to do with the ending of the world in space and time. In fact most prophecy in the Old Testament is basically a reference to the end of an old age, the present evil age and the beginning of the new age. It is about judgment and new beginnings.

Here Jesus is retelling and reworking the great story found in the prophets such as Zechariah 14, Micah 7:2-10, Isaiah 40-55, Jeremiah 7, 31:31-37, Ezekiel 34-37, Daniel 7, 9, 12, Hosea 11:1-9 and many others. Here we have examples of Jesus using the story line from the prophetic tradition and reconstructing and retelling it to focus on what was happening in his context. What God had done in the Exodus, he will at last do again, even more gloriously. There will no longer be exile for Israel, God will return to his people and be king, the temple will be rebuilt, the new covenant will begin, the time of great renewal will be here. Jesus is saying all this is happening through him. He is the Messiah, the chosen of God, the word of God, the new temple where sins are now forgiven. When the Romans destroy Jerusalem and the temple, his prophecy will be fulfilled.

Wright's point is Jesus constantly warned the nationalist resistance movement to give up their agenda of getting rid of Rome through violent action, and if not, God would act against them. This was part of the meaning of the word repentance, for both the nation and individuals were included in the call to repent. The nationalist resistance movement did not stop their militant actions, nor did the Jewish leaders and the temple authorities change their unjust and oppressive ways; therefore, the nation is punished once again for the same reasons they were previously punished by God during the time of the Assyrian and Babylonian exiles. Rome will be called by God to do the same as was done previously by the Assyrians and the Babylonians. After the fall of the temple and the end of the sacrificial system, Christianity will begin to really make its mark and expand.

Verses 32-36 continue, "From the fig tree learn its lesson: as soon as its branch becomes tender and puts forth its leaves, you know that summer is near. So also when you see these things, you know that he is near, at the very gates. Truly I tell you, this generation will not pass away until all these things have taken place. Heaven and earth will pass away, but my words will not pass away. But about that day and hour no one knows, neither the angels of heaven, nor the Son, only the Father."

Heaven and earth will pass away, but my words will never pass away is apocalyptic. There will be in the end a new heaven and new earth. The issue is how to define this generation, his coming, the gathering of the elect, and beginning and end of the kingdom. The most anyone can really say for sure is that the message is telling people to be prepared. That is the message of the following verses, whether it be the destruction of Jerusalem and the temple or the final judgment.

Verses 37-41 say, "For as the days of Noah were, so will be the coming of the Son of Man. For as in those days before the flood they were eating and drinking, marrying and giving in marriage, until the day Noah entered the ark, and they knew nothing until the flood came and swept them all away, so too will be the coming of the Son of Man. Then two will be in the field; one will be taken and one will be left. Two women will be grinding meal together; one will be taken and one will be left."

When will this happen? The context says, at the trumpet call when the elect are gathered. The trumpet call is symbolic language for a time of judgment. The elect being gathered can refer both to the beginning and spread of Christianity and the final judgment. Some believe it is at the time of Rome destroying Jerusalem and the temple where the remnant in Jerusalem who belong to Jesus are preserved for the mission Jesus gave them, while the Jewish nation is judged. In context those taken are taken in judgment. An incredible number of people died in the Roman attack on Jerusalem in 66-70

AD. They are not taken in a rapture to eternal bliss. Those left alive on earth, like Noah and those in the ark, are the remnant from the old covenant, Jews who become followers of the Christ, who will begin to make up the new Israel of God. They are the angels (translated messengers) who go into the world to gather the elect.

Verses 42-44 are the key to the message. "Keep awake therefore, for you do not know on what day your Lord is coming. But understand this; if the owner of the house had known in what part of the night the thief was coming, he would have stayed awake and would not have let his house be broken into. Therefore you also must be ready, for the Son of Man is coming at an unexpected hour." (The purpose of this whole section of the chapter is not to tell us when God will act through Christ in the power of the Spirit, but that he will act and act more than once, so be prepared.)

Verses 45-51 continue saying, "Who then is the faithful and wise slave, whom his master has put in charge of his household, to give the other slaves their allowance of food at the proper time?" (The master is God; the wise slaves are God's leaders called to take care of his people both spiritually and materially.) "Blessed is that slave whom his master will find at work when he arrives. Truly I tell you, he will put that one in charge of all his possessions. But if that wicked slave says to himself, 'My master is delayed,' and he begins to beat his fellow slaves, and eats and drinks with drunkards, the master of that slave will come on a day when he does not expect him and at an hour he does not know. He will cut him in pieces and put him with the hypocrites, where there will be weeping and gnashing of teeth."

Again this can be in reference to both that generation and the end time judgment. The nation in that generation continues to take advantage of their fellow humans through political oppression, economic exploitation, and spiritual manipulation in the name of religion as the same continues in today's generation. The parable is saying they will pay the price for their selfish and self serving actions just as they did in the past. However one interprets this chapter the theme is God is a God of both love and wrath, so be prepared. All individuals, the nations, and especially the church need to have eyes that see and ears that hear.

Chapter 25:1-13 continues with parables of judgment. This is about wisdom opposed to folly. It says, "Then the kingdom of heaven will be like this. Ten bridesmaids took their lamps and went to meet the bridegroom. Five of them were foolish, and five were wise. When the foolish took their lamps, they took no oil with them; but the wise took flasks of oil with their lamps. As the bridegroom was delayed, all of them became drowsy and slept. (The foolish were like the seed sown on rocky ground; they expected him to come shortly and did not prepare for the duration to be a long time.)

But at midnight there was a shout, 'Look here is the bridegroom! Come out to meet him.' Then all those bridesmaids got up and trimmed their lamps. The foolish said to the wise, 'Give us some of your oil, for our lamps are going out.' But the wise replied, 'No! There will not be enough for you and for us; you had better go to the dealers and buy some for yourselves.' And while they went to buy it, the bridegroom came, and those who were ready went with him into the wedding banquet (a metaphor for the judgment gathering); and the door was shut. Later the other bridesmaids came also saying, 'Lord, lord, open to us.' But he replied, 'Truly I tell you, I do not know you.' Keep awake therefore, for you know neither the day nor the hour."

The message is to prepare for the long haul; do not lose heart or become lazy and fall away. There will be a time when it is too late to repent and enter the kingdom. There is a mission to be involved in before judgment and new creation, so do not lose focus. This parable must first be applied to the nations, especially the nation of Israel, and those within the nation rejecting the agenda of the kingdom and continuing their agenda of destruction toward the Romans as a way of getting rid of them.

Second, it is a parable about both individuals, nations, and the church throughout time being prepared and making sure they stay prepared for the final coming of Jesus. The light one bears through the oil of God's grace working through the Holy Spirit, and the righteousness and fruits one bears because of the working of the Holy Spirit, must not be allowed to burn out, even though at times it can become dim. It is those who endure to the end that will be saved. Those who allow the light to burn out and return to the former way will come up empty.

The second parable of judgment covers verses 14-30. It says, "For it is as if a man going on a journey, summoned his slaves and entrusted his money to them; to one he gave five talents, to another two, to another one, to each according to his ability. (A talent represents a large sum of money.) Then he went away. The one who had received the five talents went off at once and traded with them, and made five more talents. In the same way, the one who had the two talents made two more talents. But the one who received the one talent went off and dug a hole in the ground and hid his master's money.

"After a long time, the master of those slaves came to settle accounts with them. Then the one who had received the five talents came forward bringing five more talents, saying, 'Master, you handed over to me five talents; see, I have made five more talents.' His master said to him, 'Well done, good and trustworthy slave; you have been trustworthy in a few things, I will put you in charge of many things; enter into the joy of your master.' And the one with two talents also came forward, saying, 'Master, you handed over to me two talents; see, I have made two more talents.' His master said to him, 'Well done, good and trustworthy slave; you have been trustworthy in a few things, I will put you in charge of many things; enter into the joy of your master.' Then the one who received the one talent also came forward saying, 'Master, I knew that you were a harsh man, reaping where you did not sow, and gathering where you did not scatter seed; so I was afraid, and I went and hid your talent in the ground. Here have what is yours.' (This person had a misconception about who God is, and he did not understand or realize that while God is away he still works sowing and scattering his seed through his people.)

"But his master replied, 'You wicked and lazy slave! You knew, did you, that I reap where I did not sow, and gather where I did not scatter? Then you ought to have invested my money with the bankers, and on my return I would have received what was my own with interest. So take the talent from him, and give it to the one with the ten talents. For to all those who have, more will be given, and they will have abundance; but from those who have nothing, even what they have will be taken away. As for this worthless slave, throw him into the outer darkness, where there will be weeping and gnashing of teeth.' "

The man gone on a journey who gave the talents is the Father who gives gifts to his people (called his slaves, first the nation of Israel and second his church). For the word talents one can substitute whatever gifts God gives to his people. He gives his word, different abilities, different material gifts, and different spiritual gifts. He expects us to use what he gives for God's glory, for he owns his people and the gifts he gives them. The master coming to get an account is his Son, Jesus the Messiah, first from the nation of Israel, and then his church.

The accounting happens both during this life and the final judgment. Constant watchfulness and preparation demand action that brings forth fruit. For Christians Christ is to live in and through his people doing his works in his people and through his people for his glory. All his people have is on loan from him, and he will demand an accounting. One is not saved by works, but one is not saved without works. The works are the works of God that his people allow him to work in and through them (Phil 2:12-14). For his followers it is a way they confirm their part of the covenant. In 2 Peter 1:10-11 Peter says, Therefore, brothers and sisters, be all the more eager to confirm your call and election, for if you do this, you will never stumble. For in this way, entry into the eternal kingdom of our Lord and Savior Jesus Christ will be richly provided for you.

In verses 31-33 is another parable, It says, "When the Son of Man comes in his glory, and all the angels with him, then he will sit on the throne of his glory. All the nations will be gathered before him, and he will separate people one from another as a shepherd separates the sheep from the goats, and he will put the sheep at his right hand and the goats at his left."

We know that this is about the judgment of individuals, but since God is Lord of all, it is also about the corporate judgment of nations and the institutional church. As one looks at history, it seems that civilizations and nations are judged by God. These groups are all responsible for the people living within it. Nations, the church, and institutions are also responsible to the people and to God.

The individuals who make up nations are responsible for their witness and for influencing their nation for good. God holds each person accountable and will judge them not only for what they do, but also for whether or not one attempts to influence for good individuals as well as nations and the institutions within those nations. This is part of Christ's call to go into "all" the world. This is the mission of the kingdom God gives his people. God cares about the world that people live in because the world and its nations and institutions influence people.

Individuals influence nations, and nations influence individuals; it works both ways. The following verses show how individuals, the nations, and the church shall be judged. The precedent had already been set all through the Old Testament, so what follows is really nothing new. It is only new for those who have very little or no real Old Testament background.

Verses 34-40 say, "Then the king (the Son of Man) will say to those at his right hand, 'Come, you that are blessed by my Father, inherit the kingdom that has been prepared for you from the foundation of the world; for I was hungry and you gave me food, I was thirsty and you gave me something to drink, I was a stranger (such as immigrants) and you welcomed me, I was naked and you gave me clothing, I was sick and you took care of me, I was in prison and you visited me.' (These items are symbolic of people's basic needs.) Then the righteous will answer him, 'Lord when was it that we saw you hungry and gave you food, or thirsty and gave you something to drink? And when was it that we saw you a stranger and welcomed you, or naked and gave you clothing? And when was it that we saw you sick or in prison and visited you? And the king will answer them, 'Truly I tell you, just as you did it to one of the least of these who are members of my family, you did it to me.' "

This is about taking care of the needs of the people, not wants but needs. When one takes the side of and cares for the stranger, the disadvantaged, the poor, the sick, those who can not work, or those who can not find a job, the immigrant, and the working poor, who are not paid a just wage to earn enough to meet their needs, one is caring for Christ and the things he cared for when he was on this earth. The people of Christ are called to be an extension of Christ, his eyes, his hands, his legs, his mouth until he returns in glory. Christ is to work in and through his people while he waits to return again. When this is done, they are actually caring for Christ and the things he cared for.

There are no excuses or rational analyses accepted. They are judged on how they use their influence and what they do for people in need. It must be noted the issue is not just about you personally and individually giving of yourself and your means but also about influencing the institutions of one's society to bring about the common good. The church and its people are called not only to preach and teach this but to model it. When they care for these people of God, these verses are telling the people that they are caring for Christ himself.

Verses 41-46 continue, "Then he will say to those at his left hand, 'You that are accursed, depart from me into the eternal fire prepared for the devil and his angels; for I was hungry and you gave me no food, I was thirsty and you gave me nothing to drink, I was a stranger and you did not welcome me, naked and you did not give me clothing, sick and in prison and you did not visit me. Then they will answer, 'Lord, when was it that we saw you hungry or thirsty or a stranger or sick or in prison, and did not care for you?' Then he will answer them, 'Truly I tell you, just as you did not do it to one of the least of these, you did not do it to me.' And these will go away into eternal punishment, but the righteous into eternal life." Jesus is inviting all of his creation to be transformed and join him in his kingdom. Government, along with individuals, are created by God and thus responsible to God.

Many people in America do not understand the biblical concept of group or corporate responsibility. Groups and institutions sin just as they can do good. The people of those times understood that very well; they first made the nation responsible. They believed the nation was to set the example for individuals, and then individuals will follow. Individuals make up groups, but groups can take on a personality different from many of the individuals within it. Individuals make up groups, but groups also form the thinking of individuals. For example look at the political parties. They form the thinking of the individuals within it, but not all the individuals within it believe in everything that the political party gets passed in Congress. Therefore there is a responsibility that falls on the group but not upon every individual within it.

The Bible makes both nations and individuals responsible, and the mission Christ gives his people especially makes individuals responsible to some extent for influencing the personality of the group or the corporate institutions one is associated with. Since individualism is so strong in this country, too many Americans have difficulty understanding that life under God is more than individuals only being responsible for no one but themselves. According to Scripture, churches, institutions, and nations are responsible for the common good as well as individuals to influence them for good, and all will be judged by how they respond to the kingdom teachings of Jesus.

Where is the reader in all this? This writer encourages the reader to allow the Scriptures to interpret the reader in what one thinks, what one believes and everything the reader does by asking a simple question: How would Jesus look at this if he were living today? The purpose is to allow the word of God to transform one's life. Hear what God has to say. Do not come to God's inspired word to find Scriptures to fit into your particular ideology and politics. Let the word of God form the reader's thinking and then let it be applied to the world where you live. Eliminate as much as possible trying to fit what you already believe into God's word in order to get God to approve what was learned elsewhere.

❧

Chapter 26:1-5 says, When Jesus had finished saying all these things, he said to his disciples, "You know that after two days the Passover is coming, and the Son of Man will be handed over to be crucified." Then the chief priests and the elders of the people (the leaders of the Jews) gathered in the palace of the high priest, who was called Caiaphas, and they conspired to arrest Jesus by stealth and kill him. But they said, "Not during the festival, or there may be a riot among the people."

Verses 6-13 say, Now while Jesus was at Bethany in the house of Simon the leper, a woman came to him with an alabaster jar of very costly ointment, and she poured it on his head as he sat at the table. But when the disciples saw it they were angry and said, "Why this waste? For this ointment could have been sold for a huge sum, and the money given to the poor." But Jesus, aware of this, said to them, "Why do you trouble this woman? She has performed a good service for me. For you always have the poor with you, but you will not always have me. (Since there will always be the poor they will have plenty of opportunities to help them, but there are only a few days left for Jesus on this earth.) Jesus then says, By pouring this ointment on my body she has prepared me for burial. Truly I tell you, wherever the good news is proclaimed in the whole world, what she has done will be told in remembrance of her."

Verses 14-16 say, Then one of the twelve, who was called Judas Iscariot, went to the chief priests and said, "What will you give me if I betray him to you?" They paid him thirty pieces of silver. And from that moment he looked for an opportunity to betray him. (It seems as though it finally dawned on him that the kingdom Jesus was teaching was not the one Judas was looking for.)

Verses 17-19 say, On the first day of Unleavened Bread the disciples came to Jesus saying, "Where do you want us to make the preparations for eating the Passover?" (The Unleavened Bread is another name for the Passover, and the first day is the day for getting the Passover lamb and preparing to eat it.) He said, "Go into the city to a certain man, and say to him, 'The Teacher says, my time is near; I will keep the Passover at your house with my disciples.' " So the disciples did as Jesus had directed them, and they prepared the Passover meal.

The Jews believe the Messiah will come during a Passover. Their reasoning is that Passover is the religious feast celebrating the time in Egypt that God had set the Hebrews free from slavery in Egypt. God planned to kill all first born in Egypt because Pharaoh kept changing his mind about letting the Hebrews go free. God told the Hebrews to put blood on their door posts, and he would pass over their homes and not put to death the Hebrew first born. This happened as God said, and the Hebrews escaped from Egypt and prepared for entry into the promised land. (This as well as all the Old Testament references can be seen in their context in this author's previous book, *Reading and Understanding the Old Testament: The Foundation of Judaism, Christianity, and Islam*.)

Verses 20-25 say, When it was evening he took his place with the twelve; and while they were eating, he said, "Truly I tell you, one of you will betray me." And they became greatly distressed and began to say to him one after another, "Surely not I, Lord?" He answered, "The one who has dipped his hand into the bowl with me will betray me. (They all did that.) The Son of Man goes as it is written of him (a reference to Isaiah's suffering servant, Isa 53), but woe to that one by whom the Son of Man is betrayed! It would have been better for that one not to have been born. "Judas who betrayed him, (Ps 41:9) said, "Surely not I, Rabbi?"

He replied, "You have said so." (It is interesting to note that the other disciples called him Lord, while Judas called him Rabbi.)

Verses 26-30 say, While they were eating, Jesus took a loaf of bread, and after blessing it he broke it, gave it to the disciples, and said, "Take eat; this is my body." Then he took a cup, and after giving thanks he gave it to them, saying, "Drink from it, all of you; for this is my blood of the covenant, which is poured out for many for the forgiveness of sins. I tell you, I will never again drink of this fruit of the vine until that day when I drink it new with you in my Father's kingdom." When they had sung the hymn (which would be one of the Passover hymns from Pss 115-118) they went out to the Mount of Olives. (This institutes the Lord's Supper which he will drink with them, meaning his presence will be with them, after he rises from the dead. The Eucharist will take the place of the Passover meal.)

Verses 31-35 say, Then Jesus said to them, "You will all become deserters because of me this night; for it is written (Zech 13:7), 'I will strike the shepherd, and the sheep of the flock will be scattered.' But after I am raised up, I will go ahead of you to Galilee." Peter said to him, "Even though I must die with you, I will not deny you." And so said all the disciples.

Zechariah chapters 13-14 should be read at this point. Jesus seems to be reworking his prophecy and tying it in with his actions in the temple, the institution of the Lord's Supper at the Passover, and the new covenant and new age that ends the exile and has God coming to his people as king. As the Passover related to the Exodus from Egypt is celebrated, Jesus institutes the new symbol for the new Exodus.

Verses 36-39 say, Then Jesus went with them to a place called Gethsemane; and he said to his disciples, "Sit while I go over there and pray." He took with him Peter and the two sons of Zebedee, and began to be grieved and agitated. Then he said to them, "I am deeply grieved, even to death; remain here, and stay awake with me." And going a little farther, he threw himself on the ground and prayed. "My Father, if it is possible, let this cup pass from me; yet not what I want but what you want." (The humanity of Jesus is being expressed.)

Verses 40-46 say, Then he came to the disciples and found them sleeping; and he said to Peter, "So could you not stay awake with me one hour?" Stay awake and pray that you may not come into the time of trial; the spirit indeed is willing, but the flesh is weak." Again he went away for the second time and prayed, "My Father, if this can not pass until I drink it, your will be done." Again he came and found them sleeping, for their eyes were heavy. So leaving them again he went away for the third time, saying the same words. Then he came to the disciples and said to them, "Are you still sleeping and taking your rest? See, the hour is at hand, and the Son of Man is betrayed into the hand of sinners. Get up, let us be going. See my betrayer is at hand." (Once again his disciples disappoint him. The spirit is willing, but the flesh is weak. Many of us can identify with that statement.)

Verses 47-50 say, While he was still speaking, Judas, one of the twelve arrived; with him was a large crowd with swords and clubs, from the chief priests and elders of the people. Now the betrayer had given them a sign, saying, "The one I will kiss is the man, arrest him." At once he came up to Jesus and said, "Greetings Rabbi!" and kissed him. Jesus said to him, "Friend do what you are here to do." Then they came and laid hands on Jesus and arrested him.

Verses 51-54 say, Suddenly, one of those with Jesus put his hand on his sword, drew it, and struck the slave of the high priest, cutting off his ear. Then Jesus said to him, "Put your sword back into its place; for all who take the sword will perish by the sword. (This is a prophecy that has been fulfilled over and over throughout the history of the world.) Do you think that I cannot appeal to my Father, and he will at once send me more than twelve legions of angels? But how would the scriptures be fulfilled, which say it must happen in this way?"

Verses 55-56 say, At that hour Jesus said to the crowds, "Have you come out with swords and clubs to arrest me as though I were a bandit? Day after day I sat in the temple teaching, and you did not arrest me. But all this has taken place, so that the scriptures of the prophets may be fulfilled." Then all the disciples deserted him and fled. (Once again his disciples disappoint him.)

Verses 57-58 say, Those who had arrested Jesus took him to Caiaphas the high priest, in whose house the scribes and elders had gathered. But Peter was following him at a distance, as far as the courtyard of the high priest; and going inside, he sat with the guards in order to see how this would end.

The elders are wealthy, powerful leaders selected because of their wealth and position in society. The scribes are of the Pharisees, some who support a violent overthrow of Rome. But most are priests representing the Sadducees who are supporters of Rome, for Rome gave them the privilege of position. Later they will go to the side of the militant party when the war begins. It is this group that makes up the Sanhedrin which is the religious and political ruling body of Israel's theocracy.

Verses 59-64 say, Now the chief priests and the whole council were looking for false testimony against Jesus so they might put him to death, but they found none, though many false witnesses came forward. At last two came forward and said, "This fellow said, 'I am able to destroy the temple of God and to build it in three days.' " The high priest stood up and said, "Have you no answer?

What is it that they testify against you?" But Jesus was silent. Then the high priest said to him, "I put you under oath before the living God, tell us if you are the Messiah, the Son of God." Jesus said to him, "You have said so. But I tell you, From now on you will see the Son of Man seated at the right hand of power and coming on the clouds of heaven." (This is a reference to Dan 7:12-14 and the fact that God will make his presence and judgment known; Jesus will be vindicated at Pentecost and with the destruction of Jerusalem and the temple.)

Jesus under oath says that he is the Son of Man quoted from Dan 7:12-14. The verses of Daniel say, I saw one like a human being coming with the clouds of heaven. And he came to the Ancient One and was presented before him. To him was given dominion and glory and kingship, that all peoples, nations, and languages should serve him. His dominion is an everlasting dominion that shall not pass away, and his kingship is one that shall never be destroyed.

Jesus will be put to death, for he is claiming to be the one the prophet Daniel described. The session described here is interesting because trials during Passover, and night time trials are forbidden by Jewish law. There is a remote possibility that it was not an official trial but a gathering of leaders and people to decide how they would charge him in order to get Pilate to agree to have him put to death. The Romans have to approve a death penalty.

Verses 65-68 say, Then the high priest tore his clothes (a sign of distress) and said, "He has blasphemed! Why do we need witnesses? You have heard his blasphemy. What is your verdict?" They answered, "He deserves death." Then they spat in his face and struck him; and some slapped him, saying, "Prophesy to us you Messiah! Who is it that struck you?"

Why are the chief rulers of the Jews anxious to put him to death? The answer in part is he is challenging their religious and political actions and their way of thinking, not always directly, but through the parables and teaching he is giving to his people and anyone who will listen. He is on the side of the poor and disadvantaged and continues to criticize through his teaching of the people the wealthy and powerful as oppressors for taking advantage of them. The leaders realize as more follow him, their actions will be more and more questioned and their positions of power will be in jeopardy.

The leaders of the land believe he is not a patriot, not being loyal to the traditions of Israel. He even challenges those who hate the Romans. They believe he is a traitor to the cause and leading people astray. Also, they fear he is the new king who will cast them from their power positions that has given them great wealth. So the religious and political establishment of Israel's theocracy have to find a way to put him to death.

Let us be clear, they did not want to put him to death because he said he loved everyone and wanted to die for their sins. The Father will accept his death for that theological reason, but that is not why the religious and political leaders want to kill him and eventually do. Because he claims to be Daniel's king of a new and eternal kingdom, they charge him with blasphemy. How can anyone claim to be a king of an eternal kingdom if he is not God? Thus we see there are both theological and historical reasons for Jesus being put to death.

Verses 69-75 say, Now Peter was outside sitting in the courtyard. A servant-girl came to him and said, "You also were with Jesus the Galilean." But he denied it before all of them saying, "I do not know what you are talking about." When he went out to the porch, another servant-girl saw him, and she said to the bystanders, "This man was with Jesus of Nazareth." Again he denied it with an oath, "I do not know the man." After a little while the bystanders came up and said to Peter, "Certainly you are also one of them, for your accent betrays you." Then he began to curse and swore an oath, "I do not know the man!" At that moment the cock crowed. Then Peter remembered what Jesus had said: "Before the cock crows, you will deny me three times." And he went out and wept bitterly.

Chapter 27:1-2 says, When morning came, all the chief priests and the elders of the people conferred together against Jesus in order to bring about his death. They bound him, led him away, and handed him over to Pilate the governor.

Pilate is the Roman governor of Judea, which is under Roman occupation. He holds that position from AD 26-36. His headquarters are in Caesarea on the Mediterranean shore. But during the Passover he would come to Jerusalem to keep order. Crowds of people are always in Jerusalem for the Passover; it is one of the three main holy days that all male Jews are required to attend, if they are able. Most Jews also believe that when the Messiah comes it will be during Passover. While in Jerusalem he stays at the Praetorium in the Fortress of Antonio. It is here that Jesus' mock trial is held.

Verses 3-8 say, When Judas, his betrayer, saw that Jesus was condemned, he repented and brought back the thirty pieces of silver to the chief priests and elders. He said, "I have sinned by betraying innocent blood." But they said, "What is that to us? See to it yourself." Throwing down the pieces of silver in the temple, he departed; and he went and hanged himself. (According to Matthew Judas repents. A somewhat different account is given in Acts 1:16-20.) But the chief priests taking the pieces of silver said, "It is not lawful to put them into the treasury, since they are blood money." After conferring together, they used them to buy the potter's field as a place to bury foreigners. For that reason this field has been called the Field of Blood to this day.

Verses 9-10 say, Then was fulfilled what had been spoken through the prophet Jeremiah, "And they took the thirty pieces of silver, the price of the one on whom a price had been set, on whom some of the people of Israel had set a price, and they gave them for the potter's field, as the Lord commanded me."

This text is based very loosely on Zech 11:13. Jeremiah is inaccurately listed as the source. But the name is suggested by Jeremiah's purchase of the land (Jer 32:6-15) and visit to the potter (Jer 18:1-3, 19:1-13). By examining these Scriptures one can see how loosely the early writers used Scripture. Those Scriptures actually have nothing to do with how Matthew is using these Old Testament Scriptures as he makes them a fulfillment of Judas' actions. Their use of Scripture is mainly to show that what is happening fits their story.

Verses 11-14 say, Now Jesus stood before the governor; and the governor asked him, "Are you the King of the Jews?" Jesus said, "You say so." (Probably means yes, but it is qualified because even though he is the king that Jews are waiting for, he is not the type of king they are expecting. He has already confessed to the Jewish leaders that he is the one spoken of by Daniel 7:12-14.) But when he is accused by the chief priests and elders, he does not answer. (He has already answered them.) Then Pilate said to him, "Do you not hear how many accusations they make against you?" But he gave him no answer, not even to a single charge, so that the governor was greatly amazed.

Verses 15-19 say, Now at the festival (Passover) the governor was accustomed to release a prisoner for the crowd, anyone whom they wanted. At that time they had a notorious prisoner, called Jesus Barabbas. So after they had gathered, Pilate said to them, "Whom do you want me to release for you, Jesus Barabbas or Jesus who is called the Messiah?" For he realized it was out of jealousy that they had handed him over. While he was sitting on the judgment seat, his wife sent word to him, "Have nothing to do with that innocent man, for today I have suffered a great deal because of a dream about him."

Verses 20-23 say, Now the chief priests and the elders persuaded the crowds to ask for Barabbas and to have Jesus killed. (Crowds tend to go along with mob rule.) The governor again said to them, "Which of the two do you want me to release to you?" And they said, "Barabbas." Pilate said to them, "Then what should I do with Jesus who is called the Messiah?" All of them said, "Let him be crucified!" Then he asked, "Why, what evil has he done?" But they shouted all the more, "Let him be crucified." (Because he did not ride in on a horse with an army conquering the hated Romans, they now see Jesus as an imposter.)

Verses 24-25 say, So when Pilate saw that he could do nothing, but rather that a riot was beginning, he took some water and washed his hands before the crowd, saying, "I am innocent of this man's blood; see to it yourselves." Then the people as a whole answered, "His blood be on us and our children!" (His blood was on them and their children until their children of that generation died. They experienced that with the destruction of Jerusalem and the temple forty years later. It has been wrong for Christians to use this as a justification for persecuting Jews down through history.) Verse 26 says, he released Barabbas for them; and after flogging Jesus, he handed him over to be crucified. (To flog him the Romans use a whip of knotted cord or leather, sometimes weighted with sharp bone or metal.)

The death penalty for the Jews was by stoning, but because they are under a Roman military occupation, they have to get approval before they can hand out a death sentence. Then, because it is carried out by the Romans, the death will be the Roman way for any they determine to be a revolutionary. Crucifixion is the method of choice for that conviction (see the discussion in Mark 15). Rome had the power to stop the death penalty. But Pilate knew, as the Roman representative, he could be put to death by Rome, if he goes easy on a person claiming to be a new king bringing in a new kingdom. Rome has the Herodians and the Sanhedrin who are the puppet rulers of Judea under control. They do not want to hear anything about a regime change, especially from a new king bringing in a new kingdom. Therefore Pilate is not about to upset the apple cart.

Verses 27-31 say, Then the soldiers of the governor took Jesus into the governor's headquarters, and they gathered the whole cohort around him. (A cohort of Roman soldiers is the tenth part of a legion consisting of 760 infantry and 240 cavalry.) They stripped him and put a scarlet robe on him, and after twisting some thorns into a crown, they put it on his head. They put a reed in his right hand and knelt before him and mocked him saying, "Hail, King of the Jews!" They spat on him and took the reed and struck him on the head. After mocking him, they stripped him of the robe and put his own clothes on him. Then they led him away to crucify him.

The way the scene is described is reminiscent of Psalm 22, the psalm of the righteous sufferer. The early Christians see in this psalm the explanation of what Jesus is experiencing. Matthew emphasizes that Jesus suffers as the king of the Jews in accordance with Psalm 22.

Verses 32-37 say, As they went out they came upon a man from Cyrene (modern day Libya) named Simon; they compelled this man to carry Jesus' cross. And when they came to a place called Golgotha (which means Place of a Skull), they offered Jesus wine to drink, mixed with gall (a bitter, distasteful fruit); but when he tasted it, he would not drink it. (The traditional site is now within the expanded city wall in the Church of the Holy Sepulchre.) And when they had crucified him, they divided his clothes among themselves by casting lots; then they sat down there and kept watch over him. (This fulfills Psalm 22:18.) Over his head they put the charge against him, which read, "This is Jesus the King of the Jews." (This announcement by the Romans is telling everyone that the attempted revolution by an imposter king is over.)

Verse 38 says, Then two bandits were crucified with him, one on his right and one on his left. (Griffith-Jones (2000, 37) and Wright and Borg, (1999, 88-89) state that crucifixion is only for runaway slaves, and those who rebel against Rome, and those that Rome charge with treason.)

Verses 39-44 say, Those who passed by derided him, shaking their heads and saying, "You who would destroy the temple and build it in three days, save yourself! If you are the Son of God, come down from the cross." In the same way the chief priests also, along with the scribes and elders, were mocking him, saying, "He saved others; he cannot save himself. He is the King of Israel; let him come down from the cross now, and we will believe in him. He trusts in God; let God deliver him now, if he wants to; for he said, 'I am God's Son.' " The bandits who were crucified with him also taunted him in the same way.

Verses 45-50 say, From noon on, darkness came over the whole land until three in the afternoon. (This is symbolizing that it is a dark time in the history of the world.) And about three o'clock Jesus cried with a loud voice, "Eli, Eli, lema sabachthani?" that is, "My God, my God why have you forsaken me?" (The Father allows him to experience total separation from God, for at this point all the sins of the world are upon him, past, present, and future. This quotation is from Psalm 22:1.)

When some of the bystanders heard it, they said, "This man is calling for Elijah." At once one of them ran and got a sponge, filled it with sour wine, put it on a stick, and gave it to him to drink. But the others said, "Wait let us see whether Elijah will come to save him." Then Jesus cried again with a loud voice and breathed his last. (According to popular Jewish belief Elijah is the helper of the oppressed. This narrative is shaped by Ps 22:1, 7, 8, 18, and Ps 69:21.)

The question is who killed Jesus? Unfortunately, down through the years all Jews have been blamed. But the answer is that certain Jews and certain Romans at that particular time were responsible for his death. The Jews at that time could not put anyone to death without Roman approval. The answer to who killed Jesus is given in 1 Corinthians 2:8. It says the rulers of that age put Jesus to death. We would have to even narrow that down to certain rulers of that age put him to death.

Verse 51 says, At that moment the curtain in the temple was torn in two, from top to bottom. The earth shook, and the rocks were split.

The curtain separates the holy place from the most holy place in the temple. Only the high priest is permitted to enter the most holy place one day of the year and that is on the Day of Atonement. Here the priest is in the presence of God. The severing of the curtain symbolizes that Jesus has broken down the dividing line clearing the way for anyone to come into the presence of God through him (Heb 10:19-23). This is probably symbolic history and apocalyptic language expressing the deep meaning of the event. Just because it is symbolic history does not mean it did not happen.

Verse 52 says, The tombs also were opened, and many bodies of the saints who had fallen asleep were raised. After his resurrection they came out of the tombs and entered the holy city and appeared to many. (For Christians this is symbolizing that because of Jesus the people of God have the assurance of also being raised. But for

Jews living in those times resurrection is a sign that the exile of Judah is over, no more foreign domination, the new age of justice and peace and the rule of God has arrived, and God has returned to Israel, see Ezek chapters 34, 36, and 37.)

Verses 54-56 say, Now when the centurion and those with him, who were keeping watch over Jesus, saw the earthquake and what took place, they were terrified and said, "Truly this man was God's Son." (This is also translated a son of god.) Many women were also there, looking on from a distance; they had followed Jesus from Galilee and had provided for him. Among them were Mary Magdalene, and Mary the mother of James and Joseph, and the mother of the sons of Zebedee.

Verses 57-61 say, When it was evening, there came a rich man from Arimathea, named Joseph, who was a disciple of Jesus. He went to Pilate and asked for the body of Jesus; then Pilate ordered it to be given to him. So Joseph took the body and wrapped it in a clean linen cloth and laid it in his new tomb, which he had hewn in the rock. He then rolled a great stone to the door of the tomb and went away. Mary Magdalene and the other Mary were there, sitting opposite the tomb.

Verses 62-66 say, The next day, that is, after the day of Preparation, the chief priests and the Pharisees gathered before Pilate and said, "Sir we remember what that imposter said while he was still alive, 'After three days I will rise again.' Therefore command the tomb to be made secure until the third day; otherwise his disciples may go and steal him away, and tell the people, 'He has been raised from the dead.' And the last deception would be worse than the first." Pilate said to them, "You have a guard of soldiers; go, make it as secure as you can." So they went with the guard and made the tomb secure by sealing the stone.

Chapter 28:1-7 says, After the sabbath, as the first day of the week was dawning, Mary Magdalene and the other Mary went to see the tomb. And suddenly there was a great earthquake; for an angel of the Lord, descending from heaven, came and rolled back the stone and sat on it. (Earthquakes and darkening of sun and moon highlight the apocalyptic nature of the events, a sign of the Day of the Lord, a time of judgment and great change.) His appearance was like lightning, and his clothing white as snow. For fear of him the guards shook and became like dead men. But the angel said to the women, "Do not be afraid; I know that you are looking for Jesus who was crucified. He is not here; for he has been raised, as he said. Come see the place where he lay. Then go quickly and tell his disciples, 'He has been raised from the dead, and indeed he is going ahead of you to Galilee; there you will see him.' This is my message to you."

Verses 8-10 say, So they left the tomb quickly with fear and great joy, and ran to tell his disciples. Suddenly Jesus met them and said, "Greetings!" And they came to him, took hold of his feet, and worshiped him. (In Jn 20:17 Jesus does not permit Mary Magdalene to hold on to him because he has not yet ascended to the Father.) Then Jesus said to them, "Do not be afraid; go and tell my brothers to go to Galilee; there they will see me." (Mary Magdalene and the other Mary are the first witnesses to the resurrection. The interesting aspect of this is that a witness by women is not acceptable in judgments in those times. For a special exercise on the resurrection accounts turn to the last page of the Gospel of Mark.)

Verses 11-15 say, While they were going, some of the guard went into the city and told the chief priests everything that had happened. After the priests had assembled with the elders, they devised a plan to give a large sum of money to the soldiers, telling them, "You must say, 'His disciples came by night and stole him away while we were asleep.' If this comes to the governor's ears, we will satisfy him and keep you out of trouble." So they took the money and did as they were directed. And this story is still told among the Jews to this day.

Verses 16-20 say, Now the eleven disciples went to Galilee, to the mountain to which Jesus had directed them. When they saw him, they worshiped him; but some doubted. (They simply are not expecting his resurrection, or is their doubt about worshiping him? If this is made up, would this be included? Also, Matthew is probably writing to people in churches where some continue to doubt. Some still doubt today.)

And Jesus came and said to them, "All authority in heaven and earth has been given to me. Go therefore and make disciples of all nations, baptizing them in the name of the Father and of the Son and of the Holy Spirit, and teaching them to obey everything that I have commanded you. And remember, I am with you always, to the end of the age."

Teaching them to obey everything involves a message that includes more than individual salvation. The message of the cross must be brought to bear on everything including the world of which the nations are part. We must remember that the primary message of Jesus is the in-breaking of the kingdom, which includes bringing the rule of God to the world. It is about bringing renewal and salvation to the cosmos. If we keep the message of the cross only in the individual salvation, the so-called spiritual level, we are missing and even rejecting Jesus' primary message concerning the kingdom. God is Lord of all his creation.

In the process we are in danger of repeating the ancient Gnostic heresy that believes the physical is not real; it is imaginary, for only the spirit is real. NT Wright in an address at Fordham University on March 18, 2011 said the story of the Gospels is not about escaping the world to go to heaven. It is about God's sovereign, saving rule coming to birth on earth as well as heaven. It is about how God in Jesus became king on earth as in heaven.

Yes, this is also about the salvation of the world and cosmos. We must remember God so loved the world . . . (Jn 3:16). The world means everything in it including creation itself. Romans 8:19-23 says, For the creation waits with eager longing for the revealing of the children of God; for the creation was subject to futility, not of its own will but by the will of the one who subjected it, in hope that the creation itself will be set free from its bondage to decay and will obtain the freedom of the children of God. We know that the whole creation has been groaning in labor pains until now; and not only the creation but we ourselves, who have the first fruits of the Spirit, groan inwardly while we wait for adoption, the redemption of our bodies.

The kingdom is about renewal of individuals, institutions, nations, and the world itself until Jesus returns to complete kingdom building by making all things new. If we miss this part of Jesus' message we are missing a very big part of his purpose. By making Christianity *Gnostic,* where the physical and material are split off and separated from the spiritual, many Christians and their churches are missing this very important aspect of his kingdom message.

A very big part of the message and mission of Jesus includes the world's political, economic, social, and cultural life. See the following authors in the bibliography: Horsley, Verhey, Wright, Dunn, Borg, Yoder, Wallis, and Hendricks. Christianity can not be reduced to the political, economic, and social implications, but neither can it be emptied of them. The Bible does not give us a political, economic, and social system, but it does tell us some important characteristics any system should have. The politics of Jesus is the kingdom of God's good future breaking into the world (Verhey, 388-418).

The kingdom of God challenges the world's politically oppressive systems and its economically exploitive systems and especially those using religion to legitimize themselves (see Brueggemann and Wink). For that reason Jesus was put to death by the leaders of Israel and Rome. It does not seem that on the whole he directly confronted them, but it is obvious that they understood what would happen to them, if more and more people joined Jesus in his thinking.

Any nation that wants to be under God, needs to make God and his kingdom its priority. Any nation too quick to use its military might, and allow their economic system let the rich get richer and the poor get poorer, living by a theme of the survival of the fittest, would not be approved by Jesus and the kingdom he instituted.

Many people in the United States like to think this country is God's nation, a nation of God, but is it? The issue is not: Does this nation do better than others? The question is: Does it have the characteristics of the kingdom? When Americans sing God Bless America are they putting all the responsibility on God to bless while they avoid blessing those he calls all to bless by working toward peace, justice, healing the sick, and feeding the poor?

The promise that Jesus will be with his people, the church, to the end of the age presumes an era of the church between the inauguration of God's kingdom through Jesus and its fullness at his final coming. In the old covenant God called a nation, but in the new covenant he calls a church. The church is not the kingdom but is called to make the kingdom present thus blessing the world. The old covenant was the promise; the new covenant is its fulfillment. A descendant of Abraham has now become the fulfillment of God's promise to Abraham that through a nation coming from Abraham all the world will be blessed. With the death and resurrection of Jesus, God's followers will be mystically united with the Father through his Son Jesus making him present by the power of the Holy Spirit. All creation is in the process of being created anew. All God's adopted children are now empowered by the Spirit to live a life of higher righteousness in his kingdom.

Colossians 1:13-14 says, He has rescued us from the power of darkness and transferred us into the kingdom of his beloved Son, in whom we have redemption, the forgiveness of sins. Rev 1:5-6 says, To him who loves us and freed us from our sins by his blood, and made us to be a kingdom, priests serving his God and Father, to him be glory and dominion forever and ever.

The Gospel of Matthew is about the kingdom. The call of the church is to be and make present the kingdom, but can the church do such, if it seeks the same kind of power and strength the world seeks? Can the church do this when it gets in bed with the world? Can the church do this when it no longer calls its people, its nation, and its institutions to repentance? There are many who believe the church needs to quit striving to be accepted by the world and hear again the words God spoke to the Apostle Paul in 2 Corinthians 12:9 "My grace is sufficient for you, for power is made perfect in weakness." Paul's response was, "I will boast all the more in my weaknesses, so that the power of Christ may dwell in me." (For the kingdom to make its impact on the world in which we live, it must not bear witness to itself; it must bear witness to Christ, for the power of Christ is made perfect in weakness.)

One of the great theologians of the twentieth century, Karl Barth (*Church Dogmatics*, 1, 1, 36.) said that the greatest problem for the church does not come from atheists or even those who doubt, but it comes from the corruption of its message.

THE GOSPEL OF LUKE

*The majority of scholars believe Luke's gospel was written around 80-85 AD. A small minority of scholars disagree. Scholars believe there is a good possibility he wrote from Antioch of Syria. Luke is called a physician. He is a companion of the Apostle Paul. He also writes the book of Acts which is a sequel to his gospel. Both books equal about two-fifths of the New Testament. The beginning verses say he is writing an orderly account using eye witnesses as references. Luke is both a theologian and an historian in the ancient sense of what historians were, and it seems he put his attempt at a Hellenistic (Greek) biography of Jesus in an historical context with his two volume Luke/Acts narrative. In Luke he journeys to Jerusalem, and in Acts he journeys to Rome.

*Luke is writing to inform people that Jesus is a real person, but also God's unique Son who is the world's Savior. The Roman emperor is not the lord and savior called by God to bring peace and order as he claimed; Jesus is the true Lord and Savior who will bring God's real peace to the world.

Salvation and the word *savior* mean to the Jews at that time something very different from what Christians today mean by the terms. According to NT Wright (1992, 299-301) it first means liberation from exile from the oppressive, pagan Romans. It means forgiveness of sin for the nation, a time of peace and restoration. It means the inauguration of a new covenant, where God pours out his Spirit so people are able to keep Torah from the heart. It means God is returning to his people. It means the beginning of the new age with God ruling in his kingdom through his true king, sometimes referred to as the messianic age. And it means God will restore the temple. Jesus will accomplish all of this but not in the way it was expected.

*The first application of salvation is a corporate or national salvation. Those of the old covenant become part of that salvation by obeying Torah as a way to confirm their acceptance of the covenant (2 Peter 1:10-11). It is not a salvation by works; it is all because of grace and God's love for his people. None of this happens in the manner that the Jews think it will happen. Jesus redefines all of this and applies it to himself and a new covenant. Then it is further redefined by the apostles Peter, Paul, John, and James in the rest of the New Testament. The message Jesus came to preach is the kingdom of God (Lk 4:43). The kingdom has broken into the world now, and the kingdom is about judgment and renewal both now and at the end of time.

*Salvation history is a good way to describe Luke's gospel. Yet Luke's concept of salvation and Savior come from the Old Testament prophets, especially Isaiah. Thielman (2005, 113-125) gives the example from Isaiah chapters 25-26, 40-41, 45, 52. The prophet looks forward to future deliverance from enemies at a time when a rich banquet will be prepared for all peoples, death will be destroyed, and God's people will say, this is our God in whom we trust. Let us rejoice in his salvation. The nations will forsake their idolatry, and see God the creator as Savior.

*Luke writes primarily to a Hellenistic (Greek) culture of Gentiles, those who are not Jewish. They are located throughout the Roman Empire and in particular in Asia Minor (Turkey), Syria, in the area of the peninsula of Greece, and Rome, areas where the church is first planted. For Luke, Jesus and his message are on a journey. It will lead to Jerusalem, and then to Rome and the world.

*He writes specifically to Theophilus. We do not know who he is. Some think he is probably a God-fearer, those who are non-circumcised Gentiles who go to the synagogue because they have great respect for the Jews and their religion. Others think he is a convert to Christianity or about to become a convert. Others think he supports Luke financially. Still others believe he is a Roman government administrator who Luke and Paul try to convince that Christianity is not a threat to Roman power. Luke appears to describe him as one instructed somewhat in the faith.

*This gospel is called the universal gospel because it is written to all people about the humanity of people and their human needs. Jesus wants all people not just the Jews to come to him, for he is the universal Savior for all humankind. Therefore, Luke's genealogy goes back to Adam, the first human father of all people.

*The birth narrative is detailed because Luke as a physician is very interested in such. He mentions some things that are different from Matthew. For example, Matthew has wise men, or at least leaders coming to visit Jesus at his birth in a home. Luke has poor shepherds visiting him in a lowly barnyard manger. It is possible that both visits happened but at different times, even different years, but still called birth narratives because they cover the first two years of Jesus' life.

*Luke has Jesus paying special attention to the poor masses, many of whom are being oppressed by the elite people of power and wealth who control society. He presents a special concern for the masses who are struggling to survive, those of low social status, the outcasts of society, those who do not fit in, and are not accepted by the in-crowd. All the Gospels are concerned with social justice, but Luke emphasizes this biblical concept, which has deep roots in the Old Testament, especially the prophets. A background of the Old Testament prophets makes it easier to see what is behind the teachings and actions of Jesus. Not having that background has led to many misinterpretations of Jesus' message.

*Women have a very important place in Luke's gospel. Jesus even teaches them, which is a rarity in the ancient world, for women are not considered worthy to be taught. Also prayer, the Holy Spirit, and the use of the word *Lord* are emphasized. Lord (Adonai in Hebrew) is a substitute word for (YHWH) for the Jews. The word also means savior in the Gentile pagan religions, which were numerous at the time.

*The word joy is a word Luke constantly uses. Its reference is not to an emotional high but a type of inner peace and happiness.

*Luke emphasizes the Holy Spirit. In fact when he writes the Acts of the Apostles some will call it the Acts of the Holy Spirit. Practically every page in Luke has the Holy Spirit leading something, creating, and working.

*These three gospels of Mark, Matthew, and Luke are called the Synoptic Gospels because they are very similar, even though they often see things from different perspectives and have different theologies and ways of describing things. Most scholars believe Mark wrote first, and then Matthew and Luke wrote later, but both use Mark as a source. Scholars also believe that both Matthew and Luke had a source that Mark did not have. They labeled this source Quelle (Q), a German word that means source. This source is thought to be a document that consists only of the sayings of Jesus. This source has never been found. The gospel writers also each had their own sources that none of the others had. Some of the sources may have been written but in an oral society most were oral sources. Still the writings are similar enough to be called the *Synoptics.* None of the sources have been found, but the thinking behind this is the consensus of the majority of scholars as a result of very educated and disciplined analysis over a long period of time.

*Most scholars believe that Mark writes first, possibly even 20 years before the others. Dunn (2003, 139-172) says that much of Mark is in Matthew and Luke. Only thirty verses of Mark do not appear in the other two gospels. The order in each case generally follows Mark's order. For the existence of Q (presumed to be a sayings of Jesus source) there are some two hundred verses in Matthew and Luke, which are substantially the same but missing in Mark. The theories about who writes first and why as well as other thinking about the Synoptics can be found in most books concerning the Gospels.

*All three gospels seem to emphasize the humanness of Jesus before the crucifixion as he moves toward the cross. Thus their gospels are called a Christology from below. On the other hand John is very different as he will emphasize what Jesus means to the disciples after his resurrection, emphasizing the divinity of Jesus. John's approach is called a Christology from above. Let us now take a closer look at Luke.

Chapter 1:1-4 says, Since many have undertaken to set down an orderly account of the events that have been fulfilled among us (promises of Scripture are fulfilled), just as they were handed on to us by those who from the beginning were eyewitnesses and servants of the word, I too decided, after investigating everything carefully from the very first, to write an orderly account for you, most excellent Theophilus, so that you may know the truth concerning the things about which you have been instructed.

This tells us that the writers of the Gospels used sources of information that can no longer be located. Luke is saying his information was received from eyewitnesses who also taught and preached the word and that his account is an orderly account. What he means by an orderly account is not certain. Possibly he is indicating that from all the different oral and written accounts circulating, he is putting themes and chronology together more thoroughly.

Luke is telling us he is a second generation Christian like his readers. He writes in classical Greek which indicates he is an educated convert like many of his readers who are scattered throughout the Roman Empire. Luke wants to help his non-Jewish converts trace their roots back to the historic Jesus to understand better his actions and teachings, and to follow the growth and development of the early church. He wants everyone to thoroughly understand the gospel's Jewish roots, to see that the new covenant is rooted in the old covenant, and to see that everyone's humanity goes back to Adam.

If Theophilus was a God-fearer, he probably attended a Jewish synagogue because he was tired of the different pagan religions and was impressed with the one God and teachings of the Jews. Most God-fearers had not converted officially to the religion of the Jews, even though they consistently attended the assembly. This writer would imagine that adult circumcision was always somewhat of a hindrance to completing conversion.

Verses 5-7 say, In the days of King Herod of Judea (he is an Edomite, descended from Esau and a puppet king for the Romans), there was a priest named Zechariah, who belonged to the priestly order of Abijah. (Being a priest is inherited by belonging to the family of Aaron of the Levite tribe. There are twenty-four priestly orders. The priests from the orders come from their villages to work about two weeks a year in the temple, and then they return to their homes.)

His wife is a descendant of Aaron (meaning like her husband she also is of a priestly family), and her name was Elizabeth. Both of them are righteous before God, living blamelessly according to all the commandments and regulations of the Lord. (Living blamelessly does not mean they were sinless; it means they were serious about living according to the teachings of the law.) But they had no children, because Elizabeth was barren, and both were getting on in years.

Verses 8-12 inform us that once when he is serving as priest and offering incense in the sanctuary, there appears to him an angel of the Lord. Zechariah is terrified and fear overwhelms him. Verses 13-15 say, the angel said to him, "Do not be afraid, Zechariah, for your prayer has been heard. Your wife Elizabeth will bear you a son, and you will name him John. You will have joy and gladness, and many will rejoice in his birth, for he will be great in the sight of the Lord. He must never drink wine or strong drink; even before his birth he will be filled with the Holy Spirit.

This means he is to be a Nazirite, a person dedicated to the service of the Lord by vows, never to drink intoxicants, and never cutting his hair. Numbers chapter 6 explains what being a Nazirite entails. Verses 16-17 say, He will turn many of the people of Israel to the Lord their God. With the spirit and power of Elijah he will go before him, to turn the hearts of parents to their children, and the disobedient to the wisdom of the righteous, to make ready a people prepared for the Lord."

Verses 18-20 say, Zechariah said to the angel, "How will I know this is so? For I am an old man, and my wife is getting on in years." The angel replied, "I am Gabriel. I stand in the presence of God, and I have been sent to speak to you this good news. But now, because you did not believe my words, which will be fulfilled in their time, you will become mute, unable to speak, until the day these things occur." In (21-23) when he went out from the temple sanctuary, the people who were outside praying realized he had seen a vision while in the sanctuary. When his time of service ended, he went to his home. Verses 24-25 say, After those days his wife Elizabeth conceived, and for four months she remained in seclusion and gave praise to the Lord.

The following is called the *Annunciation*. Verses 26-33 say, In the sixth month the angel Gabriel was sent by God to a town in

Galilee called Nazareth, to a virgin engaged to a man whose name was Joseph, of the house of David. (Gabriel appeared many years before to Daniel, 8:16, 9:21.) The virgin's name was Mary. And he came to her and said, "Greetings favored one! The Lord is with you." But she was much perplexed by his words and pondered what sort of greeting this might be.

The angel said to her, "Do not be afraid, Mary, for you have found favor with God. And now, you will conceive in your womb and bear a son, and you will name him Jesus (a Greek form of the Hebrew Joshua meaning God saves). He will be great, and he will be called Son of the Most High, and the Lord God will give to him the throne of his ancestor David. He will reign over the house of Jacob forever, and of his kingdom there will be no end."

From this the Catholic faith begins to develop the Hail Mary prayer, a prayer whose purpose is to show respect for the woman who bore the world's Savior but also to ask for her prayers. Catholics believe that followers of Jesus who die are alive, so they can pray for the people on earth just as those living on earth can. It is not worship of her, even though that does happen by some of the uneducated. The Annunciation tells us that Jesus is the one promised that would come from the line of David, and he would be God's Son.

In verses 34-35 Mary said to the angel, "How can this be since I am a virgin?" (This is an appropriate biological question.) The angel said to her, "The Holy Spirit will come upon you, and the power of the Most High will overshadow you; therefore the child to be born will be holy. He will be called Son of God. (Many scholars deny a virgin birth. Some deny it because they reject the miracles of the Bible. Others believe it is simply a literary device to illustrate Jesus was unique. Others say, if by the Holy Spirit, God can create the world, could he not also bring forth his child from a virgin?)

Verses 36-38 say, And now your relative Elizabeth in her old age has also conceived a son; and this is the sixth month for her who was said to be barren. For nothing will be impossible with God." Then Mary said, "Here am I, the servant of the Lord; let it be with me according to your word." Then the angel departed from her. (Christians say, the response by Mary is to be the response of all who claim to be serious followers of the Christ.)

Verses 39-42 say, In those days Mary set out and went with haste to a Judean town in the hill country, where she entered the house of Zechariah and greeted Elizabeth. When Elizabeth heard Mary's greeting, the child leaped in her womb. And Elizabeth was filled with the Holy Spirit and exclaimed with a loud cry, "Blessed are you among women, and blessed is the fruit of your womb. (These are more words of the Catholic Hail Mary prayer.) Verses 43-45 continue, And why has this happened to me, that the mother of my Lord comes to me? For as soon as I heard the sound of your greeting, the child in my womb leaped for joy. And blessed is she who believed that there would be a fulfillment of what was spoken to her by the Lord."

Verses 46-56 include what is called the *Magnificat* (so called from the first word of the Latin translation). It is a praise hymn that echoes the Old Testament Hannah's song over her son Samuel's birth (I Sam 2:1-10) in which God is also praised for the salvation of the lowly and oppressed. Verses 46-56 say, And Mary said, "My soul magnifies the Lord, and my spirit rejoices in God my Savior, for he has looked with favor on the lowliness of his servant. Surely, from now on all generations will call me blessed; for the Mighty One has done great things for me, and holy is his name. His mercy is for those who fear him from generation to generation. He has shown strength with his arm; he has scattered the proud in the thoughts of their hearts. He has brought down the powerful from their thrones, and lifted up the lowly; he has filled the hungry with good things, and sent the rich away empty. He has helped his servant Israel in remembrance of his mercy, according to the promise he made to our ancestors, to Abraham and his descendents for ever." And Mary remained with her about three months (probably until Elizabeth delivered) and then returned to her home. In verses 57-58 Elizabeth gives birth to a son.

Mary's song is key for understanding Luke; it is about hope in the future for the so-called nobodies of the world. Her song is similar to Hannah's when she gave birth to Samuel (I Samuel 2:1-10). The proud will be scattered. The powerful will be brought down. The lowly will be lifted up. The hungry will be filled. The rich will be sent away. The promise made to Abraham that from him one would come that would be a blessing to all nations is being fulfilled.

As one reads the Gospels there is no doubt about the priority of Jesus for those who do not have wealth and power. Jesus will spend his time with this kind of people. In this canticle the early Christians celebrate the prophetic ministry of Jesus and summarize his earthly mission. Jesus comes to reveal the blessedness of the poor and the outcasts, and in the process oppressive and corrupt leaders feel they are being confronted.

The rich being sent away does not mean that Jesus does not want the rich. It means that because they do not accept his teaching about the poor and his siding with them, they go away or oppose him and his teaching. Jesus is more than a prophet but he is a prophet in the Old Testament sense, where power and wealth are always challenged to listen to God's word and put it in action. The comfortable are constantly told to listen with mind and heart, and to get on the side that God is on. He comes to the lowly, and those who listen to his word are empowered, and given respect and dignity. Without a reading of the Old Testament prophets and their constant criticism of those who have the power and wealth, one will not understand where Jesus is coming from.

Verses 59-66 say, On the eighth day they came to circumcise the child, and they were going to name him Zechariah after his father. But his mother said, "No; he is to be called John." They said to her, "None of your relatives have this name." Then they began motioning to his father to find out what name he wanted to give him. He asked for a writing tablet and wrote, "His name is John." And all of them were amazed. Immediately his mouth was opened and his tongue freed, and he began to speak, praising God. Fear (awe) came over all their neighbors, and all these things were talked about throughout the entire hill country of Judea. All who heard them pondered them and said, "What then will this child become?" For, indeed, the hand of the Lord was with him.

In the form of what becomes a hymn called the *Benedictus* (named for the first word in the Latin translation), verses 67-75 say, Then his father Zechariah was filled with the Holy Spirit and spoke this prophecy: "Blessed be the Lord God of Israel, for he has looked favorably on his people and redeemed them. He has raised up a mighty savior for us in the house of his servant David, as he spoke through the mouth of his holy prophets from of old, that we would be saved from our enemies and from the hand of all who hate us. Thus he has shown the mercy promised to our ancestors, and has remembered his holy covenant, the oath that he swore to our ancestor Abraham, to grant us that we, being rescued from the hands of our enemies, might serve him without fear, in holiness and righteousness before him all our days. (In this context being saved from all who hate us is a reference to being saved from the nation's enemies, which means any foreign power, especially the hated Romans in their land.)

Verses 76-79 say, "And you child will be called the prophet of the Most High; for you will go before the Lord to prepare his ways, to give knowledge of salvation to his people by the forgiveness of their sins. By the tender mercy of our God, the dawn from on high will break upon us, to give light to those who sit in darkness and in the shadow of death, to guide our feet into the way of peace." (As mentioned here, the reader will see, the theme of peace is prevalent throughout the message of Jesus. This peace is peace with God, peace with self, peace with each other, and peace with all creation.) Verse 80 says, The child grew and became strong in spirit, and he was in the wilderness until the day he appeared publically to Israel.

It is difficult to tell if forgiveness of individual sins is here being added to the concept of salvation, but if not now, it will soon be. The primary reference is first to the nation of Israel. They believe they are still dominated by a foreign power because of the nation's sin and not living properly under the law. At this point Jews believe all sin is forgiven at the temple through the sacrificial system developed in the book of Leviticus. They will learn later through John and Jesus that the forgiveness of all sin will come only through the blood of Jesus.

The message is that the nation of Israel and the people of the old covenant are being redeemed by the Savior God who is from the lineage of David, as promised by the Old Testament prophets. For Luke Jesus is the new David. The message being proclaimed is that the theological exile is over. God is showing mercy to his people. God is in the process of being made present to Israel. He is rescuing people from their enemies so they might serve him in holiness and righteousness and without fear. At the moment Rome is the enemy oppressor, but knowledge will be given soon about the true enemy, which is evil caused by sin. Light will be given to all who sit in darkness, and feet will be guided to the way of peace. This writer knows that many now misunderstand the full significance of these words just as they will miss the full significance of the meaning behind the kingdom that Jesus comes to establish.

In relation to sin and evil the key is to focus on the importance of forgiveness of sin and serving God in holiness and righteousness first for the nation of Israel, and then for a new nation of God, the church, made up of all God's people. The new people will then individually receive forgiveness within the covenant made with the church, a covenant built upon the blood of Jesus. Thus forgiveness of sin is both corporate and individual. Both are the concern of Scripture.

Chapter 2:1-2 says, In those days a decree went out from Emperor Augustus that all the world should be registered. This was the first registration and was taken while Quirinius was governor of Syria. (Palestine is a province of Syria ruled by Rome. Luke is specific, for he wants to put everything in historical context. Quirinius is the Roman governor of Syria and is responsible to Augustus. Most scholars believe the dating of the tax registration is off by a few years, but there may have been two rulers with the name Quirinius. Even so, the time and years are very close. The purpose is to show that Jesus was born under an oppressive Roman dictatorship.)

Augustus (Gaius Octavius) rules as Caesar or Emperor from 27 BC to 14 AD. He is worshiped by many throughout the Roman Empire as lord and savior, and as the one who brought peace to the world (Pax Romana). But Luke is writing to say Jesus is the real Lord and Savior who brings peace to the world, and this peace comes through the kingdom he is announcing. This is not good news to Augustus, who is not interested in hearing about a regime change. This Lord and Savior coming into the world will not be an oppressive king ruling through fear and military action like

Augustus, but one who brings peace through respect, dignity, and without war.

Verses 3-5 say, All went to their own towns to be registered. Joseph also went from the town of Nazareth in Galilee to Judea, to the city of David called Bethlehem, because he was descended from the house and family of David. (Both Joseph and Mary are descendants of David. The Old Testament is filled with prophecies that the one to come will be from David's royal line.) He went to be registered with Mary, to whom he was engaged and who was expecting a child.

An engagement usually lasts for a year, and to break it one has to make official divorce papers. The fact that she is expecting a child is not acceptable during an engagement and can result in her death by stoning. Any female who is not a virgin could be divorced and even put to death according to Old Testament law (Deut 33:13-21).

Nazareth is a small peasant village in Galilee, four miles from Sepphoris, which is the largest city in Galilee and the center of the Herodian administration during Jesus' childhood years. It is destroyed by the Romans in 4 BC because of a rebellion against the Romans. Later it is rebuilt by one of Herod's sons, Herod Antipas, who also rebuilds Tiberius, which becomes the biggest city in the area and the place of his administration.

Verses 6-7 say, While they were there, the time came for her to deliver her child. And she gave birth to her firstborn son, and wrapped him in bands of cloth, and laid him in a manger (a feed box for animals), because there was no place for him in the inn. (A firstborn son is considered a blessing, has a privileged role, and a right to the largest part of the inheritance. According to Catholic teaching, firstborn is a Semitic legal term signifying inheritance rights and does not necessarily imply subsequent births.)

On the whole Matthew tells the story somewhat differently, for

Matthew does not mention the registration for enrollment, and does not have him in Nazareth coming to Bethlehem. Matthew has the family in a house located in Bethlehem and is visited by magi, who are thought to be royalty or, at least, from the upper class. Luke has the family visited by shepherds.

Hill (2004, 88-100) and Brown (1993) point out similarities and differences of the infancy accounts. There are some major differences. Most scholars agree that the stories are not meant to be exact history but are inspired theological reflections or meditations drawn from the Hebrew Scriptures developed after the resurrection to show why Jesus was born and that he is the Messiah, the Son of God. Against charges that he is illegitimate, it is explained that his birth is from God and from a mother who is blessed and holy.

Some of the similarities of the narratives are the following. Both parents are named Mary and Joseph with Davidic descent. Both stories include an angelic annunciation, conception through the Holy Spirit, the intended naming of Jesus, and his designated role of Savior. Both stories place the birth in Bethlehem during the reign of Herod the Great, and point out that he was raised in Nazareth.

Some of the differences are the following. Matthew's genealogy differs considerably from Luke's. Matthew traces Joseph's lineage back to Abraham; Luke goes back to Adam. Matthew traces through kings from David, while Luke traces through Nathan the prophet, who was a son of David (1 Chron 3:5). Jesus will be both king and prophet. Matthew focuses more on Joseph; Luke pays more attention to Mary. Matthew has Jesus born in a house in Bethlehem, not while engaged, but after they have been married. Then after a visit from the wise men (magi), they flee to Egypt to protect the child's life, and then they settle in Nazareth. In Luke the engaged couple travel from Nazareth to Bethlehem for a census. Here Jesus is born and laid in a manger. Then after a visit from shepherds, the family goes not to Egypt but to Nazareth. The different writers highlight different details to express teachings they think are important.

On the other hand, if one looks closely at Matthew, chapter one may simply be to tell of Joseph's experience with an angel and the virgin birth without Matthew mentioning things such as he came from Nazareth and being born in a manger. He does not mention them because he is not concerned about them, and they do not fit with his purpose. Matthew's chapter two then jumps to the incident with Herod two years later because Matthew is interested in showing that Jesus like Moses survives the ruler's attempt to kill all male babies and like Moses he will come out of Egypt to bring salvation to the people. If this is correct, a number of the differences between Matthew and Luke can be eliminated. But it also eliminates the coming of the wise men as a Christmas story because it happened approximately two years after his birth.

Luke always stresses the fact that Jesus is a Jew, but not only a Jew, but a universal Savior coming into the world for all humanity. Luke stresses a strong concern for the poor and oppressed. Matthew does also, but his priority is to show that Jesus is the one foretold in the Old Testament Scriptures, and he is the fullest expression of what Moses began and God's plan.

Many scholars believe that the birth accounts are theological meditations or reflections on the birth of Jesus, and not meant to be history. That does not mean that it is all a theological myth and no history is involved. They are based on a historical happening. Many serious scholars believe that the birth stories were formulated from oral narratives after the resurrection to express the divinity of Jesus. Oral expressions in an oral society circulated for 40-50 years before they were written. The key themes remain stable but specific details are different depending upon theological emphasis as inspired by the Holy Spirit. Of course, others believe if God could create the world out of nothing, he could surely send his Son into the world through a virgin birth.

Luke, the historian, keeping with what happened at the birth of Jesus in (8-11) says, In that region there were shepherds living in the fields, keeping watch over their flock by night. Then an angel of the Lord stood before them, and the glory of the Lord shone around them, and they were terrified. But the angel said to them, "Do not be afraid; for see—I am bringing you news of great joy for all the people: to you is born this day in the city of David a Savior, who is the Messiah, the Lord."

Luke is saying that Jesus is the Messiah, the Savior, and the Lord; it is not the Roman emperor or any government and its leader, or any nation and its leader. Throughout history there have been many who have tried to make their country their savior and lord.

Verses 12-14 say, "This will be a sign for you: you will find a child wrapped in bands of cloth and lying in a manger." (Some translate it swaddling clothes, which were wrappings used by the poor.) And suddenly there was with the angel a multitude of the heavenly host, praising God and saying, "Glory to God in the highest heaven, and on earth peace among those he favors!" (From these verses comes the beginning of the *Gloria* sung in the liturgy of many churches.)

The Roman emperor is considered the world's savior who is the lord of all. He has brought peace to the known world. So Jesus being called the Savior and Lord, bringing another kind of peace, and announcing that the kingdom of God is near, will be in conflict with those in power at the time. This conflict will be over who is the real Savior and Lord of the kingdom, and what is that kingdom to look like. Luke wants to highlight this issue. Jesus announcing the kingdom of God is near will get the attention of those in power, both the Romans and the Jews, as we shall see.

Verses 15-20 say, When the angels had left them and gone

into heaven, the shepherds said to one another, "Let us now go to Bethlehem to see this thing that has taken place, which the Lord has made known to us." So they went with haste and found Mary and Joseph, and the child lying in the manger. When they saw this, they made known what had been told them about this child; and all who heard it were amazed at what the shepherds told them. But Mary treasured all these words and pondered them in her heart. The shepherds returned glorifying and praising God for all they had heard and seen, as it had been told to them. (Luke stresses this because glorifying and praising God is what all of the followers of Jesus are to do when they come to worship and hear the Scriptures read and sung.)

Verses 21-24 say, After eight days had passed, it was time to circumcise the child; and he was called Jesus, the name given by the angel before he was conceived in the womb. When the time came for their purification according to the law of Moses (Ex 13:2, 11-17, Lev 5:1-15), they brought him to Jerusalem to present him to the Lord (as it is written in the law of the Lord, "Every firstborn male shall be designated as holy to the Lord"), and they offered a sacrifice according to what is stated in the law of the Lord, "a pair of turtle doves or two young pigeons."

This offering is acceptable for those who can not afford the sacrifice of the more expensive animals that are required. Luke portrays the holy family as humble and poor, staying in a barnyard, visited by poor shepherds, and not able to offer much at the temple. The offering is part of the ceremony of redeeming the firstborn. The ceremony is about buying back or redeeming the child from God through an offering. In ancient times the firstborn son is to be set aside for God. A way is developed for the parents to redeem the son. In this way the parents state that the child belongs to God who is loaning him to this family for the time being.

Verses 25-32 say, Now there was a man in Jerusalem whose name was Simeon; the man was righteous and devout, looking forward to the consolation of Israel, and the Holy Spirit rested on him. (To those people the consolation of Israel has to do with setting Israel free from the system of foreign domination.) It had been revealed to him by the Holy Spirit that he would not see death before he had seen the Lord's Messiah. Guided by the Spirit, Simeon came into the temple; and when the parents brought in the child Jesus, to do for him what was customary under the law, Simeon took him in his arms and praised God saying, "Master, now you are dismissing your servant in peace, according to your word; for my eyes have seen your salvation, which you have prepared in the presence of all peoples, a light for revelation to the Gentiles and for glory to your people Israel."

These words of Simeon inspired by the Holy Spirit praising God and declaring his saving purpose for both the nation and individuals throughout history are often used at the close of Christian worship. They are called the Nunc Dimittis, which is Latin for its first words. Did Simeon now know the full meaning of the word salvation, even as it relates to individuals? At this time practically no one would see the full significance of salvation. It will not be fully understood until after the crucifixion and resurrection.

Verses 33-35 say, And the child's father and mother were amazed at what was being said about him. (The astonishment of Jesus' parents is difficult to reconcile with all that happened surrounding Jesus' birth. This may be a sign that some of the infancy stories were originally passed along independently of one another and were developed after the resurrection to explain the supernatural aspect of his birth.) Then Simeon blessed them and said to his mother Mary, "This child is destined for the falling and the rising of many in Israel, and to be a sign that will be opposed so that the inner thoughts of many will be revealed—and a sword will pierce your own soul too."

Verses 36-38 say, There was also a prophet, Anna the daughter of Phanuel, of the tribe of Asher. She was of a great age, having lived with her husband seven years after her marriage, then as a widow to the age of eighty-four. She never left the temple but worshiped there with fasting and prayer night and day. (The main purpose of a prophet is not to predict the future but to speak for God and proclaim his truth for the people of the time.) At that moment she came, and began to praise God and to speak about the child to all who were looking for the redemption of Jerusalem. (Notice in the minds of the people the first purpose is the redemption of Jerusalem and the nation.)

Verses 39-40 say, When they had finished everything required by the law of the Lord, they returned to Galilee, to their own town of Nazareth. The child grew and became strong, filled with wisdom; and the favor of God was upon him. (Luke does not mention a trip to Egypt. Matthew has them going to Egypt for two years, for his theology is to emphasize that Jesus is the new Moses called out of Egypt to set his people free. In Luke nothing is mentioned about Jesus childhood until he is twelve years old.)

Verses 41-47 say, Now every year his parents went to Jerusalem for the festival of the Passover. And when he was twelve years old, they went up as usual for the festival. When the festival was ended and they started to return, the boy Jesus stayed behind in Jerusalem, but his parents did not know it. Assuming that he was in the group of travelers, they went a day's journey. Then they started to look for him among their relatives and friends. When they did not find him, they returned to Jerusalem to search for him. After three days they found him in the temple, sitting among the teachers, listening to them and asking them questions. And all who heard him were amazed at his understanding and his answers.

Verses 48-50 say, When his parents saw him, they were astonished; and his mother said to him, "Child, why have you treated us like this? Look your father and I have been searching for you in great anxiety." He said to them, "Why were you searching for me? Did you not know that I must be in my Father's house?" But they did not understand what he said to them.

The purpose of the narrative is to show he is God's Son. Again, it is surprising that they do not understand, which indicates the possibility of a later development of the infancy stories that were added into the gospel. Verses 51-52 say, Then he went down with them and came to Nazareth and was obedient to them. His mother treasured all these things in her heart. And Jesus increased in wisdom and in years, and in divine and human favor. (We must remember his humanity, and the fact that he has to mature.)

In chapter 3:1-2 Luke again historically situates his context by saying, In the fifteenth year of the reign of Emperor Tiberius (26-27AD), when Pontius Pilate was governor of Judea, and Herod (Antipas) was ruler of Galilee, and his brother Philip ruler of the region of Ituraea and Trachonitis, and Lysanius ruler of Abiline, during the high priesthood of Annas and Caiaphas, the word of God came to John son of Zechariah in the wilderness.

When Herod the Great dies his territory is split among his sons. Pilate is sent as a military commander of Judea to take the place of Archelaus who is so corrupt and brutal that Rome removes him. The powers of the region are the Roman emperor represented by Pilate, the Herod family, and the Jewish high priest with the Sanhedrin, the ruling body of the Jews. The Jewish tradition is that the high priest will come from Moses' brother Aaron, but the system is corrupted when the Romans appoint who they desire.

In verses 3-6 John says, He went into all the region around the Jordan, proclaiming a baptism of repentance for the forgiveness of sins, as it is written in the book of the words of the prophet Isaiah, "The voice of one crying out in the wilderness: 'Prepare the way of the Lord, make his paths straight. Every valley shall be filled, and every mountain and hill shall be made low, and the crooked shall be made straight, and the rough ways made smooth; and all flesh shall see the salvation of God.' "

This is an Old Testament metaphor for being set free from exile and preparing the way for the coming of the Messiah. According to Borg and Wright (1999, 32-33) as long as Israel is dominated by another country and in bondage to oppressive political, economic, and religious structures, they are still in exile. The promise of forgiveness spoken of by prophets like Isaiah, Jeremiah, and Ezekiel had not yet been fulfilled. That was the situation through to the time of Jesus. For a thorough discussion on Jewish thinking on the meaning of exile at the time of the second temple, see Wright (1999, 268-279).

Preparing for the coming of Christ always involves preparing to have one's sins forgiven by repentance, which is being sorry for past sins and being ready to change one's ways. The call for repentance is for the nation and individuals in relation to the covenant. The first call of the Old Testament prophets was for the nation to repent of its unjust actions toward those in their own nation. Israel went into exile twice because of their worship of idols, their unjust political, economic, and social actions toward their own people, and not listening to the prophets about making war. They had been warned to make God's agenda their own agenda, but they refused (see any of the prophets, especially Amos, Isaiah, and Jeremiah).

Second, the Old Testament people of God as individuals are called to repent in relation to the covenant God made with the nation. The only change in the new covenant is that individuals are called to repent in relation to the covenant God made with the church. Covenant is always first a corporate agreement to which individuals are called to participate. In Scripture everything, including individuals, is always related to the whole.

This idea of corporate repentance involving the call to the nation to repent is contrary to the thinking of many Americans. This is because they are living in a nation that focuses on individualism and most are not familiar with the prophets, or the concept of how covenant works. Another problem is sitting under teachers that do not use the prophets as the Scriptures use them. Instead many use the prophets mainly in an attempt to make them predict everything that will take place at the end of time. This is not the function or purpose of the prophets. In Scripture the prophets always call both individuals and the nation to change their ways. One never exists without the other.

In verses 7-9 John said to the crowds that came out to be baptized by him, "You brood of vipers! Who warned you to flee from the wrath to come? Bear fruits worthy of repentance. Do not begin to say to yourselves, 'We have Abraham as out ancestor'; for I tell you, God is able from these stones to raise up children from Abraham. Even now the ax is lying at the root of the trees; every tree therefore that does not bear good fruit is cut down and thrown into the fire."

John is working in the transition stage and is calling individuals to repent, for a new group is being prepared to be the new Israel of God. John is telling them that if they think they are safe from the wrath to come because they can trace their descent to Abraham, they are badly mistaken. The fact that they belong to the nation of Israel is not good enough, for it is sin filled and needs to repent also. They need to change their actions, or they will be thrown into the fire of hell. Moderns do not like this language, but it is the language of Scripture indicating an adverse end for those refusing to repent and adapt to the ways proclaimed by Jesus.

Verses 10-14 say, And the crowds asked him, "What then should we do?" In reply he said to them, "Whoever has two coats must share with anyone who has none; and whoever has food must do likewise." (The answer is share with those in need, especially food and clothing.) Even tax collectors came to be baptized, and they asked him, "Teacher, what should we do?" He said to them, "Collect no more than the amount prescribed for you." (In other words do not take advantage of the people by using your authority and power.) Soldiers also asked him, "And what should we do?" He said to them, "Do not extort money from anyone by threats or false accusations, and be satisfied with your wages."

Because soldiers are not paid much, they use fear tactics and their power to shake down people to get money and favors from them. They are to end those actions and be satisfied with what they have. He does not tell them to get out of the army, for law and order are important. Latourette (1975, 242-244) says in the first three hundred years of Christianity very few soldiers are found to be part of the worshiping community and often are refused admission into the church. But John simply tells them not to use their power and authority in a way that does wrong to people. Police action to protect people from wrong doing is never spoken against.

Verses 15-17 say, As the people were filled with expectation, and all were questioning in their hearts concerning John, whether he might be the Messiah, John answered all of them saying, "I baptize you with water; but one who is more powerful than I is coming; I am not worthy to untie the thong of his sandals. He will baptize you with the Holy Spirit and fire. His winnowing fork is in his hand, to clear his threshing floor and to gather the wheat into his granary; but the chaff he will burn with the unquenchable fire." (John's water baptism is only a preparation, but the baptism of Jesus will include the Spirit that takes away sin, see Acts 2:38, Rom 8:9-11, Titus 3:5, 1 Peter 3:18-20). The baptism with fire is not explained, but it is often a symbol of judgment and even cleansing (Mt 7:19, 13:40-42, Heb 6:7-8).

Verses 18-20 say, So with many other exhortations, he (John) proclaimed the good news to the people. But Herod (Antipas) the ruler, who had been rebuked by him because of Herodias, his brother's wife, and because of all the evil things Herod had done, added to them all by shutting up John in prison. (This is explained in detail in Mark 6:14-29.)

Verses 21-22 say, Now when all the people were baptized, and when Jesus also had been baptized and was praying, the heaven was opened, and the Holy Spirit descended upon him in bodily form like a dove. (It does not say a dove came upon him, but it was like a dove.) And a voice came from heaven, "You are my Son, the Beloved; with you I am well pleased." (This is from Psalm 2:7. You are my son; today I have begotten you. And Isa 42:1 says, Here is my servant, whom I uphold, my chosen, in whom my soul delights; I have put my spirit upon him; he will bring forth justice to the nations (see comments in Mk 3:9-10 and Mt 3:17).

In verses 23-38 a genealogy of Jesus through Joseph is given that is somewhat different from the one through Joseph that Matthew gives. Some think since Luke emphasizes women it is the genealogy of Mary, and Heli may have been Joseph's father-in-law. Others think while Matthew traces through David, Luke traces through the prophet Nathan, the son of David (1 Chron 3:5) to show that Jesus is both king and prophet. The real importance of the genealogy is that Luke's purpose is to trace Jesus back to Adam the father of all humans because he is primarily writing to Gentiles. Matthew's purpose is to trace Jesus back to Abraham the father of the Jews because he is primarily writing to a Jewish population. Both include David, for it is important to show that Jesus is from David.

∽๏๛

After the baptism of Jesus, chapter 4:1-2 says, Jesus, full of the Holy Spirit, returned from the Jordan and was led by the Spirit in the wilderness, where for forty days he was tempted by the devil. He ate nothing at all during those days, and when they were over, he was famished. (Luke emphasizes the work of the Holy Spirit.)

As soon as a commitment is made the devil goes to work. The Spirit will lead Jesus and be his help. The wilderness is a dangerous place inhabited by wild beasts, bandits, and according to the people of the time many demons. With Moses Israel spent forty years of testing in the wilderness and failed, but Jesus will be successful, and he will overcome the devil's temptations.

From the time of the second temple (the time of Nehemiah and Ezra) to the time of Jesus, covering at least four hundred years, the hope was that when Yahweh (God) becomes king, Israel will be set free from exile, foreign domination will be ended, evil will be defeated, God himself will return to Zion, and the temple will be rebuilt. Up to the time of Jesus none of this has happened, and now Rome dominates the land. How this becomes fulfilled will be in a manner different from what is expected.

Jesus will liberate the people from bondage to Rome in a way different from what is thought. He liberates them from evil, but the liberation is from the evil (sin) that is behind Rome but not deliverance from the nation of Rome. God returns in the person of Jesus. Jesus becomes the new Torah. The temple is rebuilt in Jesus as he becomes the new temple where forgiveness of sin takes place and the new spiritual house, the new Israel, is built (see 1 Peter 2:4-

8). This return of God in the form of Jesus, the Messiah, the Son of God who does not conquer the Romans and rid them from the land is different from expectation. But the way Jesus fulfills God's plan defines the end of Israel's exile; the old is fulfilled and the new begins.

At the close of the forty days, verses 3-4 say, The devil said to him, "If you are the Son of God, command this stone to become a loaf of bread." Jesus answered, "It is written, 'One does not live by bread alone.' "

The devil recognizes him as the Son of God and tempts him to use his power for his own benefit and prove to people that he can give them the material things they need and want. Do miracles to give them what they want, and then they will follow you is the devil's temptation. Base your ministry on what satisfies their wants. Jesus knows this does not work, for when what they want is satisfied, they will want more, and if they do not get it, they will go away, or demand more. Their discipleship becomes based upon the wrong reason. Jesus answers Satan by quoting Scripture from Deut 8:3.

Verses 5-8 say, Then the devil led him up and showed him in an instant all the kingdoms of the world. And the devil said to him, "To you I will give their glory and all this authority; for it has been given over to me, and I give it to anyone I please. If you then will worship me, it will be yours." Jesus answered him, "It is written, 'Worship the Lord your God, and serve only him.' " (This is from Deut 6:13.)

The world's glory is wealth, fame, and position, and the world's power is authority to lord it over everyone. Because the masses of people fall into the devil's temptation and make those things their way of life rather than the things of God, the devil has authority over the things of the world and can give it to Jesus. Satan wants Jesus to work with him in a partnership, and the condition is that Jesus serves Satan. The devil wants Jesus to use his calling as prophet, priest, and king for his evil purposes and the glories of the world. But Jesus will not give his allegiance to the ways of the world and the devil. He will serve the Father only. Matthew states, one can not serve both God and mammon (wealth, 6:24).

In verses 9-11, Then the devil took him to Jerusalem, and placed him on the pinnacle of the temple, saying to him, "If you are the Son of God, throw yourself down from here, for it is written, 'He will command his angels concerning you, to protect you,' and 'On their hands they will bear you up, so that you will not dash your foot against the stone.' " Verses 12-13 say, Then Jesus answered him, "It is said, 'Do not put the Lord your God to the test.' " When the devil had finished every test, he departed from him until an opportune time.

The devil is never finished. Luke writes this to illustrate that the temptations of Jesus are the same for his people and their churches. Note that even the devil quotes Scripture quoting Ps 91:11-12 and Deut 6:16. The devil is saying give the people sensations, make them feel good, keep them excited, give then what they want, and then the crowds will follow you. It is the old idea of giving the people bread and circuses. Satan is saying that the masses of people do not really understand the deeper issues, and are not really interested so take advantage of them and get them to follow you by appealing only to their senses. Do not bother giving them anything deep or profound to think and act upon. They will not take the time to grasp them, and are not interested.

Verses 14-19 say, Then Jesus, filled with the power of the Holy Spirit, returned to Galilee, and a report about him spread through all the surrounding country. He began to teach in their synagogues and was praised by everyone. When he came to Nazareth, where he had been brought up, he went to the synagogue on the sabbath day, as was his custom. He stood up to read, and the scroll of the prophet Isaiah was given to him. He unrolled the scroll and found the place where it was written: "The Spirit of the Lord is upon me, because he has anointed me to bring good news to the poor. He has sent me to proclaim release to the captives and recovery of sight to the blind, to let the oppressed go free, to proclaim the year of the Lord's favor."

Good news to the poor, release to captives, sight for the blind, and setting the oppressed free. These quotes from Isaiah 61:1-3 and 58:6-14 represent social justice issues. This teaching becomes one of the main reasons the governing leaders of Israel and Rome, those of wealth and power, will have Jesus put to death. He will challenge their oppression of the people by the content of his teaching to the apostles, to the common people, and when the authorities come to question him. He usually does not confront directly the authorities, but they realize as he gathers more and more followers their position and practices will be in jeopardy.

There is no way people today can say social justice issues are personal opinion and individual matters of only leftists and liberals. They are the plain teachings of Jesus and the prophets and are found on practically every page of Scripture. Those who disagree have not read the prophets or Jesus, or else they are in denial of what they teach and choose to ignore them. Keep in mind, at this time, the Scriptures for these people are found in the Old Testament. In the end Jesus is put to death for teaching about a kingdom that was coming whose values were totally different from the thinking and actions of the leadership of Israel, especially that of the Sanhedrin.

The Sanhedrin is the theocratic system of governing Israel making the political, economic, social, and religious decisions for the nation. Their oppressive temple system is the center of wealth and power in Israel and the leadership. The system has become politically oppressive and economically exploitive, and all of it done in the name of God, just as their ancestors before them had governed.

Jesus will be put to death because he stands against their system of advocating an alternative vision, one that is not grounded in the kingdom of God. Even though Jesus opposes any violent revolutionary activity, his kingdom threatens their worldly kingdom, so they have to figure out a way to eliminate him. Anyone who reads the four Gospels and the Prophets knows God is concerned about the whole person and anything that eliminates their dignity. He is Lord of all, even governments and their systems.

Gnosticism is not a characteristic of the Bible. Avoiding or escaping from the world because anything physical or material is evil is not a teaching in the Bible. There is no neat separation of the so-called spiritual issues from the real issues of life that have meaning to humankind. It is not really possible for Christianity to ignore these things because they are not "spiritual" issues. That was not the approach of Christ. Those who believe such are succumbing to the thinking of the Enlightenment Age, which was an age where anti-religion leaders wanted to eliminate any religious thinking from the world's issues, so they could do what they wanted in politics, economics, and social issues.

When the religion of Christ becomes a pie in the sky religion concerned only with individual salvation, it distorts Christianity and ignores the kingdom Jesus came to preach. Even so, it is important to note that there is no complete political, economic, or social system, or any system of individual, or social ethics in Scripture. But these issues are not avoided and are a concern throughout Scripture. And although no complete system is given, a way to think about these issues is given to the serious reader of both the Old Testament and the New Testament.

The reader must always keep in mind that the kingdom of God

is to be very different from the kingdoms of this world that have become permeated with greed and self concern. Because of this, many in Israel will oppose him just as is done in our world today. The prayer of Jesus that says, "Your kingdom come. Your will be done on earth as well as heaven," must not be forgotten. Governments as well as individuals are created by God and responsible to him.

After quoting Isaiah he tells the people Isaiah was referring to him. Verses 20-21 say, he rolled up the scroll, gave it back to the attendant, and sat down. The eyes of all in the synagogue were fixed on him. Then he began to say to them, "Today this scripture has been fulfilled in your hearing." (Some appreciate what he says, but many do not, and they insinuate since he grew up in the area, how could he be the one Isaiah was referring to? Jesus in (24) answered, "Truly I tell you, no prophet is accepted in the prophet's hometown." (The problem is usually too much familiarity. The expert is most often the one who is from out of town.)

Since Jesus is a prophet in the Old Testament tradition, he reminds them that the great prophets Elijah and Elisha were also rejected by their people. He reminds them instead they went to the Gentiles. Verses 28-30 say, When they heard this, all in the synagogue were filled with rage. They got up, drove him out of town, and led him to the brow of the hill on which their town was built, so that they might hurl him off the cliff. But he passed through the midst of them and went on his way.

It is not much different today. When people, including religious people, do not like the Scriptures used to oppose their ideologies and actions, they attempt to slander or get rid of the messenger, sometimes even using violence. Miraculously, Jesus is able to get away from their attempted violence.

Verses 31-32 say, He went down to Capernaum, a city in Galilee, and was teaching them on the sabbath. They were astounded at his teaching, because he spoke with authority. (Jesus made reasonable sense and spoke as though God is speaking through him. As we see in Matthew's Sermon on the Mount he reinterprets many of their teachings and even eliminates some of their Scriptures such as their purity laws, dietary food laws, and worship laws.)

Verses 33-37 say, In the synagogue there was a man who had the spirit of an unclean demon, and he cried out with a loud voice, "Let us alone! What have you to do with us, Jesus of Nazareth? Have you come to destroy us? I know who you are, the Holy One of God." But Jesus rebuked him saying, "Be silent, and come out of him!" When the demon (representing evil) had thrown him down before him, he came out of him without having done him any harm. They were all amazed and kept saying to one another, "What kind of utterance is this? For with authority and power he commands the unclean spirits, and they come!" And a report about him began to reach every place in the region. (The demons recognize him, but his own people, and their religious leaders do not.)

In verses 38-39 Jesus heals Peter's mother-in-law, and she immediately gets up and serves them. (Some people are surprised that Peter is married, but the current Roman Catholic position of not permitting priests to marry is simply a church discipline or practice that can change. Even today there are a few Roman Catholic priests who are married. They are former Protestant clergy who converted to the Catholic Church.)

Verses 40-43 say, As the sun was setting, all those who had any who were sick with various kinds of diseases brought them to him; and he laid his hands on each of them and cured them. Demons also came out of many, shouting, "You are the Son of God." But he rebuked them and would not allow them to speak, because they knew he was the Messiah.

Jesus has control over the demons. Jesus does not allow them to speak because he does not want their witness. First, demons have no credibility. Second, at this point, he does not want to be labeled as the Son of God or Messiah, for this will cause more concern to the current governing authorities than he wants to deal with right now. He needs more time to prepare his disciples. He knows the governing authorities will eventually want him dead, for his kingdom presents a way totally opposite from their kingdom.

The way any world system works is with power always comes money and perks that bring more money and power. It happens because those with power create ways and laws that make it happen. Those with power and money have the power to make decisions to benefit themselves and their benefactors at the expense of others. That brings oppression as well as even more money and power. To see the system in action today, one does not have to watch other nations just watch the working of Congress and state legislatures. The wealthy continue to greatly benefit while the middle class and the poor, who have no legislators or special interest group representing them, suffer even though they may get another can of spam to pacify them. It becomes obvious why those in power fear the nature of the kingdom of God that Jesus represents. It is no different today.

Verses 42-44 say, At daybreak he departed and went into a deserted place. And the crowds were looking for him; and when they reached him, they wanted to prevent him from leaving them. But he said to them, "I must proclaim the good news of the kingdom of God to the other cities also; for I was sent for this purpose." So he continued proclaiming the message in the synagogues of Judea.

It is important to note here a purpose for which Jesus is sent: to declare the kingdom of God. He is declaring the virtues, values, and vision of God. The kingdom is being made present in the actions and teachings of Jesus. He is called to renew and reconcile all things, meaning individuals, nations, their system of government, all their institutions, and all God's creation, visible and invisible. This is basically what he is saying in verses 16-20.

Colossians 1:15-20 says, He is the image of the invisible God, the firstborn of all creation; (meaning he has the inheritance rights) for in him all things in heaven and earth were created, things visible and invisible, whether thrones or dominions or rulers or powers—all things have been created through him and for him. He himself is before all things, and in him all things hold together . . . and through him God was pleased to reconcile to himself all things, whether on earth or in heaven by making peace through the blood of the cross.

Luke 20:41-43, Acts 2:35, 7:49, Heb 1:13, 10:14 all quote Ps 110:1 where the Father tells the Lord, the Messiah, to come beside him while he makes all his enemies, all that oppose him, his footstool, meaning until all is in subjection to him. The writer of 1 Corinthians 15:24-25 adds in the end when Christ comes in judgment, he will hand the kingdom over to God the Father, after he has destroyed every ruler and every authority and power. For he must reign until he has put all his enemies under his feet.

Everything in creation must be renewed, conformed, and remodeled to Christ or be destroyed. This is what the kingdom now breaking into the earth is about, and this is the mission given to all his followers. Followers of Jesus either believe that, and adjust their thinking and actions about life's issues and serve the purposes of God, or by their thinking and actions oppose the teaching of Scripture and continue to serve their own interests. All things are reconciled to God by the blood of the cross not just individuals. The kingdom is not about individual ethics only but also about social ethics; God is Lord of all things. As in the Old Testament the message is also for nations and institutions.

If the teachings of Jesus were not intended to have any effect upon the world and its institutions, the Jewish and Roman leaders would have ignored him. The values he taught were in conflict with the virtues and values of the ruling elites of both Israel and Rome. Jesus' challenge of the new kingdom of God will get him put to death.

Chapter 5:1-7 says, Once while Jesus was standing beside the lake of Gennesaret (Sea of Galilee), and the crowd was pressing in on him to hear the word of God, he saw two boats there at the shore of the lake; the fishermen had gone out of them and were washing their nets. One boat was Simon's, and he asked him to pull out a little way from the shore, and there he taught the crowds from the boat. When he had finished speaking, he said to Simon, "Put out into the deep water and let down your nets for a catch." Simon answered, "Master, we have worked all night long but have caught nothing. Yet if you say so, I will let down the nets." When they had done this, they caught so many fish that their nets were beginning to break. So they signaled their partners in the other boat to come and help them. And they came and filled both boats, so that they began to sink (see Jn 21:4-8).

Verses 8-11 say, when Simon Peter saw it, he fell down at Jesus' knee saying, "Go away from me, Lord, for I am a sinful man!" For he and all who were with him were amazed at the catch of fish that they had taken; and so also were James and John, sons of Zebedee, who were partners with Simon. (They are beginning to become aware of the fact that there is really something different about Jesus.) Then Jesus said to Simon, (Peter) "Do not be afraid; from now on you will be catching people." When they had brought their boats to shore, they left everything and followed him.

Notice that Jesus is concerned with the every day life of his people and is moved to help them. Out of gratitude Peter recognizes the holiness of Jesus and responds by worshiping him. In the process he recognizes he needs Jesus in all areas of his life. He recognizes one of the primary reasons for which Jesus came unto this earth. Jesus, like many of the world's great religious leaders, is followed by so many because he is concerned with the whole person and their needs. When Christ's church ignores the needs of the common people it does so at its own peril.

Even so, Christianity is different from all the world's religions in two major ways: Christianity centers on the cross (the forgiveness of sins) and the resurrection. Its leader rose from the dead to continue forgiving and preparing a place for those he has forgiven. No other leader in any of the world's religions makes the claim Christ made. Not one of them came to forgive sin, and not one of them claimed to rise from the dead. Christianity does not make any claim that it is more moral than any of the other religions, but it does make the claim that it is different from all other religions with the cross and resurrection.

Verses 12-16 say, Once when he was in one of the cities, there was a man covered with leprosy. When he saw Jesus, he bowed with his face to the ground and begged him, "Lord, if you choose, you can make me clean." Then Jesus stretched out his hand, touched him, and said, "I do choose. Be made clean." Immediately the leprosy left him. And he ordered him to tell no one. "Go," he said, "and show yourself to the priest, and, as Moses commanded, make an offering for your cleansing, for a testimony to them." But now more than ever the word about Jesus spread abroad; many crowds would gather to hear him and to be cured of their diseases. But he would withdraw to deserted places and pray.

Jesus is a Jew, so he works within the Old Testament (covenant) system that is his heritage. A leper is not permitted among people, so he has to be pronounced clean by a priest before he can be admitted back into normal society. Now more than ever the word spreads about Jesus as Jesus heals the people, and then sets himself apart in prayer.

In verses 17-26 while he was teaching, the crowds were so great that some men carrying a paralyzed man on a bed went up on the roof and let the man down to Jesus through the tiles of the roof. (Mark 2:1-12 says that they removed the roof having dug through it.) Verse 20 says, When he saw their faith, he said, "Friend, your sins are forgiven you." Then the scribes and the Pharisees in (21) began to question, "Who is this that is speaking blasphemies? Who can forgive sins but God alone?" (That is the point Jesus is making, but they are not going to accept him as God or Messiah and will declare him an imposter. In their system forgiveness of sins is only in the temple through their system of animal sacrifices with the priests, and Jesus is ignoring this.)

When Jesus perceived their questionings in (22-24) he answered them, "Why do you raise such questionings in your heart? Which is easier to say, 'Your sins are forgiven you,' or to say, 'Stand up and walk'? But so that you may know that the Son of Man has authority on earth to forgive sins"—he said to the one who was paralyzed—"I say to you, stand up and take your bed and go your home." Verses 25-26 say, Immediately he stood up before them, took what he had been lying on, and went to his home, glorifying God. Amazement seized all of them, and they glorified God and were filled with awe, saying, "We have seen strange things today."

Jesus uses this healing to point out that he heals both physically and spiritually and to point out that he has the authority to do what only God can do, forgive sin. He is showing them that he is the fulfillment of the prophets. The prophets had said that at the end of the exile and the beginning of the new age, God himself will return and feed the people with justice (see Ezek 34:15-16) and sins will be forgiven (Isa 53).

Verses 27-28 say, After this he went out and saw a tax collector named Levi, sitting at the tax booth; and he said to him, "Follow me." And he got up, left everything, and followed him. (Many of the tax collectors are notoriously dishonest and hated by the people. The salary they make is based on how much they can add on to what they have to pay the governing authorities, who are the Romans and the Herods. Some of these tax collectors take huge advantage of the common people and become very wealthy. Is there anything new in the world?)

Verses 29-32 say, Then Levi gave a great banquet for him in his house; and there was a large crowd of tax collectors and others sitting at the table with them. The Pharisees and their scribes were complaining to his disciples, saying "Why do you eat and drink with tax collectors and sinners?" Jesus answered, "Those who are well have no need of a physician, but those who are sick; I have come to call not the righteous but sinners to repentance."

The laws of the Pharisees basically say, if you are not in agreement with someone in your practices of religion, especially with their ritual laws of table fellowship including their ceremonial cleansings and food laws, you are not to eat with that person, because it makes you unclean or unholy and unfit for worship. According to the Pharisees, eating with a Gentile is unthinkable. Jesus pays no attention to their man-made laws, and it upsets them. He sees them becoming self-righteous and thinking they are without sin. Those who follow their laws to the letter call those who do not follow their rituals, sinners. In the process this keeps them from taking God's light to the world, which God had previously commanded. These dietary laws are part of the so-called works of righteousness that Jesus opposed.

Many of the common people are disgusted with what religion is becoming, and are looking for a return to the real meaning of religion. Jesus knows there is no possibility of the self-righteous coming to him for forgiveness of sin because they do not recognize their need. So he calls to follow him those who the Pharisees call sinners. They are the people who see their own sins as well as the sins of the nation and know that forgiveness and healing is necessary.

Verses 33-35 say, then they said to him, "John's disciples, like the disciples of the Pharisees, frequently fast and pray, but your disciples eat and drink." Jesus said to them, "You can not make wedding guests fast while the bridegroom is with them, can you? The days will come when the bridegroom will be taken away from them, and then they will fast in those days."

Jesus is using Zech 8:19. His point is while Jesus is with them it is time to celebrate. There will be much time later to fast. The heart of the new teaching is to celebrate the presence of Jesus. Later the early Christians will fast and pray. It is important to note that Jesus describes his follower's relationship to him as a marriage, for he is the bridegroom.

Verses 36-39 say, He also told them a parable: "No one tears a piece from a new garment and sews it on an old garment; otherwise the new will be torn, and the piece from the new will not match the old. And no one puts new wine into old wineskins; otherwise the new wine (when it ferments) will burst the skins and will be spilled, and the skins will be destroyed. But new wine must be put into fresh wineskins. And no one after drinking old wine desires new wine, but says, 'The old is good.' "

The new teachings of Jesus are bursting the seams of the religious leaders' interpretations and teachings of the old law. Many of the Pharisees in particular are too rigid to accept Jesus who can not be contained in their biblical interpretations and their tradition of man-made rules. Their pious conservatism has made them inflexible and keeps them from accepting new teachings. Is this also a lesson for some of today's religious people?

❧❦❧

Chapter 6:1-2 says, One sabbath while Jesus was going through the grain fields, his disciples plucked some heads of grain, rubbed them in their hands, and ate them. But some of the Pharisees said, "Why are you doing what is not lawful on the sabbath?"

In Jewish legal tradition there are thirty-two categories of activities forbidden on the Sabbath. The disciples are not stealing, for the law told farmers to leave the edges of their fields so travelers and the poor could eat. The problem according to the Pharisees is that they are rubbing the grain in their hands. They call this harvesting; thus the Pharisees say they are working on the Sabbath, a violation of the law. Actually it is not a violation of God's law but a violation of their man-made tradition of laws. The Pharisees think the laws of their religious system have all the answers to anything that surfaces. This is the same thinking of many fundamentalists today. The Pharisees can not accept Jesus because he is too liberal in his use of the law; he is not fitting into their system. Does the reader think that there are Christians today who attempt to make Jesus fit into their small boxes?

Verses 3-5 say, Jesus answered, (1 Sam 21: 4-6) "Have you not read what David did when he and his companions were hungry? He entered the house of God and took and ate the bread of the Presence, which it is not lawful for any but the priests to eat, and gave some to his companions?" Then he said to them, "The Son of Man is lord of the sabbath."

Jesus reminds them that need takes precedence over their man-made religious laws, and if David interpreted the law in such manner, how much more can the Son of Man. Jesus refers to himself not only as Lord of the Sabbath but the Son of Man who is Lord of the Sabbath. The people would immediately recognize that Jesus is referring to himself as the son of man (not capitalized in the Old Testament) from the book of Daniel that said one like a human being would establish an eternal kingdom (see Dan 7:12-14). The *Aramaic* translation for one like a human being is son of man.

Verses 6-9 say, On another sabbath he entered the synagogue and taught, and there was a man whose right hand was withered. The scribes and the Pharisees watched him to see whether he would cure on the sabbath, so that they might find an accusation against him. Even though he knew what they were thinking, he said to the man who had a withered hand, "Come and stand here." He got up and stood there. Then Jesus said to them, "I ask you, is it lawful to do good or to do harm on the sabbath, to save life or destroy it?"

Verses 10-11 say, After looking around at all of them, he said to him, "Stretch out your hand." He did so, and his hand was restored. But they were filled with fury and discussed with one another what they might do with Jesus. (They see Jesus as being disloyal to the nation and its tradition. Getting rid of Jesus and preserving the nation's religious and social tradition are more important to them than helping people in need. Does the reader see any of that in today's world?)

Verses 12-16 say, Now during those days he went out to the mountain to pray; and he spent the night in prayer to God. (Before Jesus does anything, he prays.) And when day came, he called his disciples and chose twelve of them, whom he also named apostles: Simon, whom he named Peter, and his brother Andrew, and James, and John, and Philip, and Bartholomew, and Matthew, and Thomas, and James son of Alphaeus, and Simon, who was called the Zealot, and Judas, son of James, and Judas Iscariot, who became a traitor.

Apostle, meaning sent out, is not always limited to twelve, (see Rom 16:7, Acts 14:14) but preserving the concept of the basic twelve is important, for the twelve apostles are going to take the place of the twelve tribes of Israel. Some of the names are different from Matthew's list. A traditional answer is that some of them are known by two names, possibly a Jewish name and a Gentile translation. Simon is also called Peter and Cephas. Matthew is called Levi. Bartholomew is thought to be the same as Nathaniel. Judas the son of James is also called Thaddaeus.

Verses 17-19 say, He came down with them and stood on a level place, with a great crowd of his disciples and a great multitude of people from all Judea, Jerusalem, and the coast of Tyre and Sidon. They had come to hear him and be healed of their diseases; and those who were troubled with unclean spirits were healed. And all in the crowd were trying to touch him, for power came out from him and healed all of them.

Verses 20-23 say, "Blessed are you who are poor, for yours is the kingdom of God. Blessed are you who are hungry now, for you will be filled. Blessed are you who weep now, for you will laugh. Blessed are you when people hate you, and when they exclude you, revile you, and defame you, on account of the Son of Man. Rejoice in that day and leap for joy, for surely your reward is great in heaven; for that is what their ancestors did to the prophets." (Harassment even comes from those who call themselves believers but who have become immersed in the ways of the world. The same happened to the prophets in the time of the Old Testament, and Jesus is basically going to be put to death by his fellow Jews.)

Luke puts a different twist on the Beatitudes which is the name for the beginning of Jesus' Sermon on the Mount. Luke has his words being made on a plain, or flat place, and he puts many of them in economic terms. There is consolation to the poor who trust

God, but a warning to the wealthy that trust man, themselves, and their material goods. Luke is saying there is going to be a great reversal and relates the words to Mary's Magnificat (see 1:46-56).

As one reads the Old Testament it is plain that the prophets are killed by the wealthy and powerful leaders in Israel and Judah's theocracy because the prophets challenge their religious, political, economic, and social decision making. Jesus is saying it is not going to be any different now. He is also saying they are going to be blessed, even though many are going to be put to death. When people today stay unaware of the prophetic tradition of the Old Testament, they tend to misinterpret and even distort the meaning of the life and death of Jesus and why many were martyred for his cause. The Old Testament was the Bible of Jesus and the Jews of his time.

Verses 24-26 continue, "But woe to you who are rich, for you have received your consolation. Woe to you who are full now, for you will be hungry. Woe to you who are laughing now, for you will mourn and weep. Woe to you when all speak well of you, for that is what their ancestors did to the false prophets."

The false prophets tell the comfortable what they want to hear, and the people of comfort encourage, reward and speak well of those false prophets. Jesus is saying it is no different now. Jesus is saying as in those days it is now the same, for too many people of comfort concern themselves only with preserving the status quo which preserves their own interests. In the name of religion they politically and economically exploit the masses to benefit themselves, and in the process attempt to destroy those who oppose them. Does the reader believe it is different in our time?

Then in verses 27-31 Jesus says, "But I say to you that listen, Love your enemies, do good to those who hate you, bless those who curse you, pray for those who abuse you. If anyone strikes you on the cheek, offer another also, and from anyone who takes away your coat do not withhold even your shirt. Give to anyone who begs from you; and if anyone takes away your goods, do not ask for them again. Do to others as you would have them do to you."

These are not commands to be followed legalistically as timeless laws but by the spirit in which they were intended in the situation of those times. When Jesus teaches, his concern is primarily about developing a character that pleases God; it is about, virtues, values, the development of attitudes, dispositions, proper motivations and intentions. The message is do not act like the people who are selfish, greedy, abuse power, and take advantage of you. Follow the teachings of Jesus who said to lose self for the well being of others, use any power and wealth you have for the common good, and then do to others as you would have them do to you, if you were in their situation. It is about being at peace with God and others of God's creation. He is saying that doing the opposite is not the approach of the kingdom.

Numerous scholars like NT Wright, Marcus Borg, and George Caird are convinced that the primary purpose of these teachings is not only to teach the virtues, values, and vision of the new kingdom but to inform the resistance party that they need to exchange their agenda of violence against the Romans for the agenda of Jesus or they, the city, and the temple will be destroyed. Therefore verses 27-31 are ways they need to begin to act toward the Romans because if they continue their path of resistance and violence they will be doomed. Of course, we know the resistance party (Zealots) and many Pharisees and those who sympathize with them will ignore Jesus' teachings, and Rome will do exactly what Jesus said they would do.

In verses 32-34 Jesus says, "If you love those who love you, what credit is that to you? For even sinners love those who love them.

If you do good to those who do good to you, what credit is that to you? For even sinners do the same. If you lend to those from whom you hope to receive much again, what credit is that to you? Even sinners lend to sinners, to receive as much gain." Verses 35-36 continue saying, "But love your enemies, do good, and lend, expecting nothing in return. Your reward will be great, and you will be children of the Most High; for he is kind to the ungrateful and the wicked. Be merciful just as your Father is merciful."

Jesus is asking his followers what they are doing that is different from those who are in love with the ways of the world. That is also a good question for his followers even today. Jesus is not asking people to feel love, for sometimes it is difficult to change feelings. But he is calling his people to act differently from the people of the world. Many times humans can not feel love, but they can always act in the ways of love.

People can always make a decision to be kind, do good, do what is best for people, be helpful, be merciful, be compassionate, not seek to get even, be patient, be humble, be gentle, and not be rude, arrogant, irritable, resentful, selfish, and insisting on one's own way (1 Cor 13:4-7). If we would all do to others as we would have them do to us, the world would change and become more like the kingdom of God. Doing this even when one does not feel like it is not being a hypocrite, for it is doing what Jesus calls his people to do. In the process, sometimes feelings will change.

Verses 37-38 say, "Do not judge, and you will not be judged; do not condemn, and you will not be condemned. Forgive and you will be forgiven; give and it will be given to you . . . for the measure you give will be the measure you get back." (These are just to expand on the idea to do unto others as you would have them do unto you. Do not judge or condemn in ways you would not want to be judged or condemned by others. See this writer's commentary on judging in Matthew 7.)

He continues in verses 39-42, "Can a blind person guide a blind person? Will not both fall into a pit? A disciple is not above the teacher, but everyone who is fully qualified will be like the teacher. Why do you see the speck in your neighbor's eye but do not notice the log in your own eye? Or how can you say to your neighbor, 'Friend, let me take out the speck in your eye' when you yourself do not see the log in your own eye? You hypocrite, first take the log out of your own eye, and then you will see clearly to take the speck out of your neighbor's eye."

Jesus gives the proper way to make judgments. Look within yourself and compare your thinking and actions to the teachings of Jesus, be aware of and deal with your imperfections, and then you will be able to look at another's thinking and actions and possibly be of help to them. Again, a person who tries to do right and fails is not a hypocrite. Neither are those who do what is right even though they may not feel like it. A hypocrite is blinded by his own sin and is only interested in covering up his own sins and exposing another's sin, or rationalizing his sin by pointing out the same sin in another.

Verses 43-45 continue, "No good tree bears bad fruit, nor again does a bad tree bear good fruit; for each tree is known by its fruit. Figs are not gathered from thorns, nor are grapes gathered from a bramble bush. The good person out of the good treasure of the heart produces good, and the evil person out of the evil treasure produces evil; for it is out of the abundance of the heart that the mouth speaks." (Jesus constantly stresses that the heart is key to everything.)

In verses 46-49 Jesus says, "Why do you call me 'Lord, Lord' and do not do what I tell you? I will show you what someone is like who comes to me, hears my word, and acts on them. That one is like a man building a house, who dug deeply and laid the foundation on rock; when a flood arose, the river burst against that house but could not shake it, because it had been well built. But the one who hears and does not act is like a man who built a house on the ground without a foundation. When the river burst against it, immediately it fell, and great was the ruin of that house." (These are those who hear and ignore him, but they are also those who hear and call him Lord, but do not have the commitment to act on his teachings.)

Matthew takes three chapters for his Sermon on the Mount; Luke takes one chapter for his Sermon on the Plain. Are they the same with one being an adaption from Jesus' one sermon, or are they two different messages by Jesus in two different contexts? Most scholars believe they were derived from different collections of words from Jesus that were passed on orally until Matthew and Luke put them into writing. It should be obvious that Jesus would teach the same things in different ways in different situations.

One other point that must be emphasized is the virtues and values behind these situational teachings are not just for individuals. If one reads the Old Testament, the message from God is first to the covenant made with Abraham for the nation of Israel, and then to individuals. In the New Testament a new covenant is made through Christ with the church. The church through individuals will take the message of Jesus and his kingdom to more individuals and to all the nations of the world. If one is serious about Scripture, the church can not be eliminated.

A mistake in interpretation is to override the way of thinking with those in the East who wrote Scripture with the thinking of those of us who live in the West. Making Scripture apply only to individuals and not nations or institutions within nations, and isolating Scripture to only so-called spiritual applications is an example of mistaken interpretation, which is very close to the ancient heresy of Gnosticism. Nations, institutions, and churches are physical and material and have character. They are also to conform themselves to the characteristics of the kingdom.

Chapter 7:1 says, After Jesus had finished all his sayings in the hearing of the people, he entered Capernaum. Verses 2-5 tell us that a centurion had a slave he valued who was close to death. He sent Jewish elders to ask Jesus to come and heal the slave. In (5) the elders earnestly told Jesus, "He is worthy of you doing this for him, for he loves our people, and it is he who built our synagogue for us." Jesus went with them and when he neared the house the centurion sent friends in (6-8) to say to him, "Lord, do not trouble yourself, for I am not worthy to have you come under my roof; therefore I did not presume to come to you. But only speak the word, and let my servant be healed. For I also am a man set under authority, with soldiers under me; and I say to one, 'Go' and he goes, and to another, 'Come,' and he comes, and to my slave, 'Do this,' and the slave does it."

Verses 9-10 say, When Jesus heard this he was amazed at him, and turning to the crowd that followed him, he said, "I tell you not even in Israel have I found such faith." When those who had been sent returned to the house, they found the slave in good health.

Even though the first followers of Jesus are Jews, the majority reject him and in the long run, it will be Gentiles that make the movement a success. Here Jesus accepts the faith of a Gentile. When the reader compares the same incident in Mt 8:5-13 and Jn 4:46-53, it is noticed that the story is told in three different ways, but the basic message and main theme stay the same. The details are changed either inadvertently or for the purposes of each writer. An analysis of the three stories highlights the process of passing along orally from one village to another the things Jesus said and did.

Dunn (2003, 205-210) documents a man named Kenneth Bailey who lived more than thirty years in a Middle Eastern village whose culture was oral. Bailey describes how narratives are passed along stressing how the basic theme is always the same but flexibility in exact details is adjusted to the different audiences. Bailey's experience can be seen first hand by comparing the following narratives.

To examine this issue in more detail compare the following narratives: the stilling of the storm (Mk 4:35-41, Mt 8:23-27, Lk 8:22-25); the Syrophoenician woman (Mk 7:24-30, Mt 15:21-28); the healing of the possessed boy (Mk 9:14-27, Mt 17:14-18, Lk 9:37-44); the dispute about greatness (Mk 9:33-37, Mt 18:1-5, Lk 9:46-48); and the widow's mite (Mk 12:41-44, Lk 21:1-4).

After comparing the written versions it is obvious that the information from the Scripture writers comes from different oral performances that were being passed on in a culture, as Bailey describes, where few could read or write. Bailey describes this as *informal, controlled oral tradition*. This idea is also very obvious in the three conversion accounts of the Apostle Paul in Acts 9:1-22, 22:1-21, 26:9-23. When one examines the inspired Scriptures carefully, the fundamentalist belief that every word is God's exact word, and the way the narratives are described is historically accurate in all the details, must be put to rest. That concept has nothing to do with inspiration simply because the writer's purpose is not exact history as we moderns understand history.

In verses 11-13 Jesus goes to Nain, a town about twenty-five miles south of Capernaum. A widow whose only son has died is passing through the city gate. (No burials are allowed within a Jewish town; they have to be outside the city gate, so they are passing through the city gate. The death of a widow's only son is not only a time of deep sorrow but an economic catastrophe. She will have no legal inheritance and will be dependent on charity.) Verse 13 says, When the Lord saw her, he had compassion for her and said to her, "Do not weep." (Constantly Luke uses the word Lord for Jesus to indicate he is God (YHWH). Lord (Adonai) is the Old Testament word Jews substitute for God because they do not feel they are worthy to say his name.)

In verse 14 he touched the bier and said, "Young man, I say to you, rise!" Verses 15-17 say, The dead man sat up and began to speak, and Jesus gave him to his mother. Fear (awe) seized all of them; and they glorified God saying, "A great prophet has risen among us!" and "God has looked favorably upon his people!" This word about him spread throughout Judea and all the surrounding country. (Those Jesus raised from the dead were resuscitations not resurrections, for those he raised will eventually die again.)

Jesus touching the casket is a violation of Old Testament purity laws, for one can not touch the dead or the casket containing the dead, for it will make them unclean. One then has to offer a sacrifice at the temple to be purified. Jesus is in the process of reinterpreting many of the Old Testament laws.

In Ezekiel 37:1-28 rising from the dead is a sign that the nation is being set free from exile. The Jews in those times associate the time when the dead will rise as the beginning of the new age and the reign of God. Therefore, Jesus is concerned about the word spreading about him, for he knows the Jewish and Roman authorities are plotting against him. As the word spreads concerning him and what he is doing, he knows the authorities will be gathering more support against him. Because he is preaching a kingdom different from their interests, he knows his time is getting short, and he needs more time to teach his disciples. The fact that he is not yet arrested is due to his itinerant style. At this point he is just scattering seed anywhere he can and moving along as he works at teaching his disciples more thoroughly.

In verses 18-20 the disciples of John reported these things to John, so in (19) he sent them to Jesus to ask, "Are you the one who is to come or are we to wait for another?" Verses 21-23 say, Jesus had just then cured many people of diseases, plagues, and evil spirits, and had given sight to many who were blind. And he answered them, "Go and tell John what you have seen and heard: the blind receive their sight, the lame walk, and lepers are cleansed, the deaf hear, the dead are raised, the poor have good news brought to them. And blessed is anyone who takes no offense at me." (John is concerned and confused, for Jesus is approaching things somewhat differently from John. John is rough and gruff while Jesus is mild and compassionate. Jesus' quotes from Isaiah 35:1-10 as a sign of the new king and the new age.)

In verses 24-26 Jesus asks the people what they expected to see when they went out to see John? Did they expect someone who was wealthy, dressed in fine clothes, who bends with the wind in what he believes? Did they expect a prophet? Then Jesus tells them that John is a prophet and more than a prophet. In verses 27-28 Jesus says, "This is the one about whom it is written, 'See, I am sending my messenger ahead of you, who will prepare your way before you.' I tell you, among those born of women no one is greater than John; yet the least in the kingdom of God is greater than he."

This is an *eschatological* metaphor. It is saying that those who are coming into the kingdom that Jesus is in the process of establishing now will be part of the end time eternal kingdom that is in the process of breaking in upon the earth. This will be greater than what is on earth up to this time.

Verses 29-30 say, And all the people who heard this, including the tax collectors, acknowledged the justice of God, because they had been baptized with John's baptism. But by refusing to be baptized by him, the Pharisees and the lawyers (scribes) rejected God's purpose for themselves. (Acknowledging the justice of God is acknowledging the righteousness of God's plan of salvation for the nation of Israel and the people.)

In verses 31-32 Jesus compares them to children in the marketplace who do not know what they want and are never satisfied. In verses 33-35 Jesus says, "For John the Baptist has come eating no bread and drinking no wine and you say, 'He has a demon'; the Son of Man has come eating and drinking, and you say, 'Look, a glutton and a drunkard, a friend of tax collectors and sinners!' Nevertheless wisdom is vindicated by all her children."

Because they are not open to God's message, they reject everything that is contrary to their preconceived notions. The Pharisees' main objection is not so much with their dietary habits but with Jesus exposing their hypocrisy. Wisdom's children are the followers of Jesus and John. These followers are living transformed lives. Their righteous living demonstrates the wisdom Jesus and John taught. It is interesting to note that Jesus obviously enjoyed life as well as a good party.

Verses 36-38 present an incident with a lesson dealing with a self-righteous and judgmental Pharisee, and a humble woman who recognizes who Jesus is and her need for him. A meal with a Pharisee provides an occasion to discuss who is acceptable in God's kingdom. The incident begins when one of the Pharisees asks Jesus to eat with him. While Jesus is there, a woman who is a sinner comes bringing an alabaster jar of ointment. Standing behind Jesus she begins weeping and bathing his feet in tears and drying them with her hair. Verse 39 says, Now when the Pharisee who had invited him saw it, he said to himself, "If this man were a prophet, he would have known who and what kind of woman this is who is touching him—that she is a sinner."

Pharisees do not have table fellowship with anyone they judge as a sinner, for they believe it will make them ritually unclean. Again, by this woman touching him Jesus will be made unclean according to their law. To understand these laws more thoroughly, one needs some Old Testament background. The more one understands the Old Testament, the easier it is to understand what is happening in the New Testament.

Verses 40-43 say, Jesus spoke up and said to him, "Simon I have something to say to you." "Teacher," he replied, "speak." "A certain creditor had two debtors; one owed five hundred denarii, and the other fifty. When they could not pay, he canceled the debts for both of them. Now which of them will love him more?" Simon answered, "I suppose the one for whom he cancelled the greater debt." And Jesus said to him, "You have judged rightly."

Verses 44-47 say, Then turning toward the woman, he said to Simon, "Do you see this woman? I entered your house; you gave me no water for my feet, but she has bathed my feet with her tears and dried them with her hair. You gave me no kiss, but from the time I came in she has not stopped kissing my feet. You did not anoint my head with oil, but she has anointed my feet with ointment. Therefore, I tell you, her sins, which were many, have been forgiven; hence she has shown great love. But the one to whom little is forgiven, loves little."

Jesus is saying to Simon, look how much greater her love is for me than yours. The woman knows the meaning and importance of forgiveness, but the Pharisee does not. He probably does not even believe that he has much sin to even forgive. Water for the feet, a kiss, and oil are the usual gestures of Middle Eastern hospitality.

Then in verses 48-50 Jesus said to the woman, "Your sins are forgiven." But those who were at the table with him began to say among themselves, "Who is this that even forgives sins?" And he said to the woman, "Your faith has saved you; go in peace." (Jesus confounds them because he forgives sins that are not committed against him but sins committed against God and others. Their thinking is that only God can do such, but that is his point.)

Chapter 8:1-3 says, Soon afterwards he went on through cities and villages, proclaiming and bringing good news of the kingdom of God. The twelve were with him, as well as some women who have been cured of evil spirits and infirmities: Mary called Magdalene, from whom seven demons had gone out, and Joanna, the wife of Herod's steward Chuza, and Susanna, and many others, who provide for them out of their resources.

We must not forget that according to Luke the good news of the kingdom of God is the primary message Jesus is sent to give. Eternal life and the eternal way have broken into the earth. It is this kingdom, a way of life different from the values of the current kingdom, which startles both the Romans and the leaders of the Jews. It is they who have the religious and political power. This writer encourages the reader to be familiar with the books of Verhey, Wright, Wallis, Dunn, Borg, Crossan, Hill, and Horsley. These writers have much to say about the political, economic, and social processes of the time and the effect of Jesus upon the political leaders. These books are listed in the bibliography.

Traditionally it was said that Mary Magdalene was a prostitute, but there is no record of that belief. Scripture simply says that Jesus cast seven demons from her, something he had done with many different people. Seven is the Jewish number meaning complete.

Verses 4-8 say, When a great crowd gathered and people from town after town came to him, he said in a parable: "A sower went out to sow his seed; and as he sowed, some fell on the path and was trampled on, and the birds of the air ate it up. Some fell on the rock; and as it grew up, it withered for lack of moisture. Some fell among thorns, and the thorns grew up with it and choked it. Some fell into good soil, and when it grew, it produced a hundredfold." As he said this, he called out, "Let anyone with ears to hear listen!" In verses 9-10 his disciples asked him what this parable meant. He said, "To you it has been given to know the secrets of the kingdom of God; but to others I speak in parables, so 'looking they may not perceive, and listening they may not understand.' "

This saying taken from the prophet Isaiah is directed mainly to the people of power and comfort–those not interested in hearing or learning, those wanting to get rid of him. One reason he speaks in parables is to make them try to figure out what he is saying. He does this mainly to slow down their attempt to kill him and to give him more time to teach his disciples.

Verses 11-15 say, "Now the parable is this: The seed is the word of God. The ones on the path are those who have heard; then the devil comes and takes away the word from their hearts, so that they may not believe and be saved. The ones on the rock are those who, when they hear the word receive it with joy. But these have no root; they believe only for awhile and in a time of testing fall away. As for what fell among the thorns, these are the ones who hear; but as they go on their way, they are choked by the cares and riches and pleasures of life, and their fruit does not mature. But as for that in the good soil, these are the ones who, when they hear the word, hold it fast in an honest and good heart, and bear fruit with patient endurance."

Luke wants his readers to look in the mirror and determine if they or we are path people, rock people, thorn people or good soil people, and if good soil people how good? Luke also wants his readers and listeners to ask what part they are playing in allowing the kingdom of God to break into the world through them.

In verses 16-18 Jesus says, "No one after lighting a lamp hides it under a jar, or puts it under a bed, but puts it on a lampstand, so that those who enter may see the light. For nothing is hidden that will not be disclosed, nor is anything secret that will not become known and come to the light." (Luke is saying that when Christ's light illuminates his people, they are to let others see it by what they say and do. He is also saying that in the end all will be evaluated by Christ's light.) Jesus then warns his listeners by saying, "Then pay attention to how you listen; for to those who have (an understanding of God's word), more will be given; and from those who do not have, even what they seem to have will be taken away."

If people are not growing and deepening their understanding of God's word, they are actually losing some of what they did know and understand. This is true simply because over time the world's thinking and ways seep in and replace what previously one was sure of and understood as God's way. Luke focuses on how one hears. He is saying if one listens closely and works at understanding, one will continue to understand more deeply and in the process grow to greater maturity as a disciple of Christ. But if one does not work at it, one will lose the understanding and maturity previously gained.

It is like a muscle. If it is exercised it gets stronger, but if not exercised, it becomes flabby and useless. It has been said that most people's understanding of religion is not much higher than a fourth grade level, and there is very little education to advance improvement upon that level. For too many people after confirmation, education seems to stop, and in the confirmation process, at the most, only the bare basics are learned.

Verses 19-21 say, Then his mother and his brothers came to him, but they could not reach him because of the crowd. And he was told, "Your mother and your brothers are standing outside, wanting to see you." But he said to them, "My mother and my brothers are those who hear the word of God and do it."

These verses are to be understood in the context of the previous verses. Readers can be assured that Jesus then went to see his mother and brothers, but first he uses the situation to teach an important concept. Christians have a genetic family but also a divine family. One becomes a member of that divine family by hearing the word of God and doing it. Jesus is not degrading his genetic family, but he is teaching about priorities.

Verses 22-25 say, One day he got into a boat with his disciples, and he said to them, "Let us go across to the other side of the lake." So they put out, and while they were sailing, he fell asleep. A windstorm swept down on the lake, and the boat was filling with water, and they were in danger. They went to him and woke him up, shouting, "Master, Master, we are perishing!" And he woke up and rebuked the wind and the raging waves; they ceased, and there was calm. He said to them, "Where is your faith?" They were afraid and amazed, and said to one another, "Who then is this, that he commands even the winds and the water, and they obey him?"

Luke is saying Jesus is God, for only God can control nature. When the Jews wanted to express God's power and authority they spoke of his mastery over the sea or water (Ps 65:7-8, 89:9, 93:3-4, 107:29). The picture of Jesus stilling the storm makes the claim that he is God. That which was said of God in the Old Testament is now said of Jesus. Borg (2001, 207) illustrates some metaphorical meanings that could be the purpose of the story. Some of them are the following: Without Jesus, you do not get anywhere. Without Jesus, you are at sea and in the dark. Following Jesus may put you in difficult situations. Jesus takes away fear. Jesus comes to you in distress. Jesus stills the storms of life. Call upon Jesus, and he will be there to help.

Borg is suggesting that most readers should not get bogged down in debates about whether or not this narrative, or others like it, actually happened but concentrate on what the story means. Whether or not something happened in most cases is not the issue and has nothing to do with transformation of the heart or the inspiration of Scripture. Some scholars like Borg do not believe the incident actually happened, and that it is a metaphor developed by the church to teach theological truths. Borg states this not to deny the miracles of Jesus but to be honest as an historian.

Others disagree with Borg saying if God can create the world, he surely can do what he wills in and with his creation. Although that is true, Borg's point that the issue is the meaning of the story for those people in those times, and what it means to Christians today is important in being transformed. Proving history is important, but at this point, one is not able to prove or disprove the miracles, so the next best thing is to look for the meaning or theology behind the events.

In verses 26-39 is an incident in the land of the Gerasenes located east of Galilee. A man from the city was living in the tombs and, for a long time had worn no clothes. An unclean spirit often had seized him, so he was kept under guard and kept in chains. The man would break the bonds and be driven by the demon into the wilds. Verse 28 says, When he saw Jesus, he fell down before him and shouted at the top of his voice, "What have you to do with me, Jesus, Son of the Most High God? I beg you, do not torment me"–for Jesus had commanded the unclean spirit to come out of the man. In verse 30 Jesus then asked him, "What is your name?" He said "Legion"; for many demons had entered him. They begged him not to order them to go back into the abyss.

Verses 32-33 say, on the hillside a large herd of swine was

feeding; and the demons begged Jesus to let them enter these. So he gave them permission. Then the demons came out of the man and entered the swine, and the herd rushed down the steep bank into the lake and was drowned. In Matthew and later in Luke Jesus said if by the Spirit of God, I cast out demons, then the kingdom of God has come upon you.

In (34-37) after the people were told what happened, they came out and they saw the man who had the demons seated at the feet of Jesus healed and in his right mind. And they were afraid. The people asked Jesus to leave them. So he got into the boat and returned. (Neither the in-breaking kingdom of God nor a person being healed of a terrible disease is their interest. Profits are more important than a man's health being restored. Does that sound familiar?)

Verses 38-39 say, The man from whom the demons had gone begged that he might be with him; but Jesus sent him away saying, "Return to your home, and declare how much Jesus has done for you." So he went away, proclaiming throughout the city how much Jesus had done for him.

This is Gentile territory. Jesus uses this man to prepare the territory for the future planting of churches. With most people their mission field is with their own family and friends. An interesting study is to compare how Luke tells this incident with how Matthew 8:28-34 and Mark 5:1-20 explain the incident. More interpretation of this incident can be seen by turning to those Scriptures explained in this book. Also debated is the nature of the narrative. Is it history, or a parable, and if its roots are in history, how much of it is actual history? But according to Borg those things are not what is important; the meaning of the narrative is first in importance. On this side of the divide, it will never be determined how much is actual history and how much is not. Although history is important, it is not absolutely necessary in expressing theology. For example some of the best theology is expressed through hymns.

In verses 40-56 Jesus continues healing. A synagogue leader named Jairus begs Jesus to come to his house and help his only daughter who is dying. On the way as the crowds press in on him, a woman who has been suffering hemorrhages for twelve years comes up behind him and touches the fringe of his clothes, and immediately she is healed. Verse 43 tells us that she had spent all she had on physicians, and no one could cure her. Verses 45-46 say, Jesus asked, "Who touched me?" When all denied it, Peter said, "Master, the crowds surround you and press in on you." But Jesus said, "Someone touched me; for I noticed that power had gone out from me."

Verses 47-48 say, When the woman saw that she could not remain hidden, she came trembling; and falling down before him, she declared in the presence of all the people why she had touched him, and how she had been immediately healed. He said to her, "Daughter, your faith has made you well; go in peace."

This chapter is showing that Jesus by the Spirit defeats evil and heals. Therefore his people are to set as one of their primary tasks to stand against all evil and to help people overcome evil. This can be done by one's example and bearing one another's burdens. In the process they are to be of help in whatever leads to healing. Again, it is important to note that healing the blind, the deaf, enabling the lame to walk is taken from Old Testament passages like Isa 29:18-19 and 35:3-6 that refer to the age to come and the outpouring of the Spirit. Jesus models the in-breaking kingdom for his disciples.

Verses 49-53 say, While he was still speaking, someone came from the leader's house to say, "Your daughter is dead; do not trouble the teacher any longer." When Jesus heard this, he replied, "Do not fear. Only believe, and she will be saved." When he came to the house, he did not allow anyone to enter with him, except Peter,

James, and John, and the child's father and mother. (Peter, James, and John will also be the only ones with him at the transfiguration.) They were all weeping and wailing for her; but he said, "Do not weep; for she is not dead but sleeping." And they laughed at him, knowing that she was dead.

But verses 54-56 say, he took her by the hand and called out, "Child get up!" Her spirit returned, and she got up at once. Then he directed them to give her something to eat. Her parents were astounded; but he ordered them to tell no one. (He directs her to eat to show it is not her ghost that he raised. The raising of the dead is a sign that the new age has come.)

Jesus astounds everyone with these two incidents. By a woman touching him with a blood issue, he will be declared unclean by their religious laws and not permitted to enter worship. It is the same with touching a dead person. Jesus will declare these laws null and void. This will be to the amazement of the Jews and to the anger of the religious leaders, who will declare him a traitor to their nation and its traditions.

In chapter 9:1-2 Jesus calls the twelve together and gives them power and authority over all demons and to cure diseases, and he sends them out to proclaim the kingdom of God and to heal. (These two verses have much to say to today's Christians and their churches about their mission: Proclaim the kingdom and teach what it involves, stand against all evil, and do something about the healthcare of people.) In verses 3-5 Jesus told them to take nothing with them, and if the people do not welcome them, move on. (This clearly shows that he does not come to offer his followers prosperity and wealth.) Verse 6 says, they departed and went through the villages, bringing the good news and curing diseases everywhere.

Verses 7-9 mention that when Herod (Antipas) hears about all these actions of Jesus he is perplexed. He had beheaded John the Baptist. Herod wonders if John has risen from the dead. He along with others wonder if this one called Jesus can even be Elijah or one of the prophets who has risen from the dead.

Verses 10-11 tell us that when the disciples return to Jesus, they go to Bethsaida for some privacy, but the crowds find out and follow him. Verse 11 says, he welcomed them and spoke to them about the kingdom of God and healed those who needed to be cured.

In verses 12-17 the day is coming to a close, and there is nothing to eat. Jesus tells his disciples to give the people something to eat, but they only have five loaves and two fish. There are five thousand men not counting the women and children. Jesus tells his disciples to organize them into groups of fifty. Verses 15-17 say, They did so and made them all sit down. And taking the five loaves and two fish, he looked up to heaven, and blessed and broke them, and gave them to the disciples to set before the crowd. And all ate and were filled. What was left over was gathered up, twelve baskets of broken pieces. (This is obviously extraordinary, for all four gospel writers mention it.)

Verses 18-19 say, Once when Jesus was praying alone, with only the disciples near him, he asked them, "Who do the crowds say I am?" They answered, "John the Baptist; but others, Elijah; and still others, that one of the ancient prophets has arisen." Verse 20 says, He said to them, "But who do you say that I am?" Peter answered, "The Messiah of God." (This is the question Luke wants all people to answer, for it determines one's philosophy or theology as far as one's thinking and actions are concerned.)

Verses 21-22 say, He sternly ordered and commanded them not to tell anyone, saying, "The Son of Man must undergo great suffering, and be rejected by the elders, chief priests, and scribes, and be killed, and on the third day be raised." (The disciples ignore this latter statement, for they do not believe this could possibly happen. So he tells them not to tell anyone because they do not have the right idea of who he is. He needs more time to teach them and prepare them for who he is, what the kingdom is really about, and what is going to happen.)

In verses 23-26 Jesus says, "If any want to become my followers, let them deny themselves and take up their cross daily and follow me. For those who want to save their life will lose it, and those who lose their life for my sake will save it. What does it profit them if they gain the whole world, but lose or forfeit themselves? Those who are ashamed of me and my words, of them the Son of Man will be ashamed when he comes in his glory and the glory of the Father and the holy angels. But truly I tell you, there are some standing here who will not taste death before they see the kingdom of God."

The issue here is the choice of gaining the world or the kingdom. One leads to death the other to life. He is giving them instruction on how both the world and the kingdom of God are gained. Losing self and replacing it with the "Christ self" is the way to life. This is what picking up the cross is about: dying to self and living for Christ and his purposes. This is not a one time decision but a daily decision. The symbols are the cross and resurrection. The cross symbolizes putting self to death and putting on the "Christ self." Colossians chapter 3:1-17 gives a fuller description of what one is to put on and what one is to put off. The resurrection symbolizes rising to a new way of life, a life that shows a new way of thinking and acting (Rom 6:2-23, 12:1-21).

Luke is asking his readers which one they are in the process of choosing, their selfish desires and interests for themselves, their nation and the world, or the desires and interests of Christ. He tells them they will soon see the kingdom come in glory. Apparently he is in reference to Acts chapter 2 with the visual coming of the Spirit and what is called the official beginning of the kingdom. He promises that when he is with his Father, he will send the Spirit, which will be his real presence and real power with his people. Then believers will be responsible for carrying on his work until he comes at the end time to bring in the final, perfected kingdom. At this point they do not understand, for they still believe he is the one to throw out the Romans and set up a political kingdom with them ruling the nation and being served by the people.

Verses 28-36 present the transfiguration of Jesus. Now about eight days after these sayings Jesus took with him Peter and John and James, and went up on the mountain to pray. And while he was praying, the appearance of his face changed, and his clothes became dazzling white. Suddenly they saw two men, Moses and Elijah, talking to him. They appeared in glory and were speaking of his departure, which he was about to accomplish in Jerusalem. Now Peter and his companions were weighed down with sleep; but since they had stayed awake, they saw his glory and the two men who stood with him. Just as they were leaving him, Peter said to Jesus, "Master it is good for us to be here; let us make three dwellings, one for you, one for Moses, and one for Elijah"–not knowing what he said. While he was saying this, a cloud came and overshadowed them; and they were terrified as they entered the cloud. Then from the cloud came a voice that said, "This is my Son my Chosen; listen to him!" When the voice had spoken, Jesus was found alone. And they kept silent and in those days told no one any of these things they had seen. (In Scripture God and his judgments are often made present through a cloud.)

This is an event that begins in prayer and leads to an intense mystical experience. Mt 17:9 uses the word vision, meaning another dimension is made present to them. The message is that Jesus is

God's final revelation. He is the one who is to be listened to and to whom all things are to be submitted. The Old Testament is now to be understood and brought to fulfillment through Christ, his words and actions. When Jesus previously said some would not die before they see the kingdom, some think he is also referring to what Peter, James, and John saw in the transfiguration.

In verses 37-43 Jesus heals a man's only son who has convulsions caused by a demon. Verses 43-45 say, And all were astounded at the greatness of God. While everyone was amazed by all he was doing, he said to his disciples, "Let these words sink into your ears: The Son of Man is going to be betrayed into human hands." But they did not understand this saying; its meaning was concealed from them, so that they could not perceive it. And they were afraid to ask him about this saying. (They like many of us only want to hear the positive, for the negative is too difficult to deal with.)

In verses 46-48 an argument arose among them as to which one is the greatest. Jesus told them the least among all of you is the greatest. His example to them is a little child who is the least of all in the world's superiority-inferiority system. Again Jesus upturns the values of the world and makes them think about what greatness is in the eyes of God.

In verses 49-50 John said, "Master we saw someone casting out demons in your name, and we tried to stop him, because he does not follow with us." But Jesus said to him, "Do not stop him; for whoever is not against you is for you." (The disciples of Jesus are not to sit in judgment of those who do good and are not followers. He is teaching to be open to others and accept the action of God in unexpected people and places. The message is to be careful drawing boundaries around who God approves. Mark 8:40 agrees with what Jesus said, but Mt 12:30 disagrees. The key is the context.)

In verses 51-56 Jesus sets his face to go to Jerusalem in order to be taken up. James and John go ahead to Samaria to prepare the way, but the Samaritans do not accept them. James and John say to Jesus, "Lord do you want us to command fire to come down from heaven and consume them?" But Jesus rebuked them, and they went on.

Verses 57-58 say, As they were going along the road, someone said to him, "I will follow you wherever you go." And Jesus said to him, "Foxes have holes, and birds of the air have nests; but the Son of Man has nowhere to lay his head."

Notice Jesus does not say all he has to do is believe. He does not tell him how easy it is to be a follower. In fact he tries to discourage him. Basically, Jesus tells him to count the cost, for true discipleship is far more than just believing to be saved eternally. In fact that is a topic Jesus rarely discusses. The book of James 2:19 says, even the demons believe. How different that is from many churches today whose only goal seems to be to count the numbers and the money and to feel good about how many are in church on Sunday morning.

Verses 59-62 say, To another he said, "Follow me." But he said, "Lord, first let me go and bury my father." But Jesus said, "Let the dead bury their own dead; but as for you go and proclaim the kingdom of God." (Since Jewish law lays a great responsibility on taking care of parents, the man is probably asking Jesus to wait until his father dies, and then he will come into and work in the kingdom.) Along the same lines in (61) another said, "I will follow you Lord; but let me first say farewell to those at my home." Jesus said to him, "No one who puts a hand to the plow and looks back is fit for the kingdom of God." (Notice the language is not to go get people saved, but to go and proclaim the kingdom. The difference is that the kingdom is concerned with making Jesus present in every day activity and the transformation of individuals and the world. Then eternity will take care of itself.)

This writer believes these sayings of Jesus are examples of Jesus using hyperboles to stress an important teaching. Nothing is to interfere with the call of Jesus. Jesus is not telling either of them to reject one's family, nor is he stating a timeless ethic, but he is challenging them with what their idol may be, or whatever is interfering with them making a commitment to him. The teaching is that anyone who makes something more important than Jesus and the kingdom of God has an idol.

These examples are metaphors teaching that nothing is to get in the way of serious discipleship. Also, Jesus does not advocate the teaching of just believe, meaning head knowledge only. Second Thessalonians 2:13 tells us that both belief in the truth and sanctification in the Spirit (growing in holiness) are necessary. His message is to count the cost, and if one is not willing to do so, it seems Jesus is not interested in that person's witness.

Chapter 10:1-3 says, After this the Lord appointed seventy others and sent them on ahead of him in pairs to every town and place where he had intended to go. He said to them, "The harvest is plentiful, but the laborers are few; therefore ask the Lord of the harvest to send out laborers into the harvest. Go on your way. See, I am sending you out like lambs in the midst of wolves." (The call is to harvest for the kingdom. They are being sent out in their own land in a trial run to prepare for their future work.)

Let us take a look at what being in the midst of wolves may mean even for our time. The job Jesus sends his laborers to do will not be easy. Most of the world will not really be interested in the message. The messengers will be attacked by those who oppose the virtues, values, and vision of the kingdom. There will be many martyrs. As time goes on others will change the message. Some will co-opt the real message making it a pie in the sky message of personal salvation at no cost to them. Instead of being changed by the message of the kingdom, some will change the message by accepting what they want to hear and ignoring the rest. Others will read it only in service of their own personal power and interests or their nation's power and interests. The comfortable will read it to justify themselves and their culture's values, even as the rich get richer and the poor get poorer.

Economic exploitation and greed will become institutionalized as a way of economics in a system based too much on the survival of the fittest. Those not surviving or having difficulty surviving will be blamed for having no initiative. The poor will be considered lazy instead of being the victims as a result of decisions made by the wealthy and powerful who control government to benefit themselves, and take advantage of those without wealth and power. What is true of a minority that take advantage of the system will be made to appear as though it is the majority. The working poor will be taken advantage of by an unjust wage system (James 5:1-5). Scripture taken out of context will be used to justify their actions. Oppression will become a way of politics and economics producing a broken society and culture. The Bible will be used to develop a religion accommodated to the world and a nation's conventional wisdom. Wars will be initiated in the name of Christ. Defense of the nation will be used to attack other nations for political purposes and economic gain. All of these things are directly opposite of what Jesus said and did.

All of these things and more are what Jesus is referring to when he says I will send you out like lambs in the midst of wolves, for when there is an attempt to correct the injustice of the status quo, the comfortable begin to howl. The Scriptures will be used by all types of people as a weapon to judge others and to justify their unjust actions. Also, when people's misunderstanding or distortion of Scripture is pointed out to them, they will muster all their resources against the messenger just as they will do to Jesus. Jesus knows he will be put to death for challenging hypocrisy, self centeredness, and greed, so he tells his real followers that the same will happen to them; they will be like lambs in the midst of wolves.

Seventy is one number the Jews use for the nations; the number represents going into all the world. In the Old Testament God chose the Israelites to reveal himself, but he expected them to reveal him to the nations. They were to be a light to the nations, a city set upon the hill, but they failed to be obedient to God's call, even thinking the Gentiles were not worthy of God. When Jesus sends out the twelve, they are to go to the Jews, but the seventy will later symbolize they are to go to the whole world, to the Gentiles.

In verses 4-9 Jesus gives them their instructions. He tells them to take nothing and to depend on God and the people they teach to supply their needs. Whatever house you enter say peace to the house. Stay in one house; do not change houses. Accept whatever hospitality is offered, for the laborer deserves to be paid. Cure the sick who are there; tell them that the kingdom of God has come near. In verses 10-12 they are instructed to move on, if a town does not accept them, and to tell them it will be more tolerable for Sodom than for that town.

Then in verses 13-15 Jesus lists towns that are rejecting him such as Chorazin, Bethsaida and Capernaum. He says to them woe to you. (In Scripture cities, towns, and nations are judged. According to Jesus their judgment will be when the Romans destroy them in the war of 66-70 AD.) Verse 16 says, "Whoever listens to you listens to me, and whoever rejects you rejects me, and whoever rejects me rejects the one who sent me. (Jesus makes it plain that by rejecting him, they are rejecting God, for it is God who sent him.)

Verses 17-18 say, The seventy returned with joy, saying, "Lord in your name even the demons submit to us!" He said to them, "I watched Satan fall from heaven like a flash of lightning." (Jesus envisions the fall of Satan through their ministry, another way of saying the eschatological (end-time) battle between good and evil has begun, and in the name of Jesus victory will be won.)

Verses 19-20 say, "See, I have given you authority to tread on snakes and scorpions, and over all the power of the enemy; and nothing will hurt you. Nevertheless, do not rejoice in this, that the spirits submit to you, but rejoice that your names are written in heaven." (He is saying not to be enamored by the temporary power given to them. The reader will see in the book of Acts and the letters of Paul this temporary power given to the disciples. The disciples will be given the same basic powers Jesus has.)

Verse 21 says, At that same hour Jesus rejoiced in the Holy Spirit and said, "I thank you, Father, Lord of heaven and earth, because you have hidden these things from the wise and intelligent and have revealed them to infants; yes, Father, for such was your gracious will. (The so-called wise and intelligent are not open to teachings that are not in agreement with their thinking, while those considered infants in Christ are open to learn and change their ways.)

Verses 22-23 continue, All things have been handed over to me by my Father; and no one knows who the Son is except the Father, or who the Father is except the Son and anyone to whom the Son chooses to reveal him." (He is choosing a small group to carry out his mission.) Then turning to the disciples, Jesus said to them privately, "Blessed are the eyes that see what you see! For I tell you that many prophets and kings desired to see what you see, but did not see it, and to hear what you hear, but did not hear it." (Jesus is always referring back to the Old Testament.)

Jesus chooses to go to the poor, the nobodies of the world. He knows the so-called wise and the comfortable are not interested, nor are they willing to risk all they have for his cause, a cause the people of the world will reject. Even though many will accept him in name, mainly because they want eternal life, they will actually ignore his key teachings.

Verses 25-37 contain the parable of the Good Samaritan. Verse 25 says, a lawyer stood up to test Jesus. "Teacher," he said, "what must I do to inherit eternal life?" (Eternal life is also translated, the age to come. According to Jesus, the kingdom, eternal life, the age to come, renewal of both individuals and all God's creation, is breaking into the world now.) He said to him, "What is written in the law? What do you read there?" He answered, "You shall love the Lord your God with all your heart, and with all your soul, and with all your strength, and with all your mind; and your neighbor as your self." And he said to him, "You have given the right answer; do this, and you shall live."

But wanting to justify himself he asked Jesus, "And who is my neighbor?" Jesus replied, "A man was going down from Jerusalem to Jericho, and fell into the hands of robbers, who stripped him, beat him, and went away, leaving him half dead. Now by chance a priest was going down that road; and when he saw him, he passed by on the other side. So likewise a Levite, when he came to the place and saw him, passed by on the other side. But a Samaritan while traveling came near him; and when he saw him, he was moved with pity. He went to him and bandaged his wounds, having poured oil and wine on them. Then he put him on his own animal, brought him to an inn, and took care of him. The next day he took out two denarii, gave them to the innkeeper, and said, 'Take care of him; and when I come back, I will repay you whatever more you spend.'

Which of these three, do you think, was a neighbor to the man who fell into the hands of the robbers?" He said, "The one who showed him mercy." Jesus said to him, "Go and do likewise."

From this parable a neighbor is defined both as one who helps his fellow human in need and the fellow human in need. The one who helps is a neighbor, and the one being helped is also a neighbor. The priest and the Levite (clergymen) are either too busy to help, or they are occupied with other interests. The man who helps, who the parable declares as a neighbor, is a Samaritan.

Samaritans are half Jew and half Gentile as a result of intermarriages begun in 722 BC. The land had been divided between the north (Israel) and the south (Judah). The Assyrians conquered the northern nation of Israel and took all the competent people into exile. Those that remained intermarried with the Assyrians. According to Judah, they eventually corrupted the religion. These are the Samaritans, and they are hated by most of the people of Judah (Jews). Jesus makes this man of mercy, the hated Samaritan, the hero of the story. Jesus is always turning conventional wisdom upside down.

Who are the modern day people who pass on by when they see people who are hurting? Could it be those who want to deny health care to the poor or to those who can not afford decent care? An issue here is that compassion leads to costly care. Even so, should this not be a priority for those who say Jesus is their model? Let us take a closer look at the story of the good Samaritan. Suppose the good neighbor leaves the inn and continues down the road and sees another person hurting, and then continues and sees another, and then continues and sees another. His personal finances are now depleted. How can he now be a good neighbor? That is the question for us today when close to fifty million people have no health care and many others can only afford a poor plan. Is health care only for the comfortable and wealthy? Is not the care of people's health a responsibility of a nation for its people? Do the people of this nation only care about the survival of the fittest or the wealthiest?

The parable for today must deal with the "for profit health care providers" and "health care policy makers" groups that were not in the society in which Jesus lived. Allen Verhey (2000, 480-486) says that today's good Samaritan needs to insist on some consideration for a health care policy that assures the hurting the care they need. The parable can not be reduced just to policy in today's world where close to fifty million people in the U.S. are without health care because of its exorbitant costs, but policy can not be ignored. Both private business and government must work together to provide the answer, and today's good Samaritan needs to be involved in bringing about the help needed. There are those who say government needs to stay out of it, but is not government God's creation also and accountable to him? It appears to this writer that the greatest healer in history would be concerned and do something about the problem. Does the reader think Jesus would promote a system based on profits only as the solution? Why or why not?

This writer finds it sad that many who have Medicare, do not want more government spending for others to have it, even as they support more government spending for wars. They reject something Jesus cared about to support something Jesus opposed. How does the reader think Jesus would approach this issue? Does the reader believe he would say everyone should fend for himself? Would he agree that only those who have the money should have health care? Would he say whoever has more, more shall be given, and whoever does not have much that which he has will be taken away? Services for those in need continue to be stripped in order to benefit the desires of the comfortable and wealthy. All is supported by worldly reason and a Scripture verse every once in awhile taken out of context. This writer can not find anything in the teachings of Jesus to support such activity. In fact on practically every page of Scripture, the opposite is seen. Over and over Scripture warns about the selfish use of money.

Jim Wallis (2005, 212) states there are 2,350 verses in the Bible on the poor and God's response to injustice. One of every sixteen verses in the New Testament is about the poor and the subject of money. In the first three gospels (the Synoptics) it is one out of every ten verses, and in the book of Luke, it is one in seven. In all these verses there is nothing that favors the comfortable, and there are many warnings to them. When is the last time the reader heard a sermon on these issues from the pulpit of their church?

Today, in America those on the right are constantly warning about a drift toward socialism, even communism because of government using tax money to help people, but those on the left need to begin warning of a drift toward an oligopoly, or plutocracy, or at the very extreme right, fascism. The more government uses tax money to benefit corporations and the more government works together with corporations to control the masses to benefit themselves, then the more the drift is to the right.

When this happens, corporations benefit at the expense of the middle class, who have to make up for the tax breaks to the rich and in the process lose badly needed services. Meanwhile, the politicians get big returns from the corporations and big money to finance their campaigns to stay in power and to continue to take care of them. Since the legislators made it all legal, it is not called a system of bribes and kickbacks.

Corporations must make a profit, but where is the line between reasonable profits and greed? Instead of corporations outsourcing jobs, what is their responsibility to create jobs and provide a decent wage structure for the laborers in their own society? When their profits are bursting at the seams, what is their responsibility to provide healthcare to their workers? What confounds the mind of this author is people receiving these benefits from their employer or the government, but they are opposed to such when it applies to someone else. Is that not the height of selfishness?

In verses 38-42 as they went on their way, he entered a certain village, where a woman named Martha welcomed him into her home. She had a sister named Mary, who sat at the Lord's feet and listened to what he was saying. But Martha was distracted by her many tasks; so she came to him and asked, "Lord, do you not care that my sister has left me to do all the work by myself? Tell her then to help me." But the Lord answered her, "Martha, you are worried and distracted by many things; there is need of only one thing. Mary has chosen the better part, which will not be taken away from her."

An interesting note is Jesus again upturning the conventional wisdom of society. Women were not to be taught in their society. Jesus again challenges the status quo. One thing Jesus is not; he is not conservative. That is something that can not even be debated. He challenges conventional religion, politics, economics, and social policy. The status quo and returning to the old ways of doing things are not his way of doing things. His approach to living life is always to model how to best love God and love one's neighbor. And that is done by serving one's neighbor, and doing to others as one would like done to them.

In the Martha and Mary incident being a disciple of Jesus means that a relationship with him and listening to him is first in importance, and then serving others comes out of one's relationship to Jesus. Martha is distracted from listening to Jesus because she is very busy, even though what she is doing is important. The incident is about priorities. Of first importance is one's relationship to Jesus, listening to his word, and understanding the nature of his kingdom;

this is to order all priorities. One's ideas about life are not to come from the world's ideas but from one's relationship to Jesus and the kingdom that he came to preach.

Chapter 11:1-4 says, He was praying in a certain place, and after he finished, one of his disciples said to him, "Lord teach us to pray, as John taught his disciples." He said to them, "When you pray, say: Father, hallowed be your name. Your kingdom come. Give us each day our daily bread. And forgive us our sins, for we ourselves forgive everyone indebted to us. And do not bring us to the time of trial. (Compare with Mt 6:9-13 to see that the structure is the same but the wording is different. This is another example of how things were passed on orally in different communities for approximately fifty years until the different writers wrote down what they received.)

We can call God Father because through Jesus we become his adopted sons and daughters. In saying hallowed be your name believers recognize his holiness and praise him. In praying your kingdom come, one prays for his kingdom to break into this world more fully. In praying for daily bread, the prayer is for people to have the physical bread needed as well as spiritual bread. In praying for forgiveness of sin and debts, the person praying states that in receiving God's mercy they will also grant mercy to those who have sinned against them and who are indebted to them. Finally in asking not to be brought to the time of trial, the person prays to be able to overcome temptations and to be delivered from evil.

In verses 5-8 he said to them, "Suppose one of you has a friend, and you go to him at midnight and say to him, 'Friend, lend me three loaves of bread; for a friend of mine has arrived, and I have nothing to set before him.' And he answers from within, 'Do not bother me; the door has already been locked, and my children are with me in bed; I cannot get up and give you anything.' I tell you even though he will not get up and give him anything because he is his friend, at least because of his persistence he will get up and give him whatever he needs. (The idea is even though you may not get what you first pray for, stay in communication with God. God will take care of your needs, not necessarily your wants but your needs.)

Verses 9-13 say, "So I say to you, Ask and it will be given you; search, and you will find; knock, and the door will be opened for you. For everyone who asks receives, and everyone who searches finds, and for everyone who knocks, the door will be opened. Is there anyone among you who, if your child asks for a fish, will give a snake instead of a fish? Or if the child asks for an egg, will give a scorpion? If you then, who are evil, know how to give good gifts to your children, how much more will the heavenly Father give the Holy Spirit to those who ask him." (God cares about the needs of his people. When these verses are used elsewhere it is usually in the context of receiving the fruits and gifts of the Holy Spirit, whose purpose is to form the character of God's people and make them instruments of the kingdom.)

In verses 14-16 he casts out a demon from a mute person, and the person begins to talk. But some claim he casts out the demon by Beelzebul, the ruler of the demons. Others kept demanding a sign from him to test him. But in verses 17-23 Jesus said, "Every kingdom divided against itself becomes a desert, and house falls on house. If Satan also is divided against himself, how will his kingdom stand?–for you say that I cast out the demons by Beelzebul. Now if I cast out demons by Beezebul, by whom do your exorcists cast them out? Therefore they will be your judges. But if it is by the finger of God that I cast out demons, then the kingdom of God has come to you. When a strong man, fully armed, guards his castle, his property is safe. But when one stronger than he attacks him and overcomes him, he takes away his armor in which he trusted and divides his plunder. Whoever is not with me is against me, and whoever does not gather with me scatters."

In Luke 9:50 and Mk 9:38-41 Jesus said the opposite. He said, if one is not against us he is with us. But the difference is the different context as the reader will soon see. In this conflict there is no middle ground. Jesus is being opposed. Jesus is the strong man who has invaded Satan's domain and is plundering it. This is the sign that the kingdom of God is breaking in upon God's creation. Evil is in the process of being defeated.

In verses 24-26 Jesus said, "When the unclean spirit has gone out of a person, it wanders through waterless regions looking for a resting place, but not finding any, it says, 'I will return to my house from which I came.' When it comes it finds it swept and put in order. Then it goes and brings seven other spirits more evil than itself, and they enter and live there; and the last state of that person is worst than the first."

Jesus is saying it is not enough to have your sins forgiven and be swept clean of evil. If one's heart is not filled with the Holy Spirit and the gifts and fruit of the Spirit, and if one is not born of God and transformed, evil will return even in greater magnitude than previously. This is not only a teaching for individuals but also used in reference to the nation of Israel. In the past God sent Assyria in 722 BC and then Babylonia in 586 BC to punish his people and send them into exile. But Israel seems to keep repeating its sins, and each time gets worse than the last. Now, if the nation is forgiven but rejects Christ, then without Christ and the Holy Spirit they will return to their past, and the last state will be worse than the first. Formerly their ancestors killed the prophets, and now they will kill him and those who follow him. God will again punish the nation. This time he will use the Romans.

Verses 27-28 say, While he was saying this, a woman in the crowd raised her voice and said to him, "Blessed is the womb that bore you and the breasts that nursed you!" But he said, "Blessed rather are those who hear the word of God and obey it." (Jesus is not really denying what she said, but again is setting priorities.)

Verses 29-30 say, When the crowds were increasing, he began to say, "This generation is an evil generation; it asks for a sign, but no sign will be given to it except the sign of Jonah." (The sign of Jonah was repentance offered to the Gentiles, and they repented.) Verse 32 says, "The people of Nineveh will rise up at the judgment with this generation and condemn it, because they repented at the proclamation of Jonah, and see, something greater than Jonah is here."

The people of Nineveh, who were Gentiles, repent after Jonah spent three days in the big fish and came out. Jesus, the perfect Son of God, comes to his own people, is put to death, and then after three days rises from the dead, but his people do the opposite of the people of Nineveh; they refuse to repent.

In verses 33-36 Jesus says, "No one after lighting a lamp puts it in a cellar, but on the lampstand so that those who enter may see the light. Your eye is the lamp of your body. If your eye is healthy, your whole body is full of light; but if it is not healthy, your body is full of darkness. Therefore consider whether the light in you is not darkness. If then your whole body is full of light, with no part of it in darkness, it will be as full of light as when a lamp gives you light with its rays.

The light is Christ. A healthy eye represents spiritual insight and understanding because one has allowed the light to fill the mind and body. If there is darkness it is because one is taking the eye off the mark. Luke is saying to his readers be filled with the light of Christ, and let your light shine.

Verses 37-41 say, While he was speaking, a Pharisee invited him to dine with him; so he went in and took his place at the table. The Pharisee was amazed to see that he did not first wash before dinner. (The washing has nothing to do with sanitation. It is part of the ritual purity laws to symbolize the washing away of contamination in case something declared unclean is touched. These laws were originally for priests but now forced upon the people.) In (39) the Lord said to him, "Now you Pharisees clean the outside of the cup and of the dish, but inside you are full of greed and wickedness. You fools! Did not the one who made the outside make the inside (hearts) also? So give for alms those things that are within; (from the heart) and see, everything will be clean for you." (Jesus insists that the inner life is even more important than the outer life. One will not be able to cover up their greed and wickedness with a life of hypocrisy.)

In verses 42-44 Jesus says, "But woe to you Pharisees! For you tithe mint and rue and herbs of all kinds, and neglect justice and the love of God; it is these you ought to have practiced, without neglecting the others." (They are meticulous about tithing everything to the temple, even the most simple of things, like their garden herbs, but they really do not love God, for they neglect social justice, which is God's concern for the disadvantaged. They give to the church and use this to rationalize their greed and non-concern for the poor.) "Woe to you Pharisees! For you love to have the seat of honor in the synagogues and to be greeted with respect in the marketplaces. Woe to you! For you are like unmarked graves, . . ." (They are defiling themselves without realizing it. They wash on the outside but refuse to be washed on the inside.)

Verses 45-46 say, One of the lawyers (usually called scribes) answered him, "Teacher, when you say these things, you insult us too." And he said, "Woe also to you lawyers! For you load people with burdens hard to bear, and you yourselves do not lift a finger to ease them." (The religious leaders load people down with burdensome religious demands based on their man made rules.)

Verses 47-52 say, "Woe to you! For you build the tombs of the prophets whom your ancestors killed. So you witness and approve of the deeds of your ancestors; for they killed them, and you build their tombs. Therefore also the Wisdom of God said, 'I will send them prophets and apostles, some of whom they will kill and persecute,' so that this generation may be charged with the blood of all the prophets shed since the foundation of the world, from the blood of Abel to the blood of Zechariah, who perished between the altar and the sanctuary. Yes, I tell you, it will be charged against this generation. Woe to you lawyers! For you have taken away the key of knowledge; you did not enter (the kingdom) yourselves, and you hindered those who were entering." (He is not applying these statements to all Pharisees just to the leadership attempting to destroy him and the extremists.)

He reminds them that during the reign of King Joash, Zechariah tried to clean up corrupt worship and religion and they killed him (2 Chron 24:17-22). Now, they control the Scriptures by their authority, but because they do not really understand their deepest meaning, they erroneously interpret them. Then they surround the people with man made rules that distort the Scriptures. They also hinder the people from entering the kingdom with their bad examples. Instead of modeling the Scriptures too many of them model arrogance and greed. Does the reader think these Scriptures have any bearing on what is happening today? Why?

Verses 53-54 say, When he went outside, the scribes and the Pharisees began to be very hostile toward him and to cross examine him about many things, lying in wait for him, to catch him in something he might say. (If the reader wants to follow Jesus and experience what he experienced just begin to criticize the hypocritical actions of those in power who call themselves followers of Christ but deny his teachings. It will not take long to begin to experience what Jesus experienced.)

Chapter 12:1-3 says, Meanwhile, when the crowds gathered by the thousands, so that they trampled on one another, he began to speak first to his disciples, "Beware of the yeast of the Pharisees, that is, their hypocrisy. Nothing is covered up that will not be uncovered, and nothing secret that will not become known. Therefore whatever you have said in the dark will be heard in the light, and what you have whispered behind closed doors will be proclaimed from the housetops. (The hypocrisy of those who are religious, then and now, and the true condition of all hearts will be revealed on judgment day. Therefore, his message is to receive forgiveness and get your heart right with God.)

Verses 4-7 say, "I tell you, my friends, do not fear those who kill the body, and after that can do nothing more. But I will warn you whom to fear: fear him who, after he has killed, has authority to cast into hell. Yes, I tell you, fear him! Are not five sparrows sold for two pennies? Yet not one of them is forgotten in God's sight. But even the hairs of your head are all counted. Do not be afraid; you are of more value than many sparrows." Verses 8-9 say, "And I tell you, everyone who acknowledges me before others, the Son of Man will also acknowledge before the angels of God; but whoever denies me before others will be denied before the angels of God." (This denial is not only by words but by actions.)

Verse 10 says, "And everyone who speaks a word against the Son of Man will be forgiven; but whoever blasphemes against the Holy Spirit will not be forgiven. (Jesus said that when he is raised up, he will send the Holy Spirit as his presence to continue his work on earth. That is humanity's last chance. If in the end the work of the Holy Spirit is rejected, there will no longer be any hope.) Verses 11-12 say, When they bring you before the synagogues, the rulers, and the authorities, do not worry about how you are to defend yourselves or what you are to say; for the Holy Spirit will teach you at that very hour what you ought to say." (This is fulfilled in the book of Acts.)

Verses 13-15 say, Someone in the crowd said to him, "Teacher, tell my brother to divide the family inheritance with me." But he said to him, "Friend, who set me to be a judge or arbitrator over you?" And he said to them, "Take care! Be on your guard against all kinds of greed; for one's life does not consist in the abundance of possessions." (Notice how often greed is mentioned in the Gospels. In Col 3:5 greed is called an idol. Of course, this writer does not know anyone who thinks their greed is greed. Does the reader know any such person? Rarely does this writer miss a church service, but it is not remembered the last time a sermon or homily was heard on greed.)

Then in (16-21) he told them a parable: "The land of a rich man produced abundantly. And he thought to himself, 'What should I do, for I have no place to store my crops?' Then he said, I will do this: I will pull down my barns and build larger ones, and there I will store all my grain and my goods. And I will say to my soul, 'Soul, you have ample goods laid up for many years; relax, eat, drink, be merry.' But God said to him, 'You fool! This very night your life is being demanded of you. And the things you have prepared, whose will they be?' So it is with those who store up treasures for themselves but are not rich toward God." (Jesus calls the selfish and the greedy, fools.)

There is no sin in taking care of oneself and in preparing for the future, but there is sin when God is left out and ignored. If one lives only for wealth and material things with no concern to spread the wealth to help those less fortunate, one will face judgment in dire straits. The rich man is the one who is poor in the sight of God. His greed trapped him in his possessions, but at his death he lost them all. The rich man is usually the one that most people envy, but in God's sight he is a fool.

In American society "spreading the wealth" is a negative term unless it is spread upward. Anytime help is offered to the disadvantaged by the government, the comfortable and wealthy complain. But most government money (tax money) does not go to the disadvantaged or welfare recipients; it goes to the wealthy and to big corporations, mainly through laws that favor them with grants and tax breaks. Then government has to make up for this by taxing the middle class more. This is called corporate welfare and spreading the wealth upward, and not a word is said about it. Why? Is not this socialism for the wealthy? Sometimes this writer has to wonder if this country's economic theory is about practicing socialism for big corporations and many businesses while practicing capitalism with those in the middle class. It is the middle class that has to make up for the massive tax breaks and benefits given to corporations and big business. This practice is usually justified by saying jobs need to be created, but even so, is it a reversed socialism? But the question is: Where are the jobs? Many people believe most of their tax money goes to support welfare, but that is not even close. For an interesting look at where your tax dollar goes, see page seventy.

Part of the answer of why nothing seems to be said is that the media is big money owned by big money, and those in Congress and state legislatures are also big money controlled by the special interests of big money. It used to be called bribes and kickbacks, but since the lawmakers made it legal, it is now called lobbying. It seems that only big money is represented in government and the media. The media is to the left on cultural issues such as gay rights and abortion but very far to the right on money issues. Of course, according to them it is always for good reasons. Now, only those with big money can even run for office. These people including the media are not going to criticize what benefits them. This writer is quite sure that if Jesus were on earth today, he would expose this injustice and call them, fools.

After he tells his disciples not to get trapped in greed, verses 22-26 say, He said to his disciples, "Therefore I tell you, do not worry about your life, what you will eat, or about your body, what you will wear. For life is more than food, and the body more than clothing. Consider the ravens: they neither sow nor reap, they have neither storehouse nor barn, and yet God feeds them. Of how much more value are you than birds! And can any of you by worrying add a single hour to your span of life? If then you are not able to do so small a thing as that, why do you worry about the rest?

Verses 27-34 say, "Consider the lilies, how they grow: they neither toil nor spin; yet I tell you, even Solomon in all his glory was not clothed like one of these. But if God so clothes the grass of the field, which is alive today and tomorrow is thrown into the oven, how much more will he clothe you–you of little faith! And do not keep striving for what you are to eat and what you are to drink, and do not keep worrying. For it is the nations of the world (those motivated, not by the kingdom, but by the things of the world) that strive after these things, and your Father knows that you need them. Instead strive for his kingdom, and these things will be given to you as well."

"Do not be afraid, little flock, for it is your Father's good pleasure to give you the kingdom. Sell your possessions, and give alms. Make purses for yourselves that do not wear out, an unfailing treasure in heaven, where no thief comes near and no moth destroys. For where your treasure is, there your heart will be also."

This message is to his disciples. It is also primarily a message for the "haves" and not the "have nots." Everyone is not called to spread the wealth by selling their possessions and giving them to the needy, but for some that is the call. But everyone is called to not let their possessions be their priority or controlling interest. And everyone is called to be of benefit to those in need in someway by what they have and by their moral support. Greed and self interest are not the call of Jesus to those who follow him.

This is not saying to ignore preparing for the future. In one sense this is a metaphor not to strive for your wants and the riches of the world, but to give alms and to trust God. God will take care of your needs. Our wants are often the problem and what gets most people off the path to true life. Jesus knew as a general statement that the more people have, the more they want, and the more they are concerned to protect it. In this writer's experience it also seems the less people have the more they seem willing to share. When the Scriptures are taken seriously, it is no wonder the Enlightenment leaders and their followers today want to keep religion out of politics and economics, especially when it comes to money issues.

So Jesus tells them to focus down instead of up and see that help goes to those in need. Again, this message is not just for individuals, but for nations, institutions, and all of God's creation. Everything created is to be under God's reign and accountable to him. Because much of America is controlled by a philosophy of individualism, which incidentally is not God's controlling philosophy, many reject this thinking that opposes greed and self interest as necessary for the efficient working of our economic system.

Jesus tells people that they can not have two masters, so strive for the kingdom and these things will be given to you. Romans 14:17 says, the kingdom of God is not food and drink but righteous (also translated justice, meaning social justice) and peace and joy in the Holy Spirit. Luke wants his audience to ask themselves where their hearts really are. Is it more concerned for striving after the kingdom that leads to life or striving after the things that lead to death?

Verses 35-40 say, "Be dressed for action and have your lamps lit: be like those who are waiting for their master to return from the wedding banquet, so that they may open the door for him as soon as he comes and knocks. Blessed are those slaves whom the master finds alert when he comes; . . . You must also be ready, for the Son of Man is coming at an unexpected hour."

In verses 41-44 Peter said, "Lord are you telling this parable for us or for everyone?" And the Lord said, "Who then is the faithful and prudent manager whom his master will put in charge of his slaves, to give them their allowance of food at the proper time? Blessed is that slave whom his master will find at work when he arrives. Truly I tell you, he will put that one in charge of all his possessions.

Verses 45-48 say, "But if that slave says to himself, 'My master is delayed in coming,' and if he begins to beat the other slaves, men and women, and to eat and drink and get drunk, the master of that slave will come on a day when he does not expect him and at an hour that he does not know, and he will cut him in pieces, and put him with the unfaithful. (The man is unrighteous with no concern for others.) That slave who knew what his master wanted, but did not prepare himself or do what was wanted will receive a severe beating. But the one who did not know and did what deserved a beating will receive a light beating. From everyone to whom much has been given, much will be required; and to whom the one has been entrusted, even more will be demanded."

It is this writer's opinion in addition to being a message to individuals it is also a reference to the Jewish leaders who the Master (God, the Father) put in charge of his people. And the coming of God is a reference to his judgment upon them in AD 70 when the city of Jerusalem and the temple are destroyed. The context, especially the following verses, (54-56) leads one to that conclusion. Even so, the principle that to whom much is given much is required is something to pay attention to as far as a Christian's responsibility toward God.

Verses 49-53 say, "I came to bring fire on the earth, and how I wish it were already kindled! I have a baptism with which to be baptized, and what stress I am under until it is completed! Do you think that I have come to bring peace to the earth? No, I tell you, but rather division! From now on five in one household will be divided, three against two and two against three; they will be divided: father against son and son against father, mother against daughter and daughter against mother, mother-in-law against her daughter-in-law and daughter-in-law against mother-in-law."

He is saying everyone, including the nation, is not going to accept his message because its values are different from the values of the world. Jesus demands a transformed life and a commitment to him and his teachings. He will be the believer's new priority. This will cause conflict between people and families.

In other places Jesus did come to bring peace. In fact in Mt 5:9 he says, "Blessed are the peacemakers." The key to interpreting Scripture is being true to the different situations or contexts. One of the reasons there are many interpretations is that contexts are ignored and individuals pick and choose the Scriptures that best fit what they want to believe, and then ignore those that do not fit their beliefs.

Verses 54-56 say, He also said to the crowds, "When you see a cloud rising in the west, you immediately say, 'It is going to rain'; and so it happens. And when you see the south wind blowing, you say, 'There will be scorching heat'; and it happens. You hypocrites! You know how to interpret the appearance of earth and sky, but why do you not know how to interpret the present time? (Jesus is specifically referring to what is and will happen in his time era, but it can be applied to all times.)

Verses 57-59 say, "And why do you not judge for yourselves what is right? Thus when you go with your accuser before a magistrate, on the way make an effort to settle the case, or you may be dragged before the judge, and the judge hand you over to the officer, and the officer throw you in prison. I tell you, you will never get out until you have paid the very last penny."

Jesus is using a metaphor to say that when judgment comes, which is a reference to dealing with the Romans as well as the destruction of Jerusalem and the temple, they will wish they had taken another path. This is also a good message for individuals to reconcile with each other and work out their problems in a fair and just manner because when one goes before the judge, it may be too late.

Chapter 13:1-5 says, At that very time there were some present who told him about the Galileans whose blood Pilate had mingled with their sacrifices. He asked them, "Do you think that because these Galileans suffered in this way they were worse sinners than all other Galileans? Verse 3 says, No, I tell you; but unless you repent, you will all perish as they did. Or those eighteen who were killed when the tower of Siloam fell on them—do you think they were worse offenders than all the others living in Jerusalem? No, I tell you; but unless you repent, you will all perish just as they did."

Neither of these incidents is mentioned elsewhere, and there is no other information about them. This teaching of Jesus has multiple meanings for both the individual and the nation. First of all, everyone is eventually going to die and face the judgment, so the call is to repent and be an instrument of the kingdom or perish.

Second, just because a catastrophe comes, it does not mean God has brought it upon the people. Earlier Matthew (5:45) taught that the rain falls on both the just and the unjust.

Third, this writer believes that in those times the primary message is to the nation about oppression of their own people and its resistance movement. Jesus is from the tradition of the Old Testament prophets, and this was their constant message. Jesus is basically telling them that if the nation does not repent of its oppression of its people and its agenda to violently throw out the Romans, the nation will be judged, and in the process, even innocent people will be hurt. This writer encourages the reader to spend time with the Old Testament prophets. The more the prophets and their concerns are understood, the more one will understand Jesus, who was a prophet in the Old Testament tradition, and whose Scriptures were the same as their Scriptures.

The nation will be judged just as the northern kingdom (Israel) was judged by the Assyrians in 722 BC and taken into exile, and just as the kingdom of the south (Judah) was judged in 586 BC when the Babylonians destroyed Jerusalem and the temple, and took the people into exile. The prophets warned those people in those times with this same message. Jesus is basically repeating their message. He is saying, if the nation does not repent, God, this time, will use Rome to again destroy Jerusalem and the temple. The result was that they rejected Jesus and did not repent and change their agenda to Jesus' kingdom of God agenda. Consequently, in AD 70 the city of Jerusalem and the temple were destroyed. His prophetic words were fulfilled. History again repeated itself.

In verses 6-9 he tells a parable supporting this writer's interpretation. Jesus says, "A man had a fig tree planted in his vineyard; and he came looking for the fruit on it and found none. So he said to the gardener, 'See here! For three years I have come looking for fruit on this fig tree, and still I find none. (Fruit has reference to the ways of God.) Cut it down! Why should it be wasting the soil?' He replied, 'Sir let it alone for one more year, until I dig around it and put manure on it. If it bears fruit next year, well and good; but if not, you can cut it down.' " (In the other gospels Jesus uses the fig tree to symbolize the nation and the temple. God is always patient waiting for repentance and fruit bearing.)

Verses 10-13 say, Now he was teaching in one of the synagogues on the sabbath. And just then there appeared a woman with a spirit that had crippled her for eighteen years. She was bent over and quite unable to stand up straight. When Jesus saw her, he called her over and said, "Woman, you are set free from your ailment." When he laid his hands on her, immediately she stood up straight and began praising God.

Verses 14-17 say, But the leader of the synagogue, indignant because Jesus had cured on the sabbath, kept saying to the crowd, "There are six days in which work ought to be done; come on those days and be cured, and not on the sabbath day." But the Lord answered him and said, "You hypocrites! Does each of you on the sabbath untie his ox or his donkey from the manger, and lead it away and give it water? And ought not this woman, a daughter of Abraham whom Satan bound for eighteen long years, be set free from this bondage on the sabbath day?" (They care more for animals than people.) When he said this, all his opponents were put to shame; and the entire crowd was rejoicing at all the wonderful things he was doing. (Again, Jesus exposes their hypocrisy, to the delight of the crowd.)

In verses 18-21 He said therefore, "What is the kingdom of God like? And to what should I compare it? It is like a mustard seed that someone took and sowed in the garden; it grew and became a tree, and the birds of the air made nests in its branches." And again he said, "To what should I compare the kingdom of God? It is like yeast that a woman took and mixed in with three measures of flour until all of it was leavened."

Jesus is saying the kingdom is going to begin small, and then it will grow, and in the process bit by bit make an impact on God's creation as more and more people become transformed by the kingdom. As these new people of God become carriers of the kingdom, it will continue to grow and make an impact on individuals and everything in the world until Jesus returns in the end to finalize the new heaven and new earth.

Jesus went through one town and village after another, teaching as he made his way to Jerusalem. Verses 23-30 say, Someone asked him, "Lord, will only a few be saved?" He said, "Strive to enter through the narrow door; for many, I tell you, will try to enter and not be able. When once the owner of the house has got up and shut the door, and you begin to stand outside and to knock at the door, saying, 'Lord open to us,' then in reply he will say to you, 'I do not know where you come from.' Then you will begin to say, 'We ate and drank with you, and you taught in our streets.' But he will say, 'I do not know where you come from; go away from me, all you evil doers!' There will be weeping and gnashing of teeth when you see Abraham and Isaac and Jacob and all the prophets in the kingdom of God, and you yourself thrown out. Then people will come from east and west, from north and south, and will eat in the kingdom of God. Indeed, some are last who will be first, and some are first who will be last."

Again, this is first a message to the nation of Israel. It is called an *eschatological reversal*. The nation is expecting God to set them free from the Romans. Instead he will judge them, as he did in the past, this time through the Romans. Second it is a message to all those who believe that they are God's people to not get over confident. Many are going to think they belong, but because of their life, their actions, and what they stand for, they are going to be denied entrance.

The message is for individuals to strive to enter through the narrow door. The door is wide for those who try to enter by the way of the world's conventional wisdom. The wisdom from God is the message of Jesus and the kingdom. This is the narrow way. I Corinthians 1:18-25 tells us that the message about the cross is foolishness to those who are perishing, but to us who are being saved it is the wisdom and power of God. God has made foolish the wisdom of the world.

The people of God are constantly warned to exchange the wisdom of the world for the wisdom of God. The message is not just believe and go to church once in awhile, and then everything will be wonderful. The message is strive; strive to enter by the narrow way. Thus believing is just the beginning. There is a responsibility Jesus puts on all those wanting to follow him. There is a whole way of thinking and a whole way of life to be adapted to, which results in a major transformation.

Verses 31-34 say, At that very hour some Pharisees came and said to him, "Get away from here, for Herod wants to kill you." (Many Pharisees are open to Jesus.) He said to him, "Go and tell that fox for me, 'Listen, I am casting out demons and performing cures today and tomorrow, and on the third day I finish my work. (Calling Herod a fox is very dangerous.) Yet today, tomorrow, and the next day I must be on my way, because it is impossible for a prophet to be killed outside of Jerusalem.'

In verse 34 Jesus says, Jerusalem, Jerusalem, the city that kills the prophets and stones those that are sent to it! How often have I desired to gather your children together as a hen gathers her brood under her wings, and you were not willing! (Jesus and his agenda of peace and reconciliation oppose their militant nationalism. It is the way he offers to keep them from destruction, but they refuse.) Then in (35) he says, See, your house is left to you. And I tell you, you will not see me until the time comes when you say, 'Blessed is the one who comes in the name of the Lord.' "

Jesus is saying as Ezekiel (chapter 11) says, God and his presence are leaving the temple, and it will be left unprotected to its fate (also Mt 23:38). Like Jeremiah he is being called a traitor to Israel's national aspirations, even as he claims he is the true spokesperson for the Father. He tells them he will be vindicated, and when he is, his people will say, blessed is he who comes in the name of the Lord. He is later vindicated in three events: his resurrection, his sending of the Spirit to the church in Acts 2, and in AD 70 when Rome destroys the city and the temple. Jesus then is verified as the new temple of God.

Jesus as a prophet knows he will be put to death as the Old Testament prophets were and for the same reasons. Among other things the prophets stood against militant nationalism and for social justice against wealth and power. Wealth and power always react negatively to those who challenge their power and their political, economic, and social decisions. The prophets were usually put to death because they challenged the conventional thinking of the status quo designed to benefit selfish interests at the expense of the common good. The same will happen to Jesus, and the harassment will occur to those who echo Jesus throughout time.

Chapter 14:1-6 says, Jesus was going to the house of a leader of the Pharisees to eat a meal on the sabbath, they were watching him closely. Just then, in front of him, there was a man who had dropsy (a condition of severe fluid retention). And Jesus asked the lawyers

(scribes) and the Pharisees, "Is it lawful to heal on the sabbath or not?" But they were silent. So Jesus took him and healed him and sent him away. Then he said to them, "If one of you has a child or an ox that has fallen into a well, will you not immediately pull it out on a sabbath day?" And they could not reply to this. (Their Sabbath laws are top priority, even more important than helping a human in need. Though, they would help animals. Jesus shows them they are distorting the purpose of God's laws.)

Verses 7-11 say, When he noticed how the guests chose the places of honor, he told them a parable. "When you are invited by someone to a wedding banquet, do not sit down at the place of honor, in case someone more distinguished than you has been invited by your host; and the host who invited both of you may come and say to you, 'Give this person your place,' and then in disgrace you would start to take the lowest place. But when you are invited, go and sit down at the lowest place, so that when your host comes, he may say to you, 'Friend, move up higher'; then you will be honored in the presence of all who sit at the table with you. For all who exalt themselves will be humbled, and those who humble themselves will be exalted."

In the kingdom the arrogant will lose the place they believe is theirs. Only those who humble themselves before God will be honored. Being humble and not thinking more of oneself than one should is a key teaching throughout Scripture.

In verses 12-14 he said to the one who invited him, "When you give a luncheon or a dinner, do not invite your friends or your brothers or your relatives or rich neighbors, in case they may invite you in return, and you would be repaid. But when you give a banquet, invite the poor, the crippled, the lame, and the blind. And you will be blessed, because they cannot repay you, for you will be repaid at the resurrection of the righteous."

Again, this is not a hard and fast timeless law; it is given to shape character and attitude and to make one think about those who Jesus made a priority, and to remind them of the type of people who will be at the salvation banquet. It is to humble his disciples and make them co-creators with him in his work. It is to take their thinking and actions to a higher level. Jesus is also teaching that one is to do right not for an earthly reward, but for the sake of what is good and for the kingdom. Do not be thinking of yourself and the favors you may get from whom you take care of, think of those in need as Christ did.

Verses 15-20 say, One of his dinner guests on hearing this, said to him, "Blessed is anyone who will eat bread in the kingdom of God!" Then Jesus said to them, "Someone gave a great dinner and invited many. At the time for the dinner he sent his slave to say to those who had been invited, 'Come; for everything is ready now.' But they all alike began to make excuses. The first said to him, 'I have bought a piece of land, and I must go out and see it; please accept my regrets.' Another said, 'I have bought five yoke of oxen, and I am going to try them out; please accept my regrets.' Another said, 'I have just been married, and therefore I cannot come.' (These people are too busy with the things of the world to pay attention to God and his kingdom. Can the reader see any similarity to that today?)

Verses 21-24 say, "So the slave returned and reported this to his master. Then the owner of the house became angry and said to the slave, 'Go out at once into the streets and lanes of the town and bring in the poor, the crippled, the blind, and the lame.' (Notice it is the same type of people as in the previous parable.) And the slave said, 'Sir what you ordered has been done, and there is still room.' Then the master said to the slave, 'Go out into the roads and lanes, and compel people to come in, so that my house may be filled. For

I tell you, none of those who were invited will taste my dinner.' "

This is a parable that refers both to the kingdom of God that is now breaking into the world and the final kingdom in its completion symbolized by the salvation banquet. It is also to inform us that many who think they will be at the banquet will be surprised when they are left out.

Verses 25-26 say, Now large crowds were traveling with him; and he turned and said to them, "Whoever comes to me and does not hate father and mother, wife and children, brothers and sisters, yes, and even life itself, cannot be my disciple."

Again, this is not to be taken literally. Jesus is not saying to hate father and mother as well as life itself. The message is about priorities in hyperbolic form, a method of teaching that Jesus constantly uses. Jesus often tells people that he and the kingdom are to be first in priority. The message is also saying not to let anyone interfere with your call to follow Christ and his teachings. The word hate can be understood as "love less."

William Most (1994, 70) says that the Hebrew and Aramaic languages lack the degrees of comparison, such as good, better, best, or clear, clearer, clearest. Without these they found other ways to talk. We see an example here with love and hate. It really means that he loves one more and the other less based on their decisions. God does not hate anyone, and he certainly is not telling anyone to hate their parents. Again this is a problem for those who want to take everything literally and do not understand the nature of different languages and interpretation methodology.

He elaborates on this in (27-33) by saying, "Whoever does not carry the cross and follow me cannot be my disciple. (Carry the cross is a metaphor meaning to crucify self or to lose self interests and replace them with Christ's interests, and then follow his ways.) For which of you, intending to build a tower, does not first sit down and estimate the cost, to see whether he has enough to complete it? (Before people say they want to be a follower of Christ, they need to see if they are willing to follow through with Jesus' agenda.) Otherwise when he has laid a foundation and is not able to finish, all who see it will begin to ridicule him, saying, 'This fellow began to build but was not able to finish.' Or what king, going out to wage war against another king, will not sit down first and consider whether he is able with ten thousand to oppose the one who comes against him with twenty thousand? If he cannot, then, while the other is still far away, he sends a delegation and asks for the terms of peace. So therefore, none of you can become my disciple, if you do not give up all your possessions."

His point is one will not complete the call that involves going against the world's wisdom and the odds of success, if there is more trust in one's possessions and the things of the world than in him and his teachings of wisdom. Love of possessions and money is what keeps many from following and supporting the agenda of Jesus. It is also what causes some to twist his agenda into their agenda and attempt to cover it up by calling themselves after his name.

The statement that one has to give up all possessions to follow him is an hyperbole to guide one in setting priorities. As one reads through the Gospels Jesus does not tell everyone to do such. He does tell a rich young man to do so because his possessions were his priority and were interfering with his commitment to him. In setting priorities, it is obvious that the thinking of Jesus is not the thinking of most people today, including many of those who call themselves Christians. As a quick example just think of the reasons many decide to run for government office and the reasons many people vote for whom they vote. For too many is it not for what benefits their own selfish interests? Of course, this writer does not know any politician or voter who believes that about themselves.

Does the reader know anyone who does so?

In verses 34-35 Jesus says, "Salt is good; but if salt has lost its taste, how can its saltiness be restored? It is fit neither for the soil nor for the manure pile; they throw it away. Let anyone with ears to hear listen!"

If salt loses its flavor (taste), it becomes bland and no longer preserves food. Salt was a major way of preserving food in those times of no electricity. When salt loses its saltiness, the salt is no longer of much value. Jesus is saying, if Christians blend into the world with its interests and values, and avoid the cost of standing up for and with him and the kingdom's values and priorities, then they are no longer of value to him and the kingdom.

Chapter 15:1-7 says, Now all the tax collectors and sinners were coming near to listen to him. And the Pharisees and scribes were grumbling and saying, "This fellow welcomes sinners and eats with them." So he told them this parable: "Which one of you having a hundred sheep and losing one of them, does not leave the ninety-nine in the wilderness and go after the one that is lost until he finds it? When he has found it, he lays it on his shoulders and rejoices. And when he comes home, he calls together his friends and neighbors, saying to them, 'Rejoice with me, for I have found my sheep that was lost.' Just so, I tell you, there will be more joy in heaven over one sinner who repents than over ninety-nine righteous persons who need no repentance."

Repentance is about a change of heart and transformation. The ninety-nine may be a reference to the Pharisees and scribes or even most Jews from the old covenant, who believe they are the righteous and see no need to repent and follow Jesus, who they believe is a renegade.

Verses 8-10 say, "Or what woman having ten silver coins, if she loses one of them, does not light a lamp, sweep the house, and search carefully until she finds it? When she has found it, she calls together her friends and neighbors saying, 'Rejoice with me, for I have found the coin that I had lost.' Just so, I tell you, there is joy in the presence of the angels of God over one sinner who repents."

God's concern and compassion for those who repent and are transformed to the kingdom's way of thinking and living are highlighted. God never gives up on anyone. The next parable illustrates what the previous two parables have been saying.

Verses 11-24 say, Then Jesus said, "There was a man who had two sons. The younger of them said to his father, 'Father, give me the share of the property that will belong to me.' So he divided his property between them. A few days later the younger son gathered all he had and traveled to a distant country, and there he squandered his property in dissolute living. When he had spent everything, a severe famine took place throughout that country, and he began to be in need. So he went and hired himself out to one of the citizens of that country, who sent him to his fields to feed the pigs. He would gladly have filled himself with the pods that the pigs were eating; and no one gave him anything.

"But when he came to himself he said, 'How many of my father's hired hands have bread enough and to spare, but here I am dying of hunger! I will get up and go to my father, and I will say to him, "Father, I have sinned against heaven and before you; I am no longer worthy to be called your son; treat me like one of your hired hands." ' So he set off and went to his father. But while he was still far off, his father saw him and was filled with compassion; he ran and put his arms around him and kissed him. Then the son said to him, 'Father, I have sinned against heaven and before you; I am no longer worthy to be called your son.' But the father said to his slaves, 'Quickly, bring out a robe–the best one–and put it on him; put a ring on his finger and sandals on his feet. And get the fatted calf and kill it, and let us eat and celebrate; for this son of mine was dead and is alive again; he was lost and is found!' " And they began to celebrate.

Exile and restoration is the main theme. The man went into exile but with repentance he is restored. The story shows how the father goes out to meet the sinner returning home and how quickly the father is willing to restore him and bestow his grace of forgiveness upon one who repents; it also shows how much joy he has on repentance. The father is representing God the Father. The younger son represents those Jews who are repenting and joining Jesus and his kingdom agenda to become the new Israel.

Verses 25-32 continue, "Now the elder son was in the field; and when he came and approached the house, he heard music and dancing. He called one of the slaves and asked what was going on. He replied, 'Your brother has come, and your father has killed the fatted calf, because he has got him back safe and sound.' Then he became angry and refused to go in. His father came out and began to plead with him. But he answered the father, 'Listen! For all these years I have been working like a slave for you, and I have never disobeyed your command; yet you have never given me even a young goat so that I might celebrate with my friends. But when this son of yours (not his brother?) came back, who has devoured your property with prostitutes, you killed the fatted calf for him!' Then the father said to him, 'Son you are always with me, and all that is mine is yours. But we had to celebrate and rejoice, because this brother of yours was dead and has come to life; he was lost and has been found.' "

The true Israel is coming to its senses and returning to the Father as both Jeremiah (chapter 31) and Ezekiel (chapter 11) had foretold. They are given a new heart with a new spirit making a new covenant. Those who oppose are defining themselves as being outside the family. Many think the elder son represents the arrogant, self righteous religious leaders representing the nation, who resent salvation going to others who do not follow meticulously how things have always been, and who reject their man made religious laws as well as opposing their agenda against Rome.

For us today Luke is asking his reader who they identify with in the story. Is their attitude more like the welcoming, loving, full of grace Father, who allows sinners and the imperfect to return and begin to work on the deeper transformation of the heart? Or is their attitude like the younger son who was willing to change his thinking and be transformed, returning to the father, even as a slave? Or is their attitude like the elder son who was not willing to repent for he does not think he has any need to repent? Or like the elder son who has been in the group forever and wants things the way they have always been, and certainly does not want contaminated by someone who is unclean or different?

Chapter 16:1-4 says, Then Jesus said to his disciples, "There was a rich man who had a manager, and charges were brought to him that this man was squandering his property. So he summoned him and said to him, 'What is this that I hear about you? Give me an accounting of your management, because you cannot be my manager any longer.' Then the manager said to himself, 'What will I do, now that my master is taking my position away from me? I am not strong enough to dig, and I am ashamed to beg. I have decided what to do so that, when I am dismissed as manager, people may welcome me into their homes.'

Verses 5-9 say, "So, summoning his master's debtors one by one, he asked the first, 'How much do you owe my master?' He answered, 'A hundred jugs of olive oil.' He said to him, 'Take your bill, sit down quickly, and make it fifty.' Then he asked another, 'And how much do you owe?' He replied, 'A hundred containers of wheat.' He said to him, 'Take your bill and make it eighty.' And his master commended the dishonest manager because he had acted shrewdly; for the children of this age are more shrewd in dealing with their own generation than are the children of light. And I tell you, make friends for yourselves by means of dishonest wealth so that when it is gone, they may welcome you into the eternal homes.

This has always somewhat baffled readers. The dishonest manager is being commended for his dishonesty. But notice he is not rehired. The point of the parable is not to encourage dishonesty. Dishonesty is a value the people of the world use in their world to advance themselves and take advantage of people. People of the kingdom are not to use those values. But people of the kingdom are to live with kingdom values and use the things of this world in a wise way to advance the kingdom and prepare themselves, others, and the kingdom for final perfection. It is probable that the amounts he forgave were the excess profits he made from the people.

Verses 10-13 say, "Whoever is faithful in very little is faithful also in much; and whoever is dishonest in very little is dishonest also in much. If then you have not been faithful with the dishonest wealth, who will entrust to you the true riches? And if you have not been faithful with what belongs to another, who will give you what is your own? No slave can serve two masters; for a slave will either hate the one and love the other, or be devoted to the one and despise the other. You cannot serve God and wealth."

The point is one must choose and be faithful to light or darkness, to the things that represent God or the things that represent what opposes God. They can not exist together. You can not serve both. So the parable is saying, if followers of Christ would use their money in being as faithful to the kingdom's values as well as the people of the world use their money to be faithful to the world's values, the kingdom would make great strides.

Verses 14-15 say, The Pharisees who were lovers of money, heard all this, and they ridiculed him. (They, like many today who justify their selfishness and greed, do not like the fact that Jesus says that one can not serve God and money, for they want to have it both ways.) So he said to them, "You are those who justify yourselves in the sight of others; but God knows your hearts; for what is prized by human beings is an abomination in the sight of the God." (Jesus is saying that what many humans prize most are the world's values, wealth, and methods of obtaining it. Then they seek to justify their greed. One way they attempt to do this is by giving a few alms, but their heart is hard, see 21:1-4.)

Verses 16-18 say, The law and the prophets were in effect until John came; since then the good news of the kingdom of God is proclaimed, and everyone tries to enter it by force. "But it is easier for heaven and earth to pass away, than for one stroke of a letter in the law to be dropped."

For Luke there are three time periods: the law and the prophets, John the Baptist, and Jesus proclaiming the good news of the kingdom. Jesus is saying that all have abiding validity, but Jesus has the authority to interpret everything for the new age through his words and actions. The themes, virtues, values, principles, and vision of the new law are being made present in Jesus as the fulfillment of the old. The verse saying that people are trying to enter the kingdom by force may be a reference to the revolutionary party trying to force their agenda and call it God's will. It may be like the people of our time declaring war against their enemies and then singing patriotic songs.

Then in verse 18 he gives an interpretation of the law. Jesus says, "Anyone who divorces his wife and marries another commits adultery, and whoever marries a woman divorced from her husband commits adultery."

The value in the kingdom is staying forever with one's married partner. According to this teaching remarriage is adultery. Can adultery be forgiven? In the final kingdom there will be no divorce but also no war. As the kingdom breaks in at different times in different ways until completed by Jesus, one has to wonder in the real world of hard hearts, if there is a just war, could there also be a just divorce and remarriage?

Or is it wrong to permit both a just war, a just divorce and a just remarriage? How can one be accepted and not the other? Many, even numerous Catholics, ask how it is possible for the priest who gave communion to the pilot who dropped bombs on Hiroshima and Nagasaki to be forgiven and continue to say Mass, and the bomber be forgiven and continue to receive communion, but the one who is divorced and remarried not be allowed to receive communion? This is a question Catholic scholars must reconcile. On the other hand Protestant scholars, who make the claim of sola (only) Scripture, have to reconcile how many Protestants can grant divorce and allow remarriage practically at will as they ignore these verses.

Luke in verses 19-21 says, "There was a rich man who was dressed in purple and fine linen and who feasted sumptuously every day. (Purple is made from a dye that was very expensive. Only royalty and the very rich have anything colored purple.) And at his gate lay a poor man named Lazarus, covered with sores, who longed to satisfy his hunger with what fell from the rich man's table; even the dogs would come and lick his sores."

His medical plan, like many today, is for the dogs. Verhey

(2002, 479) says that even today the poor must scavenge and beg for crumbs from the vast supplies of medicine controlled by the wealthy, the drug corporations, and wealthy congressional leaders. This writer finds it incredible that the Congress consistently votes to keep their government health care while denying it to their constituents because they call it socialism. In the same vein many of the elderly who love their government sponsored health care, and refuse to surrender it, want to deny it to others because they want to pay less taxes and cut the federal budget.

Verses 22-26 say, "The poor man died and was carried away by the angels to be with Abraham. The rich man also died and was buried. "In Hades, where he was being tormented, he looked up and saw Abraham far away with Lazarus by his side. He called out, 'Father Abraham, have mercy on me, and send Lazarus to dip the tip of his finger in water and cool my tongue; for I am in agony in these flames.' But Abraham said, 'Child, remember that during your lifetime you received your good things, and Lazarus in like manner evil things; but now he is comforted here, and you are in your agony. Besides all this, between you and us a great chasm has been fixed, so that those who might want to pass from here to you cannot do so, and no one can cross from there to us.'

In verses 27-31 "He said, 'Then, father, I beg you to send him to my father's house—for I have five brothers—that he may warn them, so that they will not also come into this place of torment.' Abraham replied, 'They have Moses and the prophets; they should listen to them.' He said, 'No, father Abraham; but if someone goes to them from the dead, they will repent.' He said to him, 'If they do not listen to Moses and the prophets, neither will they be convinced even if someone rises from the dead.' "

The context of the narrative of the rich man goes back to verses 13-14 that mention lovers of money, and that one can not serve

God and wealth. The rich man may have been a good man as far as the world sees things. His problem in God's eyes was that he does not care about those who have nothing or little to eat, and who have health problems and no way to get healed. He does not care about the nobodies of the world that Jesus cared for; his concern was for his own comfort and wealth. He may have even looked with disdain upon Lazarus as too lazy to work. This is usually the cry from comfortable people to justify their lack of compassion. They have been so comfortable for so long that they no longer understand what is happening in the world outside of their comfort zone. The rich man needed to be transformed and begin looking at reality outside of his comfort zone. He needed to begin to look at life from the point of Jesus.

The story is actually a call to repentance before it is too late, for once one's life is over there does not seem to be any movement from the place of torment to paradise. The other issue is that there are only the Scriptures to warn anyone of what the future holds. The rich man asks that someone from the dead go to warn his family of that reality, but Luke is saying that will not happen, and it will not work. Luke knows that Jesus rose from the dead, and people still do not listen. The narrative states that if one will not listen to the Scriptures, they will not listen to one who rises from the dead. Can this also be a message to the church? Are the Scriptures being taught and emphasized as a priority in churches today, and if so, are the people making them a priority in their lives? If not, why not?

In chapter 17:1-5 Jesus said to his disciples, "Occasions for stumbling are bound to come, but woe to anyone by whom they come! It would be better for you if a millstone were hung around your neck and you were thrown into the sea than for you to cause one of these little ones to stumble. Be on your guard! If another disciple sins, you must rebuke the offender, and if there is repentance, you must forgive. And if the same person sins against you seven times a day, and turns back to you seven times and says, 'I repent,' you must forgive." (Again, hyperbole is used to state the case. Other places it says if you do not forgive, you will not be forgiven, Mt 6:15.)

In verses 5-6 the apostles said to the Lord, "Increase our faith!" (This needs to be the attitude of all of Jesus' followers.) The Lord replied, "If you had faith the size of a mustard seed, you could say to this mulberry tree, 'Be uprooted and planted in the sea,' and it would obey you." (Jesus often speaks in metaphors. He is saying that he will do wonders with your faith, even if your faith is small. He says this because anyone who asks him to increase their faith has the right attitude.)

Verses 7-10 say, "Who among you would say to your slave who has just come in from plowing or tending sheep in the field, 'Come here at once and take your place at the table'? Would you not rather say to him, 'Prepare supper for me, put on your apron and serve me while I eat and drink; later you may eat and drink'? Do you thank the slave for doing what was commanded? So you also, when you have done all that you were ordered to do, say 'We are worthless slaves; we have done only what we ought to have done!' "

Jesus is warning his disciples not to think they deserve or can earn a reward for serving him. He may be alluding to some of the Pharisees who think God is obligated to reward them for their correct observance of the law. Many of them call themselves, the righteous ones. Jesus is telling them that in serving God, doing what is right, and doing good works are expected. It is a basic requirement of being a disciple. Even with perfect faith, people would still be indebted to the God who created and gave individuals all they have and made them what they are. The message is that one does not enter the eternal kingdom by works, but also one does not enter it without works. One can not earn salvation, but one can earn a loss of it.

Verses 13-14 say, On the way to Jerusalem Jesus was going through the region between Samaria and Galilee. As he entered a village, ten lepers approached him. Keeping their distance, they called out, saying, "Jesus, Master, have mercy on us." When he saw them he said to them, "Go and show yourselves to the priests." As they went, they were made clean.

According to Leviticus chapter 13 lepers are not permitted in society; they are kept in a colony, and if anyone sees them walking along, they are required to warn others by yelling out loud the word "unclean." If any are cured, the priest on pronouncing them healed, enables them to re-enter society.

Verses 15-16 say, Then one of them, when he saw that he was healed, turned back, praising God with a loud voice. He prostrated himself at Jesus' feet and thanked him. And he was a Samaritan. (Samaritans are disliked by the Jews because they are Jews intermarried with foreigners as a result of the invasion of Assyria in 722 BC. The Jews believe them to be half breeds who corrupted God's teachings.) Verses 17-19 say, Jesus asked, "Were not ten made clean (healed)? But the other nine, where are they? Was none of them found to return and give praise to God except this foreigner?" Then he said to him, "Get up and go on your way; your faith has made you well."

Luke pinpoints the essence of the story by saying, he is a (despised) Samaritan. Samaritans were rejected by the Jews for being unholy. The story is about grace. The story is teaching his people to be accepting, to reject no one at all. No one! Who are the rejects in our society today, and what is the reader's attitude toward them? Graciousness (compassion, grace, patience) is a Christian virtue the followers of Christ are called to display.

Verses 20-21 say, Once Jesus was asked by the Pharisees when the kingdom of God was coming, and he answered, "The kingdom of God is not coming with things that can be observed; nor will they say, 'Look here it is!' or 'There it is!' For in fact the kingdom of God is among you." (The Greek word can be translated both within and among you. This is because the kingdom is both within and among you, for Christ makes himself present within his people and then through them to be among his people.)

Jesus is informing them that the kingdom will not be a worldly kingdom to throw out the Romans or a kingdom set up by the Jews to rule the world as it was in the time of David. Jesus is instituting a different kind of kingdom. He is telling them that the kingdom has already broken into the world. The kingdom is where Jesus and his values are made present. When this happens the kingdom is made present to individuals, the world, its nations, and their institutions influencing all for good. In this way the world begins to change.

This is not the type of kingdom they are expecting, nor the type of kingdom some of his followers in America want to hear about either. Unfortunately too many of his followers want to keep Jesus as a "spiritual" experience only divorced from everyday life. Others want his message to apply only to individuals. They will want to translate the Greek word as the kingdom is in you and avoid the kingdom is among you. But in trying to isolate Jesus they ignore all the other kingdom passages.

If the church and the followers of Jesus are called to advance his kingdom and if they claim to be disciples representing his interests, then they must make his interests and his priorities their interest and priority, and that includes the political, economic, and social implications of his teachings. The church is not to be involved itself in power politics, but it is to challenge power politics, not to gain power, but to see that power works for what Christ stood for. God is Lord of all not just our so-called spiritual life. That is the implication of the kingdom breaking into the real world that darkness keeps trying to push back. One must stand with God's word, and be willing to stand with and for the things he stood for, as well as take the side of those with whom Jesus sided. In the process of doing so, when suffering (mental or physical) comes, one must be willing to suffer as Jesus did.

Verses 22-37 say, Then he said to his disciples, "The days are coming when you will long to see one of the days of the Son of Man, and you will not see it. They will say to you, 'Look there!' or 'Look here!' Do not go, do not set off in pursuit. For as the lightning flashes and lights up the sky from one side to the other, so will the Son of Man be in his day. But first he must endure much suffering and be rejected by this generation. Just as it was in the days of Noah, so too it will be in the days of the Son of Man. They were eating and drinking, and marrying and being given in marriage, until the day Noah entered the ark, and the flood came and destroyed all of them.

"Likewise, just as it was in the days of Lot; they were eating and drinking, buying and selling, planting and building, but on the day that Lot left Sodom, it rained fire and sulfur from heaven and destroyed all of them–it will be like that on the day that the Son of Man is revealed. On that day, anyone on the housetop who has belongings in the house must not come down to take them away; and likewise anyone in the field must not turn back. Remember Lot's wife. Those who try to make life secure will lose it, but those who lose their life will keep it. I tell you on that night there will be two in one bed; one will be taken and the other left. There will be two women grinding meal together; one will be taken and the other left." Then they asked him, "Where Lord?" He said to them,

"Where the corpse is, there the vultures will gather."

First of all, according to Wright, Caird, Borg and others this is about the teaching of Jesus and him being vindicated when Rome comes in AD 70 destroying the temple and the city of Jerusalem. He often tells the people to change their agenda of violence against the Romans, or they will be destroyed by Rome. Jesus is talking about two types of people: those who accept his agenda and those who reject it. In context of these verses the one taken is taken in judgment, not in a rapture to bliss. The many thousands of Jews killed in the Roman war of 60-70 are the corpses that the vultures gather for their food. Those who lose their life for his life will safely escape this incident and will go into the world with his message. As a second fulfillment of Scripture it can also be applied to the end of time and final judgment. Again those taken are taken in judgment while God's people are transformed to perfection within the new heaven and new earth. The message over and over is about repenting, which is not a very popular message.

Chapter 18:1 says, Then Jesus told them a parable about their need to pray always and not to lose heart. He said, "In a certain city there was a judge who neither feared God nor had respect for people. In that city there was a widow who kept coming to him and saying, 'Grant me justice against my opponent.' For awhile he refused; but later he said to himself, 'Though I have no fear of God and no respect for anyone, yet because this widow keeps bothering me, I will grant her justice, so that she will not wear me out by continually coming.' And the Lord said, "Listen to what the unjust judge says. And will not God grant justice to his chosen ones who cry to him day and night? Will he delay long in helping them? I tell you, he will quickly grant justice to them. And yet, when the Son

of Man comes, will he find faith on earth?"

The message is to be persistent in prayer; it may be a long time before prayer is answered to your benefit, but do not give up. The good and loving Father knows when the time is ready, or even if what you are praying for is in his plan, and best for all involved. The last sentence is interesting. Will faith be found when the Son of Man comes? The faith he is talking about is real committed faith such as the kind Luke has been discussing, not the superficial kind.

He also told this parable in (9-14) to some who trusted in themselves that they were righteous (represented by some of the Pharisees) and regarded others with contempt. "Two men went up to the temple to pray, one a Pharisee and the other a tax collector. The Pharisee, standing by himself, was praying thus, 'God, I thank you that I am not like other people: thieves, rogues, adulterers, or even like this tax collector. I fast twice a week; I give a tenth of all my income.' But the tax collector standing far off, would not even look up to heaven, but was beating his breast and saying, 'God, be merciful to me, a sinner!' I tell you, this man went down to his house justified rather than the other; for all who exalt themselves will be humbled, but all who humble themselves will be exalted."

If one does not see oneself as a sinner, it will be impossible to be justified. The message is that no matter what one does, a person can not justify himself, for people can not eliminate their own sins. In Christian thinking only the grace of God can do that through the blood of Christ. There is no sin in heaven, and sin must be eliminated before entry. No one can enter heaven with their sins upon them (Rev 21:27, 22:14-15). The Pharisee saw himself as righteous; therefore, he saw no reason to repent of his sins. In fact he probably thought he was sinless because he followed all the outward laws and rituals.

In verses 15-17 people are bringing infants to him and the

disciples try to stop them, but Jesus orders them to let them come. In (17) he says, whoever does not receive the kingdom of God as a little child will never enter it. (This is referring to trusting and accepting the kingdom completely as Jesus teaches it with no alterations.)

In verses 18-23 a certain ruler asked him, "Good Teacher, what must I do to inherit eternal life?" (This is also translated to enter into life.) Jesus said to him, "Why do you call me good? No one is good but God alone." (Jesus is asking him if he knows why or how he is using the word good.) Jesus said, "You know the commandments: 'You shall not commit adultery; You shall not murder; You shall not steal; You shall not bear false witness; Honor your father and mother.' " (These are the social commandments. He does not mention to believe in one God only and to have no idols. He is saving those for later.) He replied, "I have kept all these since my youth." When Jesus heard this he said to him, "There is still one thing lacking. Sell all that you own and distribute the money to the poor, and you will have treasure in heaven; then come, follow me." But when he heard this, he became sad; for he was very rich. (That command makes many people sad.)

His wealth is most important to him, and he is not going to give any of it to the poor or those in need. Jesus is enabling this man to see that he is violating the worship of the one God only and to have no idols. His idols are his wealth and possessions. Jesus enables him to see that he is not loving God with all his heart and his neighbor as himself, which is the summary of the whole law.

In verses 24-27 Jesus looked at him and said, "How hard it is for those who have wealth to enter the kingdom of God! Indeed, it is easier for a camel to go through the eye of a needle than for someone who is rich to enter the kingdom of God." (Here Semitic exaggeration is used.) Those who heard it said, "Then who can be saved?" He replied, "What is impossible for mortals is possible for God."

The teaching is that no one can save themselves, even with their money and wealth, but money and wealth can keep one from salvation. But God can even save the rich, if they follow his teachings, receive the Spirit and his merciful grace as God's gift to them, and then have compassion on those less fortunate (Mt 25:31-46).

Verses 28-30 say, Then Peter said, "Look, we have left our homes and followed you." And he said to them, "Truly I tell you, there is no one who has left house or wife or brother or parents or children, for the sake of the kingdom of God, who will not get back very much more in this age, and in the age to come eternal life." (Jesus recognizes their commitment, and again states the kingdom of heaven breaking in upon the earth has even higher priority than one's family.)

Verses 31-34 say, Then he took the twelve aside and said to them, "See, we are going up to Jerusalem, and everything that is written about the Son of Man by the prophets will be accomplished. For he will be handed over to Gentiles; and he will be mocked and insulted and spat upon. After they have flogged him, they will kill him, and on the third day he will rise again." But they understood nothing about all these things; in fact what he said was hidden from them, and they did not grasp what was said. (They are not expecting anything like this and can not conceive of it, but later they will remember what he said.)

Verses 35-43 say, As he approached Jericho, a blind man was sitting by the roadside begging. When he heard a crowd going by, he asked what was happening. They told him, "Jesus of Nazareth is passing by." Then he shouted, "Jesus, Son of David, have mercy on me!" (In calling him the Son of David he recognizes him as the Messiah.) Those who were in front sternly ordered him to be quiet; but he shouted even more loudly, "Son of David, have mercy on me!" Jesus stood still and ordered the man to be brought to him; and when he came near, he asked him, "What do you want me to do for you?" He said, "Lord, let me see again." Jesus said to him, "Receive your sight; your faith has saved you." Immediately he regained his sight and followed him, glorifying God; and all the people, when they saw it, they praised God. (The man had spiritual sight; now he has physical sight.)

Chapter 19:1-6 says, He entered Jericho and was passing through it. A man was there named Zacchaeus; he was a chief tax collector and was rich. (He is probably a supervisor of those collecting taxes for the Romans.) He was trying to see Jesus, but because of the crowd he could not, because he was short in stature. (Who is short of stature, Zacchaeus or Jesus?) So he ran ahead and climbed a sycamore (fig) tree to see him, because he was going to pass that way. When Jesus came to the place, he looked up and said to him, "Zacchaeus, hurry and come down; for I must stay at your house today." So he hurried down and was happy to welcome him. (Can you imagine his shock when Jesus looks up in the tree, calls him by name, and then tells him to come down because he is going to his house?)

Verses 7-10 say, All who saw it began to grumble and said, "He has gone to be the guest of one who is a sinner." Zacchaeus stood there and said to the Lord, "Look, half my possessions, Lord, I will give to the poor; and if I have defrauded anyone of anything, I will pay it back four times as much." Then Jesus said to him, "Today salvation has come to this house, because he too is a son of Abraham. For the Son of Man came to seek and to save the lost." (In 4:43 Luke says that his purpose is to preach the kingdom. Here he says his purpose is to seek the lost. Summed up these two purposes are what he was about and what he continues to be about.)

Notice that Jesus is not telling him to sell all he has and give it to the poor as he did the rich young ruler, but Zacchaeus knows he is to help the poor. He has the right attitude, and it is the heart that concerns Jesus. By faith he has responded to Jesus' message. Apparently, he had been listening to Jesus as he went about teaching. The grace of God comes into his life, and he is transformed.

Verses 11-15 say, As they were listening to this, he went on to tell a parable, because he was near Jerusalem, and because they supposed that the kingdom of God was to appear immediately. So he said, "A nobleman went to a distant country to get royal power for himself and then return. He summoned ten of his slaves, and gave them ten pounds, and said to them, 'Do business with these until I come back.' But the citizens of his country hated him and sent a delegation after him saying, 'We do not want this man ruling over us.' When he returned, having received royal power, he ordered these slaves, to whom he had given the money, to be summoned so that he might find out what they had gained by trading.

Verses 16-21 say, "The first came forward and said, 'Lord, your pound has made ten more pounds.' He said to him, 'Well done good slave! Because you have been trustworthy in a very small thing, take charge of ten cities.' Then the second came saying, 'Lord your pound has made five pounds.' He said to him, 'And you, rule over five cities.' Then the other came, saying, 'Lord here is your pound. I wrapped it up in a piece of cloth, for I was afraid of you, because you are a harsh man; you take what you did not deposit, and reap what you did not sow.' (This writer imagines this man thought the noble man was a harsh man because he made people responsible for the gifts he gave, and then judged them for their actions.)

Verses 22-27 continue, "He said to him, 'I will judge you by your own words, you wicked slave! You knew, did you, that I was a harsh man, taking what I did not deposit and reaping what I did not sow? (He probably said that as a tongue in cheek remark.) Why then did you not put my money into the bank? Then when I returned, I could have collected it with interest.' He said to the bystanders, 'Take the pound from him and give it to the one who has ten pounds.' And they said to him 'Lord he has ten pounds!' 'I tell you, to all those who have more will be given; but from those who have nothing, even what they have will be taken away. But as for these enemies of mine who did not want me to be king over them—bring them here and slaughter them in my presence.' " (This is about bearing fruit for God.)

The first application of this parable is to Israel. God is coming to judge Israel (see verses 41-44). The status quo is not acceptable. God gives his people gifts to be used for his purposes. Second, the ideas behind the parable can be applied to the followers of Jesus throughout time. Christ through the power of the Holy Spirit gives his people gifts for the progress and advancement of the kingdom, and he will judge his people for the manner in which they use them. All that we have is God's gift. People, whether it be the old Israel of God or the new Israel of God, will be judged on whether or not they make God the king of their lives and respond accordingly.

Verse 27 is a strong warning to those who do not make Jesus the king of their total lives including their wealth. They will be slaughtered in his presence. There are many Christians who do not really believe this statement, and many of them have created for themselves a Jesus that is not the one found in the New Testament. Yes, he is a God of love, mercy, and grace for those who have made him king of their lives and are working for the agenda of his kingdom, but for those who are not, the story is different.

Verses 28-35 say, After he had said this, he went on ahead, going up to Jerusalem. (Luke always has Jesus on a journey to Jerusalem, for it is here he will go to the cross and rise from the dead.) When he had come near Bethphage and Bethany, at the place called the Mount of Olives, he sent two of his disciples saying, "Go into the village ahead of you, and as you enter it you will find tied there a colt that has never been ridden. Untie it and bring it here. If anyone asks you, 'Why are you untying it?' just say this, 'The Lord needs it.' " So those who were sent departed and found it as he had told them. As they were untying the colt, its owners asked them, "Why are you untying the colt?" They said, 'The Lord needs it.' Then they brought it to Jesus; and after throwing their cloaks on the colt, they set Jesus on it.

Verses 36-40 say, As he rode along, people kept spreading their cloaks on the road. As he was now approaching the path down from the Mount of Olives, the whole multitude of the disciples began to praise God joyfully with a loud voice, for all the deeds of power that they had seen, saying, "Blessed is the king who comes in the name of the Lord! Peace in heaven, and glory in the highest heaven!" some of the Pharisees in the crowd said to him, "Teacher, order your disciples to stop." He answered, "I tell you, if these were silent, the stones would shout out."

Jesus riding on a donkey is a reference to the prophesy of Zechariah (9:9) that says, "Rejoice heartily, O daughter Zion, shout for joy, O daughter Jerusalem! See your king shall come to you; a just savior is he, meek, and riding on an ass."

This king comes not on a conquering war horse, but on a beast of burden representing humbleness and peace. Unfortunately, many of his believers down through history have never understood this message. When did Jesus become pro war, pro guns, and pro rich, even pro America in whatever it does? Those ideas are not in Scripture. They are the creation not of patriots but American nationalists, many are militants and actually call themselves Christians. There is a big difference between a patriot and a nationalist.

Verses 41-44 say, As he came near and saw the city, he wept over it, saying, "If you, even you, had only recognized on this day the things that make for peace! But now they are hidden from your eyes. Indeed, the days will come upon you, when your enemies will set up ramparts around you and surround you, and hem you in on every side. They will crush you to the ground, you and your children within you, and they will not leave within you one stone upon another; because you did not recognize the time of your visitation from God."

Like Jeremiah (Jer 7) before him Jesus laments over what will be the destruction of Jerusalem and the temple because the leaders and many of the people refuse to listen. This is around 33 AD, and the total destruction will not happen until 70 AD, but Jesus knows what will happen and weeps. Jesus has been trying to convince the people to change their agenda of arrogance, oppression, and violence for his agenda of the kingdom, an agenda of humbleness, justice, and peace. But like in the time of the prophet Jeremiah, it is not going to happen, and the city and the temple will be destroyed again by a foreign power. This time it will be also for failure to accept the Messiah. Unfortunately, most people down through time do not learn from history.

Verses 45-48 say, he entered the temple and began to drive out those who were selling things there; and he said, "It is written, 'My house shall be a house of prayer'; but you have made it a den of robbers."

Too often this has been displayed as an uncontrolled, emotional display of anger by Jesus, but that is not true. The incident needs to be understood within the symbolic actions of the prophetic tradition of Israel, and then his actions become nothing more than enlivened symbolic actions prophesying the temple and nation's future judgment and destruction.

The temple has become a place where people are being taken advantage of in the name of religion. People coming from distant lands to worship at the temple are being charged outrageous prices to exchange their money and to buy the animals to sacrifice as part of their worship. The temple leaders, responsible to the Sanhedrin, have become corrupt oppressors, who have institutionalized greed and the oppression of their own people. Jesus simply does what the prophet Jeremiah did before him; he criticizes their actions and warns them and the nation, and the resistance movement bent on a violent overthrow of their enemy that if they do not change their ways, both Jerusalem and the temple are going be destroyed. (To get a better idea of the nation's oppression read Jeremiah, Isaiah, or Amos, which is the shorter book.)

The temple has become like the barren fig tree, no longer producing fruit. Many of the disadvantaged in the land see the temple as a symbol of everything that is taking advantage of them. They see the leaders as a rich, corrupt aristocracy in cahoots with the Romans by taking their lands, overtaxing them and keeping the masses indebted to them. The light of the leaders has dimmed through their systemic injustice. Later when the militant nationalistic rebels attack the temple, the first thing they will do is destroy all the tax records. The temple then becomes the center of the revolution against Rome. Later an incredible number of Jews will be killed as the Romans destroy the temple and the city. Jesus had warned them over and over that this would occur, but it was to no avail.

Verses 47-48 say, Every day he was teaching in the temple. The chief priests, the scribes, and the leaders of the people kept looking for a way to kill him; but they did not find anything they could do, for all the people were spell bound by what they heard.

Those opposing him are the wealthy leaders in religion, politics and commerce. They have several reasons for getting rid of Jesus. He has damaged business in the temple. In addition he keeps preaching against injustice and constantly criticizes the rich and their policies, since his teaching favored the poor over the rich. But most important he claims a new kingdom is coming soon, and they are not interested in a regime change.

Chapter 20:1-8 says, One day, as he was teaching the people in the temple and telling the good news, the chief priests and the scribes came with the elders and said to him, "Tell us, by what authority are you doing these things? Who is it that gave you this authority?" He answered them, "I will also ask you a question, and you tell me; Did the baptism of John come from heaven, or was it of human origin?" They discussed it with one other, saying, "If we say, 'From heaven,' he will say, 'Why did you not believe him?' But if we say, 'Of human origin,' all the people will stone us; for they are convinced that John was a prophet." So they answered that they did not know where it came from. Then Jesus said to them, "Neither will I tell you by what authority I am doing these things."

If they agree John is a prophet, they will have to accept what he says about Jesus, but they are not willing to do so. Under these circumstances Jesus decides that it is a waste of time trying to convince them of anything.

Verses 9-13 say, He began to tell the people this parable: "A man planted a vineyard, and leased it to tenants, and went to another country for a long time. (The owner of the vineyard is God. The vineyard is Israel. The tenants are the religious leaders.) When the season came, he sent a slave (his prophets) to the tenants in order that they might give him his share of the produce of the vineyard;

but the tenants beat him and sent him away empty handed. Next he sent another slave; that one also they beat and insulted and sent away empty handed. And he sent still a third; this one also they wounded and threw out. Then the owner of the vineyard (the Father) said, 'What shall I do? I will send my beloved son; perhaps they will respect him.'

Verses 14-16 say, "But when the tenants saw him, they discussed it among themselves and said, 'This is the heir; let us kill him so that the inheritance may be ours.' So they threw him out of the vineyard and killed him. (They killed Jesus.) What then will the owner of the vineyard do to them? He will come and destroy those tenants and give the vineyard to others." When they heard this, they said, "Heaven forbid!"

The people can not believe that the tenants will be destroyed and David's kingdom given to the Gentiles, so they cry out in disbelief. Verses 17-18 say, But he looked at them and said, "What does this text mean: 'The stone that the builders rejected has become the cornerstone'? Everyone who falls on that stone will be broken into pieces; and it will crush anyone on whom it falls." (This is a quote from Psalm 118:22. Jesus shows the unbelieving leaders that their rejection of Jesus had been prophesied in Scripture.)

Verses 19-20 say, When the scribes and chief priests realized that he had told this parable against them, they wanted to lay hands on him at that very hour, but they feared the people. So they watched him and sent spies who pretended to be honest, in order to trap him by what he said, so as to hand him over to the jurisdiction and authority of the governor. (The Roman governor is Pontius Pilate. He is the final judge and authority of all cases deserving death in the Roman territory.)

Verses 21-26 say, "Teacher, we know that you are right in what you say and teach, and you show deference to no one, but teach the way of God in accordance with the truth. Is it lawful for us to pay taxes to the emperor, or not?" But he perceived their craftiness and said to them, "Show me a denarius (a coin). Whose head and whose title does it bear?" They said, "The emperor's." He said to them, "Then give to the emperor the thing that is the emperor's, and to God the things that are God's." And they were not able in the presence of the people to trap him by what he said; and being amazed by his answer, they became silent.

The question they are asking centers on whether a theocracy, a state under God's leadership, should pay taxes to a pagan government. The answer is that the political domain one lives under and receives services from has the right to be paid taxes. But in the process one must give God his due. The leaders want him to choose one over the other, which will put him in jeopardy with the one not chosen, but he does not fall into their trap. (See Mk 12:13-17 for an additional perspective.)

Verses 27-33 say, Some of the Sadducees, those who say there is no resurrection, came to him and asked him a question, "Teacher, Moses wrote for us that if a man's brother dies, leaving a wife but no children, the man shall marry the widow and raise up children for his brother. (This is called the levirate law.) Now there were seven brothers; the first married, and died childless; then the second and the third married her, and so in the same way all seven died childless. Finally the woman also died. In the resurrection, therefore, whose wife will the woman be? For the seven had married her." (This is a trick question, for the Sadducees did not believe in a resurrection.)

Jesus in (34-40) said to them, "Those who belong to this age marry and are given in marriage; but those who are considered worthy of a place in that age and in the resurrection from the dead neither marry nor are given in marriage. Indeed they cannot die anymore, because they are like angels and are children of God, being children of the resurrection. And the fact that the dead are raised Moses himself showed, in the story about the bush, where he speaks of the Lord as the God of Abraham, the God of Isaac, and the God of Jacob. Now he is God not of the dead, but of the living; for to him all of them are alive." Then some of the scribes (Pharisees who believe in a resurrection) answered, "Teacher, you have spoken well. For they no longer dared to ask him another question."

Jesus confirms there is more than one state of existence, and life after death is not an extension of this life. It is something altogether different. Also he is not saying people will not be with or recognize their loved ones. In the spirit world there will be perfect love.

Then in verses 41-44 he said to them, "How can they say that the Messiah is David's son? For David himself says in the book of Psalms, (110:1) 'The Lord said to my Lord, "Sit at my right hand, until I make your enemies your footstool." ' David thus calls him Lord; so how can he be his son?" (Later when they see Jesus at the right hand of the Father, they will understand. He is the Son of David, but not his real son. The Son of David as used is a reference to the Messiah and the one who will continue David's kingship. Luke casts Jesus as the new David.)

Verses 45-47 say, In the hearing of all the people he said to the disciples, "Beware of the scribes, who like to walk around in long robes, and love to be greeted with respect in the marketplaces, and to have the best seats in the synagogues and places of honor at banquets. They devour widows' houses and for the sake of appearance say long prayers. They will receive the greater condemnation.

When people of trust use their position to further their own comfort and selfish interest at the expense of the common good, God is not pleased. This reference to the evil conduct of the religious leaders forms the backdrop for the following prediction of the destruction of the temple and eventually the city. This attitude of Jesus toward the attitude of religious leaders stands for all time; it is not just for this situation.

❧❦❧

Chapter 21:1-4 says, He looked up and saw rich people putting their gifts into the treasury; he also saw a poor widow put in two copper coins. He said, "Truly I tell you, this poor widow has put in more than all of them; for all of them have contributed out of their abundance, but she out of her poverty has put in all she had. (Being generous is being expressed not by what one gives but by what one has left after one gives. Jesus always looks at things differently than humans. As one reads through the Gospels, it is obvious that Jesus is never impressed with the thinking and actions of the rich.)

Verses 5-8 say, When some were speaking about the temple, how it was adorned with beautiful stones and gifts dedicated to God, he said, "As for these things that you see, the days will come when not one stone will be left upon another, all will be thrown down." They asked him, "Teacher, when will this be, and what will be the sign that this is about to take place?" (The question is in reference to the destruction of the temple.) And he said, "Beware that you are not led astray; for many will come in my name and say, 'I am he!' and, 'The time is near!' Do not go after them."

Verses 9-11 say, "When you hear of wars and insurrections, do not be terrified; for these things must take place first, but the end will not follow immediately." Then he said to them, "Nation will rise against nation, and kingdom against kingdom; there will be great earthquakes, and in various places famines and plagues; and there will be dreadful portents and great signs from heaven." (What makes these verses a challenge is that these things occur in every age.)

Verses 12-19 say, "But before this occurs, they will arrest you and persecute you; they will hand you over to synagogues and prisons, and you will be brought before kings and governors because of my name. This will give you an opportunity to testify. So make up your minds not to prepare your defense in advance; for I will give you words and a wisdom that none of your opponents will be able to withstand or contradict. You will be betrayed even by parents and brothers, by relatives and friends; and they will put some of you to death. You will be hated by all because of my name. But not a hair of your head will perish. By your endurance you will gain your souls. (All of this is fulfilled in the book of Acts, but it is possible that there will be multiple fulfillments throughout history.)

Verses 20-24 say, "When you see Jerusalem surrounded by armies, then know that its desolation has come near. Then those in Judea must flee to the mountains, and those inside the city must leave it, and those out in the country must not enter it; for those are days of vengeance, as a fulfillment of all that is written. Woe to those who are pregnant and to those who are nursing infants in those days! For there will be great distress on the earth and wrath against this people; they will fall by the edge of the sword and be taken away as captives among the nations; and Jerusalem will be trampled on by the Gentiles, until the times of the Gentiles are fulfilled.

Jerusalem will be controlled by Gentiles until it is time for them to no longer control it. By the end of the New Testament all that the Old Testament foretold is fulfilled except the elimination of the Gentiles from Rome and the final coming and judgment. This whole chapter is basically about the destruction of the temple and Jerusalem in AD 70 and that which leads to it.

Verses 25-28 continue, "There will be signs in the sun, the moon, and the stars, and on the earth distress among the nations confused by the roaring of the sea and the waves. People will faint from fear and foreboding of what is coming upon the world, for the powers of the heavens will be shaken. Then they will see 'the Son of Man coming in a cloud' with power and great glory. Now when these things begin to take place, stand up and raise your heads, because your redemption is drawing near."

This whole section is apocalyptic literature, which is a special form of literature used to discuss times of great change and acts of judgment by God. Seeing the Son of Man coming in a cloud is apocalyptic literature for describing God's presence and with his coming a judgment. God's presence in Scripture is usually associated with clouds. The author believes the application of this is a reference to the day of Pentecost in Acts chapter two as well as the destruction of Jerusalem and the temple in AD 70. Wright (1992, 459-464) believes it is all a metaphor for both the destruction of the temple and Jerusalem vindicating Jesus as a fulfillment of his prophecy.

In 2 Thess 2:2 the Apostle Paul writing in the early 50s says, the day of the Lord is already here. This writer believes it may also be possible to apply these verses to the end times, for the concepts of prophecy repeat themselves. The prophets and Jesus are always current, for the thinking behind the prophets repeats itself over and over throughout history.

Then in verses 29-33 he told them a parable: "Look at the fig tree and all the trees; as soon as they sprout leaves you can see for yourselves and know that summer is already near. So also, when you see these things taking place, you know that the kingdom of God is near. Truly I tell you this generation will not pass away until all these things have taken place. Heaven and earth will pass away, but my words will never pass away.

Although this statement is true, it is still being used as a metaphor for that generation, and the main thrust of his message is that the temple and city are going to be destroyed because the people reject the kingdom message of Jesus for a message of violence against Rome. By the time Luke is writing this, the generation of Jesus has passed away. At least fifty years have passed. It was approximately 85 AD, and the temple and city had been destroyed in 70 AD. Luke is saying the prophecy of Jesus has been fulfilled (21:22).

Jesus is telling his disciples and those who listen to be prepared for what is mainly going to occur in their time, but the call to be prepared does seem to be also stretched across time. Verses 34-36 say, "Be on guard so that your hearts are not weighed down with dissipation and drunkenness and the worries of this life, and that day catch you unexpectedly, like a trap. For it will come upon all who live in the face of the whole earth. Be alert at all times, praying that you may have the strength to escape all these things that will take place, and to stand before the Son of Man."

The people think that if the temple is destroyed it will be the end of the world. So even though Jesus is primarily talking about the destruction of the temple, it may be possible that he is applying many of the same themes to the end times. What makes things intriguing in interpreting these verses is that many of these signs have been regular occurrences throughout history. The reader is encouraged to read the comments to this subject in Mt 24 and Mk 13.

Verses 37-38 say, Every day he was teaching in the temple, and at night he would go out and spend the night on the Mount of Olives, as it was called. And all the people would get up early in the morning to listen to him in the temple. (The temple has many so-called porches where people could gather to hear teachers.)

Chapter 22:1-2 says, Now the festival of Unleavened Bread, which is called the Passover, was near. The chief priests and the scribes were looking for a way to put Jesus to death, for they were

afraid of the people. Verses 3-6 say, Then Satan entered Judas called Iscariot, who was one of the twelve; he went away and conferred with the chief priests and officers of the temple police about how he might betray him to them. They were greatly pleased and agreed to give him money. So he consented and began to look for an opportunity to betray him to them when no crowd was present.

Verses 7-13 say, Then came the day of Unleavened Bread, on which the Passover lamb had to be sacrificed. So Jesus sent Peter and John saying, "Go and prepare the Passover meal for us that we may eat." They asked him, "Where do you want us to make preparation for it?" "Listen," he said to them, "when you have entered the city, a man carrying a jar of water will meet you; follow him into the house he enters and say to the owner of the house, 'The teacher asks you, "Where is the guest room, where I may eat the Passover with my disciples?" ' He will show you a large room upstairs already furnished. Make preparations for us there. So they went and found everything as he had told them; and they prepared the Passover meal.

Verses 14-20 say, When the hour came, he took his place at the table, and the apostles with him. He said to them, "I have eagerly desired to eat this Passover with you before I suffer, for I tell you, I will not eat it until it is fulfilled in the kingdom of God. (When he rises to the right hand of God, his presence will again be with them through the Holy Spirit.) Then he took a cup, and after giving thanks he said, "Take this and divide it among yourselves; for I tell you that from now on I will not drink of the fruit of the vine until the kingdom of God comes." Then he took a loaf of bread, and when he had given thanks, he broke it and gave it to them, saying, "This is my body, which is given for you. Do this in remembrance of me. And he did the same with the cup after supper, saying, "This cup that is poured out for you is the new covenant in my blood."

Jesus transforms the old covenant Passover meal into the Eucharist or Lord's Supper for the new covenant. The first covenant was confirmed by the sprinkling of the blood of an animal; the new covenant is confirmed by the blood of Jesus. When the Jews celebrate the Passover they remember the Exodus and that God had told them if they sprinkled blood on their lintel and two door posts, the angel of death would pass over them, and they would be set free from Egypt (Ex 12:23). Through the blood of the new covenant Jesus passes over the sins of his people. The Lord's Supper (Eucharist) is what Jesus institutes as the sign for what he will do for those who confirm the new covenant.

Verses 21-23 say, "But see, the one who betrays me is with me, and his hand is on the table. For the Son of Man is going as it has been determined, but woe to that one by whom he is betrayed!" Then they began to ask one another, which one of them it could be who would do this.

Verses 24-27 say, A dispute also arose among them as to which one of them is to be regarded as the greatest. But he said to them, "The kings of the Gentiles lord it over them; and those in authority over them are called benefactors. But not so with you; rather the greatest among you must become like the youngest, and the leader like one who serves. For who is greater, the one who is at the table or the one who serves? Is it not the one at the table? But I am among you as one who serves." (Again Jesus turns the conventional wisdom of the world upside down.)

Verses 28-30 say, "You are those who have stood by me in my trials; and I confer on you, just as my father has conferred on me, a kingdom, so that you may eat and drink at my table in my kingdom, and you will sit on thrones judging the twelve tribes of Israel."

Because they are in the kingdom (Col 1:13, Rev 1:6), when they participate in the Eucharist, they will be eating and drinking with him, for his presence will be with them. To sit on the thrones judging Israel is a symbolic reference to their responsibility of going to their fellow Jews calling them to repentance in order to bring them into the kingdom. The twelve represent the beginning of a restored Israel, an Israel that is forgiven. The exodus is over, the new age is beginning, the new covenant is beginning, God is now among his people through Jesus.

The nations and Jews who reject the twelve's message of repentance will not be in the kingdom, for they bring judgment upon themselves by rejecting Jesus (Jn 3:18). Jesus through the cross will take the exile upon himself and as he rises to be with the Father the new exodus is here, an exodus from sin. Those picking up their cross by being transformed or born of God become the new people of God, the new Israel of God. Israel is restored. But they must be constantly aware of Satan.

In verses 31-34 Jesus says, "Simon, Simon, listen! Satan has demanded to sift all of you like wheat, but I have prayed for you that your own faith may not fail; and you, when once you have turned back, strengthen your brothers." And he said to him, "Lord, I am ready to go with you to prison and death!" Jesus said, "I tell you, Peter, the cock will not crow this day, until you have denied three times that you know me."

Verses 35-38 say, He said to them, "When I sent you out without a purse, bag, or sandals, did you lack anything?" They said, "No not a thing." He said to them, "But now, the one who has a purse must take it, and likewise a bag. And one who has no sword must sell his cloak and buy one. For I tell you the scripture (Isa 53:12) must be fulfilled in me, 'And he was counted among the lawless' and indeed what is written about me is being fulfilled." They said, "Lord, here are two swords. He replied, "It is enough."

Jesus is telling them to prepare for the struggle and to not be a burden to others as they take the message of the kingdom. The swords are not for war making. They are a symbol of the struggle before them. They are to use them only to protect themselves against wild animals and robbers who attempt to attack them as they travel throughout the empire's lonely roads and mountain trails. To use a passage like this as a proof text for war making, as some of the more militant Christians do, is ridiculous and a distortion of interpreting God's holy word.

Verses 39-42 say, He came out and went, as was his custom, to the Mount of Olives; and the disciples followed him. When he reached the place, he said to them, "Pray that you will not come into the time of trial." Then he withdrew from them about a stone's throw, knelt down, and prayed, "Father if you are willing, remove this cup from me; yet not my will but yours be done."

Verses 43-44 say, Then an angel from heaven appeared to him and gave him strength. In his anguish he prayed more earnestly, and his sweat became like great drops of blood falling down on the ground. (Other ancient authorities lack these verses. Even though the sweat was like drops of blood, not drops of blood, it has been said that others have sweated something like blood under extreme stress.)

Verses 45-46 say, When he got up from prayer, he came to the disciples and found them sleeping because of grief, and he said to them, "Why are you sleeping? Get up and pray that you may not come into the time of trial." (Only Luke, the physician, says they are sleeping because of grief. Grief can be very energy draining.)

Verses 47-51 say, While he was still speaking, suddenly a crowd came, and the one called Judas, one of the twelve, was leading them. He approached Jesus to kiss him, "Judas, is it with a kiss that you are betraying the Son of Man?" When those who were around him saw what was coming, they asked, "Lord, should we strike with the sword?" Then one of them struck the slave of the high priest and cut off his right ear. But Jesus said, "No more of this!" (This answers the question on the use of the sword in the previous verses.) And he touched his ear and healed him.

Then in (52-53) Jesus said to the chief priests, the officers of the temple police, and the elders who had come to him, "Have you come out with swords and clubs as if I were a bandit? When I was with you day after day in the temple, you did not lay hands on me. But this is your hour, and the power of darkness."

Verses 54-59 say, Then they seized him and led him away, bringing him into the high priest's house. But Peter was following at a distance. When they had kindled a fire in the middle of the courtyard and sat down together, Peter sat among them. Then a servant-girl, seeing him in the firelight, stared at him and said, "This man also was with him." But he denied it, saying, "Woman, I do not know him." A little later someone else, on seeing him, said, "You also are one of them." But Peter said, "Man, I am not." Then about an hour later still another kept insisting, "Surely this man also was with him; for he is a Galilean." (It is like a southerner or a northerner; one from either place knows the other by their speech.)

Verses 60-62 say, But Peter said, "Man, I do not know what you are talking about!" At that moment while he was still speaking, the cock crowed. The Lord turned and looked at Peter. Then Peter remembered the word of the Lord, how he had said to him, "Before the cock crows today, you will deny me three times." And he went out and wept bitterly. (We should not be too hard on Peter, for he is among the few who had the courage to follow him this far.)

Verses 63-65 say, Now the men who were holding Jesus began to mock him and beat him; they also blindfolded him and kept asking him, "Prophesy! Who is it that struck you?" They kept heaping many other insults on him. (His role as God's true prophet is being mocked just as it was with the Old Testament prophets.) Verse 66 says, When the day came, the assembly of the elders of the people, both chief priests and scribes, gathered together, and they brought him to their council.

The council is called the Sanhedrin. It is dominated by the priests who are Sadducees. The council is in control of all temple activity. The Sadducees only accept the Pentateuch, the first five books of the Old Testament. They do not accept the rest, nor do they accept the oral law of the Pharisees, and they do not believe in the resurrection, spirits, or angels.

The Sanhedrin is the highest ruling body for the Jews. Rome gave the Jews authority to rule in most local issues. This is done through the Sanhedrin, who rules in both religious and political matters that affect the Jews. The high priest is the president. In addition to the aristocratic Sadducees, there are also some Pharisees, who are mainly the scribes, and elders. Those who make up the Sanhedrin are the wealthiest and most powerful people of Judea making all religious, political, social, and economic policies. Luke's description of a day meeting and not a night meeting as described by Mark and Matthew is likely, for a night meeting would have been illegal.

Verses 67-71 say, They said, "If you are the Messiah, tell us." He replied, "If I tell you, you will not believe; and if I question you, you will not answer. But from now on the Son of Man will be seated at the right hand of the power of God." (They would recognize this statement as him referring to himself as the Son of Man, one like a human being, given an eternal kingdom by God the Father of Dan 7:12-14.) All of them asked, "Are you, then, the Son of God?" He said to them, "You say that I am." Then they said, "What further testimony do we need? We have heard it ourselves from his own lips!" (They will interpret this as blasphemy, sufficient reason to condemn him to death.)

Chapter 23:1-3 says, Then the assembly rose as a body and brought Jesus before Pilate. (Pilate's seat of government is normally in Caesarea but moved to Jerusalem during the Passover, for the time of Passover is especially volatile.) They began to accuse him saying, "We found this man perverting our nation, forbidding us to pay taxes to the emperor, and saying that he himself is the Messiah, a king." (These accusations are political, and could be understood as fomenting revolt.) Then Pilate asked him, "Are you the king of the Jews?" He answered, "You say so."

Verses 4-5 say, Then Pilate said to the chief priests and the crowds, "I find no basis for an accusation against this man." But they were insistent and said, "He stirs up the people by teaching throughout all of Judea, from Galilee where he began even to this place. (Obviously, he did not hide his teaching from the people or the leaders.)

Verses 6-7 say, When Pilate heard this he asked whether the man was a Galilean. And when he learned he was under Herod's jurisdiction, he sent him off to Herod, who was himself in Jerusalem at the time. (This is Herod Antipas, tetrarch of the northern regions of Galilee and Perea, a son of Herod the Great. He is the one who had John the Baptist killed. Later he will be banished to France by the Roman emperor Caligua, who was emperor from 37-41 AD. Caligua ordered a statue of himself to be put in the temple, but fortunately he died before it happened, thus saving mass riots in Jerusalem.)

Verses 8-12 say, When Herod saw Jesus, he was very glad, for he had been wanting to see him for a very longtime, because he had heard about him and was hoping to see him perform some sign. He questioned him at some length, but Jesus gave him no answer.

The chief priests and the scribes stood by, vehemently accusing him. Even Herod with his soldiers treated him with contempt and mocked him; then he put an elegant robe on him (suggesting a royal mockery), and sent him back to Pilate. That same day Herod and Pilate became friends with each other; before this they had been enemies. (This will be used as a fulfillment of prophecy, see Ps 2:1-2, Acts 4:24-26. Herod and Pilate become friends because Pilate is recognizing Herod's authority. Later Caligua will retire Pilate. There are different legends about where he went and what happened to him.)

In verses 13-16 Pilate then called together the chief priests, the leaders, and the people, and said to them, "You brought me this man as one who was perverting the people; and here I have examined him in your presence and have not found this man guilty of any of your charges against him. Neither has Herod, for he sent him back to us. Indeed, he has done nothing to deserve death. I will therefore have him flogged and release him." Verse 17 is missing, but some ancient authorities add, Now he was obliged to release someone for them at the festival.

Verses 18-23 say, Then they all shouted out together, "Away with this fellow! Release Barabbas for us! (This is a man who some believe had been put in prison for an insurrection that had taken place in the city, and for murder.) Pilate, wanting to release Jesus, addressed Jesus; but they kept shouting, "Crucify, crucify him!" A third time he said to them, "Why, what evil has he done? I have found in him no ground for the sentence of death; I will therefore have him flogged and then release him." But they kept urgently demanding with loud shouts that he should be crucified; and their voices prevailed. (It is interesting how quickly a crowd can change its position from less than a week ago, when he triumphantly rode in on a donkey.) So in (24-25) Pilate gave his verdict that their demand should be granted. He released the man they asked for, the one who had been put in prison for insurrection and murder, and he handed Jesus over as they wished. (When the crowd thought he was going to bring a revolution to get rid of the Romans, they cheered him, but when they see him in defeat, they turn against him.)

Verses 26-31 say, As they led him away, they seized a man, Simon of Cyrene, who was coming from the country, and they laid the cross on him, and made him carry it behind Jesus. A great number of the people followed him, and among them were women who were beating their breasts and wailing for him. But Jesus turned to them and said, "Daughters of Jerusalem, do not weep for me, but weep for yourselves and your children. For the days are surely coming when they will say, 'Blessed are the barren and the wombs that never bore, and the breasts that never nursed.' Then they will begin to say to the mountains, 'Fall on us'; and to the hills, 'Cover us.' For if they do this when the wood is green, what will happen when it is dry?"

He says this in reference to the day when the Romans destroy the temple and the city. These women will rejoice that they have no children, for if the innocent Jesus, the green tree, has to suffer so much, what will be the fate of the dry tree, guilty Jerusalem? In other words if they put to death one who was not really a revolutionary against Rome, what will they do with the real revolutionaries who will oppose Rome in a war between AD 66-70?

Hosea writes of that time in 10:1-15. In reference to Israel he says that their heart is false; now they must bear their guilt. The sin of Israel shall be destroyed. Thorns and thistles shall grow up on their altars. They shall say to the mountains, Cover us, and to the hills, Fall on us . . . I shall come against the wayward people to punish them . . . You have plowed wickedness, you have reaped injustice, you have eaten the fruit of lies. Because you have trusted in your power and in the multitude of your warriors, therefore the tumult of war shall rise against your people and all your fortresses shall be destroyed . . . He tells them that when mothers were dashed in pieces with their children, it shall be done to you because of your great wickedness. In AD 70, like in the past, it all came to be again. Jesus uses old prophecies and applies them to new situations because prophecy seems to repeat itself.

Verses 32-38 say, Two others also, who were criminals, were led away to be put to death with him. When they came to the place that is called The Skull, they crucified Jesus there with the criminals, one on his right and one on his left. Then Jesus said, "Father forgive them; for they do not know what they are doing." And they cast lots to divide his clothing (Ps 22:18). And the people stood by, watching, but the leaders scoffed at him, saying, "He saved others; let him save himself if he is the Messiah of God, his chosen one." The soldiers also mocked him, coming up and offering him sour wine, and saying, "If you are the King of the Jews, save yourself!" There was also an inscription over him, "This is the King of the Jews."

Rome's official reason for his death is that he is a revolutionary. Pilate had to have a reason for Rome. The charge was not true. He may be considered revolutionary in his thinking, but he was not a revolutionary declaring violence against Rome.

Verses 39-43 say, One of the criminals who was hanged there kept deriding him and saying, "Are you not the Messiah? Save your self and us!" But the other rebuked him saying, "Do you not fear God, since you are under the same sentence of condemnation? And we indeed have been condemned justly, for we are getting what we deserve for our deeds, but this man has done nothing wrong." Then he said, "Jesus, remember me when you come into your kingdom." He replied, "Truly I tell you, today you will be with me in paradise."

Verses 44-49 say, It was now about noon, and darkness came over the whole land until three in the afternoon, while the sun's light failed; and the curtain of the temple was torn in two. Then Jesus crying out with a loud voice said, "Father, into your hands I commend my spirit." Having said this, he breathed his last. When the centurion saw what had taken place, he praised God and said, "Certainly this man was innocent." And when all the crowds who had gathered there for this spectacle saw what had taken place, they returned home, beating their breasts. But all his acquaintances, including the women who had followed him from Galilee, stood at a distance, watching these things.

The sun light failing symbolizes that it is a dark time for the world. The curtain in the temple in the Old Testament kept everyone away from the presence of God except the high priest, who entered one day each year, the Day of Atonement. Being torn in two symbolizes that God's presence is now available to all who come to him.

Verses 50-56 say, Now there was a good and righteous man named Joseph, who though a member of the council, had not agreed to their plan and action. He came from the town of Arimathea, and he was waiting expectantly for the kingdom of God. This man went to Pilate and asked for the body of Jesus. Then he took it down, wrapped it in a linen cloth, and laid it in a rock-hewn tomb where no one had ever been laid. It was the day of Preparation, and the sabbath was beginning. (This is the day the Passover lambs are sacrificed. Luke is saying Jesus is the true Passover lamb that takes away the sin of the world.) The women who had come with him from Galilee followed, and they saw the tomb and how the body was laid. Then they returned, and prepared spices and ointments. On the sabbath day they rested according to the commandment.

Chapter 24:1-7 says, But on the first day of the week, at early dawn, they came to the tomb, taking the spices they had prepared. They found the stone rolled away from the tomb, but when they went in, they did not find the body. While they were perplexed about this, suddenly two men in dazzling clothes stood beside them. The women were terrified and bowed their faces to the ground, but the men said to them, "Why do you look for the living among the dead? He is not here but has risen. Remember how he told you, while he was still in Galilee, that the Son of Man must be handed over to sinners, and be crucified, and on the third day rise again."

Verses 8-12 say, Then they remembered his words, and returning from the tomb, they told all this to the eleven and all the rest. Now it was Mary Magdalene, Joanna, Mary the mother of James, and the other women with them who told this to the apostles. But these words seemed to them an idle tale, and they did not believe them. But Peter got up and ran to the tomb; stooping and looking in, he saw the linen cloths by themselves; then he went home, amazed at what happened. (In the ancient world, it is much out of character to appear first to women, for their witness was not considered acceptable.)

Verses 13-18 say, Now on that same day two of them were going to a village called Emmaus, about seven miles from Jerusalem, and talking with each other about all these things that had happened. While they were talking and discussing, Jesus himself came near and went with them, but their eyes were kept from recognizing him. And he said to them, "What are you discussing with each other while you walk along?" They stood still, looking sad. Then one of them, whose name is Cleopas, answered him, "Are you the only stranger in Jerusalem who does not know the things that have taken place there in these days?"

Verses 19-24 say, He asked them, "What things?" They replied, "The things about Jesus of Nazareth, who was a prophet mighty in deed and word before God and all the people, and how our chief priests and elders handed him over to be condemned to death and crucified him. Yes, and besides all this, it is now the third day since these things took place. Moreover, some women of our group astounded us. They were at the tomb early this morning, and when they did not find his body there, they came back and told us that they had indeed seen a vision of angels who had said he was alive. Some of those who were with us went to the tomb and found it just as the women had said; but they did not see him."

Verses 25-27 say, Then he said to them, "Oh, how foolish you are, and how slow of heart to believe all that the prophets have declared! Was it not necessary that the Messiah should suffer these things and then enter into his glory?" Then beginning with Moses and all the prophets, he interpreted to them the things about himself in all the scriptures. (It is too bad the exact verses he interpreted were not written. Luke writes this to show that Jesus is the promised one, the fulfillment of what the prophets wrote.)

Verses 28-31 say, As they came near the village to which they were going, he walked ahead as if he were going on. But they urged him strongly, saying, "Stay with us, because it is almost evening and the day is now nearly over." So he went in to stay with them. When he was at the table with them, he took bread, blessed and broke it, and gave it to them. Then their eyes were opened, and they recognized him; and he vanished from their sight.

Luke writes this to state when there is breaking of the bread, the Eucharist, also called the Lord's Supper, Jesus is made present for that moment. Calvin, Luther, Wesley, the Orthodox, Episcopalians, and Roman Catholics all believe that in some way Jesus is made present in the Lord's Supper. The way that occurs is not agreed upon, but they all believe in some way Christ is made present in the eating of the bread and the drinking of the wine. Verse 32 says, They said to each other, "Were not our hearts burning within us while he was talking to us on the road, while he was opening the scriptures to us?" (Luke is saying that when the Scriptures are opened, listened to and read, Jesus also makes himself present to us.)

Verses 33-35 say, That same hour they got up and returned to Jerusalem; and they found the eleven and their companions gathered together. They were saying, "The Lord has risen indeed, and he has appeared to Simon!" Then they told what had happened on the road, and how he had been made known to them in the breaking of the bread. (Again, Luke emphasizes that Jesus is made present in the breaking of the bread.)

Verses 36-43 say, While they were talking about this, Jesus himself stood among them and said to them, "Peace be with you." They were startled and terrified, and thought that they were seeing a ghost. He said to them, "Why are you frightened, and why do doubts arise in your hearts? Look at my hands and my feet; see that it is I myself. Touch me and see; for a ghost does not have flesh and bones as you see that I have." And when he had said this, he showed them his hands and his feet. While in their joy they were disbelieving and still wondering, he said to them, "Have you anything here to eat?" They gave him a piece of boiled fish, and he took it and ate it in their presence. (The heresy of *Docetism,* a form of *Gnosticism,* states Jesus does not have a body. He is only a spirit; therefore, he did not rise in a physical body. Luke is stressing the opposite.)

Verses 44-47 say, Then he said to them, "These are my words that I spoke to you while I was still with you—that everything written about me in the law of Moses, the prophets, and the psalms must be fulfilled." Then he opened their minds to understand the scriptures, and he said to them, "Thus it is written, that the Messiah is to suffer and to rise from the dead on the third day, and that repentance and forgiveness of sins is to be proclaimed in his name to all nations, beginning from Jerusalem. (This can be stated by putting together Isa 53 with Dan 7:12-14. Up to this point no one had put them together like this.)

In verses 48-49 Jesus says, You are witnesses of these things. And see, I am sending upon you what my Father promised; so stay here in the city until you have been clothed with power from on high." (The Apostle Paul in 2 Cor 1:20 said, "For in him every one of God's promises is a yes." He is saying that all the God-given promises in the Old Testament find their "yes" in Christ. He is their fulfillment as Luke is stating.)

Verses 50-53 say, Then he led them out as far as Bethany, and lifting up his hands, he blessed them. While he was blessing them, he withdrew from them and was carried up into heaven. (Liturgically, this is called the Ascension.) And they worshiped him, and returned to Jerusalem with great joy; and they were continually in the temple blessing God. (Luke ends his gospel with the people praising God, which is what his people are to do until he comes at the end.)

Luke writes to inform people that Jesus is a real historical person who lived in historical time. He is God's Son and the Savior of Israel and the world. The Roman emperor is not the lord and savior called by God to bring peace and order; those titles are reserved only for Jesus. And he is not like the saviors of the many mystery cults of the time, who were mythical. Salvation history is a good way to describe Luke's gospel. Yet Luke's concept of *savior* and *salvation* first comes from the story of Israel and especially Old Testament prophets like Isaiah, and it is to the nation of Israel. Then it is further adapted to a remnant of individual Jews to become the new Israel, and then to the church established on the day of Pentecost as stated in chapter two of Luke's book of the Acts of the Apostles, and then to all individuals throughout the world.

Luke says, While Jesus was blessing them, he withdrew from them and was carried up into heaven. In Acts 1:9 he adds, he was lifted up, and a cloud took him out of their sight. Luke is describing Daniel 7:12-14 that says, I saw one like a human being (Son of Man) coming with the clouds of heaven. And he came to the Ancient One (Ancient of Days) and was presented before him. To him was given dominion and glory and kingship, that all peoples, nations, and languages should serve him. His dominion is an everlasting dominion that shall not pass away, and his kingship is one that shall not be destroyed. (Luke is saying Jesus is the new David, the one all the prophets said would come; he is the fulfillment of Daniel's prophecy. Being taken up into heaven is Luke's way of saying Jesus was transported to another dimension.)

The prophets looked forward to future deliverance from their enemies at a time when a rich banquet would be prepared for all peoples, death would be destroyed, and God's people would say, this is our God in whom we trust. Let us rejoice in his salvation. The prophets speak of a time when God's punishment of the nation for its sin would end. Israel would be at peace, and God's glory would be present with them. It is a time of the restoration of Israel, a time that the nation will recognize that God is with his people. The nations will forsake their idolotry, and see God the Creator as Savior. It is the time that Israel's exile will be over. No foreign country will dominate them. Evil will be defeated. God will return to Israel. There would be the beginning of a new covenant, and a new age with all the nations coming to Israel (see Isa 52:7-12, 54:4-8, Zeph 3:14-20, Ps 145:10-13, Pss 93, 96, 97).

According to all of NT Wright's books and many others, Jews did not interpret that language to mean the end of the world as we know it, for it means the exile is over and the new age and the new covenant is beginning and is to be preached to all nations.

Luke is writing to say all this did take place but not in the way expected. The reader must remember this was written fifty plus years after the death, crucifixion, and resurrection of the Jewish Jesus when most believers were still basically from the Jewish people.

In summary Luke has Jesus saying he came to preach the kingdom and to seek and to save the lost. He pays special attention to the poor masses, the people oppressed by the elite people of power and wealth, both Jewish and Roman, who control society. He has a special concern for women, the masses who are struggling to survive, those of low social status, the outcasts of society-those who do not fit in and are not accepted by the in-crowd. Matthew has kings, or at least leaders, coming to visit Jesus and bowing down to him, either at his birth or within the first two years of his life, and it takes place in a home; Luke has poor shepherds visiting him in a lowly barnyard manger. All three Synoptic gospels are concerned with social and economic justice, but Luke emphasizes this biblical concept, which has deep roots in the Old Testament, especially the Exodus and the Prophets.

Women have a very important place in Luke's gospel. Jesus even teaches them, which is a rarity in the ancient world. Also prayer, the Holy Spirit and the use of the word *Lord* are emphasized. Lord is a substitute word for YHWH (God) for the Jews. The word means savior in the Gentile pagan religions that are also called the mystery religions. The word joy is a word Luke constantly uses. Its reference is not to an emotional high but a type of inner peace and happiness. Luke emphasizes the Holy Spirit. In fact when he writes Acts some will say it should be called the Acts of the Holy Spirit. Practically every page in Luke has the Holy Spirit leading something, creating, and working.

These three gospels of Mark, Matthew, and Luke are called the Synoptic Gospels because they are very similar, even though they often see things from different angles and sometimes emphasize different theologies. All three gospels emphasize the humanness of Jesus as he moves toward the cross. Thus their gospels are called a Christology from below. On the other hand John will be very different, since he will emphasize this side of the cross, the resurrection of Jesus, and the divinity of Jesus. John's approach is called a Christology from above. Let us now look at the Gospel of John.

THE GOSPEL OF JOHN

*The majority of scholars believe this non-Synoptic Gospel was probably written between 90-100 A.D, and most likely the gospel was completed by the disciples of John's school. A small minority of scholars disagree. It is the last gospel written and is probably the only account written by someone who was with Jesus from the beginning.

*This gospel is the most spiritual, theological, philosophical, mystical, symbolic, and sacramental in that it stresses Christ from above-his divinity. It is an expression of what the Christians, after the cross and resurrection, finally believe.

*Light and darkness are constantly used to contrast good and evil, God and the things of the world. If light weakens, darkness takes its place.

*There is an emphasis on experiencing the presence of God through the material things of God's creation. John emphasizes the incarnation-the divine Son taking on flesh and becoming human. He writes to counter *Docetism* a form of *Gnosticism* that believes the body is evil, and says that Jesus did not have real flesh and a real body. It just appeared that he did.

*John looks beyond the appearance of things to stress their underlying meaning. In John Jesus overturns the tables in the temple at the beginning of his ministry while in the Synoptics he does it at the end of his ministry. John puts it at the beginning, for it is the key to understanding the final decision of why the Jewish leaders put Jesus to death. John wants to highlight this particular action of Jesus and stress the meaning of this event.

*In John there are no parables, no exorcisms, and few metaphors pointing to the kingdom and its importance. The kingdom is now established, so the emphasis is on the King. The new age is in operation; the kingdom is advancing.

*John uses many symbols to point to the mystery of who Jesus is. He says his purpose is to prove that Jesus is the Messiah, God's unique Son and that through believing one may have life in his name (19:31).

*John has the "I am" passages which Jesus uses to tell who he is. Remember when God revealed his name to Moses he said YHWH meaning, "I am who I am." This is explained in the author's previous book on the Old Testament (47-48). Jesus said I am the bread of life, the good shepherd, the way, the truth, and the light, the light of the world, the resurrection and the life, and the true vine. He uses "I am" 54 times, and he speaks of God his Father 118 times. According to John, Jesus has no doubt who he is and why he took on flesh.

*Because he is the Lamb of God his death takes place on the day of preparation of the Passover lamb. In the Synoptics Jesus dies on the day of Passover. In John he is being prepared as the new Passover lamb. He is the Passover lamb whose bones are not broken (Ex 12:46). There is no longer a need for Passover lambs or any animal sacrifice. Jesus is the Lamb of God; he is the new and final Passover lamb that takes away the sin of the world. Jesus is the source of living water meaning the Holy Spirit. In John, Jesus gives Peter a certain authority by telling him to feed his lambs. His lambs will be the children of God called to sacrifice themselves for the things of Jesus and his kingdom that has broken in upon the earth.

*John has no real birth story, but he does stress the Word, who is from the beginning and becomes incarnate (becomes flesh). In a sense John is creating a new Genesis. He intends his teachings to be interpreted in the light of a total narrative that goes back to the beginning of creation and comes through the story of Israel. Jesus is the true shepherd, God himself coming into the world to shepherd his sheep just as Ezekiel 33 foretold.

*There are no exorcisms. Jesus overcomes evil by his word. He is the logos, meaning word, who becomes flesh and lives among us. He takes the place of Torah. He is the new *shekinah* (presence of God). He takes the place of the temple. At the end of the first chapter of Genesis is the creation of the human in the image of his creator. At the end of John chapter one is Jesus the divine image-bearer, the *logos* becoming human to enable humans to see and understand God's wisdom in the flesh. The climax in John is at the end when Thomas says, My Lord and my God.

*John has Jesus' public activity fitting into one year mainly in Jerusalem and Judea while the Synoptics put most things in Galilee and in a three-four year period. John's concern is to inform people who Jesus is and that he is from above and is divine.

*Instead of a reinterpretation of the Mosaic Law, which is the main topic of many of Jesus' short synoptic discourses, he has only one new commandment, and that is to love. Love is the summary of the law and the real distinguishing mark of discipleship. John has Jesus saying, "I give you a new commandment, that you love one another. Just as I have loved you, you also should love one another." On the whole John's discourses are long themes or speeches, not individual separated units as in the Synoptics.

*John says nothing about Jesus' second coming, for he stresses that Jesus is present now through the Holy Spirit, and the fact that eternal life has now begun on this earth. The kingdom has officially broken in upon the earth. Jesus is most present through Word and the Eucharist, and when his people are together in his name. Although he represents the bread and wine as sacramental life giving symbols, he substitutes foot washing for the Eucharist at the Last Supper to emphasize humble service. John says that the meal took place the day before the Passover.

*Instead of the cry of despair at the cross as in Mark, Jesus simply says, "It is finished." He accomplishes his purpose. His death is a glorification. John's continual use of the term "lifting up" denotes the exaltation, the triumph of the cross.

Now, let us look at the Gospel of John. Verses 1-18 seem to be part hymn and part poem expressing John's theology that Jesus is the Father's supreme revelation and his interpreter. Then in 19-51 a series of witnesses come to identify Jesus.

John 1:1-5 says, In the beginning was the Word, and the Word was with God, and the Word was God. He was in the beginning with God. All things came into being through him, and without him not one thing came into being. What has come into being in him was life, and the life was the life of all people. The light shines in the darkness, and the darkness did not overcome it.

The Word who is Jesus is also said here to be divine; he is with God in the beginning. He and the Father are involved together in creation. Although it appears that darkness does overcome the light at the cross, at the resurrection light overcomes darkness. As long as the light shines darkness will not overcome the light, but when light does not shine, there is darkness. The Gospels will inform us that his followers will be his shining light.

Verses 6-9 say, there was a man sent from God, whose name was John (the Baptist not the Apostle John). He came as a witness to testify to the light, so that all might believe through him. He himself was not the light, but he came to testify to the light. The true light, which enlightens everyone, was coming into the world. (The Quakers believe this light that enlightens everyone is put into hearts and is the inner light given to all at birth. If one follows this light salvation will come.)

Verses 10-13 say, He was in the world, and the world came into being through him; yet the world did not know him. He came to what was his own (the Jewish people), and his own people did not accept him. But to all who received him, who believed in his name, he gave power (grace) to become children of God, who were born, not of blood or the will of the flesh or of the will of man, but of God.

John is saying that one personally must believe in Jesus the light, receive him, and thus receive the power (grace) to become born of God. Then one becomes a child of God. One can no longer be permanently considered a child of God by being born into this by heritage, such as belonging to the right nation, church, or group. Each individual must eventually decide to receive him into their lives, and let him, through his grace, do his work in them and through them. This is the process of being born of God and becoming a child of God. No other human being can do it for you. When Peter gives the first sermon in Acts 2, and calls people to receive Christ, he instructs the people after they ask him what they should do (see 2:36-47).

Verse 14 continues, And the Word became flesh and lived among us, (the incarnation) and we have seen his glory, the glory as of a father's only son, full of grace and truth. (The followers of Jesus must not only apply the meaning of the resurrection to their lives but also the meaning of the incarnation. Jesus' life, not just his death, is to have meaning to his followers and change their lives where they become people of grace and truth to the glory of God.)

Verses 15-17 say, John testified to him and cried out, "This was he of whom I said, 'He who comes after me ranks ahead of me because he was before me.' " From his fullness we have all received, grace upon grace (available to all and never exhausted). The law indeed was given through Moses; grace (unmerited favor) and truth (God's final truth) came through Jesus Christ.

The law of Moses was written on stone, a minimum law to be obeyed, but grace and truth, God's unlimited grace and love, are now written on the heart by the Spirit that Christ sends to those born of God to help them love to the maximum degree possible for humans. Verse 18 says, No one has ever seen God. It is God the only Son, who is close to the Father's heart, who has made him known.

Verses 19-23 say, This is the testimony given by John when the Jews sent priests and Levites from Jerusalem to ask him, "Who are you?" He confessed and did not deny it, but confessed, "I am not the Messiah." And they asked him, "What then? Are you Elijah?" He said, "I am not." "Are you the prophet?" He answered, "No." Then they said to him, "Who are you? Let us have an answer for those who sent us. What do you say about yourself?" He said, "I am the voice of one crying in the wilderness, 'Make straight the way of the Lord,' " as the prophet Isaiah said (40:3).

To understand what John is saying it would be a good idea to read all of Isaiah 40. John is saying that the exile is almost over. The presence of God (the glory of the Lord) is about to be announced. The word he brings will last forever. He is the shepherd who will feed his flock. He is the everlasting God, the creator, who gives power to the weak and strengthens the powerless.

Verses 24-28 say, Now they had been sent from the Pharisees. They asked him, "Why then are you baptizing if you are neither the Messiah, nor Elijah, nor the prophet?" John answered them, "I baptize with water. Among you stands one whom you do not know, the one who is coming after me; I am not worthy to untie the thong of his sandal." This took place in Bethany across the Jordan where John was baptizing. (They can not understand who gives him the authority to baptize Jews. Up to this time the primary purpose of one baptizing in water is to baptize Gentiles who are becoming Jews.)

In verse 29 the next day he saw Jesus coming toward him and declared, "Here is the Lamb of God who takes away the sin of the world!"

He is called the Lamb of God because he will take the place of all the Old Testament animal sacrifices for sin, including the Passover lamb. It is important to say a few words on the biblical concept of sin. In the Old Testament thinking of the prophets, sin is not just about individual sin but includes the sin of the world, meaning institutional sin, and the sin of nations. Jesus, a prophet from the Old Testament tradition, accepts the notion that there is corporate sin as well as individual sin. Most Americans, because of their emphasis on individualism, do not have a very good understanding of corporate and institutional sin.

Americans as well as most of the world's nations tend to make all sin individual sin, which misconstrues the total nature of biblical sin. Biblical morality is both personal and social. Making the personal God private and ignoring the social aspects of God's concern only allows power and wealth to keep religion out of the social and economic aspects of life, which enables them to politically oppress and economically exploit. Keeping God private was one of the goals that came from the Enlightenment. It was developed by politicians and the powerful and wealthy in order to have the freedom to do whatever they wanted without interference from the church. But God is not just Lord of one's individual private life, but the Lord of all life. Compassion is both individual, social, and public. Public compassion and social justice is to benefit the common good. See in particular in the bibliography Stephen Mott's book, *Biblical Ethics and Social Change* and Allen Verhey's book *Remembering Jesus: Christian Community and the Moral Life*, and any of the morality writings by Roman Catholic writers.

Social justice is not for liberals only; it is the teaching of Jesus and the prophets. Ignoring this biblical concept may be this century's greatest heresy, for it is key to advancing the kingdom, the kingdom that Jesus said to pray about in the Lord's prayer. Jesus said when you pray say, Your kingdom come. Your will be done on earth as in heaven. Karl Barth, the great Reformed theologian, constantly warned that the great problem of the church is heresy, the corruption of its message, and not paganism or doubt (Church Dogmatics, 1, 1, 36).

The thinking of the Jews in those times is that when the sin of the nation and its sins of oppression are forgiven, the new age and new covenant will begin. Those individuals who respond to the call of repentance receive forgiveness for their individual sins and are transferred into the new covenant sealed by Jesus' blood. This new covenant is the corporate covenant made with the church to which individuals are added. They become his people and he becomes their God.

People in America do not usually think that way, but that is the thinking Scripture portrays. Americans tend to focus on the responsibility of individuals only. Individuals do make up the church, but first there is the covenant established with the corporate church to which individuals are added. This is called the new covenant. The same is true with the old covenant that permeates the Old Testament. It was first made with the nation, and then individuals were joined to it.

This thinking is especially difficult for Americans who have been trained in the concept of individualism only, stressing personal liberties over social obligations, which the extremists falsely call socialism. Thus they tend to become blinded to how social systems, and institutions shape their lives. They become blind as to how the community or any institution shapes the thinking of individuals. As an example think how the political party one belongs to shapes the thinking of its people, or how the church one belongs to shapes one's thinking about issues, and how they think about other churches, or how special interests determine how a government representative votes. Individuals do make up groups, but groups influence individuals to think like the group.

The writers of Scripture from the Old Testament prophets to Jesus and to the Apostle Paul railed against unjust institutions calling not only for individual conversion but for the social transformation of entire communities and institutions. Institutions, nations, and communities have their own distinctive character that model example and shape individual character. As long as we think we are individuals only, our social obligations will be weak, and our concept of justice will be only about protecting our own personal freedoms and punishing those we think are threatening us.

Because too many Americans no longer understand how corporate sin influences individuals, they no longer have a healthy concept of and compassion for the common good as well as the need for social justice. Part of the problem is a lack of understanding the themes of the Old Testament, especially the primary purpose of the prophets, and the fact that Jesus comes out of the tradition of those prophets to establish the kingdom of God. We must not forget the prayer of Jesus, "Your will be done on earth as it is in heaven." All of this is important to understand when readers come in contact with the biblical concept of sin. Government and the structures that make it function are all created by God and thus also accountable to God.

In verses 30-34 John, in reference to Jesus, says, "This is he of whom I said, 'After me comes a man who ranks ahead of me because he was before me.' I myself did not know him; but I came baptizing for this reason, that he might be revealed to Israel." And John testified, "I saw the Spirit descending from heaven like a dove, and it remained on him. I myself did not know (recognize) him, but the one who sent me to baptize with water said to me, 'He on whom you see the Spirit descend and remain is the one who baptizes with the Holy Spirit.' And I myself have seen and have testified that this is the Son of God." (The water baptism of John is just to prepare individuals and the nation of Israel for the one whose water baptism will bring the Holy Spirit that actually washes away the sin of people, see Acts 2:38, Titus 3:5. Also see comments on the baptism of Jesus in Mt 3:13-17, Mk 1:9-11, Lk 3:21-23.)

Verses 35-42 say, The next day John again was standing with two of his disciples, and as he watched Jesus walk by, he exclaimed, "Look here is the Lamb of God!" The two disciples heard him say this, and they followed Jesus. When Jesus turned and saw them following, he said to them, "What are you looking for?" They said to him, "Rabbi" (which translated means teacher), "where are you staying?" He said to them, "Come and see." They came and saw where he was staying, and they remained with him that day. It was about four o'clock in the afternoon. One of the two that heard John speak and followed him was Andrew, Simon Peter's brother. He first found his brother Simon and said to him, "We have found the Messiah" (which is translated Anointed). He brought Simon to Jesus, who looked at him and said, "You are Simon son of John. You are to be called Cephas" (which is translated Peter).

Verses 43-49 say, The next day Jesus decided to go to Galilee. He found Philip and said to him, "Follow me." Now Philip was from Bethsaida, the city of Andrew and Peter. Philip found Nathanael and said to him, "We have found him about whom Moses in the law and also the prophets wrote, Jesus son of Joseph from Nazareth." Nathanael said to him, "Can anything good come out of Nazareth?" Philip said, "Come and see." When Jesus saw Nathanael coming toward him, he said of him, "Here is truly an Israelite in whom there is no deceit!" Nathanael asked him, "Where did you get to know me?" Jesus answered, "I saw you under the fig tree before Philip called you." Nathanael replied, "Rabbi, you are the Son of God! You are the King of Israel!" (Nathanael obviously is impressed that Jesus knows his character without ever meeting him.)

In verses 50-51 Jesus answered, "Do you believe because I told you that I saw you under the fig tree? You will see greater things than these." And he said to him, "Very truly I tell you, you will see heaven opened and the angels of God ascending and descending upon the Son of Man." (The writer alludes to Jacob's dream (Gen 28:12) that through the people of Jacob, God would reveal himself. They would be the mediators of God's message. Now, Jesus will be the mediator of God's message.)

Chapter 2:1-5 says, On the third day there was a wedding in Cana of Galilee, and the mother of Jesus was there. Jesus and his disciples had also been invited to the wedding. When the wine gave out the mother of Jesus said to him, "They have no wine." And Jesus said to her, "Woman, what concern is that to you and to me? My hour has not yet come." His mother said to one of the servants, "Do whatever he tells you."

In those days a wedding could be a week long. Jesus enjoys a good celebration. Addressing his mother as woman is a respectful address. By telling the servant to do what he says shows trust in Jesus in whatever he says or does. He then yields to her request. This will be the first of seven signs. In John a sign points to a deeper theological truth. The basic message throughout John's themes will be the same as 2 Corinthians 5:17. The old ways are passing away, and the new ways are coming in. An abundance of wine is a symbol of the messianic age breaking in (see Amos 9:13-14, Joel 3:18), and this festival is a symbol of the Eucharist or even the messianic banquet where the wine never runs out and the best is saved for last (Borg, 2001; 204-205). Marriage and the wedding feast are obvious imagery for the restoration of Israel (Isa 49:18, 54:1-8, 62:4-6, Hos 2:19-20).

Verses 6-11 say, Now standing there were six stone water jars for the Jewish rites of purification, each holding twenty or thirty gallons. Jesus said to them, "Fill the jars with water." (It seems the fundamentalists, who believe the Bible says alcohol is forbidden, stop reading at this verse.) And they filled them up to the brim. He said to them, "Now draw some out, and take it to the chief steward." And so they took it. When the steward tasted the water that had become wine, and did not know where it came from . . . the steward called the bridegroom and said to him, "Everyone serves the good wine first, and then the inferior wine after the guests have become drunk. But you have kept the good wine until now." (The theme is the old law is passing away, for the new has arrived.) Jesus did this, the first of his signs in Cana of Galilee, and revealed his glory; and his disciples believed in him. Verse 12 says, After this he went down to Capernaum with his mother, his brothers, and his disciples, and they remained there a few days. (John says nothing about his brothers not believing in him.)

The purpose of Jesus is to reveal himself as God's final revelation and to reveal God's kingdom through his presence. So in the process he transforms whatever is natural into new life and purpose. John put this in the beginning of his gospel because his whole message is about transformation and making all things new. Jesus is about the transformation of individuals, the world, and everything that makes up the world. It is not a private message only to individuals. That thinking is not a modern day creation, for it was part of the ancient heresy known as Docetic Gnosticism.

Many scholars say Gnosticism was not an issue in those times, for it developed later. But this writer does not agree. Gnosticism is the basis of Hinduism and Buddhism that had been well established five hundred years before in the East. There is no reason not to believe that the Gnostic philosophy had penetrated the area to some extent.

John now mentions the temple incident that the other gospel

writers do not mention until the end of their writings. Jesus will not only become the new Torah, but he will also become the new temple of God. The temple incident and what it symbolizes will be one of the major reasons he will eventually be put to death. This is why John expresses it early in his writing. By writing that Jesus is the Lamb of God that takes away sin, he wants to stress that Jesus has become the new temple of God where sins are now forgiven and all are united as one. For the Jews the temple is the main center of worship that will unite the nations. For the Jews it is where the daily animal sacrifices for many things including the sins of the people are made. Every male who can is obligated to come to the temple each year for the three major holy days of Passover, Pentecost, and Booths (Tabernacles).

Verses 13-17 say, The Passover of the Jews was near, and Jesus went up to Jerusalem. In the temple he found people selling cattle, sheep, and doves, and the money changers seated at the tables. Making a whip of cords, he drove all of them out of the temple, both the sheep and the cattle. He also poured out the coins of the money changers and overturned their tables He told those who were selling the doves, "Take these things out of here! Stop making my Father's house a market place." His disciples remembered that it was written, "Zeal for your house will consume me." (This is Ps 69:9.)

Too often this is displayed as an emotional display of anger by Jesus, but that is not quite true. The incident is to be understood within the symbolic actions of the prophetic tradition of Israel. Then his actions become nothing more than enlivened symbolic actions, an object lesson, prophesying judgment on the temple and its destruction, as well as the reason for its destruction. The temple has become a place where people are fleeced in the name of religion, and it represents what the leaders of the nation have done to the people of Israel. The temple controlled by the Sanhedrin was the centralized economic institution dominating the nation's economy.

People coming from distant lands to worship at the temple are being charged outrageous prices to exchange their money and to buy the animals to sacrifice as part of their worship. The temple leaders have become corrupt oppressors who have institutionalized greed and the oppression of their own people. Jesus simply does what the prophet Jeremiah did before him. He criticizes their actions and warns them, the nation, and the resistance movement, bent on a violent, militant overthrow of Rome that if they do not change their ways both Jerusalem and the temple will be destroyed. The leaders do not appreciate the message Jesus is giving them and will continue to give them. Twenty-five years later Jesus' prophecy will be fulfilled. Because of its importance, it becomes another reason John places the temple incident at the beginning of his gospel.

The temple has become like the barren fig tree, no longer producing fruit. Many of the disadvantaged in the land, as well as Jesus, see the temple as everything that is taking advantage of them. They see the leaders as a rich, corrupt aristocracy in cahoots with the Romans taking their lands, overtaxing them, and keeping the masses indebted to them. Their light has dimmed through their systemic injustice. Later when the nationalistic rebels attack the temple, the first thing they do is destroy all the tax records. The temple then becomes the center of the revolution against Rome.

The Sanhedrin consists of seventy religious and political leaders of Israel in charge of the temple. Most of the priests are the Sadducees who are working closely with the Romans in order to keep their power positions. They are among the wealthiest in Israel. In the process the Pharisees, many who are scribes and have joined the resistance movement, want him out of the way because he is not an observant Jew and is opposing their traditions. Also the

READING AND UNDERSTANDING THE GOSPELS

Zealots, who led the resistance movement, want him gone because he is not a loyal, flag waving patriot. Jesus condemns their attitude and warns them to repent, to change their violent agenda for his kingdom's agenda.

Verses 18-25 say, The Jews then said to him, "What sign can you show us for doing this?" (They are asking him what his authority is to treat the temple this way.) Jesus answered them, "Destroy this temple, and in three days I will raise it up." The Jews then said, "This temple has been under construction for forty-six years, and you will raise it up in three days?" But he (Jesus) was speaking of the temple of his body. After he was raised from the dead, his disciples remembered that he had said this; and they believed the scripture and the word that Jesus had spoken.

When he was in Jerusalem during the Passover festival, many believed in his name because they saw the signs that he was doing. But Jesus on his part would not entrust himself to them, because he knew all the people and needed no one to testify about anyone; for he himself knew what was in everyone.

Jesus understands how superficial faith can be as his parable of the farmer sowing seed expresses. He knows these particular Jews have no desire to believe in him. The temple that is standing is the one rebuilt by Zerubbabel over five hundred years before and had been remodeled by Herod the Great starting forty-six years ago and is still in progress. It will be finished by Herod Antipas and then totally destroyed in AD 70.

⚜

In chapter 3 the theme of newness continues. Verses 1-5 say, Now there was a Pharisee named Nicodemus, a leader of the Jews. He came to Jesus by night and said to him, "Rabbi, we know that you are a teacher who has come from God; for no one can do these signs that you do apart from the presence of God." (With the word "we," he may be representing a group of people.) Jesus answered him, "Very truly I tell you, no one can see the kingdom of God without being born from above (born of God)! Nicodemus said to him, "How can anyone be born after having grown old? Can one enter a second time into the mother's womb and be born?" Jesus answered, "Very truly, I tell you, no one can enter the kingdom of God without being born of water and Spirit."

Baptism is associated with the new birth also in the following: Jn 1:33, 3:22-23, Acts 2:38, 8:36, Rom 6:4, 1 Cor 6:11, 12:13, Eph 5:26, Titus 3:5, 1 Peter 3:18-22, Ezek 36:25-27. Nicodemus comes to Jesus in the darkness of night, but in the process receives light.

Verses 6-10 say, "What is born of flesh is flesh, and what is born of the Spirit is spirit. (Being born from above is about transformation and new life.) Do not be astonished that I said to you, 'You must be born from above.' The wind blows where it chooses, and you hear the sound of it, but you do not know where it comes from or where it goes (Ezek 37:5-10). So it is with everyone who is born of the Spirit." Nicodemus said to him, "How can these things be?" Jesus answered him, "Are you a teacher of Israel, and yet do not understand these things?"

Verses 11-15 say, "Very truly, I tell you, we speak of what we know and testify to what we have seen; yet you do not receive our testimony. If I have told you about earthly things (like the parable of the wind) and you do not believe, how can you believe if I tell you about heavenly things? No one has ascended into heaven except the one who descended from heaven, the Son of Man. And just as Moses lifted up the serpent in the wilderness, so must the Son of Man be lifted up (Numbers 21:9), that whoever believes in him has eternal life."

Participation in God through the one who has descended from

and ascended to heaven is eternal life, and it begins now with the in-breaking kingdom. For a reference to Moses lifting up the serpent in the wilderness and other Old Testament references, see Numbers 21. Nicodemus will appear again in chapters seven and nineteen.

In verses 16-17 Jesus then says to Nicodemus, "For God so loved the world that he gave his only Son, so that everyone who believes in him may not perish but may have eternal life. Indeed, God did not send the Son into the world to condemn the world, but in order that the world might be saved through him."

Sometimes Scripture uses *world* in a positive sense and other times in a negative sense. When used as God's creation, it is used positively. The world and individuals are now broken because of sin, so the Father sends the Son to redeem and renew the world. In the end the world will be created new, along with individuals, and there will be a new heaven and new earth. Being created new begins now and is a process that will be completed at the return of Christ.

The Apostle Paul in Rom 8:18-24 says, I consider that the sufferings of this present time are not worth comparing with the glory about to be revealed to us. For the creation waits with eager longing for the revealing of the children of God; for the creation was subjected to futility, not of its own will but by the will of the one who subjected it, in hope that creation itself will be set free from its bondage to decay and will obtain the freedom of the glory of the children of God. We know that the whole creation has been groaning in labor pains until now; and not only the creation, but we ourselves, who have the first fruits of the Spirit, groan inwardly while we wait for adoption, the redemption of our bodies. For in hope we were saved.

Then, in verse 18 after Jesus says that he did not come into the world to condemn the world but to save it, Jesus says, "Those who believe in him are not condemned; but those who do not believe are condemned already, because they have not believed in the name of the only Son of God."

It must be noted that according to these Scriptures all are condemned until they believe. They are condemned because of their sin, and according to Scripture all have sinned, and nothing unclean will enter into heaven (Rom 3:21-26, Rev 21:22-27). But it must be remembered that even the demons believe (James 2:19). Water and the Spirit as stated above and repentance for sin are part of belief, and faith must be brought to completion (James 2:18-26). This comes through God's grace and the working of the Holy Spirit (Phil 2:12-13). We are not saved by works, but we are not saved without works, but the works are the works of God that he works through his people as Philippians states. Augustine says (Epistle 194.5.29): "When God crowns your merits, he crowns nothing other than his own gifts."

Verses 19-21 say, And this is the judgment, that the light has come into the world, and people loved darkness rather than light because their deeds were evil. For all who do evil hate the light and do not come to the light, so that their deeds may not be exposed.

This is a good explanation as to why the world continues to be in a mess. People judge themselves by not coming to the light. They do not want to be changed and transformed into people of the light, for they enjoy darkness and do not believe in God. But those who do what is true come to the light, so that it may be clearly seen that their deeds have been done in God. Again, salvation comes to those whose deeds are done in God by God. If God's light is within, it is God who is doing the works in his people and through his people (Phil 2:12-13).

Verses 22-23 say, After this Jesus and his disciples went into the Judean countryside, and he spent some time there with them and baptized. (Chapter 4:1-2 says Jesus himself did not baptize but his disciples did.) John also was baptizing at Aenon near Salim because water was abundant there; and people kept coming and were being baptized . . . (The fact that water is abundant tells us this baptism probably is an immersion in water. The Geek word baptize means immerse.)

Verses 25-30 say, Now a discussion about purification arose between John's disciples and a Jew. They came to John and said to him, "Rabbi, the one who was with you across the Jordan, to whom you testified, he is baptizing, and all are going to him." John answered, "No one can receive anything except what has been given from heaven. You yourselves are my witnesses that I said, 'I am not the Messiah, but I have been sent ahead of him.' He who has the bride is the bridegroom. The friend of the bridegroom, who stands and hears him, rejoices greatly at the bridegroom's voice. For this reason my joy has been fulfilled. He must increase, but I must decrease." (John the Baptist makes it plain where he stands in relation to Jesus at a time when there is some confusion.)

In verses 31-36 Jesus continues, The one who comes from above is above all; the one who is of the earth belongs to the earth and speaks about earthly things. The one who comes from heaven is above all. He testifies to what he has seen and heard, yet no one accepts his testimony. Whoever has accepted his testimony has certified this, that God is true. He whom God has sent speaks the words of God, for he gives the Spirit without measure. The Father loves the Son and has placed all things in his hands. (The Father-Son relationship is key to Jesus' authority as revealer of God.) Verse 36 says, Whoever believes in the Son has eternal life; whoever disobeys the Son will not see life, but must endure God's wrath.

Wrath is the consuming fire of God's holiness. The writer makes it plain who Jesus is. He also makes it plain that obeying him is necessary for salvation, for he says, whoever disobeys the

Son will not see life, but must endure God's wrath. This is contrary to numerous preachers, especially the television preachers whose message is all anyone has to do is believe. Believing is key, but remember even the demons believe. It is plain the Scriptures teach that one can not reach heaven by works, but one also does not reach heaven without God's grace working in and through those he calls to obedience. Without obedience there is no faith (James 2:14-28, and Hebrews 11).

In chapter 4 Jesus leaves Judea to go to Galilee, and he passes through Sychar (near Shechem) in Samaria near the plot of ground where Joseph, Jacob's son, is buried and near Jacob's well. Since he is tired, he sits by the well. It is about noon. Verses 7-9 say, A Samaritan woman came to draw water, and Jesus said to her, "Give me a drink." (His disciples had gone to the city to buy food.) The Samaritan woman said to him, "How is it that you, a Jew, ask a drink of me, a woman of Samaria?"

Jews do not share things in common with Samaritans. Jews consider them apostates from the one true religion, and they believe they will be made unclean, or unfit for worship even by talking to them. Also, a respectable religious, male Jew would never be seen talking to or receiving anything from a woman in public. Therefore she is surprised.

Verses 10-15 say, Jesus answered her, "If you knew the gift of God, and who it is that is saying to you, 'Give me a drink.' You would have asked him, and he would have given you living water." The woman said to him, "Sir, you have no bucket, and the well is deep. Where do you get that living water? Are you greater than our ancestor Jacob, who gave us the well, and with his sons and his flocks drank from it?" Jesus said to her, "Everyone who drinks of this water will be thirsty again, but those who drink of the water that I will give them will never be thirsty. The water that I will give will become in them a spring of water gushing up to eternal life." The woman said to him, "Sir, give me this water, so that I may never be thirsty or have to keep coming here to draw water."

She misunderstands what he says because she is taking literally everything he says. Living water means running water, but Jesus is talking about something deeper. He is talking about the soul that searches for God and is satisfied by the Spirit of God. The Spirit fills a person and overflows out to touch others. Jesus is referring to Isaiah (49:10) and Jeremiah (17:13) and Psalms (36:9). When Jesus speaks of bringing people to the water that quenches thirst forever, he is stating he is the Messiah bringing in the new age. Also see Ezekiel 47 and Revelation 22.

Verses 16-20 say, Jesus said to her, "Go, call your husband, and come back." The woman answered him, "I have no husband." Jesus said to her, "You are right in saying, 'I have no husband'; for you have had five husbands, and the one you have now is not your husband. What you said is true!" The woman said to him, "Sir, I see that you are a prophet. Our ancestors worshiped on this mountain (Mt Gerizim), but you say that the place where people must worship is in Jerusalem."

The Samaritans only accept the first five books of the Bible and reject the oral law of tradition. They built their own temple on Mt Gerizim to keep their people from going to the Jerusalem temple to worship. The current Samaritans originated when the Jewish women, who remained in the land after most were exiled, married the foreign Assyrians who had plundered and conquered the north. This occurred in 722 BC after the land had been divided into the north (Israel) and the south (Judea). This mixture of people became known as Samaritans. The people of the north and the people of the south became bitter enemies. As the years went by, the Samaritans and the Jews got further and further apart.

In verses 21-24 Jesus said to her, "Woman, believe me, the hour is coming when you will worship the Father neither on this mountain nor in Jerusalem. (Jesus is saying worship will not be in the Samaritan or the Jewish temple.) You worship what you do not know; we worship what we know, for salvation is from the Jews. But the hour is coming, and is now here, when the true worshipers will worship the Father in spirit and truth, for the Father seeks such as these to worship him. God is spirit, and those who worship him must worship him in spirit and truth.

He does not define exactly what that means, so an educated guess must be made. Worshiping in spirit must be with a right attitude through the power of the Holy Spirit. The things of the Spirit must be related to one's life, and then the life lived offered to God in the right spirit. The things of the Spirit are its gifts and fruit. So from one's spirit through the Holy Spirit, one is to worship God in every day living by using the gifts God gives to honor and glorify him. The gifts of the Spirit are those spiritual and material things or talents God gives. The fruit of the Spirit is love, joy, peace, patience, kindness, generosity, faithfulness, gentleness, and self control. So as we live by those characteristics to honor God, he is being worshiped. This is one aspect of worship and a very important one.

He also says to worship in truth. The Scriptures tell us his word is truth. So God's people are to worship God by listening to his word. The Scripture also says Jesus is the Father's truth. So we worship Jesus by doing what he says. This includes the Eucharist, for on its institution he tells them to do it in remembrance of him, for as two or three are gathered together, he is being made present in their midst. When God's people come together to worship him, listening to his word, and participating in the Lord's Supper are two very important items to include.

Verses 25-26 say, The woman said to him, "I know that the Messiah is coming" (who is called the Christ). "When he comes, he will proclaim all things to us." Jesus said to her, "I am he, the one who is speaking to you."

I am (YHWH) is the name for God in the Old Testament. John uses this to state Jesus' identity. John like the other gospels has Jesus revealing himself to women, which is shocking in those times. Speaking to a woman in public is not socially acceptable, and a woman's witness is not even accepted in a court of law.

Verses 27-30 say, Just then his disciples came. They were astonished that he was talking with a woman, but no one said, "What do you want?" or, "Why are you speaking with her?" Then the woman left her water jar and went back to the city. She said to the people, "Come and see a man who told me everything I have ever done. He cannot be the Messiah, can he?" They left the city and were on their way to him. (Obviously, she is impressed and sees the need to get an opinion from others.)

Verses 31-38 say, Meanwhile the disciples were urging him, "Rabbi, eat something." But he said to them, "I have food to eat that you do not know about." So the disciples said to one another, "Surely no one has brought him something to eat?" Jesus said to them, "My food is to do the will of him who sent me and to complete his work. Do not say, 'Four months more then comes the harvest'? But I tell you, look around you, and see how the fields are ripe for harvesting. The reaper is already receiving wages and is gathering fruit for eternal life, so that sower and reaper may rejoice together. For here the saying holds true, 'One sows and another reaps.' I sent you to reap that for which you did not labor. Others have labored, and you have entered into their labor."

The sowers of the seed are the work of Moses and the prophets, and now Jesus and his disciples are to continue sowing seed so they and those that follow can begin to reap the harvest. And the harvest includes the Samaritans who are coming out as a result of the woman's witness to them. In this chapter Jesus teaches what the real food and water are. God's word is the food and the Holy Spirit is the water. This is the spiritual food that brings life. Without the proper food and water, one can not exist physically or spiritually.

Verses 39-42 say, Many Samaritans from that city believed in him because of the woman's testimony, "He told me everything I have ever done." (In other words he revealed her sins to her.) So when the Samaritans came to him, they asked him to stay with them; and he stayed there two days. And many more believed because of his word. They said to the woman, "It is no longer because of what you said that we believe, for we have heard for ourselves, and we know that this is truly the Savior of the world." (It is important to note that the Roman emperor goes by the title of the savior of the world, but John is saying the real and true Savior of the world is now being revealed.)

Verses 43-48 say, When the two days were over, he went from that place to Galilee . . . When he came to Galilee, the Galileans welcomed him, since they had seen all that he had done in Jerusalem at the festival; for they too had gone to the festival. Then he came again to Cana in Galilee where he had changed the water into wine. Now there was a royal official whose son lay ill in Capernaum. (Cana to Capernaum is about 15-20 miles.) His son was at the point of death. Then Jesus said to him, "Unless you see signs and wonders you will not believe."

Verses 49-54 say, The official said to him, "Sir, come down before my little boy dies." Jesus said to him, "Go; your son will live." The man believed the word that Jesus spoke to him and started on his way. (He did not need signs and wonders to believe, for he already believed.) As he was going down, his slaves met him and told him that his child was alive. So he asked them the hour he began to recover, and they said to him, "Yesterday at one in the afternoon the fever left him." The father realized that this was the hour when Jesus had said to him, "Your son will live." So he himself believed, along with his whole household. Now this was the second sign that Jesus did after coming from Judea to Galilee.

In chapter 5 Jesus went to a festival (religious holy day) in Jerusalem. There was a pool there by the Sheep Gate called Bethzatha where the blind, lame, and paralyzed lay hoping to be healed. Verses 5-7 say, One man was there who had been ill for thirty-eight years. (That does not mean he was at the pool for thirty-eight years, but he obviously is not a newcomer.) When Jesus saw him lying there and knew he had been there a long time, he said to him, "Do you want to be made well?" (This is a legitimate question; a minority of people do not want to be healed and take on the responsibilities of life.) The sick man answered, "Sir, I have no one to put me into the pool when the water is stirred up; and while I am making my way, someone else steps down ahead of me."

An underground stream bubbles up once and awhile, and the people believe it is possible to be healed if one gets into it in time. This may be in someway similar to the Roman Catholic belief of what occurs at Lourdes in France.

Verses 8-13 say, Jesus said to him, "Stand up, take your mat and walk." At once the man was made well, and he took up his mat and began to walk. (He did not need to go into the water; Jesus heals him.) Now that day was a sabbath. So the Jews (the Pharisees) said to the man who had been cured, "It is the sabbath; it is not lawful for you to carry your mat. (It is true the law says not to work on the

Sabbath, but the law does not define carrying a mat as work. This is a law that the Pharisees have developed to build a fence around the law to make sure no one violates the basic law. Possibly this man is a homeless man who uses his mat to sleep on.) But he answered them, "The man who made me well said to me, 'Take up your mat and walk.' "

They asked him, "Who is the man who said to you, 'Take it up and walk'?" Now the man who had been healed did not know who he was, for Jesus had disappeared in the crowd that was there. (Their rules defining work on the Sabbath are more important to them than having a man restored to health. Jesus is teaching that a person being restored to good health is far more important than any law.)

Verses 14-15 say, Later Jesus found him in the temple and said to him, "See, you have been made well! Do not sin anymore, so that nothing worse happens to you." The man went away and told the Jews that it was Jesus who had made him well.

Possibly the man is leading a life devoid of God so Jesus is telling him to come to him and be transformed, to be born from above. It is also possible he had become paralyzed many years before by doing something he should not have been doing, but we do not know the background of this man.

Verses 16-17 say, Therefore the Jews (certain religious leaders of the Jews) started persecuting Jesus, because he was doing such things on the sabbath. But Jesus answered them, "My Father is still working, and I also am working." (He is saying his Father works and does what is good and right on the Sabbath or any day, so he does the same on the Sabbath.) Verse 18 says, for this reason the Jews were seeking all the more to kill him, because he was not only breaking the sabbath, but was also calling God his Father, thereby making himself equal with God.

Verses 19-21 say, Jesus said to them, "Very truly, I tell you, the Son can do nothing on his own, but only what he sees the Father doing; for whatever the Father does, the Son does likewise. (Jesus is saying that he and the Father are one in what they say and do.) The Father loves the Son and shows him all that he himself is doing; and he will show him greater works than these, so that you will be astonished. Indeed just as the Father raises the dead and gives them life, so also the Son gives life to whomever he wishes (even to those the religious leaders think do not deserve it).

Verses 22-24 say, "The Father judges no one but has given all judgment to the Son, so that all may honor the Son just as they honor the Father. Anyone who does not honor the Son does not honor the Father who sent him. Very truly, I tell you, anyone who hears my word and believes him who sent me has eternal life, and does not come under judgment, but has passed from death to life."

These statements say much to Christians; it is key to understanding who Jesus is. Jesus is saying that he and the Father are one, and that he has been sent into this world by the Father. All that he says and does comes from his Father. Life and judgment come to all through the Son, and the Father is worshiped through the Son. If the Son is not worshiped the Father is not worshiped. He is also saying that eternal life has begun now.

Verses 25-27 say, "Very truly, I tell you, the hour is coming, and now is here, when the dead will hear the voice of the Son of God, and those who hear will live. For just as the Father has life in himself, so he has granted the Son also to have life in himself; and he has given him authority to execute judgment, because he is the Son of Man." (Again, life and judgment come through Jesus, the Christ. Being called the Son of Man goes back to the prophesy of Daniel 7:12-14.)

Verses 28-30 say, "Do not be astonished at this; for the hour is coming when all who are in their graves will hear his voice and will come out–those who have done good, to the resurrection of life, and those who have done evil to the resurrection of condemnation. I can do nothing on my own. As I hear, I judge; and my judgment is just, because I seek to do not my own will but the will of him who sent me."

The sign of the dead rising is first a reference to Mt 27:52-53 that occurred after Jesus' death saying, The tombs also were opened, and many bodies of the saints who had fallen asleep were raised. After his resurrection they came out of the tombs and entered the holy city and appeared to many. Many Jews believe that when people are raised from the dead, the Messiah has come and the new age has begun. Jesus is saying, the kingdom is near, and I am the Messiah.

NT Wright (1992, 211) says that by the first century the term resurrection had functioned for a long time as a symbol and metaphor for the total reconstitution of Israel, the return from exile, and the final redemption. Ezekiel 37 spoke of the return in terms of Israel the nation awakening from the grave. It is the metaphorical resurrection of the reconstitution of a theocratic Israel, probably under a Messiah. The foreign conqueror will be gone, the exile will be over, and Israel's sins will be forgiven. God will now be ruling through his chosen one, his very presence would be back in Israel, and the nations will come. It would be the beginning of the new age.

This message in (28-30) of the necessity of doing good for eternal life is a problem for those who can not comprehend how that fits in with salvation as a free gift of God. But it is the same message throughout Scripture. In interpreting Scripture, one can not take some verses and ignore others. As stated previously, we are not saved by works, but we are not saved without works either.

All must confirm their part of the covenant by their obedience. Faith is belief and obedience. Peter in 2 Peter 1:10-11 says, Therefore, brothers and sisters, be all the more eager to confirm your call and election, for if you do this, you will never stumble. For in this way, entry into the eternal kingdom of our Lord and Savior Jesus Christ will be richly provided for you. Those who are struggling to understand those statements need to refer again to the beginning of the book in the section of the New Testament on the principle of complementarity and the paradoxes of faith as well as Phil 2:12-14, James 2:14-26 among many others. It should be remembered that when a life is surrendered to God, it is God through his grace who does the works in and through a person, and then as St Augustine said, God accounts those works to the individual.

In verses 31-35 Jesus mentions John the Baptist's testimony about him saying that he knows that his testimony is true. But in verses 36-38 Jesus says, I have a testimony greater than John's. The works that the Father has given me to complete, the very works I am doing, testify on my behalf that the Father has sent me. (The works are his miracles confirming his words.) You have never heard his voice or seen his form, and you do not have his word abiding in you, because you do not believe him whom he has sent.

Verses 39-44 say, You search the scriptures because you think that in them you have eternal life; and it is they that testify on my behalf. (Their Scriptures are the Old Testament.) Yet you refuse to come to me to have life. I do not accept glory from human beings. (He is saying no human standards apply to him.) But I know that you do not have the love of God in you. I have come in my Father's name, and you do not accept me; if another comes in his own name, you will accept him. How can you believe when you accept glory from one another and do not seek the glory that comes from the one who alone is God? (They are like many today who seek glory and praise from each other without giving thought to what God thinks of their actions.)

Verses 45-47 say, "Do you think I will accuse you before the Father; your accuser is Moses, on whom you have set your hope. If you believed Moses, you would believe me, for he wrote about me. But if you do not believe what he wrote, how will you believe what I say?" (This chapter is very important to Christians, for it tells who Jesus is in relation to God the Father, and what he does, and what he is going to do.)

In chapter 6 Jesus went to the other side of the Sea of Galilee also called the Sea of Tiberias. Large crowds kept following because they saw the signs he was doing for the sick. Jesus went up the mountain and sat there with his disciples and saw a large crowd coming toward him. It was near the Passover. Jesus tested Philip in verses 5-10 by saying, "Where are we to buy bread for these people to eat?" He said this to test him, for he knew what he was going to do. Philip answered, "Six months wages would not buy enough bread for each of them to get a little." One of his disciples, Andrew, Simon Peter's brother said to him, "There is a boy here who has five barley loaves and two fish. But what are they among so many people?" Jesus said, "Make the people sit down." Now there was a great deal of grass in the place; so they sat down about five thousand in all. (The Synoptics say it was five thousand not counting women and children. In those times women and children were not counted. Barley bread was the food of the poor.)

Verses 11-15 say, Then Jesus took the loaves, and when he had given thanks, he distributed them to those who were seated, so also the fish, as much as they wanted. When they were satisfied, he told his disciples, "Gather up the fragments left over, so that nothing may be lost." (That is a good message to our throw away generation.) So they gathered them up, and from the fragments of the five barley loaves, left by those who had eaten, they filled twelve baskets. When the people saw the sign he had done, they began to say, "This is indeed the prophet who is to come into the world." When Jesus realized that they were about to come and take him by force to make him king (a political king to oppose Rome), he withdrew again to the mountain by himself. (This is the only miracle recorded by all four Gospels.)

Verses 16-21 say, When evening came, his disciples went down to the sea, got into a boat, and started across the sea to Capernaum. It was now dark, and Jesus had not yet come to them. The sea became rough because a strong wind was blowing. When they had rowed about three or four miles, they saw Jesus walking on the sea and coming near the boat, and they were terrified. But he said to them, "It is I; do not be afraid." Then they wanted to take him into the boat, and immediately the boat reached the land toward which they were going. (The writer is saying Jesus is God, for he is Lord of the elements, Ps 65:7-8, 89:8, 93:3-4, 107:29-30. The presence of Jesus eliminates fear.)

Verses 22-24 say, The next day the crowd that had stayed on the other side of the sea saw that there had been only one boat there. They also saw that Jesus had not got into the boat with his disciples, but that his disciples had gone away alone. Then some boats from Tiberias came near the place where they had eaten the bread after the Lord had given thanks. So when the crowd saw that neither Jesus nor his disciples were there, they themselves got into the boats and went to Capernaum looking for Jesus.

Verses 25-27 say, When they found him on the other side of the sea, they said to him, "Rabbi, when did you come here?" Jesus answered them, "Very truly, I tell you, you are looking for me, not because you saw signs, but because you ate your fill of the loaves. Do not work for the food that perishes, but for the food that endures to eternal life, which the Son of Man will give you. For it is on him that God the Father has set his seal."

He tells them to work for the food that feeds the soul, the food he has to offer them, for the Father has sent him into the world for that very purpose. There are many people in the world who hunger and thirst for God, for justice including social justice, for meaning in life, and for the deeper things of the Spirit. John is saying Jesus is the answer to that hunger. Jesus is the bread of life and the water of life that satisfies that hunger and that thirst.

Verses 28-34 say, Then they said to him, "What must we do to perform the works of God?" Jesus answered, "This is the work of God that you believe in him whom he has sent." (Even believing is God's work.) So they said to him, "What sign are you going to give us then, so that we may see it and believe you? What work are you performing? Our ancestors ate the manna in the wilderness; as it is written, 'He gave them bread from heaven to eat.' " Then Jesus said to them, "Very truly, I tell you, it was not Moses who gave you the bread from heaven. For the bread of God is that which comes down from heaven and gives life to the world." They said to him, "Give us this bread always." (They do not really understand, so he explains in the following verses.)

Verses 35-40 say, Jesus said to them, "I am the bread of life. Whoever comes to me will never be hungry, and whoever believes in me will never be thirsty. But I said to you that you have seen me and yet do not believe. Everything that the Father gives me will come to me, and anyone who comes to me I will never drive away; for I have come down from heaven, not to do my own will, but the will of him who sent me. (This writer believes that God chooses some and not others for specific tasks, but as it says, anyone can come to him, and he will not drive them away.) And this is the will of him who sent me, that I should lose nothing of all that he has given me, but raise it up on the last day. This is indeed the will of my Father, that all who see the Son and believe in him may have eternal life; and I will raise them up in the last day."

The food that is eternal that will raise one up is the food for the soul that only Jesus can give. Belief or unbelief is a mystery known only to God, but no one who comes for that food will be rejected. Belief is God's gift of grace for whoever comes. Belief is a work of God and involves a relationship where Jesus lives in and through those who believe and in the process lose self for the Christ self. It is for those who say as the Apostle Paul said, I have been crucified with Christ; and it is not I who live, but it is Christ who lives in me. And the life I now live in the flesh I live by faith in the Son of God, who loved me and gave himself for me (Gal 2:19-20). The whole process is the sanctification process of God working through his grace.

Verses 41-46 say, Then the Jews began to complain about him because he said, "I am the bread that came down from heaven." They were saying, "Is not this Jesus, the son of Joseph, whose father and mother we know? How can he now say, 'I have come down from heaven'?" Jesus answered them, "Do not complain among yourselves. No one can come to me unless drawn by the Father who sent me; and I will raise that person up on the last day. It is written in the prophets, 'And they shall all be taught by God.' Everyone who has heard and learned from the Father comes to me. Not that anyone has seen the Father except the one who is from God; he has seen the Father."

God's grace begins its work through the word of God. Jesus is saying when one is exposed to him and his word, one is hearing and learning from God. God's grace can work in mysterious ways, and God's grace is meant for all, but God's gift of free will also allows one to reject his grace.

Verses 47-51 say, "Very truly, I tell you, whoever believes has eternal life. I am the bread of life. Your ancestors ate the manna in the wilderness, and they died. This is the bread that comes down from heaven, so that one may eat of it and not die. I am the living bread that came down from heaven. Whoever eats of this bread will live forever; and the bread that I will give for the life of the world is my flesh." (The other gospels present the institution of the Lord's Supper; John skips its institution but explains its meaning as he explains what happens when one comes to the supper.)

In verses 52-59, The Jews then disputed among themselves, saying, "How can this man give us his flesh to eat?" So Jesus said to them, "Very truly, I tell you, unless you eat the flesh of the Son of Man and drink his blood, you have no life in you. Those who eat my flesh and drink my blood have eternal life, and I will raise him up on the last day; for my flesh is true food and my blood is true drink. Those who eat my flesh and drink my blood abide in me, and I in them. Just as the living Father sent me, and I live because of the Father, so whoever eats me will live because of me. This is the bread that came down from heaven, not like that which your ancestors ate, and they died. But the one who eats this bread will live forever." He said these things while he was teaching in the synagogue at Capernaum.

These teachings about eating his flesh and drinking his blood are similarly understood by the early church fathers, the Roman Catholic Church, the Orthodox Catholic Church, many in the Episcopal Church, Martin Luther, John Calvin, and John Wesley, to explain what happens at Eucharist or the communion of the Lord's Supper. They all believe in some way that one in a mystical way truly takes the real presence of Jesus within them. Even though they all explain how that happens in different ways, they all believe in a mystical real presence. It will be some of the followers of the above leaders who will later reject a real presence and make the Lord's Supper a memorial only to the point that today among Protestants it is very dominant. Roman Catholics believe the bread and wine become the actual body and blood of Christ. Lutherans believe Christ is present in, with, and under the bread and wine, but the bread and wine stays bread and wine. Some of the Reformed churches (Presbyterians, United Church of Christ, Disciples of Christ) believe that by the power of the Holy Spirit through the bread and wine one eats and drinks Christ, but most believe it is a memorial only. The Orthodox believe basically as the Roman Catholics do. Episcopalians or Anglicans are mixed as some believe as the Roman Catholics do while others believe as the Reformed churches do and still others believe as the Baptists do who think it is only a memorial.

Verses 60-62 say, "When many of the disciples heard it, they said, This teaching is difficult; who can accept it?" (This makes it plain that nobody understood the intention of Jesus' words as a remembrance or memorial only.) Jesus being aware that his disciples were complaining about it, said to them, "Does this offend you? Then what if you were to see the Son of Man ascending to where he was before?" (The miracle of his resurrection will confirm the truth of what he is saying about himself and the Eucharist, also called the communion of the Lord's Supper.)

Verses 63-65 say, "It is the spirit that gives life; the flesh is useless. (In other words without the Spirit making things happen the body is just the body, flesh is just flesh, bread is just bread, and wine is just wine. It is the Spirit sent by the Father and the Son that brings life to all things (Rom 8:5-11). The words that I have spoken to you are spirit and life. But among you there are some who do not believe." For Jesus knew from the first who the one was that did not believe, and who the one was that would betray him. And he said,

"For this reason I have told you that no one can come to me unless it is granted by the Father."

This is simply saying that it is all initiated and brought about through God's grace. This supernatural mystery will take place through the work of the Holy Spirit. There is nothing humans can do to make any of this happen, for it is all a work of the Father, the Son, and the Holy Spirit. His grace is either accepted by those who believe or rejected as Judas apparently did.

Verses 66-71 say, Because of this many of his disciples turned back and no longer went about with him. So Jesus asked the twelve, "Do you also wish to go away?" Simon Peter answered him, "Lord, to whom can we go? You have the words of eternal life. We have come to believe and know that you are the Holy One of God." Jesus answered them, "Did I not choose you, the twelve? Yet one of you is a devil." He was speaking of Judas son of Simon Iscariot, for he, though one of the twelve, was going to betray him.

Judas chooses not to believe that God is supernaturally behind the words and actions of the Son, so he chooses to reject Jesus and turns him in to the authorities. Others believe the reason he does this is to force Jesus into action. In other words he chooses to make it all a human work by forcing Jesus to begin a revolution that will overthrow the Romans and begin a new government with them in charge. Either way Judas rejects the supernatural working of God, believing they are in charge of making things happen.

In chapter 7 Jesus went about in Galilee. He did not go to Judea, for the leaders of the Jews were looking for an opportunity to kill him. His brothers, who did not believe in him, told him to go to Judea to the Jewish festival of Booths so people could see his works and become well known. But Jesus in verses 5-10 said, "My time has not yet come, but your time is always here. The world cannot hate you, but it hates me because I testify against it that its works are evil. (This will be one of the major reasons the leaders of the world in that time will put him to death.) Go to the festival yourselves. I am not going to this festival, for my time has not yet fully come." Later he went in secret.

His brothers not believing in him, coupled with Joseph and Mary not understanding his actions at the temple when he was twelve years old, and that he said he was not going but then changed his mind and went certainly authenticates these Scriptures. A false gospel would eliminate these parts. The false gospel accounts that circulated in early Christian history whitewashed any thing that appeared negative and then described many preposterous miracles Jesus supposedly did during his childhood. See the non-canonical gospels later in this book.

There are some who would say that the information about his brothers and Joseph and Mary are also cause to question the virgin birth accounts as actual history and interpret them as a theological meditation that simply describes Jesus as God's unique Son and Messiah. Others would say the brothers' reactions, at this time, are typical of a brotherly rivalry. His being human is coming out as is the humanness of Joseph and Mary.

Verses 11-18 say, The Jews were looking for him at the festival and saying, "Where is he?" And there was considerable complaining about him among the crowds. While some were saying, "He is a good man," others were saying, "No, he is deceiving the crowd." Yet no one would speak openly about him for fear of the Jews (leaders of the Jews). About the middle of the festival Jesus went up into the temple and began to teach. The Jews were astonished at it saying, "How does this man have such learning, when he has never been taught." Then Jesus answered them, "My teaching is not mine but his who sent me. Anyone who resolves to do the will of God will know whether the teaching is from God or whether I am speaking on my own. Those who speak on their own seek their own glory; but the one who seeks the glory of him who sent him is true, and there is nothing false in him."

In verses 19-24 Jesus said, "Did not Moses give you the law? Yet none of you keeps the law. Why are you looking for an opportunity to kill me?" The crowd answered, "You have a demon! Who is trying to kill you?" Jesus answered them, "I performed one work, and all of you are astonished. Moses gave you circumcision (it was from Abraham), and you circumcise a man on the sabbath. If a man receives circumcision on the sabbath in order that the law of Moses may not be broken, are you angry with me because I healed a man's whole body on the sabbath? Do not judge by appearances, but judge with right judgment." (Jesus exposes their double standard. Their man-made laws say they can circumcise on the Sabbath, but they can not heal.)

Verses 25-31 say, Now some of the people of Jerusalem were saying, "Is this not the man whom they are trying to kill? And here he is, speaking openly, but they say nothing to him! Can it be that the authorities really know that this is the Messiah? Yet we know where this man is from; but when the Messiah comes, no one will know where he is from." Then Jesus cried out as he was teaching in the temple, "You know me, and you know where I am from. I have not come on my own. But the one who has sent me is true, and you do not know him. I know him because I am from him, and he sent me." Then they tried to arrest him, but no one laid hands on him, because his hour had not yet come. (The Father determines when that time is to be.) Yet many in the crowd believed in him and were saying, "When the Messiah comes, will he do more signs than this man has done?"

Verses 32-34 say, The Pharisees heard the crowd muttering such things about him, and the chief priests (Sadducees) and Pharisees sent temple police to arrest him. (The Pharisees and the Sadducees do not get along with each other, but here they unite to send the temple police to arrest him.) Jesus then said, "I will be with you a little while longer, and then I am going to him who sent me. You will search for me, but you will not find me; and where I am, you cannot come."

Verses 35-36 say, The Jews said to one another, "Where does this man intend to go that we will not find him? Does he intend to go to the Dispersion among the Greeks and teach the Greeks? What does he mean by saying, 'You will search for me and you will not find me' and 'Where I am, you cannot come'?" (The Dispersion is the name given to area outside Judea where the Greek speaking Jews live.)

Verses 37-39 say, On the last day of the festival, the great day, while Jesus was standing there, he cried out, "Let anyone who is thirsty come to me, and let the one who believes in me drink. As the scripture has said, 'Out of the believer's heart shall flow rivers of living water.' " Now he said this about the Spirit, which believers in him were to receive; for as yet there was no Spirit, because Jesus was not yet glorified.

This took place at the festival of Booths commemorating the wilderness wanderings (Lev 23:39-43). For seven days water is carried in a golden pitcher from the Spring of Gihon and the Pool of Siloam to the temple as a reminder of the water from the rock in the desert (Num 20:2-13), and as a symbol of hope for the coming messianic deliverance (Isa 12:3). During this festival of water-drawing, prayers for water (rain) are uttered and libations are poured over the altar in the temple. In an agricultural society these prayers are very important.

Some Old Testament verses of interest are the following. Isa 12:3 says, With joy you will draw water from the wells of salvation. And you will say in that day: Give thanks to the Lord, call on his name; make known his deeds among the nations; proclaim that his name is exalted. Zech 14:8,16, 20-21 say, On that day living waters shall flow out from Jerusalem, half of them to the eastern sea and half to the western sea . . . On that day there shall be inscribed on the bells on the horses 'Holy to the Lord.' . . . and every cooking pot in Jerusalem and Judah shall be sacred to the Lord of Hosts, . . . and there shall no longer be traders in the house of the Lord of Hosts on that day. Zech 13:1 says, On that day a fountain shall be opened for the house of David and the inhabitants of Jerusalem, to cleanse them from sin and impurity.

Ezekiel 47:1-12 is all about the flowing of water. Verses 9-12 say, Wherever the water goes, every living creature that swarms will live . . . Their leaves will not wither nor their fruit fail, but they will bear fresh fruit every month, because the water for them flows from the sanctuary. Their fruit will be for food, and their leaves for healing. Rev 22:1-2 says, Then the angel showed me the river of the water of life, bright as crystal, flowing from the throne of God and of the Lamb through the middle of the street through the city. On either side of the river is the tree of life, with its twelve kinds of fruit, producing its fruit each month; and the leaves of the tree are for the healing of the nations.

Water is a symbol for the Holy Spirit. Jesus and the people of his culture were accustomed to speaking in metaphors. When Jesus sends the Spirit, it is to fill the believer, and as the believer continues to drink of it there is an overflow that come out of the person and touches those with whom the believer comes in contact. The Spirit is later defined as life in Christ Jesus through the Holy Spirit while the believer lives and abides in Jesus, and Jesus lives in and abides in the believer through the Holy Spirit.

Verses 40-44 say, When they heard these words, some in the crowd said, "This is really the prophet." Others said, "This is the Messiah." But some asked, "Surely the Messiah does not come from Galilee, does he? Has not the scripture said that the Messiah is descended from David and comes from Bethlehem, the village where David lived?" So there was a division in the crowd because of him. Some of them wanted to arrest him, but no one laid hands on him.

Verses 45-52 say, Then the temple police went back to the chief priests and Pharisees, who asked them, "Why did you not arrest him?" The police answered, "Never has anyone spoken like this!" Then the Pharisees replied, "Surely you have not been deceived too, have you? Has anyone of the authorities or of the Pharisees believed in him? But this crowd, which does not know the law—they are accursed." Nicodemus, who had gone to Jesus before, and who was one of them, asked, "Our law does not judge people without first giving them a hearing to find out what they are doing, does it?" They replied, "Surely you are not also from Galilee, are you? Search and you will see that no prophet is to arise from Galilee."

These leaders sound like those today who interpret the Constitution as strict constitutionalists about everything they want and accuse their opposition of not believing in the Constitution. Then something comes up they do not like about the Constitution, they want to change it. They complain about activist judges from the other party, but say nothing about their own activist judges. This fits in line with those who interpret the Bible in a fundamentalist way; they do the same with the Constitution. Only what benefits them can be ignored or changed.

⌒⌘⌒

In chapter 8 Jesus goes to the Mount of Olives. This is east of Jerusalem and separated from the city by the valley of Kidron. Then the next morning he goes to the temple. The following incident is omitted in some of the most ancient manuscripts. It appears to be an authentic incident but was possibly not originally in the Gospel of John.

All the people came to him, and he sat down and began to teach them. Verses 3-6 say, The scribes and the Pharisees brought a woman who had been caught in adultery; and making her stand before all of them, they said to him, "Teacher, this woman was caught in the very act of committing adultery. (Where is the man?) Now in the law Moses commanded us to stone such a woman. Now what do you say?" They said this to test him, so that they may have some charge to bring against him. Jesus bent down and wrote with his finger on the ground. (No one knows what he is writing. Perhaps he is listing their sins.)

In verses 7-11, When they kept on questioning him, he straightened up and said to them, "Let anyone among you who is without sin be the first to throw a stone at her." (Is this a good question to ask ourselves when we avidly support capital punishment?) And once again he bent down and wrote on the ground. When they heard it they went away, one by one, beginning with the elders; and Jesus was left alone with the woman standing before him. Jesus straightened up and said to her, "Woman, where are they? Has no one condemned you?" She said, "No one, sir." And Jesus said, "Neither do I condemn you. Go your way, and from now on do not sin again." (He is not dismissing her sin. He made a judgment on it, and then shows her mercy.)

Much has been made of the fact that Jesus does not condemn her, but it is apparent that it is the time of forgiveness and not condemnation. He judges her sin, but does not condemn her to death. He tells her to go and sin no more. The religious leaders represent the people of the world, who are always ready to condemn those other than themselves. Jesus represents God, who is always ready to forgive and give a person hope and another chance.

During the festival of Booths big golden lamps were lit. Verses 12-16 say, Again Jesus spoke to them, saying, "I am the light of the world. Whoever follows me will never walk in darkness but will have the light of life" (see Isa 60:1-3). Then the Pharisees said to him, "You are testifying on your own behalf; your testimony is not valid." Jesus answered, "Even if I testify on my own behalf, my testimony is valid because I know where I have come from and where I am going, but you do not know where I come from and where I am going. You judge by human standards; I judge no one (by human standards). Yet even if I do judge, my judgment is valid; for it is not I alone who judge, but I and the Father who sent me (see 5:22-24).

Verses 17-20 say, "In your law it is written that the testimony of two witnesses is valid. I testify on my own behalf, and the Father who sent me testifies on my behalf." Then they said to him, "Where is your Father?" Jesus answered, "You know neither me nor my Father. If you knew me you would know my Father also." He spoke these words while he was teaching in the treasury of the temple, but no one arrested him because his hour had not come.

Verses 21-27 say, Again he said to them, "I am going away, and you will search for me, but you will die in your sin. Where I am going, you cannot come." (They will die in their sin because they will not come to Jesus to receive forgiveness, see 3:17-21.) Then the Jews said, "Is he going to kill himself? Is that what he means by saying, 'Where I am going you cannot come'?" He said to them, "You are from below. I am from above; you are of this world; I am not of this world. I told you that you would die in your sins, for you will die in your sins unless you believe that I am he." They said to him, "Who are you?" Jesus said to them, "Why do I speak to you at all? I have much to say about you and much to condemn; but the one who sent me is true, and I declare to the world what I have heard from him." They did not understand that he was speaking to them about the Father.

In verses 28-30 Jesus said, "When you have lifted up the Son of Man, then you will realize that I am he and that I do nothing on my own, but I speak these things as the Father instructed me. And the one who sent me is with me; he has not left me alone, for I always do what is pleasing to him." As he was saying these things, many believed him.

Verses 31-32 say, Then Jesus said to the Jews who had believed in him, "If you continue in my word, you are truly my disciples; and you will know the truth, and the truth will make you free." (He is talking about the truth that frees one from sin and Satan and delivers one from the things of the world that control and destroy a person. As usual they do not understand yet that Jesus is the way, the truth, and the life.) They answered him, "We are descendants of Abraham and have never been slaves to anyone. What do you mean by saying, 'You will be made free'?"

Verses 33-36 say, Jesus answered them, "Very truly, I tell you, everyone who commits sin is a slave to sin. The slave does not have a permanent place in the household; the Son has a place there forever. So if the Son makes you free, you will be free indeed." (It is Jesus that sets one free from the things of the world that control and destroy.)

In verses 37-38 Jesus said, "I know that you are descendants of Abraham; yet you look for an opportunity to kill me because there is no place in you for my word. I declare what I have seen in the Father's presence; as for you, you should do what you have heard from the Father." (Christians believe when there is no place in a person's life for God's word, they are again, in their own way, putting Jesus to death.)

Verses 39-43 say, They answered him, "Abraham is our Father." Jesus said to them, "If you were Abraham's children, you would be doing what Abraham did, but now you are trying to kill me, a man that has told you the truth I heard from God. This is not what Abraham did. You are indeed doing what your father (Satan) does." They said to him, "We are not illegitimate children; we have one Father, God himself." Jesus said to them, "If God were your Father, you would love me, for I came from God and now I am here. I did not come on my own, but he sent me. Why do you not understand what I say? It is because you cannot accept my word."

Jesus continues in 44-47, "You are from your father, the devil, and you choose to do your father's desires. He was a murderer from the beginning and does not stand in the truth, because there is no truth in him. When he lies, he speaks according to his own nature, for he is a liar and the father of lies. But because I tell you the truth, why do you not believe me? Whoever is from God hears the words of God. The reason you do not hear them is that you are not from God."

This is very strong talk not considered very cool by today's standards. Jesus always challenges sin and hypocrisy. After listening to Jesus, how does the reader think educational leaders would deal with him, if he applied to teach at their school or university? How many churches does the reader think would hire him? How many politicians would listen to him, make known and apply his teachings to their situation? How many leaders of corporate America would want him as their leader? What does the reader think leaders in the world or leaders in America would do with him today?

In verse 48, The Jews answered him, "Are we not right in saying that you are a Samaritan and have a demon? (This is also typical of today. When one has no answer, it becomes a time to call names.)

In 49-53 Jesus answered, "I do not have a demon; but I honor my Father, and you dishonor me. Yet I do not seek my own glory; there is one who seeks it and he is the judge. Very truly, I tell you, whoever keeps my word will never see death." The Jews said to him, "Now we know that you have a demon. Abraham died, and so did the prophets; yet you say, 'Whoever keeps my word will never taste death.' Are you greater than out father Abraham, who died? Who do you claim to be?"

In verses 54-56 Jesus answered, "If I glorify myself, my glory is nothing. It is my Father, who glorifies me, he of whom you say, 'He is our God,' though you do not know him. But I know him; if I would say I do not know him, I would be a liar like you. But I do know him, and I keep his word. Your ancestor Abraham rejoiced that he would see my day; he saw it and was glad.

How did Abraham see it? Possibly in the attempted sacrifice of Isaac which is the typology for the lamb sacrificed as God's only Son, see Gen 22, or possibly he is referring to the fact that Abraham is now alive with the Father in heaven. *Aqudeh* is the term uses by the Jews for the binding and sacrifice of Isaac.

Then in verses 57-59 the Jews said to him, "You are not yet fifty years old, and have you seen Abraham?" Jesus said to them, "Very truly, I tell you, before Abraham was I am." (Remember that "I am" is the name for YHWH when Moses met him in the burning bush.) So they picked up stones to throw at him, but Jesus hid himself and went out of the temple.

In chapter 9:1-5 as Jesus walked along, he saw a man blind from birth. His disciples asked him, "Rabbi, who sinned, this man or his parents that he was born blind?" Jesus answered, "Neither this man nor his parents sinned; he was born blind so that God's works might be revealed in him. We must work the works of him who sent me while it is day; night is coming when no one can work. As long as I am in the world, I am the light of the world." (The question of who are the real sinners continues throughout the chapter.)

Verses 6-12 say, When he had said this, he spat on the ground and made mud with the saliva and spread the mud on the man's eyes, saying to him, "Go, wash in the pool of Siloam" (which means sent). Then he went and washed and came back able to see. The neighbors and those who had seen him before as a beggar began to ask, "Is this not the man who used to sit and beg." Some were saying, "It is he." Others were saying, "No, but it is someone like him." He kept saying, "I am the man." But they kept asking, "Then how were your eyes opened?" He answered, "The man called Jesus made mud, spread it on my eyes, and said to me, 'Go to Siloam and wash.' Then I went and washed and received my sight." They said to him, "Where is he?" He said, "I do not know."

Verses 13-17 say, They brought to the Pharisees the man who had formerly been blind. Now it was a sabbath day when Jesus made the mud and opened his eyes. (The Pharisees will determine that making the mud is working on the Sabbath.) Then the Pharisees began to ask him how he had received his sight. He said to them, "He put mud on my eyes. Then I washed, and now I see." Some of the Pharisees said, "This man is not from God, for he does not observe the sabbath." But others said, "How can a man who is a sinner perform such signs?" And they were divided. So they said again to the blind man, "What do you say about him? It was your eyes he opened." He said, "He is a prophet."

Verses 18-23 say, The Jews did not believe that he had been born blind and had received his sight until they called the parents of the man who had received his sight and asked them, "Is this your son, who you say was born blind? How then does he see?" His parents answered, "We know that this is our son, and that he was born blind; but we do not know how it is that now he sees, nor do we know who opened his eyes. Ask him; he is of age. He will speak for himself." His parents said this because they were afraid of the Jews; for the Jews had already agreed that anyone who confessed Jesus to be the Messiah would be put out of the synagogue. Therefore his parents said, "He is of age; ask him."

Verses 24- 27 say, So for the second time they called the man who had been blind, and they said to him, "Give glory to God! (In other words, tell the truth.) We know that this man is a sinner." He answered, "I do not know whether he is a sinner. One thing I do know, that though I was blind, now I see." They said to him, "What did he do to you? How did he open your eyes?" He answered them, "I have told you already, and you would not listen. Why do you want to hear it again? Do you also want to be his disciples?"

Then in verses 28-34 they reviled him saying, "You are his disciple, but we are disciples of Moses. We know that God has spoken to Moses, but as for this man, we do not know where he comes from." The man answered, "Here is an astonishing thing! You do not know where he comes from, and yet he opened my eyes. We know that God does not listen to sinners, but he does listen to one who worships him and obeys his will. Never since the world began has it been heard that anyone opened the eyes of a person born blind. If this man were not from God, he could do nothing." They answered him, "You were born entirely in sins, and are you trying to teach us?" And they drove him out. (Again, because they are not open to hear and learn, in their frustration, they attack his character. See Isa 6:9-10, 35:5-6, 42:6-7, 16-20.)

Jesus heard that they had driven him out, and when he found him, he said, "Do you believe in the Son of Man?" He answered, "And who is he, sir? Tell me so that I may believe in him." Jesus said to him, "You have seen him, and the one speaking with you is he." He said, "Lord, I believe." And he worshiped him. Jesus said, "I came into this world for judgment so that those who do not see may see, and those who do see may become blind." Some of the Pharisees near him heard this and said to him, "Surely we are not blind are we?" Jesus said to them, "If you were blind you would not have sin. But now that you say, 'We see,' your sin remains." (Because they refuse to acknowledge their blindness, their sins remain in them. Proud refusal to admit their blindness demonstrates their sin.)

Again Jesus performs a physical miracle to show that he can heal spiritually. This narrative is written primarily to demonstrate that Jesus can and will heal the spiritually blind, if they do not close their ears and their eyes but open them to his words and actions. It is also to show that we are all blind at birth, and that knowledge and understanding does not usually come all at once; it is progressive. But one must remain open to new learning and new understanding. The story tells us that not only are we born blind, but the arrogant religious people who claim to know all the answers remain blind.

Real learning comes after one eliminates their "know it all" attitude. The leaders remain ignorant of the underlying meaning of God's teachings because they refuse to let his word interpret their thinking and ideology. Instead they use what they want from Scripture, usually out of context, to support only what they want to believe and do, and to support their greed, pride, lies, and wickedness. The method of some of the religious leaders of that day has had no shortage of users throughout history and in our times. The message of John is that with a new healing, and a new birth, one will begin to understand and have new insight.

In chapter 10 verses 1-6 Jesus says, "Very truly, I tell you, anyone who does not enter the sheepfold by the gate but climbs in by another way is a thief and a bandit. The one who enters by the gate is the shepherd of the sheep. The gatekeeper opens the gate for him, and the sheep hear his voice. He calls his own sheep by name and leads them out. When he has brought out all his own, he goes ahead of them, and the sheep follow him because they know his voice. They will not follow a stranger, but they will run from him because they do not know the voice of strangers." Jesus used this figure of speech with them, but they did not understand what he was saying to them. (Jesus often speaks in metaphors, but because many always take literally what he says, they do not understand his underlying meaning. Ezekiel 34 serves as the background for this chapter. It would be advantageous for the reader to read that chapter in the Old Testament.)

In verses 7-10 Jesus said to them, "Very truly, I tell you, I am the gate for the sheep. All who came before me are thieves and bandits; but the sheep did not listen to them. I am the gate. Whoever enters by me will be saved, and will come in and go out and find pasture. The thief comes only to kill and destroy. I come that they may have life, and have it abundantly."

The concept of "life more abundantly" is more than just eternal life, which John believes starts in this life. It is participating in the kingdom. Having life more abundantly means one discovers the reason for being created. The idea is that meaning, purpose, and value to life are found in the kingdom and thus real happiness and true joy.

As the gate for the sheep, Jesus is the way one becomes a child of God, and one is added to God's people. He is the way, the truth, and the life. His agenda is the only true agenda. The thieves and bandits are the insurrectionists, the revolutionaries, those with the agenda of throwing out the hated Romans by violence. Jesus constantly tries to warn the people not to become the sheep of those people, for it will destroy them, their city, and their temple. This will happen in AD 70.

In verses 11-15 Jesus says, "I am the good shepherd. The good shepherd lays down his life for the sheep. The hired hand, who is not the shepherd and does not own the sheep, sees the wolf coming and leaves the sheep and runs away–and the wolf snatches them and scatters them. The hired hand runs away because the hired hand does not care for the sheep. I am the good shepherd, I know my own and my own know me, just as the Father knows me and I know the Father. And I lay down my life for the sheep. (The hired hand works mainly for his interests, rewards, and agenda, but Jesus works because of love for others and his created order; therefore, he lays his life down for his people.)

Verses 16-18 say, "I have other sheep that do not belong to this fold. I must bring them also, and they will listen to my voice. (No one is to be excluded; whoever comes will be protected.) So there will be one flock, one shepherd. For this reason the Father loves me, because I lay down my life in order to take it up again. No one takes it from me, but I lay it down on my own accord. I have power to lay it down, and I have power to take it up again. I have received this command from my Father."

Verses 19-21 say, Again the Jews were divided because of these words. Many of them were saying, "He has a demon and is out of his mind. Why listen to him?" Others were saying, "These are not the words of one who has a demon. Can a demon open the eyes of the blind?"

Verses 22-23 say, At that time the festival of the Dedication took place in Jerusalem. It was winter, and Jesus was walking in the temple, in the portico of Solomon. (The portico of Solomon is one of the porches on the east side of the temple. The Dedication or Hanukkah, the Feast of Lights is the rededication of the temple after its desecration by Antiochus Epiphanes, who butchered a pig on the altar in 164 BC. Today it is celebrated by Jews near the time Christians celebrate Christmas. One can read about this in 1 Maccabees 4:36-59.)

Verses 24-30 say, So the Jews gathered around him and said to him, "How long will you keep us in suspense? If you are the Messiah, tell us plainly." Jesus answered, "I have told you, and you do not believe because you do not belong to my sheep. My sheep hear my voice. I know them and they follow me. I give them eternal life, and they will never perish. No one will snatch them out of my hand. (As long as they remain his sheep they will not be taken away, but he never takes away a person's free will to reject him and his teachings.) What my Father has given me is greater than all else, and no one can snatch it out of the Father's hand. The Father and I are one."

In verses 31-33, The Jews took up stones again to stone him. Jesus replied, "I have shown you many good works from the Father. For which of these are you going to stone me?" The Jews answered, "It is not for a good work that we are going to stone you, but for blasphemy because you, though only a human being, are making yourself God." In verses 37-39 Jesus says, "If I am not doing the works of my Father, then do not believe me. But if I do them, even though you do not believe me, believe the works, so that you may know and understand that the Father is in me and I am in the Father." (Here Jesus gives the reason for his miracles.) Then they tried to arrest him again, but he escaped from their hands.

In verses 40-42, He went away again across the Jordan to the place where John (the Baptist) had been baptizing earlier, and he remained there. Many came to him, and they were saying, "John performed no sign, but everything that John said about this man was true." And many believed in him there. (This is the wilderness area where many of the common folk are found.)

In chapter 11:1-6 a certain man was ill, Lazarus of Bethany, in the village of Mary and her sister Martha. Mary was the one who anointed the Lord with perfume and wiped his feet with her hair; her brother Lazarus was ill. So the sisters sent a message to Jesus, "Lord he whom you love is ill." But when Jesus heard it, he said, "This illness does not lead to death; rather it is for God's glory, so that the Son of God can be glorified through it." Accordingly, though Jesus loved Martha and her sister and Lazarus, after having heard that Lazarus was ill, he stayed two days longer in the place where he was.

Verses 7-11 say, Then after this he said to the disciples, "Let us go to Judea again." The disciples said to him, "Rabbi, the Jews were just now trying to stone you, and are you going there again?" Jesus answered, "Are there not twelve hours of daylight? Those who walk during the day do not stumble, because they see the light of the world. But those who walk at night stumble, because the light is not in them." (Jesus always responds in a way that makes people think.) After saying this, he told them, "Our friend Lazarus has fallen asleep, but I am going there to awaken him." (Jesus uses sleep for his followers who die.)

The disciples in verses 12-15 said to him, "Lord, if he has fallen asleep, he will be all right." Jesus, however, had been speaking about his death, but they thought that he was referring merely to sleep. Then Jesus told them plainly, "Lazarus is dead. For your sake I am glad I was not there, so that you may believe. But let us go to him." (Jesus is telling them that what he is about to do with Lazarus is going to be for their benefit and to the glory of God.) Verse 16 says, Thomas, who was called the twin, said to his fellow disciples, "Let us also go, that we may die with him." (Thomas is starting to get it.)

Verses 17-24 say, When Jesus arrived, he found that Lazarus had already been in the tomb four days. Now Bethany was near Jerusalem, some two miles away, and many of the Jews had come to Martha and Mary to console them about their brother. When Martha heard that Jesus was coming, she went and met him, while Mary stayed at home. Martha said to Jesus, "Lord, if you had been here, my brother would not have died. But even now I know that God will give you whatever you ask of him." Jesus said to her, "Your brother will rise again." Martha said to him, "I know that he will rise again in the resurrection on the last day."

Verses 25-27 say, Jesus said to her, "I am the resurrection and the life. Those who believe in me, even though they die, will live, and everyone who lives and believes in me will never die. Do you believe this?" She said to him, "Yes, Lord, I believe that you are the Messiah, the Son of God, the one coming into the world." (Jesus is saying, everyone who lives and believes in me will never die. He is saying that eternal life has begun, Rom 6:4-5, Col 2:12, 3:1. The body eventually dies but not the spirit; later the body will be raised.)

Verses 28-32 say, When she had said this, she went back and called her sister Mary, and told her privately, "The Teacher is here and is calling you." And when she heard it, she got up quickly and went to him. Now Jesus had not yet come to the village, but was still at the place where Martha had met him. The Jews that were with her in the house, consoling her, saw Mary get up quickly and go out. They followed her because they thought that she was going to the tomb to weep there. When Mary came where Jesus was and saw him, she knelt at his feet and said to him, "Lord, if you had been here, my brother would not have died."

Verses 33-35 say, When Jesus saw her weeping, and the Jews

who came with her also weeping, he was greatly disturbed in spirit and deeply moved. He said, "Where have you laid him?" They said to him, "Lord come and see." Jesus began to weep. (Even though Jesus knew what he was going to do, his compassion for them led him to weep.) In verses 36-37 the Jews said, "See how he loved him!" But some of them said, "Could not he who opened the eyes of the blind man have kept this man from dying?"

Verses 38-44 say, Then Jesus, again greatly disturbed, came to the tomb. It was a cave, and a stone was lying against it. Jesus said, "Take away the stone." Martha, the sister of the dead man, said to him, "Lord, already there is a stench because he has been dead four days." (The custom is to bury on the same day as death.) Jesus said to her, "Did I not tell you that if you believed, you would see the glory of God?" So they took away the stone. And Jesus looked upward and said, " Father, I thank you for having heard me. I knew that you always hear me, but I have said this for the sake of the crowd standing here, so that they may believe that you sent me." When he had said this, he cried out with a loud voice, "Lazarus, come out!" The dead man came out, his hands and feet bound with strips of cloth, and his face wrapped in a cloth. Jesus said to them, "Unbind him and let him go." (Jesus always does what humans can not do, but then has humans do what they can do. After four days in the tomb, his body would have been rotting.)

Verses 45-48 say, Many of the Jews therefore, who had come with Mary and had seen what Jesus did, believed in him. But some of them went to the Pharisees and told them what he had done. So the chief priests and the Pharisees called a meeting of the council, and said, "What are we to do? This man is performing many signs. If we let him go on like this, everyone will believe in him, and the Romans will come and destroy both our holy place and our nation. (The people claiming that Jesus is the king will cause the Romans to act, for they will see this as a challenge to their rule. Their only concern is protecting their positions of power. Does that remind the reader of anything today?)

Verses 49-53 say, But one of them, Caiaphas, who was high priest that year, said to them, "You know nothing at all! (He is high priest from AD 18-36. As head of the Sanhedrin he is both a political and religious leader.) You do not understand that it is better for you to have one man die for the people than to have the whole nation destroyed." He did not say this on his own, but being high priest that year he prophesied that Jesus was about to die for the nation, and not the nation only, but to gather into one the dispersed children of God. So from that day on they planned to put him to death. (Caiaphas' prophecy is an unconscious prophecy with theological meaning. Jesus will die for the people but not in a way imagined by Caiaphas.)

Verses 54-57 say, Jesus therefore no longer walked about openly among the Jews, but went from there to a town called Ephraim in the region near the wilderness; and he remained there with the disciples. Now the Passover of the Jews was near, and many went up from the country to Jerusalem before the Passover to purify themselves. (This is a reference to ritually purifying themselves in ceremonies at the temple.) They were looking for Jesus and were asking one another as they stood in the temple, "What do you think? Surely he will not come to the festival, will he?" Now the chief priests and the Pharisees had given orders that anyone who knew where Jesus was should let them know, so that they might arrest him.

❧

Chapter 12:1-3 says, Six days before the Passover Jesus came to Bethany, the home of Lazarus, whom he had raised from the dead.

There they gave a dinner for him. Martha served, and Lazarus was one of those at the table with him. Mary took a pound of costly perfume made of pure nard (a fragment ointment used in ancient times of the valerian family), anointed Jesus' feet, and wiped them with her hair. The house was filled with the fragrance of the perfume.

Verses 4-8 say, But Judas Iscariot, one of the disciples (the one who was about to betray him), said, "Why was this perfume not sold for three hundred denarii and the money given to the poor?" He said this not because he cared for the poor, but because he was a thief; he kept the common purse and used to steal what was put into it. Jesus said, "Leave her alone. She bought it so that she might keep it for the day of my burial. You always have the poor with you, but you do not always have me." (For an interesting comparison, go to Mk 14:1-11. Also keep in mind proper burial is an important responsibility in Jewish religious thinking.)

To use this verse that says, you always have the poor with you, as an excuse to not help the poor, as some have done in our society today, is a misuse of Scripture. This is especially so when the concept of economic justice and having compassion for those in need are practically on every page of Scripture. It is interesting the loopholes the selfish and the greedy use to keep their money and possessions only for themselves and their own interests. As Jesus said in Mt 19:24, Mk 10:25, and Lk 18:25, Indeed, it is easier for a camel to go through the eye of a needle than for someone who is rich to enter the kingdom of God.

In the eyes of Jesus the issue is not the right to keep earnings to do with them as one wants. The right to a fair profit is not the issue, but it is a matter of keeping a fair balance between those who control money and those who have no control over the money system. Tied closely to this issue is an unjust wage system (James 5:1-5) and an unjust tax system, where big money gets the tax breaks, while those in the middle class make up the loss of tax money. It has always been this way. Unfortunately, too many people of power are in power to benefit themselves and their benefactors. The common good is not the primary concern of most.

Exxon just made the highest profits of any company in history and paid no tax money and got millions back because of the tax structure devised by politicians to subsidize them. Guess what the politicians get in return for that favor? According to MSNBC (1-29-2011) this is in line with many big corporations including General Electric who owns MSNBC. Involved are laws and a tax structure that allow people to make exorbitant salaries, bonuses, move jobs overseas, and then escape taxes. Apparently, the common good is no concern to them, only profits. America is returning to the Gilded Age of the robber barons of the late 1800s where government and corporations work together for their own interests exploiting workers and the middle class, who have no one to protect them. Corporations get outlandish tax benefits and profits, and politicians get money to use to get elected again, and the middle class pays for it by making up for the loss of tax revenue. It is a fact that corporations like General Electric and Exon and numerous top 500 companies paid no taxes in the year 2010 and many other years. If these companies are to be treated like individuals should not they pay the same rate the rest of us pay? In fact because of the tax structure, they got millions back. Are we moving in a wrong direction, and if so, should that be a concern to free people in a democracy?

In both testaments God's people are commanded not only to help the disadvantaged but to represent them to those in power. Allen Verhey (2002, 410-11) says, in using verse 5 and relating it to Deut 15:11, Jesus is reiterating the ancient judgment against the politics of Israel that it had forgotten the covenant and reminded those who heard him of the old command to "open your hands to the poor and needy neighbor in your land." His point is we always have the poor (8) because we are not being obedient to the covenant God made with his people. The blessings and curses of the covenant can be seen in Deut 27-30.

Verses 9-11 say, When the great crowd of the Jews learned that he was there, they came not only because of Jesus but also to see Lazarus, whom he had raised from the dead. So the chief priests planned to put Lazarus to death as well, since it was on account of him that many of the Jews were deserting and were believing in Jesus. (As far as the leaders are concerned, Jesus previously stated, even if one is raised from the dead they will not believe. Their only concern is to protect their positions of power that have given them great wealth and prestige.)

Verses 12-13 say, The next day the great crowd that had come to the festival heard that Jesus was coming to Jerusalem. So they took branches of palm trees and went out to meet him, shouting, "Hosanna! Blessed is the one who comes in the name of the Lord—the King of Israel!" (Hosanna is Hebrew for save us. The reader is reminded that for most of the crowd the words "save us" at that time is a reference to saving them from the Romans. It is only later that these words will take on a different connotation.)

Verses 14-15 say, Jesus found a young donkey and sat on it; as it is written: "Do not be afraid, daughter of Zion. Look your king is coming, sitting on a donkey's colt!" (This is from Zech 9:9. If the reader continues through Zechariah chapter 9 it states that he will end war and bring peace, and his dominion will be throughout the earth. Because of the blood of the covenant, prisoners of hope will be set free. He will make war on the enemies of God's people; he will appear over them and sound his trumpet. On that day the Lord will save his people, and they shall shine on his land. They will be the flock of his people.)

John continues in verses 16-19 saying, His disciples did not understand these things at first; but when Jesus was glorified, then they remembered that these things had been written of him and had been done to him. So the crowd that had been with him when he called Lazarus out of the tomb and raised him from the dead continued to testify. It was also because they heard that he had performed this sign that the crowd went to meet him. The Pharisees then said to one another, "You see, you can do nothing. Look the world has gone after him."

Verses 20-26 say, Now among those who went up to worship at the festival were some Greeks. They came to Philip, who was from Bethsaida in Galilee, and said to him, "Sir, we wish to see Jesus." Philip went and told Andrew; then Andrew and Philip went and told Jesus. Jesus answered them, "The hour has come for the Son of Man to be glorified. Very truly, I tell you, unless a grain of wheat falls into the earth and dies, it remains just a single grain; but if it dies, it bears much fruit. Those who love their life lose it, and those who hate their life in this world will keep it for eternal life. Whoever serves me must follow me, and where I am, there will my servant be also. Whoever serves me, the Father will honor."

First, Jesus is saying that through his death and resurrection many followers will understand and come to be his disciples. Second, he is saying that anyone who wants to follow him and become his disciple must make a decision. They must decide to have as their priority either to serve themselves and the world, or to serve Jesus and his kingdom. If one chooses to serve Jesus, then one must deny one's selfish interests and respect and live first for the interests of Jesus and the common good. What direction is the reader moving?

If one is going to make him Lord, then one needs to make a

serious attempt to think like he thought and act like he acted in all areas of life. If Jesus is Lord, then he is Lord in all areas of life and not just some areas. Jesus is teaching his followers that "self" must be buried in him in order for one to bear fruit for the kingdom. This is the message the church is to give and model. It is not to strive for power nor get involved in power politics, but it is to challenge power with the message of Christ and the kingdom.

To put this into practice means that because of one's loyalty to Christ, all our political, economic, social, cultural, religious, personal, and national priorities must be open to question and criticism. God calls his people to become aware of their blind idolatries by allowing the word of God to read them and speak to them, and then be willing to change ways of thinking and acting. Scripture needs to be read not on behalf of the powerful, the comfortable, and selfish personal interests, but read humbly on behalf of those for whom Christ cared as well as for those different from us. This means eliminating all pious, self-righteousness, and self-serving uses of the Bible.

This needs to be repeated. Scripture needs to be read on behalf of others, the poor, the powerless, those on the margins, the oppressed, the hurting, the suffering, the struggling, the sick, for these are the people of Christ's preference. Any serious reader of the Bible understands this. Why this is not a priority of many churches is an enigma. Christ and the Old Testament prophets had a preferential option for those types. Scripture teaches that love does not insist on its own way (1 Cor 13:5).

A nation that wants to believe it is under God must make God and his thinking revealed through Christ its priority. There must be a serious process of self-critical reflection, if the people of America want God to continue to bless America and its churches. Are the nation and even churches willing to be disciplined by the

New Testament narrative and read it over against themselves and not totally in a self-serving defense of its political and economic interests? Does the reader think the leaders of the world and even our own leaders in America understand this or even care to understand this? The excuses offered in opposition to this are well known and documented.

On the whole the question that needs to be asked is: Have Americans become only concerned with self? Does the reader believe the majority of American even care, and if they do, how much do they care? How about the churches? To begin to answer the question is to analyze budgets. This writer is sure the reader has heard the old adage about putting your money where your mouth is. Jim Wallis in his writings believes budgets are a moral issue whether it be a nation, church, or individual. The reader may want to take time at this point to read passages such as Mt 19:16-30, Mt 25, Lk 16:19-31, James 1:19-2:26. Actually the message is on practically every page of Scripture. Using money to glorify God is found in 2,350 verses, which makes it 1-16 in the Bible, 1-10 in the Gospels, 1-6 in Luke. It is the second most prominent theme in the Bible after idolatry, and both themes are related.

America glories in capitalism, which is good when used to benefit all, but when it is used to benefit a certain few at the expense of the rest it needs corrected. When it is used to make the rich richer and the poor poorer, it needs corrected. When it is used as a system of the survival of the fittest, it needs corrected. When it is used to eliminate other's dignity and freedom, it needs corrected. When it is used to eliminate the middle class, it needs corrected, not eliminated but corrected. The question that needs examined is the following: Is America still centered in true capitalism, or have we moved to a plutocracy, meaning government of the wealthy, by the wealthy, and for the wealthy? Is America losing its democracy?

Those on the right keep warning of a drift toward socialism, even communism, but those on the left need to begin warning about a drift toward an oligopoly, plutocracy, and at the extreme, even fascism. The more government and big corporations ignore the common good and work together to manipulate the masses for the benefit of their own selfish interests, then the more the movement is to the right. Both the warnings of the right and the left are appropriate. A balance that benefits all is needed.

Paying serious attention to the ethics of the kingdom is the way true Christianity will grow and God will be glorified, but also, in the end, God will glorify his people and their nation. His people are called to either live by their possessions or live by welcoming the kingdom of God and the king who said, I was called to preach good news to the poor, and I desire mercy not sacrifice, and who said when you pray say, Your kingdom come. Your will be done on earth as it is in heaven. Without that type of direction and compassion, people deny God's truth about their calling. In the process of making Christ first, one of the first idols to be thrown away must be greed (Col 3:5). Other important Scriptures on this new way of thinking are Rom 6:4-14, 12:1-2, Col 3:1-17.

In verses 27-33 Jesus says, "Now my soul is troubled. And what should I say–'Father, save me from this hour'? No, it is this reason I have come to this hour. Father, glorify your name." Then a voice came from heaven, "I have glorified it, and I will glorify it again." The crowd standing there heard it and said that it was thunder. Others said, "An angel has spoken to him." Jesus answered, "This voice has come for your sake, not for mine. Now is the judgment of this world; now the ruler of this world (Satan) will be driven out. And I when I am lifted up from the earth, will draw all people to myself."

He says this to indicate the kind of death he is to die. It will not be until after the cross and resurrection that people will really understand the meaning of his life. The kingdom of God and the defeat of evil are beginning. The renewal and transformation of the world are beginning through God's transformed people, and eternal life is beginning. All of this will be completed and perfected when he comes for final judgment, bringing in the new heaven and new earth.

Verses 34-36 say, the crowd answered him, "We have heard from the law that the Messiah remains forever. How can you say that the Son of Man must be lifted up? Who is the Son of Man?" Jesus said to them, "The light is with you for a little longer. Walk while you have the light, so that the darkness may not overtake you. If you walk in the darkness, you do not know where you are going. While you have the light, believe in the light, so that you may become children of the light.

This is the reason so many people have no idea who they are and why they were created. They walk in the ways of the selfish, dark world. They do not understand that God created them to be co-creators with him of all things through his light and for his light. God's people of both covenants were created to make the world aware of who God is, and who they are to be in relation to him, others and his created order. Renewal and transformation are the call. They are to continue his mission to the poor and those dominated and oppressed by the structures of society, and then to go to all in the world who will listen.

Because the Old Testament people of God chose not to advance the mission, the Father sent his Son into the world. Jesus came preaching the kingdom of God that was breaking into the world through him (Lk 4:43). This is the good news. Jesus then calls his people to understand that they were created not only to share the good news but to be the good news to all they come in contact with. The message is not and was never meant to be a Jesus and me message about one's personal salvation only. He calls all to be a part of his message and mission until he comes again.

After Jesus departed, he hid from them. Verses 37-41 say, Although he had performed so many signs in their presence, they did not believe in him. This was to fulfill the word spoken by the prophet Isaiah: "Lord who has believed our message, and to whom has the arm of the Lord been revealed?" And so they could not believe, because Isaiah also said, "He has blinded their eyes and hardened their heart, so that they might not look with their eyes, and understand with their heart and turn—and I would heal them." Isaiah said this because he saw his glory and spoke about him. (There is a Hebrew pattern that attributes direct action to God in which he really just permits. This is seen in passages like God hardened Pharaoh's heart in Ex 7:13-14, 14, 22, and 1 Sam 4:3 when the Jews were defeated, and asked why God defeated them. To them if God allowed it, then they attribute it to him because God is sovereign.)

In 2 Thessalonians 2:9-12 is an explanation of Isaiah. God did not first blind them so they could not understand. They refused to believe even through his miracles, so God then blinded them all the more. Those verses in Thessalonians say, The coming of the lawless one is apparent in the working of Satan, who uses all power, signs, lying wonders, and every kind of wicked deception for those who are perishing, because they refused to love the truth and so be saved. For this reason God sends them a powerful delusion, leading them to believe what is false, so that all who have not believed the truth but took pleasure in unrighteousness will be condemned.

Verses 42-43 say, Nevertheless many, even of the authorities, believed in him. But because of the Pharisees they did not confess it, for fear that they would be put out of the synagogue; for they loved human glory more than the glory that comes from God.

Loving human glory more than the glory that comes from God continues to be a problem in our society today. This is seen in numerous ways. There are those who completely ignore the things of Christ. But there are also those leaders who clothe themselves in the name of Christ, but they are wolves in sheep's clothing (Mt 7:15, 10:16, Lk 10:3). Then those who know no different blindly follow them. Then there are those who subtly parade their political ideology of traditional values in the name of Christianity, but their definition of traditional values is extremely narrow and lacking in compassion for the things that Jesus was compassionate about.

How are traditional values defined? Do they involve more than sexual or bodily issues? When one wants to understand the traditional values of Jesus some of the following questions need to be asked. Do traditional religious values use all ethical means to benefit the common good? Does this mean encouraging everyone, including corporations and government to help people of little wealth and power and not let them suffer and die in a culture of survival of the fittest where big money and profits rule? Do traditional values encourage individuals as well as corporations and government to create jobs, make an effort to feed the hungry, and help people get the health care they need?

Would Jesus say government needs to limit itself so the big, wealthy corporations, who pay very little taxes, can be free to take advantage of people, outsource jobs, and rape society? Would Jesus who Scripture says that with his Father created everything, which would include government, be silent about how government operates on its people? Before the reader answers read Colossians 1:15-20, 1 Cor 15:27-28, and then read the Old Testament prophets. Start with Amos, Micah, and then Jeremiah and so on.

Do traditional values include not only limiting government but limiting big money and big corporations from doing whatever they want for their own greed by taking advantage of those who are at their mercy? In a society where the rich get richer and the poor get poorer, would traditional values support more tax cuts to the wealthiest two per cent forcing the other ninety-eight per cent to make up for the loss of that tax money? Would it cut services and health care to the needy to make up for the loss of tax money? Is that the direction Jesus would take? And in discussing traditional values whose traditional values are we talking about, the values of a nation or culture, or the values of God? Read 1 Cor 6:6-16.

Would the greatest healer and peacemaker in history, who was eventually put to death by wealth and power, the religious and political authorities of the time, favor all the tax money spent on big business to make war weapons? These companies then expedite them throughout the world in the name of traditional values and taking back America. What do they believe they are taking back? Every country in the world has weapons from America including those countries we are at war with. Are these the things Jesus would promote and call traditional values? Less than .04 of 1 percent of American foreign aid goes to economic development, while the majority of foreign aid is military aid. This writer understands well the position and reasoning of those who favor such activity. Does the reader believe Jesus would look kindly upon such activity?

Philippians 3:20 says, our citizenship is in heaven, and 2:3-6 says, Do nothing from selfish ambition or conceit, but in humility regard others as better than yourselves. Let each of you look not to your own interests, but to the interests of others. (This is not referring to military interests.) Let the same mind be in you that was in Christ Jesus, . . . so that at the name of Jesus every knee should bend, in heaven and on earth and under earth, and every tongue should confess that Jesus Christ is Lord, to the glory of God the Father. (Do we eliminate verses like that from our Bibles? The primary citizenship of the followers of Jesus is to be in the kingdom, and then secondarily in the nation where one lives, for one can not have two masters.)

Scripture does not create a political and economic system but it has much to say about politics and economics, simply because its decisions affect people either for good or evil. The Bible can not be reduced to its political and economic implications but neither can it be emptied of them. All one has to do to confirm this is read the prophets and the teachings of the Gospels. When the words traditional values are thrown around, do they include anything the Old Testament prophets said? Does it include anything Jesus said? Can the reader locate the exact verses? God is concerned with the whole person and whatever has an influence for good upon them. Jesus Christ is Lord of all life not just one's so-called spiritual life. Neither the Father nor the Son separates the material from the spiritual.

Some may say that Christians should stay out of politics and economics, but they have a wrong understanding of the kingdom, and the kingdom was the primary message Jesus came to preach. The kingdom is not a political and economic kingdom, but it is not devoid of political, economic, and social issues. Jesus told his disciples, "I must proclaim the good news of the kingdom of God to the other cities also; for I was sent for this purpose (Lk 4:43)." Even in prayer he told his disciples to pray, your will be done on earth as it is in heaven. These values are kingdom values. The disciples of Jesus are called to protect the interests of the vulnerable not the interests of the powerful and wealthy. By ignoring these issues we allow the people of the world to stall the advancement of the kingdom and allow the world's values to dominate kingdom values.

If one wants to say politics is to stay out of religion, and religion is to stay out of politics, it is necessary to understand that is not a biblical idea. If God is Lord of all, that means God is Lord of one's politics and economics also. Political authority comes from God and is accountable and responsible to God. By ignoring these values, we allow the thinking of the anti-religion leaders of the Age of Enlightenment and those still captivated by its philosophy, even some who go by the name Christian, to succeed in their major purpose, which was and still is to separate any religious influence from political, economic, cultural, and social life. They do this in order to control things to benefit themselves and their influential friends, so they attempt to separate religion from life issues. Religion then becomes a pie in the sky way of life separated from life issues.

The question that comes from verse 43 is: Do our values give glory to God's way or to the way of humans? A question related to the issue is: What does love one another as I have loved you really mean (Jn 13:34-35, 15:12)? What does the greatest among you will be your servant really mean (Lk 20:24-28)? What does bear one another's burdens really mean (Gal 6:2)? This writer could go on and on with like questions. Possibly the reader can add to the list. Do we answer these questions being influenced by a culture of the love of God modeled by Christ or influenced by a culture of "me first"?

Verses 44-50 say, Then Jesus cried aloud: "Whoever believes in me believes not in me but in him who sent me. And whoever sees me sees him who sent me. I have come as light into the world, so that anyone who believes in me should not remain in the darkness. I do not judge anyone who hears my words and does not keep them, for I came not to judge the world, but to save the world. The one who rejects me and does not receive my word has a judge; on the last day the word that I have spoken will serve as judge, for I have not spoken on my own, but the Father who sent me has himself given me a commandment about what to say and what to speak. I know that his commandment is eternal life. What I speak, therefore, I speak just as the Father has told me.

Another way to put the question of verse 43 is: Do our traditional values come from the light of the words of Jesus or do they come from the darkness of the world or the world's concept of religion? As C S Lewis stated in a book titled *Mere Christianity* (54-56) humans have a decision to make. We either believe Jesus and his teachings as sent from God or declare him insane. For if any human would say what he said, those would be the only two choices to make. If the decision is one believes he is of God, then a change of thinking and action is in order.

Jesus is saying his priority in coming is to save people, not to judge them, but Jesus makes it clear that his word will be humankind's judge. John wants his readers to judge themselves by the words of Jesus so that the final judgment will be a time of joy. So in context with this chapter, are the reader's values from God's word or somewhere else? A good exercise is to list your values, what is most important to you, and then start with the prophets then move to Jesus' Sermon on the Mount and continue throughout the Gospels, and see how they match with your list. One might be in for a few surprises.

❦

Chapter 13:1-5 says, Now before the festival of the Passover, Jesus knew that his hour had come to depart from this world and go to the Father. Having loved his own who were in the world, he loved them to the end. The devil had already put it in the heart of Judas son of Simon Iscariot to betray him. And during supper Jesus, knowing that the Father had given all things into his hands, and that he had come from God and was going to God, got up from the table, took off his outer robe, and tied a towel around himself. Then he poured water into a basin and began to wash the disciples' feet and to wipe them with the towel that was tied around him.

Verses 6-11 say, He came to Simon Peter, who said to him, "Lord, are you going to wash my feet?" Jesus answered, "You do not know now what I am doing, but later you will understand." Peter said to him, "You will never wash my feet." Jesus answered, "Unless I wash you, you have no share with me." Simon Peter said to him, "Lord, not my feet only but also my hands and my head!" Jesus said to him, "One who has bathed does not need to wash, except for the feet, but is entirely clean. And you are clean, though not all of you." For he knew who was to betray him; for this reason he said, "Not all of you are clean."

The following verses interpret this teaching of Jesus to mean humble service in love of each other after one is baptized as a disciple. Once washed clean then one continues to confirm discipleship by this humble service to one's fellow humans. Foot washing is the symbol for hospitable service, for in those times after walking through that dry, dusty land, the first thing done when entering a home is to offer the washing of feet.

Verses 12-20 say, After he had washed their feet, had put on his robe, and had returned to the table, he said to them, "Do you know what I have done to you? You call me Teacher and Lord—and you are right, for that is what I am. So if I, your Lord and Teacher, have washed your feet, you ought to wash one another's feet. For I have set you an example, that you also should do as I have done to you. Very truly, I tell you, servants are not greater than their master, nor are messengers greater than the one who sent them. If you know these things, you are blessed if you do them. I am not speaking of all of you; I know whom I have chosen. But it is to fulfill the scripture (Ps 41:9), 'The one who ate my bread has lifted his heel against me.' I tell you now, before it occurs, so that when it does occur, you may believe that I am he. Very truly, I tell you, whoever receives one whom I send receives me; and whoever receives me receives him who sent me."

Verse 21 says, After saying this Jesus was troubled in spirit, and declared, "Very truly, I tell you, one of you will betray me." In (22-26) they were concerned and Jesus dipped bread in a dish and offered it to each one of them. After offering it to Judas verse 27 says, Satan entered Judas and Jesus said to him, "Do quickly what you are going to do." Verses 28-30 say, no one at the table knew why he said this to him. Some thought that, because Judas had the common purse, Jesus was telling him, "Buy what we need for the festival; or, that he should give something to the poor. So, after receiving the piece of bread, he immediately went out. And it was night.

The writer mentions night because what is going to happen is a time of darkness. It is interesting to note that John's story of Jesus final meal does not contain the institution of the Lord's Supper, but he does give the meaning of it in chapter 6. John is concerned more with the meaning of things. In this chapter he is concerned with the meaning behind Jesus washing the feet of his followers. John emphasizes things different from the Synoptics. There is no doubt he is aware of those writings and chooses to write about Jesus from a different angle.

Verses 31-34 say, When he had gone out, Jesus said, "Now the Son of Man has been glorified, and God has been glorified in him. If God has been glorified in him, God will also glorify him in himself and will glorify him at once. Little children, I am with you only a little longer. You will look for me; and as I said to the Jews so now I say to you, 'Where I am going, you cannot come.' I give you a new commandment, that you love one another. Just as I have loved you, you should love one another. (It is new because Jesus is the model of one who loves so deeply that he is willing to give his life for others.) Then verse 35 says, By this everyone will know that you are my disciples, if you have love for one another. (In Scripture love does not mean a certain feeling. It is defined by the life of Jesus and 1 Cor 13:4-7. What grade would the reader give to themselves in this area? What grade would the reader give to Christianity or your particular church in this area?)

Verses 36-38 say, Simon Peter said to him, "Lord, where are you going?" Jesus answered, "Where I am going, you cannot follow me now; but you will follow afterward." Peter said to him, "Lord, why can I not follow you now? I will lay down my life for you." Jesus answered, "Will you lay down your life for me? Very truly, I tell you, before the cock crows, you will have denied me three times."

In chapter 14:1-7 Jesus says, "Do not let your hearts be troubled. Believe in God, believe also in me. In my Father's place there are many dwelling places (sometimes translated mansions). If it were not so, would I have told you that I go to prepare a place for you? And if I go and prepare a place for you, I will come again and will take you to myself, so that where I am, there you may be also. And you know the way to the place I am going." Thomas said to him, "Lord, we do not know where you are going. How can we know the way?" Jesus said, I am the way, and the truth, and the life. No one comes to the Father except through me. If you know me, you will know my Father also. From now on you do know him and have seen him."

The way is a path or journey or a transformation. It is dying to an old way of being and thinking and being born into a new way. It is about meeting a person who has made a difference in your life.

In the person of Jesus and through Jesus one comes to the Father. This is how a person is born of God and transformed. Jesus is the Father's truth and his wisdom, and the way he chooses to bring people to him. One lives the truth by allowing Jesus to live in them and through them, pushing the old self out.

Verses 8-14 say, Philip said to him, "Lord, show us the Father, and we will be satisfied." Jesus said to him, "Have I been with you all this time Philip, and you still do not know me? Whoever has seen me has seen the Father. How can you say, 'Show us the Father'? Do you not believe that I am in the Father and the Father is in me? The words that I say to you I do not speak on my own; but the Father who dwells in me does his works. Believe me that I am in the Father and the Father is in me; but if you do not, then believe me because of the works themselves. Very truly, I tell you, the one who believes in me will also do the works that I do and, in fact, will do greater works than these, because I am going to the Father. I will do whatever you ask in my name, so that the Father may be glorified in the Son. If in my name you ask me for anything, I will do it."

The apostles will be Jesus' successors and he will send them the Holy Spirit. The greater works done will be done in the world through prayer, the Holy Spirit, and the obedience of faith. It will be greater, meaning more in number, because all the apostles are going out with the special and unique power Jesus has given to them. After that generation of apostles is over and the church is established that unique miraculous power will wane, as basic Christian history shows, but the Spirit will continue to work in a normal way and blow where it will (3:8).

Even so, his disciples throughout history have the responsibility to do what they can and to keep his mission going. His disciples are called to be his eyes, ears, hands, feet, and mouth to the world in which they live. As the Father is in Jesus and Jesus is in the Father,

Jesus will be in disciples as they are transformed and born of him. In this way the mission of Jesus is carried on until he returns (15:1-17). Jesus calls his disciples to be co-creators with him through the Spirit advancing God's kingdom in this broken world.

In verses 15-17 Jesus says, "If you love me you will keep my commandments. And I will ask the Father, and he will give you another Advocate, to be with you forever. This is the Spirit of truth, whom the world cannot receive, because it neither sees him nor knows him. You know him, because he abides with you, and he will be in you."

Verses 18-21 say, I will not leave you orphaned; I am coming to you. In a little while the world will no longer see me, but you will see me; because I live, you also will live. On that day you will know that I am in my Father, and you in me, and I in you. They who have my commandments and keep them are those who love me; and those who love me will be loved by my Father, and I will love them and reveal myself to them.

John in 1 John 3:23-24 says, And this is his commandment, that we should believe in the name of his Son Jesus Christ and love one another, just as he has commanded us. All who obey his commandments abide in him, and he abides in them. And this we know that he abides in us, by the Spirit that he has given us. (Does the Spirit of love and compassion include love, compassion, and action for those in deep need of housing, food, and health care? If so, does the reader see it in those who claim to be followers of Christ in Congress? What about the churches? What is the reason for your answer?)

Verses 22-25 say, Judas (not Iscariot) said to him, "Lord, how is it that you will reveal yourself to us, and not to the world?" Jesus answered him, "Those who love me will keep my word, and my Father will love them, and we will come to them and make our home with them. Whoever does not love me does not keep my words; and the word that you hear is not mine, but is from the Father who sent me. I have said these things to you while I am still with you.

Verses 26-27 say, But the Advocate, the Holy Spirit, whom the Father will send in my name, will teach you everything, and remind you of all I have said to you. Peace I leave with you; my peace I give to you. I do not give to you as the world gives. Do not let your hearts be troubled, and do not let them be afraid."

Jesus gives them the Spirit of peace to give to those they come in contact with. The Holy Spirit will remind them of the words of Jesus and help them apply them in new situations. Revelation will be completed by the end of the first century, but illumination will continue throughout time.

Verses 28-31 say, "You heard me say to you, 'I am going away, and I am coming to you.' If you loved me, you would rejoice that I am going to the Father, because the Father is greater than I. And now I have told you this before it occurs, so that when it does occur, you may believe. I will no longer talk much with you, for the ruler of this world (the devil) is coming. He has no power over me; but I do as the Father has commanded me, so that the world may know that I love the Father. Rise, let us be on our way. (His going away yet coming to them is probably in reference to the Holy Spirit who he will send to them.)

❧❧

In chapter 15:1-2 Jesus says, "I am the vine, and my Father is the vinegrower. He removes every branch in me that bears no fruit. Every branch that bears fruit he prunes to make it bear more fruit. (This takes us back to the verse in 14:20 where Jesus said, On that day you will know that I am in my Father, and you in me, and I in you.) Verses 3-4 continue, You have already been cleansed by the word I have spoken to you. Abide in me as I abide in you. Just as the branch can not bear fruit by itself unless it abides in the vine, neither can you unless you abide in me." (The three are connected by the Holy Spirit: God the Father, Jesus, and the disciples.)

Verses 5-6 say, "I am the vine, you are the branches. Those who abide in me and I in them bear much fruit, because apart from me you can do nothing (nothing of value for God and in his name). Whoever does not abide in me is thrown away like a branch and withers; such branches are gathered, thrown into the fire, and burned.

Verses 7-11 say, "If you abide in me and my words abide in you, ask for whatever you wish, and it will be done for you. (This is in reference to bearing much fruit as the following indicates.) My Father is glorified by this, that you bear much fruit and become my disciples. As the Father has loved me, so I have loved you; abide in my love. If you keep my commandments (teachings), you will abide in my love, just as I have kept my Father's commandments and abide in his love. For I have said these things to you so that my joy may be in you, and that your joy may be complete."

Love starts with compassion in the heart because of the love of Jesus. If love is in a heart, the heart issues forth with the same compassion for all that one has for one's child. Love and compassion are similar. The key virtue in Buddhism is compassion, but it is a form of love. The key virtue in Christianity is love, but it is rooted in compassion. These words are quite clear; there is nothing in Jesus' words advocating selfish greed, or aspects of any system that takes advantage of the powerless and grinds them down. That is the opposite of love and compassion. The promise for people participating in that type of activity is removal from the vine.

Verses 12-16 say, "This is my commandment that you love one

another as I have loved you. No one has greater love than this, to lay down one's life for one's friends. You are my friends if you do what I command you. (The reader should note the word *if*.) I do not call you servants any longer, because the servant does not know what the master is doing; but I have called you friends, because I have made known to you everything that I have heard from my Father. You did not choose me, but I chose you. And I appointed you to go and bear fruit, fruit that will last, so that the Father will give you whatever you ask him in my name." (He is talking directly to his chosen apostles, and secondarily to his disciples throughout time, especially in reference to fruit bearing.)

Verses 17-25 say, "I am giving you these commands so that you may love one another. If the world hates you, be aware that it hated me before it hated you. If you belonged to the world, the world would love you as its own. Because you do not belong to the world, but I have chosen you out of the world—therefore the world hates you. Remember the word that I said to you, 'Servants are not greater than their master.' If they persecuted me, they will persecute you; if they kept my word, they will keep yours also. But they will do all these things to you on account of my name, because they do not know him who sent me."

What is that saying to those of us who are comfortable in and with the world and do not allow Christ to bear the fruit of his kingdom through us? If the message of Jesus is just to be a loving moral person and nothing else, would the leaders of the world have put him to death? He obviously expanded his message to the government leaders otherwise they would have ignored him.

Verses 22-25 say, "If I had not come and spoken to them, they would not have sin; but now they have no excuse for their sin. Whoever hates me hates my Father also. If I had not done among them the works that no one else did, they would not have sin. But now they have seen and hated both me and my Father. (The Jewish leaders made a conscious choice to reject him, not just because of their individual sin but for the sin they are responsible for as leaders of the nation.) It was to fulfill the word that is written in their law (Ps 35:19), 'They hated me without a cause.'

Verses 26-27 say, "When the Advocate comes, whom I will send to you from the Father, the Spirit of truth who comes from the Father, he will testify on my behalf. You also are to testify because you have been with me from the beginning." (Here we have the Father, Son, and Holy Spirit giving the apostles their mission and informing them that they will receive special help from the Holy Spirit.)

Chapter 16:1-6 says, "I have said these things to you to keep you from stumbling. They will put you out of the synagogues. Indeed, an hour is coming when those who kill you will think that by doing so they are offering worship to God. And they will do this because they have not known the Father or me. But I have said these things to you so that when their hour comes you may remember that I told you about them. I did not say these things to you in the beginning, because I was with you. But now I am going to him who sent me; yet none of you asks me, 'Where are you going?' But because I have said these things to you, sorrow has filled your hearts.

Verses 7-11 continue, "Nevertheless I tell you the truth: it is to your advantage that I go away, for if I do not go away, the Advocate (Holy Spirit) will not come to you; but if I go, I will send him to you. And when he comes, he will prove the world wrong about sin and righteousness and judgment: about sin, (unbelief in Jesus) because they do not believe in me; about righteousness, (revealed in the cross and resurrection) because I am going to the Father and you will see me no longer; about judgment, (triumph over evil) because the ruler of this world has been condemned.

Verses 12-16 continue, "I still have many things to say to you, but you cannot bear them now. When the Spirit of truth comes, he will guide you into all truth; for he will not speak on his own, but will speak whatever he hears (from the Father) and he will declare to you the things that are to come. He will glorify me, because he will take what is mine and declare it to you. All that the Father has is mine. For this reason I said that he will take what is mine and declare it to you. (God has more light and truth (illumination) to come from his holy word.) "A little while, and you will no longer see me, and again a little while, and you will see me."

Verses 17-18 say, Then some of his disciples said to one another, "What does he mean by saying to us, 'A little while and you will no longer see me, and again a little while, and you will see me'; and 'Because I am going to the Father'?" They said, "What does he mean by this 'a little while'? We do not know what he is talking about."

Verses 19-24 say, Jesus knew that they wanted to ask him, so he said to them, "Are you discussing among yourselves what I meant when I said, 'A little while, and you will no longer see me, again a little while, and you will see me'? "Very truly, I tell you, you will weep and mourn, but the world will rejoice; you will have pain, but your pain will turn into joy. When a woman is in labor, she has pain, because her hour has come. But when her child is born, she no longer remembers the anguish because of the joy of having brought a human being into the world. So you have pain now; but I will see you again, and your hearts will rejoice, and no one will take your joy from me. On that very day you will ask nothing of me. Very truly, I tell you, if you ask anything of the Father in my name, he will give it to you. Until now you have not asked anything in my name. Ask and you will receive, so that your joy may be complete."

This writer believes these verses are primarily directed to his apostles and what Jesus will do for them as they plant the first churches. Second, they are directed to all believers, and in context with the Gospels, this is a reference to bearing the gifts and fruits of the Spirit.

Verses 25-28 say, "I have said these things to you in figures of speech. (Again this writer reiterates that those who say everything must be taken literally, misinterpret Scripture.) The hour is coming when I will no longer speak to you in figures, but will tell you plainly of the Father. On that day you will ask in my name. I do not say to you that I will ask the Father on your behalf; for the Father himself loves you, because you have loved me and have believed that I came from God. I came from the Father and have come into the world; again, I am leaving the world and am going to the Father."

Verses 29-33 say, His disciples said, "Yes, now you are speaking plainly, not in any figure of speech! Now we know that you know all things, and do not need to have anyone question you; by this we believe that you came from God." Jesus answered them, "Do you believe? The hour is coming, indeed it has come, when you will be scattered, each one to his home, and you will leave me alone. Yet I am not alone because the Father is with me. I have said this to you, so that in me you may have peace. In the world you face persecution. But take courage; I have conquered the world!" (Instead of telling them how wonderful things will be, if they follow him, he tells them they will suffer persecution. How different that is from many of today's religious teachers.)

All of chapter 17 is a prayer of Jesus as he prepares to depart from this world. Many believe it is John's adaption of the Lord's

Prayer. In the first 5 verses Jesus prays for himself. Verses 1-5 say, "After Jesus had spoken these words, he looked up to heaven and said, "Father, the hour has come; glorify your Son so that the Son may glorify you, since you have given him authority over all people, to give eternal life to all whom you have given him. And this is eternal life that they may know you, the only true God, and Jesus Christ whom you have sent. I glorified you on earth by finishing the work that you gave me to do. So now, Father, glorify me in your own presence with the glory that I had in your presence before the world existed."

In verses 6-19 Jesus prays for his disciples. "I have made your name known to those whom you gave me from the world. (John uses the word world in two different ways. One way is a reference to God's good creation. The other way is to make it a reference to all that is opposed to God's light.) They were yours, and you gave them to me, and they have kept your word. Now they know that everything you have given me is from you; for the words that you gave me I have given to them, and they have received them and know in truth that I came from you; and they have believed that you sent me.

"I am asking on their behalf; I am not asking on behalf of the world, but on behalf of those whom you gave me, because they are yours. All mine are yours, and yours are mine; and I have been glorified in them. And now I am no longer in the world, but they are in the world, and I am coming to you. Holy Father, protect them in your name that you have given me, so that they may be one, as we are one. While I was with them, I protected them in your name that you have given me. I guarded them, and not one of them was lost except the one destined to be lost, so that the scriptures might be fulfilled.

"But now I am coming to you, and I speak these things in the world so that they may have my joy made complete in themselves. I have given them your word, and the world has hated them because they do not belong to the world, just as I do not belong to the world. I am not asking you to take them out of the world, but I ask you to protect them from the evil one. (When God's word is applied to all of life's circumstances, and the status quo is upset, God's comfort and protection are needed.) They do not belong to the world, just as I do not belong to the world. Sanctify them in the truth; your word is truth. (Sanctification means becoming more holy until finally perfected. Sanctification comes through God's word, which leads to Jesus and the Holy Spirit.) As you have sent me into the world, so I have sent them into the world. And for their sakes I sanctify myself, so that they also may be sanctified in truth."

After praying for himself and his disciples, he prays now for the church. Verses 20-26 say, "I ask not only on behalf of these, but also on behalf of those who will believe in me through their word, that they may all be one. As you Father, are in me and I am in you, may they also be in us, so that the world may believe that you have sent me. The glory that you have given me I have given them, so that they may be one, as we are one, I in them and you in me, that they may become completely one, so that the world may know that you have sent me and have loved them even as you have loved me. (It seems obvious to this writer that Christians throughout the centuries have failed miserably in answering this part of Jesus' prayer.)

"Father, I desire that those also, whom you have given me, may be with me where I am, to see my glory, which you have given me because you loved me before the foundation of the world. Righteous Father, the world does not know you, but I know you; and these know that you have sent me. I made your name known to them, and I will make it known, so that the love with which you have loved me may be in them, and I in them." (Being in Christ and Christ being in you means being in love with everyone and everything that he loved. It means allowing Christ to continue his mission in you and through you.)

⤳◦◦⤶

In chapter 18:1-3 After Jesus had spoken these words, he went out with his disciples across the Kidron valley to a place where there was a garden, which he and his disciples entered. (John does not mention its name, which is Gethsemani, nor does he mention the agony found in the other gospels. Going east across the valley is the Mt of Olives.) Now Judas who betrayed him, also knew the place, because Jesus often met there with his disciples. So Judas brought a detachment of soldiers together with police from the chief priests and the Pharisees, and they came with their lanterns and torches and weapons.

Verses 4-10 say, Then Jesus knowing all that was to happen to him, came forward and asked them, "Whom are you looking for?" They answered, "Jesus of Nazareth." Jesus replied, "I am he." (John stresses the use of "I am." John constantly has Jesus saying that he is YHWH, 'I am" the words for God's name given at the burning bush in Exodus 3:13-15.) Judas, who betrayed him, was standing with them. When Jesus said to them, "I am he," they stepped back and fell to the ground. Again he asked them, "Whom are you looking for?" And they said, "Jesus of Nazareth." Jesus answered, "I told you that I am he. So if you are looking for me, let these men go. Then Simon Peter, who had a sword, drew it, struck the high priest's slave, and cut off his right ear. The slave's name was Malchus. Jesus in (11) said to Peter, "Put your sword back into its sheath. Am I not to drink the cup my Father gave me?" (Jesus ends the violence.)

Verses 12-18 say, So the soldiers, their officer, and the Jewish police arrested Jesus and bound him. First they took him to Annas, who was the father-in-law of Caiaphas, the high priest that year. Caiaphas was the one who had advised the Jews that it was better to have one person die for the people. Simon Peter and another disciple followed Jesus (probably John, the writer of this gospel). Since that disciple was known to the high priest, he went with Jesus into the courtyard of the high priest, but Peter was standing outside at the gate. So the other disciple, who was known to the high priest, went out, spoke to the woman that guarded the gate, and brought Peter in. The woman said to Peter, "You are not also one of this man's disciples, are you?" He said, "I am not." Now the slaves and the police had made a charcoal fire because it was cold, and they were standing around it and warming themselves. Peter was also standing with them and warming himself.

Verses 19-24 say, Then the high priest questioned Jesus about his disciples and about his teaching. (This is an honorary title for Annas because previously he had been the high priest.) Jesus answered, "I have spoken openly to the world; I have always taught in synagogues and in the temple, where all Jews come together. I have said nothing in secret. Why do you ask me? Ask those who heard what I said to them; they know what I said." When he said this, one of the police standing nearby struck Jesus on the face, saying, "Is that how you answer the high priest?" Jesus answered, "If I have spoken wrongly, testify to the wrong. But if I have spoken rightly, why do you strike me?" Then Annas sent him bound to Caiaphas the high priest.

Verses 25-27 say, Now Simon Peter was standing and warming himself. They asked him, "You are not also one of his disciples, are you?" He denied it and said, "I am not." One of the slaves of the high priest, a relative of the man whose ear Peter cut off, asked, "Did I not see you in the garden with him?" Again Peter denied it, and at that moment the cock crowed.

This story in all of the Gospels, apparently, was popular. All the Gospels, which were written from 40-70 years after this incident, show the great Peter wilting under pressure. At the time of this writing, in a time of great fear, when many Christians are being martyred, there are also many wilting under pressure like Peter. Later we will see Jesus forgives Peter, giving hope to those who refused to be martyred and who yielded under pressure like Peter did. As the reader knows, later Peter will get it all together, and according to early Christian historians, becomes a Christian martyr. There is always the offer of hope for those who fail.

Verses 28-32 say, Then they took Jesus from Caiaphas to Pilate's headquarters. It was early in the morning. They themselves did not enter the headquarters, so as to avoid ritual defilement and to be able to eat the Passover. (Entering Gentile headquarters will make them ritually unclean.) So Pilate went out to them and said, "What accusation do you bring against this man?" They answered, "If this man were not a criminal, we would not have handed him over to you." Pilate said to them, "Take him yourselves and judge him according to your own law." The Jews replied, "We are not permitted to put anyone to death." This was to fulfill what Jesus had said when he indicated the kind of death he was to die.

The Romans must approve any death penalty, and the method of death for revolutionaries is by crucifixion, so this is how he is labeled in order to approve his death. The Jewish leaders need permission to put him to death by the Romans, and the Romans permit it. Death will be by crucifixion. It is interesting to note that according to Griffith-Jones (2000, 37) and Borg and Wright (1999, 88-89) only revolutionaries charged with treason, and run away or defiant slaves are put to death by crucifixion. But in reality Jesus is not a revolutionary. He is opposed to overthrowing Rome by violence and tries to discourage the militant nationalists from doing so. Even though he is not a revolutionary in respect to a violent overthrow, his thinking is revolutionary.

Verse 33-35 say, Then Pilate entered the headquarters again, summoned Jesus, and asked him, "Are you the King of the Jews?" Jesus answered, "Do you ask this on your own, or did others tell you about me?" Pilate replied, "I am not a Jew am I? Your own nation and the chief priests have handed you over to me. What have you done?"

Pilate rules Judea as the Roman procurator from AD 26-36. He is subordinate to the Roman governor of Syria. His chief duty is to administer finances and collect taxes for the Romans. With those duties came a certain amount of political power. He is known for his insensitivity and cruelty. The headquarters are the Praetorium where the governor stays when in Jerusalem. It includes military barracks, and an outdoor courtroom used as a court of judgment. It is disputed as to its exact location, but it was close to the temple.

The details of the trial that follow vary somewhat in the four Gospels, but there are also similarities. Again in an oral society history is not used as we moderns use it, and the Gospels were never meant to be an exact historical account as moderns understand history. Numerous scholars believe that in an oral society the events of the trial, crucifixion and resurrection were organized into plays to help the people remember the key events and the theology.

As things got passed down in the 40-70 year period, before things were written, some of the details became altered because of the emphasis on different themes and different theological purposes. But the theology and the basic details, and the message remain the same. Those who deny any differences, sometimes called contradictions, do not understand the purpose of these inspired Scriptures, nor do they understand how things got passed down in an oral, ancient society.

In responding to Pilate verses 36-38 say, Jesus answered, "My kingdom is not from this world. If my kingdom were from this world, my followers would be fighting to keep me from being handed over to the Jews. But as it is, my kingdom is not from here." (Jesus is saying his kingdom is from God and not from humans, and it is not a political kingdom with earthly boundaries as theirs is.) Pilate asked him, "So you are a king?" Jesus answered, "You say that I am a king. For this I was born, and for this I came into the world, to testify to the truth. Everyone who belongs to the truth listens to my voice." Pilate asked him, "What is truth?" (Pilate is asking the right question, one that all people need to ask.) After he had said this, he went out to the Jews again and told them, "I find no case against him."

In verses 39-40 Pilate said, "But you have a custom that I release someone for you at the Passover. Do you want me to release for you the King of the Jews?" They shouted in reply, "Not this man, but Barabbas!" Now Barabbas was a bandit.

In chapter 19:1 Pilate took Jesus and had him flogged. (Flogging whips had bits of metal or bone attached to them, and they often produced severe wounds, sometimes fatal.) Verses 2-7 say, And the soldiers wove a crown of thorns and put it on his head, and they dressed him in a purple robe. They kept coming up to him saying, "Hail, King of the Jews!" and striking him on the face. Pilate went out again and said to them, "Look, I am bringing him out to you to let you know that I find no case against him." So Jesus came out, wearing the crown of thorns and the purple robe. Pilate said to them, "Here is the man!" When the chief priests and the police saw him, they shouted, "Crucify him! Crucify him!" Pilate said to them, "Take him yourself and crucify him; I find no case against him." The Jews answered him, "We have a law, and according to the law he ought to die because he has claimed to be the Son of God."

They mock him as an imposter who has finally been discovered. The Jews claim that Jesus said he is the Son of God so that will be the official and the theological reason for the Jews to put him to death. The claim that Jesus is the king of a new kingdom will be the official reason for the Romans to put him to death as a revolutionary. Both the Romans and the Jews taunt him for making these claims, but he never boldly makes these claims, for he knows what the result would be. He never makes these claims in the sense that the Jews and Romans understood them.

Verse 8 says, Now when Pilate heard this, he was more afraid than ever. (No one seems to quite understand that statement, since up to now he does not seem to have shown any fear. This writer has explained that the Roman emperor was the king who also claimed to be the son of god and savior who had brought peace to the world. If Rome knew another person was claiming the same thing and nothing was done about it, Pilate would lose his head. Possibly that was his fear.)

Verses 9-12 say, He (Pilate) entered his headquarters again and asked Jesus, "Where are you from?" But Jesus gave him no answer. Pilate therefore said to him, "Do you refuse to speak to me? Do you not know I have power to release you, and power to crucify you?" Jesus said, "You would have no power over me unless it had been given you from above; therefore the one who handed me over to you is guilty of a greater sin." (Even so, both Pilate and the Jewish leadership are responsible. Jesus is also telling Pilate from whom his power comes.) From then on Pilate tried to release him, but the Jews cried out, "If you release this man, you are no friend of the emperor.

Everyone who claims to be a king, sets himself against the emperor."

This is the bind Pilate is in. Some claim Pilate is well aware of all this and is just putting the pressure on the Jews to be responsible for Jesus' death, so the Jews could not put the blame of an innocent man on him.

Verses 13-14 say, When Pilate heard these words, he brought Jesus outside and sat on the judge's bench at a place called the Stone Pavement, or in Hebrew Gabbatha. Now it was the day of Preparation for the Passover; and it was about noon. He said to the Jews, "Here is your King!"

John mentions the exact time because this is the time that the priests in the temple begin to slaughter the Passover lambs for the peoples' sins. In the meantime Jesus is in the process of being prepared as the final Passover lamb, the Lamb of God that takes away the sin of the world. This according to Christians will take away the need for any further Passover lambs.

Verses 15-18 say, They cried out, "Away with him! Away with him! Crucify him!" Pilate asked them, "Shall I crucify your King?" The chief priests answered, "We have no king but the emperor." Then he handed him over to them to be crucified. So they took Jesus; and carrying the cross by himself, (no Simon the Cyrene?) he went out to what is called Golgotha. (Also, in Aramaic it is called the Place of the Skull, and in Latin, Calvary.) There they crucified him, and with him two others, one on either side, with Jesus between them.

First, mutually responsible for the death of Jesus are Judas, a disciple; Pilate, a Roman; and certain Jewish authorities of Jerusalem. 1 Cor 2:8 tells us the rulers of this age put Jesus to death. Second, all throughout their history the Jews were called to make a choice on who their real king was. Was it God or a human? Because too often they chose the human, they were punished by God as he allowed them to be conquered by a foreign power and sent into exile. They were exiled to Assyria in 722 BC then in 586 BC to Babylon. They now consider themselves in spiritual exile because even though they are in their own land, they are controlled by the Romans, living as conquered people.

The main concern of the authorities is to get rid of Jesus at any cost. He is too much of a challenge to their way of thinking and acting. One of their hymns at Passover declares to God, "We have no king but you." So by ignoring this hymn, once again, they confirm what their leaders have done throughout history. In the meantime let us not be deceived into thinking we are any different in these times. Let us not fool ourselves by thinking we are more holy than they. We moderns crucify him again and again both by our individual decisions, even our decisions as a church, and our decisions as a nation.

Verses 19-25 say, Pilate also had an inscription written and put on a cross. It read, "Jesus of Nazareth, King of the Jews." Many of the Jews read this inscription, because the place where Jesus was crucified was near the city; and it was written in Hebrew, in Latin, and in Greek. Then the chief priests of the Jews said to Pilate, "Do not write, 'the King of the Jews,' but, 'This man said, I am King of the Jews.' " Pilate answered, "I have written what I have written." (Pilate got them and is making them squirm.)

Verses 23-25 say, When the soldiers had crucified Jesus, they took his clothes and divided them into four parts, one for each soldier. They also took his tunic; now the tunic was seamless, woven in one piece from the top. So they said to one another, "Let us not tear it, but cast lots for it to see who will get it." This was to fulfill what the Scripture says, "They divided my clothes among themselves, and for my clothing they cast lots (Ps 22:17-18)." And that is what the soldiers did. Meanwhile, standing near the cross of Jesus were his mother, and his mother's sister, Mary the wife of Clopas, and Mary Magdalene. (Is this the same Clopas in Lk 24:18?)

Verses 26-27 say, When Jesus saw his mother and the disciple whom he loved standing beside her, he said to his mother, "Woman, here is your son." Then he said to the disciple, "Here is your mother." And from that hour the disciple took her into his home.

One wonders why she does not stay with the other brothers and sisters of the family, if they are his real brothers and sisters, or is this typical of John's symbolism? Is Jesus saying that Mary is the spiritual mother of the church, to be respected, and that all Christians are her children also? This has basically been the meaning for the Roman Catholic Church and the Orthodox Catholic church. Or is it simply saying the church is to take in the heritage of Israel? Or is it simply a statement for John to take care of his mother because she is widowed? It is thought by some early Christians that Mary stayed with John at Ephesus, which is modern day Turkey.

Verses 28-30 say, After this, when Jesus knew that all was now finished, he said (in order to fulfill the scriptures), "I am thirsty (Ps 69:21, 22:15)." A jar full of sour wine was standing there. So they put a sponge full of the wine on a branch of hyssop and held it to his mouth. (This is the thin bitter drink of the soldiers. The hyssop plant sprinkled Israelite doors with the saving blood of the Passover lamb in Ex 12:22.) When Jesus received the wine, he said, "It is finished." Then he bowed his head and gave up his spirit.

What is finished is all that God had sent him to finish for the redemption of Israel and the world. In Jewish thinking individuals are redeemed as part of Israel and being part of the covenant. Contrary to thinking in the western world, in Jewish thinking individuals are redeemed in relation to the whole. As sinful humans they will eventually be created with new resurrected bodies as will the heaven and the earth be created anew. The Gospel of John is all about transformation and new creation.

Verses 31-34 say, Since it was the day of Preparation, the Jews did not want the bodies left on the cross during the sabbath, especially because that sabbath was a day of great solemnity. (In the other gospels his death occurs on the day of Passover.) So they asked Pilate to have the legs of the crucified men broken and the bodies removed. Then the soldiers came and broke the legs of the first and of the other who had been crucified with him. But when they came to Jesus and saw that he was already dead, they did not break his legs. (Breaking the legs was an act of mercy. It prevented the one being crucified from pushing up to get a breath. It led to quick suffocation.) Instead, one of the soldiers pierced his side with a spear, and at once blood and water came out. (This shows that Jesus is dead. John is also probably using this to symbolize that water and blood will become for the church the sacraments of baptism and the Eucharist.)

Verses 35-37 say, He who saw this has testified so that you also may believe. His testimony is true, and he knows that he tells the truth. These things occurred so that the scripture might be fulfilled. "None of his bones shall be broken." And again another passage of scripture says, "They will look on the one they have pierced." (These verses are from a combination of Ps 34:20, Ex 12:46, Num 9:12. The last one is Zech 12:10.)

Verses 38-42 say, After these things, Joseph of Arimathea, who was a disciple of Jesus, though a secret one because of his fear of the Jews, asked Pilate to let him take away the body of Jesus. Pilate gave him permission; so he came and removed his body. Nicodemus, who had at first come to Jesus by night, (but now in the light) also came, bringing a mixture of myrrh and aloes, weighing about a hundred pounds. They took the body of Jesus and wrapped it with the spices in linen cloths, according to the burial system of the Jews.

Now there was a garden in the place where he was crucified, and in the garden there was a new tomb in which no one had ever been laid. And so, because it was the Jewish day of Preparation, and the tomb was nearby, they laid Jesus there.

At this point the reader should read Isaiah chapters 40, 42, 49, 50, 52, 53 and 55. Christians believe these chapters show why the early Christians were able to associate Jesus with what was prophesied in the Old Testament. It also gives some background and meaning to the cross. In the New Testament Isaiah is the most quoted book of the prophets.

Chapter 20:1-2 says, Early on the first day of the week, while it was still dark, Mary Magdalene came to the tomb and saw that the stone had been removed from the tomb. (She probably comes from Magdala on the western shore of the Sea of Galilee.) So she ran and went to Simon Peter and the other disciple, the one whom Jesus loved, (John) and said to them, "They have taken the Lord out of the tomb, and we do not know where they have laid him."

Verses 3-10 say, Then Peter and the other disciple set out and went toward the tomb. The two were running together, but the other disciple outran Peter and reached the tomb first. He bent down to look in and saw the linen wrappings lying there, but he did not go in. Then Simon Peter came, following him, and went into the tomb. He saw the linen wrappings lying there, and the cloth that had been on Jesus head, not lying with the linen wrappings but rolled up in a place by itself. (This indicates that the body was not stolen, and that he had passed through the grave clothes without unwrapping them.) Then the other disciple who reached the tomb first, also went in, and he saw and believed; for as yet they did not understand the scripture, that he must rise from the dead. Then the disciples returned to their homes.

Verse 7 says that the head cloth was rolled up and lying in a separate place. The NIV and the NKJV versions translate rolled up as folded. Folded is a more interesting translation for the following reason. In the master and slave relationship after the slave set the dining table, he would leave while the master ate. When the master was finished, he would roll up his napkin and lay it on the table, but if he left the table and folded the napkin that was a sign to the slave that he was not finished and would return. Is the writer saying Jesus will return by mentioning the cloth was folded?

Verses 11-15 say, Mary stood weeping outside the tomb. As she wept, she bent over to look in the tomb; and she saw two angels in white, sitting where the body of Jesus had been lying, one at the head and the other at the feet. They said to her, "Woman, why are you weeping?" She said to them, "They have taken away my Lord, and I do not know where they have laid him." When she had said this, she turned around and saw Jesus standing there, but she did not know it was Jesus. Jesus said to her, "Woman, why are you weeping? Whom are you looking for?" Supposing him to be the gardener, she said to him, "Sir, if you have carried him away, tell me where you have laid him, and I will take him away."

In verses 16-18 Jesus said to her, "Mary!" She turned and said to him in Hebrew, "Rabbouni!" (Rabbouni means Teacher.) Jesus said to her, "Do not hold on to me, because I have not yet ascended to the Father. (A new relationship begins with him when he ascends to the Father, so do not cling to old patterns. This also indicates he is not a ghost.) But go to my brothers and say to them, 'I am ascending to my Father and to your Father, to my God and your God.' " Mary Magdalene went and announced to the disciples, "I have seen the Lord"; and she told them that he had said these things to her. (It is interesting that in Mt 27:9-10 his disciples grabbed his feet and worshiped him, and he did not stop them.)

Verses 19-23 say, When it was evening on that day, the first day of the week, and the doors of the house where the disciples had met were locked for fear of the Jews, Jesus came and stood among them and said, "Peace be with you." After he said this, he showed them his hands and his side. Then the disciples rejoiced when they saw the Lord. Jesus said to them again, "Peace be with you." As the Father has sent me, so I send you." When he had said this, he breathed on them and said to them, "Receive the Holy Spirit. If you forgive the sins of any, they are forgiven them; if you retain the sins of any, they are retained." (To the apostles he gives the Spirit to establish the church. The church's power to forgive and retain sins is a major part of its message in being sent out, as is peace with God and peace with each other and the world.)

Verses 24-29 say, But Thomas (who was called the Twin), one of the twelve, was not with them when Jesus came. So the other disciples told him, "We have seen the Lord." But he said to them, "Unless I see the mark of the nails in his hands, and put my finger in the mark of the nails and my hand in his side, I will not believe." A week later his disciples were again in the house, and Thomas was with them. Although the doors were shut, Jesus came and stood among them and said, "Peace be with you." Then he said to Thomas, "Put your finger here and see my hands. Reach out your hand and put it in my side. Do not doubt but believe." Thomas answered him, "My Lord and my God!" Jesus said to him, "Have you believed because you have seen me? Blessed are those who have not seen and yet have come to believe." (The answer by Thomas is the theme for John. Jesus is both Lord and God.)

Verses 30-31 say, Now Jesus did many other signs in the presence of his disciples, which are not written in this book. But these are written so that you may come to believe that Jesus is the Messiah, the Son of God, and that through believing you may have life in his name. (This states the purpose of the Gospel of John.)

Chapter 21:1-3 says, After these things Jesus showed himself again to the disciples by the Sea of Tiberias; (also called Sea of Galilee) and he showed himself in this way. Gathered there together were Simon Peter, Thomas called the Twin, Nathanael of Cana in Galilee, the sons of Zebedee, and two others of his disciples. Simon Peter said to them, "I am going fishing." They said to him, "We will go with you." They went out and got into the boat, but that night they caught nothing.

Verses 4-8 say, Just after daybreak, Jesus stood on the beach; but the disciples did not know it was Jesus. Jesus said to them, "Children, you have no fish, have you?" They answered him, "No." He said to them, "Cast the net to the right side of the boat, and you will find some." So they cast it, and now they were not able to haul it in because there were so many fish. That disciple whom Jesus loved said to Peter, "It is the Lord!" When Simon Peter heard that it was the Lord, he put on some clothes, for he was naked (probably means he wore only a loin cloth), and jumped into the sea. But the other disciples came in the boat, dragging the net full of fish, for they were not far from the land, only about a hundred yards off.

Verses 9-11 say, When they had gone ashore, they saw a charcoal fire there, with fish on it, and bread. Jesus said to them, "Bring some of the fish that you have just caught." So Simon Peter went aboard and hauled the net ashore, full of large fish, a hundred fifty-three of them; and though there were so many, the net was not torn.

Why 153 fish? Knowing John's writing style, it is symbolism for something. Some think the number represents in some way the world or the world throughout time. Possibly, it is to indicate that as

Jesus fed them, they are also to feed the world through the church, both spiritually and physically.

Verses 12-14 say, Jesus said to them, "Come and have breakfast." Now none of the disciples dared to ask him, "Who are you?" because they knew it was the Lord. Jesus came and took the bread and gave it to them, and did the same to the fish. This was now the third time that Jesus appeared to the disciples after he was raised from the dead.

Verses 15-19 say, When they had finished breakfast, Jesus said to Simon Peter, "Simon son of John, do you love me more than these?" He said to him, "Yes, Lord; you know that I love you." Jesus said to him, "Feed my sheep." A second time he said to him, "Simon son of John, do you love me?" He said to him, "Yes, Lord, you know that I love you." Jesus said to him, "Tend my sheep." He said to him a third time, "Simon son of John, do you love me?" Peter felt hurt because he said to him the third time, "Do you love me?" And he said to him, "Lord, you know everything; you know that I love you." Jesus said to him, "Feed my sheep."

Peter had denied him three times, so Jesus allows him to reverse himself three times. Throughout Scripture Peter is the leader, and his name always appears first in lists of Apostles. Is Peter now officially being made the leader throughout time, setting in motion the office of Peter? The Roman Catholics believe so, but Protestants disagree. The idea behind Roman Catholic thinking is that every group needs a leader. The Orthodox Catholic Church titles their leader as the first among equals, and he does not have nearly the power as the Roman Catholic Pope.

In verse 18 Jesus says to Peter, "Very truly, I tell you, when you were younger, you used to fasten your own belt and go wherever you wished. But when you are old, you will stretch out your hands, and someone else will fasten a belt around you and take you where you do not wish to go." He said this to indicate the kind of death by which he would glorify God. After this he said to him, "Follow me." (Peter is to follow Jesus and be crucified. Early Christian writers claim that Peter was martyred under Emperor Nero between 64-68 AD.)

Verses 20-23 say, Peter turned and saw the disciple whom Jesus loved following them; he was the one that reclined next to Jesus at the supper and said, "Lord, who is it that is going to betray you?" When Peter saw him, he said to Jesus, "Lord, what about him?" Jesus said to him, "If it is my will if he remain until I come, what is that to you? Follow me!" So the rumor spread in the community that this disciple would not die. Yet Jesus did not say to him that he would not die, but "If it is my will that he remain until I come, what is that to you?"

Verses 24-25 say, This is the disciple who is testifying to these things and has written them, and we know that his testimony is true. But there are also many other things, that Jesus did, if everyone of them were written down, I suppose that the world itself could not contain the books that would be written.

This tells us that the Gospel of John as well as the other gospels are not written to tell us everything we would like to know, or even to give us an exact and complete history. They are simply written as a testimony. They are written for the purpose John stated in 20:31 "But these are written so that you may come to believe that Jesus is the Messiah, the Son of God."

This ends John. The resurrection accounts are inspired testimonies of faith reflecting on his crucifixion and resurrection. They are not meant to prove anything other than to remember and reflect upon their experiences with Jesus and to encourage others to have faith. There is no doubt in their minds concerning Jesus as a real person and rising from the dead in a bodily form. In the Gospel of John, Jesus dies in simple dignity in total control of the situation, and then rises from the dead, then appears to them at numerous times. The Gospel of John stresses the unity of God. Jesus and the Father are one through which the Holy Spirit is sent to lead and guide those who will advance the church. It is an excellent book in which to meditate upon the truths of God.

At the end of Mark there is a special exercise comparing the four Gospel accounts of the resurrection, which is helpful in understanding interpretation issues. There is no question about the four Gospels disagreeing in many details as that exercise shows. They disagree in other areas also. For example, the arrangement and selection of materials differ. Jesus baptism is not reported in all of the Gospels. The prodigal son, the good Samaritan, Lazarus and the poor homeless man, the sheep and the goats, among others are each mentioned only one time each and in different Gospels.

There are numerous differences in the Synoptics, but the greatest disagreement in details is between the Synoptics and John. But what is important is that they all agree on the basic story and its essentials. This is divine inspiration and human analysis with its imperfections working together. Or one can say it is divine inspiration, even as God allowed different people to express inspired, theological truths in their different and imperfect ways.

Luke Timothy Johnson (1996, 107-111) mentions numerous differences. He states that the narrative sequence between John and the Synoptics is very different. In John the ministry of Jesus is one year and mainly in Judea. In the Synoptics Jesus ministers for three years mainly in Galilee. In John Jesus cleanses the temple at the beginning of his ministry, but in the Synoptics he does it at the end. In John Jesus dies on the day of preparation for the Passover, but in the Synoptics he dies on the day of Passover. In John Jesus has followers with him at the cross, but in the Synoptics he is by himself. In John the empty tomb story involves Peter and John. In the Synoptics it is a group of women at the empty tomb. In John Jesus does different things and speaks in a different way from what he does in the Synoptics. In John Jesus works no exorcisms. Instead he works seven signs. In the Synoptics Jesus' exorcisms are connected to the proclamation of the kingdom. John speaks none of the parables that are all through the Synoptics. In John the controversies with the opponents often lead to long discourses, but in the Synoptics the controversies are short with a brief pronouncement made.

These are just a few of the differences. The exercise at the end of Mark deals with the resurrection accounts, but we could also include the trial and crucifixion of Jesus, some of the parables, possibly the birth accounts and some of the incidents of Jesus and people. Through all of this God is allowing humans to present the story of Jesus in different ways and from their personal perspective to appeal to different people located in different situations. Remember Jesus did not write anything, and the writers are basically giving their testimony of who Jesus is. All of these differences confirm to this author that the theological message is inspired. Otherwise, they would have smoothed out all the differences.

As stated previously ancient people did not write history as we modern people do. Keep in mind the main purpose of the Gospels is not a detailed history or a biography, even though they are a history and biography in the ancient sense. For those of us living today, the Gospels, with their basis in history, are primarily about theology, and to remember who Jesus is, and what he taught. What is important is that Jesus is real. From him we learn the many truths of God and ways of presenting them that can not be contained in the writing of any one person. We learn these truths in order to better serve God. The thinking that every word is infallibly given by God is a false theory developed by fundamentalists from a philosophy developed a couple of hundred years ago. Their purpose to prove the Bible as God's word was noble, but their methodology was and is still flawed. All scripture is inspired of God as 2 Timothy 3:16-17 says, but that fundamentalist theory can not be deduced from it as a careful reading of Scripture shows.

From reading Scripture we learn who God is, who we are, how he wants us to relate to him, how he wants us to relate to each other, and to all of God's good creation. We learn the virtues and values that please God and vices that do not, we learn about God's vision for his people and the world he created, and we learn that because of his incarnation, life, crucifixion, resurrection, and then sending his Spirit, people find the meaning and purpose for which they were created.

In looking at the story of Jesus in all the Gospels, we do see a consistent pattern and meaning. There is a very strong consistency about who he is and how to think and live life. Jesus came as God's unique Son to be a mentor to all his people, to show his people what life, suffering, and death is about, as well as how to live abundantly, as he established the beginning of his kingdom, and died for the sins of humankind.

Col 1:13-14 say, He has rescued us from the power of darkness and transferred us into the kingdom of his beloved Son in whom we have redemption, the forgiveness of sins. Rev 1:6 says, To him who loved us and freed us from our sins by his blood, and made us to be a kingdom, priests serving his God and Father, to him be glory and dominion forever and ever. Amen.

He gathered his people to continue his mission of growing the kingdom, (Your kingdom come. Your will be done in earth as it is in heaven.) welcoming everyone, especially the worst sinners and those not accepted by the people of wealth, power, and the status quo. In the meantime he calls the latter to join him in his mission. All those he calls are to be transformed as they become his eyes, ears, mouth, hands, and feet, having the mind and spirit of Christ, living in trust and obedience to him, as they wait for him to transform all things.

In 1 Cor 1:26-31 the Apostle Paul reminds everyone of whom God primarily calls, and the reason for it when he says, not many of you were wise by human standards, not many were powerful, not many were of noble birth. But God chose what is foolish in the world (foolish according to the world's wisdom) to shame the wise (those who are wise in the ways of the world); God chose what was weak in the world (according to the world's wisdom) to shame the strong (the strong in the eyes of the world); God chose what is low and despised in the world, things that are not, (not great according to the world's standards) to reduce to nothing things that are (considered great in the world), so that no one might boast on the presence of God. He is the source of your life in Christ Jesus, who became for us wisdom from God, and righteousness, sanctification, and redemption, in order that, as it is written, "Let the one who boasts, boast in the Lord."

His lowly people are called to live as he lived for the well being and service of others. They are called to participate in growing his kingdom as it breaks more fully into the world, growing like a mustard seed, transforming individuals and the world. The pattern of the Messiah is to be the pattern for being his disciple, and this means being willing to suffer mentally and/or physically for the things he suffered as they represent his wisdom and his life.

As 2 Cor 5:20-21 says, we are ambassadors for Christ, since God is making his appeal through us; we entreat you on behalf of Christ be reconciled to God. For our sake he made him to be sin who knew no sin, so that in him we might become the righteousness of God. If this pattern is not the direction of his church and its people then they are not even attempting to be his disciples.

So who is Jesus, and what did he teach? Jesus is the resurrected Lord who is now alive and present through the Holy Spirit. His transforming Spirit is now active in the church community and in the world transforming individuals, nations, institutions, and creation according to his thinking and actions. Jesus is the one who by the Spirit makes the lives of believers begin to model and live a life of faithful obedience to God and loving service to the poor, disadvantaged, and anyone in need, and willing to stand for them against the power and wealth of the world and its wisdom. This is what his life is to mean to his people. When those things are not done, one has abandoned the meaning and purpose of the four Gospels. If we in the church call ourselves followers of Christ, then we ought to believe and do what he did.

When the priority for Christians is to live according to the wisdom of the world expressed in a life of selfish individualism and no concern for the common good, living a life devoted to materialism, consumerism, guns, greed, outlandish profits, and destruction of the environment, while being overly concerned with the protection of one's things, and preoccupation of personal rights, the Gospels are being distorted. Such distortion of Christianity can find no harsher critic, no more radical rejecter, than the Jesus found in the Gospels, the Jesus who was himself emptied out for the well being of others and called his followers to do the same.

The path to transformation begins with a decision of priorities, his or ours. Thus if we and the church claim to be disciples of Christ and claim to represent his interests, we must make his interests and his priorities ours, and that includes the political, economic, and social implications of his teachings.

The church is not to be involved itself in power politics, but it is to challenge power politics in the name of Christ and his kingdom, not to gain power, but to see that power works for what Christ stood for and against. God is Lord of all not just our so-called spiritual life. That is the implication of the kingdom breaking into the real world. One must stand with God's word, and be willing to stand with and for the things he stood for, as well as take the side of those with whom Jesus sided. In the process of doing so, when suffering (mental or physical) comes, one must be willing to suffer as he suffered. The early Christians took this challenge upon themselves. The question for his followers today is: Are the followers of Jesus today willing to do the same?

THE NONCANONICAL GOSPELS

C anon is a term biblical scholars use to determine the books that are accepted by the church as Scripture. There were other writings circulating in the first four hundred years of Christianity. Why were some selected and others ignored? There are numerous answers, but a primary one centers on whether or not the writings agree with the teachings of the apostles.

There are over twenty other gospels that survived but did not make it into the New Testament, ranging in date over a period of six hundred years. Most of them are highly legendary, and if one reads them it becomes quite obvious why they did not pass the test. They can be categorized as either narrative gospels, which include stories of Jesus' words and actions, or sayings gospels, which focus on his teachings. For example the Gospel of Peter is a fragmentary narrative of Jesus' trial, death, and resurrection, including Jesus' miraculous emergence from the tomb. The Gospel of Thomas is a sayings gospel that includes 114 sayings with the right interpretation that brings eternal life.

Many of the writings that were rejected were part of one of the earliest Christian heresies known as *Gnosticism*. Some of the major ideas of the Gnostics are the following. There is a good god and an evil god. Matter is inherently evil; spirit is good. Therefore, Jesus, a good man, did not have a body. He only appeared to have a body. He was spirit only, like a ghost. He did not suffer because he did not have a body, and he did not rise from the dead with a body. Some people in the world are pure matter, but they are like the animals destined for annihilation. But others like the Gnostics have a spark of the divine within. The goal of the Gnostic religion was to escape from the material trappings of the world to allow the divine spark to return to its original spiritual home. Escape comes only by acquiring the secret knowledge necessary for salvation.

The Greek word for knowledge is *gnosis*. The only way to acquire this knowledge was for a divine emissary to come down from the spiritual realm to instruct one on what they had to know. Christ for these people represented the divine being who came to earth to teach the truth that could lead to salvation. Salvation came to those who understood the secret meaning of the words. A book titled *Lost Scriptures* by Bart Ehrman includes some of the following information, and is a good book for the reader who wants to read the texts in detail.

The Gospel of Thomas is one of the Gnostic gospels. People are fallen spirits who have fallen from the divine realm and have become entrapped in a body. The point of the Gospel of Thomas is that those who learn the secret teachings of Jesus will have eternal life. It is not by believing in his death that one finds salvation but by understanding his words. Many of the sayings found in Matthew, Mark, Luke, and John are found here; others convey the idea that the world is a realm that must be escaped, if one is to find true life.

The body is likened to a set of clothes that must be removed if one is to be saved. Salvation is not something that comes in the future through the kingdom of God. It comes by reuniting the spark within to what it came from in the divine realm. Peter tells Jesus to make Mary leave them, for women are not worthy of life. Jesus told him that he will lead her in order to make her male so she can be like a male, for every woman who makes herself male will enter the kingdom of heaven. Even though matter is not important, the Gospel of Thomas tells women that they must become like men to be saved. This is a gospel that many modern theologians deem very important, including some female theologians, which confounds the mind of this writer. It is an important book for those belonging to a group called the *Jesus Seminar.*

The Gospel of Peter is mentioned by Eusebius and other early church fathers as being heretical. It is a fragment beginning in the middle of a sentence, then ending by breaking off in the middle of a sentence. It deals with the trial, crucifixion, and resurrection. Some parts are the same but some are very different. The Jews are held to be much more responsible for Jesus' death than in the four Gospels. Jesus does not appear to suffer. It also does not make Jesus fully human. There is a bizarre description of Jesus emerging from the tomb, supported by angels as tall as the sky, himself towering above them, with the cross itself coming forth from the tomb. A voice asks if he has preached to those who have already died, and the cross answers, "Yes!"

Another is *The Secret Gospel of Mark.* Mark supposedly produced two versions of his gospel. One was for church members and the other for the spiritually elite who were able to grasp the secret mysteries of the kingdom. The gospel narrates the resurrection of a rich young man whom Jesus initiates into the mystery of the kingdom of God. Another excerpt refers to the resuscitated young man as the youth whom Jesus loved.

The Infancy Gospel of Thomas produces several narratives during the youth of Jesus. They are fictional, fanciful stories taking place between the birth of Jesus and his trip to the temple when he was twelve years old. This gospel shows Jesus on a Sabbath amusing himself by making real sparrows from the clay found in the river. When Joseph tells him he is violating the Sabbath, he claps his hands and sends the sparrows flying off, eliminating the evidence against him. Jesus hexes playmates he does not like, blinds people who criticize his behavior, and curses another youth with premature old age. Later he cures some he afflicted, even resurrecting a boy killed in a fall.

The Gospel of the Nazareans (also Nazarenes). They were Jewish Christians that preferred the book of Matthew since Matthew stressed the Jewish law. This gospel does not include the first two chapters of Matthew, which recorded the events surrounding the birth of Jesus. They did not accept Jesus as being born of a virgin. He was a natural human being who was especially chosen to be the Messiah because God considered him to be more righteous than anyone else.

The Gospel of the Ebonites. This gospel denies the divinity of Jesus saying he was only a human. But they did believe he was God's sacrifice for sin. They were vegetarians because animals had been used as sacrifices. Therefore John the Baptist did not eat locusts and wild honey but pancakes and wild honey.

The Gospel According to the Hebrews. There is much that is Gnostic in this gospel. James the brother of Jesus is important, and said he would not eat bread until Jesus was raised from sleep. Soon afterward the Lord took bread and blessed it and gave it to James telling him to eat because the Son of Man is risen.

The Gospel According to the Egyptians. Sexual activity is condemned as being opposed to the will of God. Ascetic concerns are highlighted. Desire is to be eliminated. Revelation will be complete when people shed the human body, and all thing are restored to that which is one, ultimate unity. This is a Gnostic statement.

The Gospel according to Mary. Mary Magdalene is given a high status among the apostles. In fact Levi says, Jesus loved her more than them. Jesus tells her how the human soul ascends past the four ruling powers or emanations of the world to find eternal life. This is a Gnostic teaching. Mary says that Jesus prepared them to be men. Mary has a vision that says her desire and ignorance has ended, and she is released from this world.

The Gospel of Phillip. This is another Gnostic work. The virgin birth and the resurrection are not to be taken as literal. They are symbolic expressions of a deeper truth. Light and darkness, life and death, the right and the left are one. They cannot separate from one another. Therefore, the good are not good; nor are the evil, evil; nor is life, life; nor is death, death. Most of this Gnostic thinking is still very popular in Far Eastern religions. When one takes on Christ, one is no longer a Christian but Christ himself. Mary Magdalene was Jesus' lover. She was his consort. It was common in the pagan world for gods to have female consorts. Another teaching is that the world came into being through an error.

The Proto-Gospel of James. This gospel narrates events that took place before Jesus birth, although it does include an account of the birth. The author claims to be James the half brother of Jesus. He is assumed to be Joseph's son by a previous marriage. The book provides a legendary account of Mary's birth to a wealthy Jew named Joachim and his wife Anna. An angel appeared to Anna and told her she would give birth to a girl who would be known throughout the world. Anna said she would offer the girl to be a servant of God. She gave birth to her after the sixth month and named her Mary. Jesus was born in a cave in Bethlehem. An unbelieving midwife performed an inspection of Mary and assured her virginity. She was brought up in the temple and married at twelve to Joseph, an old widower chosen miraculously to be her husband. Mary then worked as a seamstress for the curtain in the temple.

The Epistle to the Apostles. This gospel contains a post-resurrection dialogue with Jesus and his followers. Jesus provides them with secret teachings that are different from his public teachings. These secret teachings become the basis for the true religion. This is a Gnostic teaching, but much of the gospel opposes the views of two famous Gnostics, Simon Magnus and Cerinthus. It does teach that the flesh arises with the spirit, and that opposes Gnostic teaching.

The Apocalypse of Peter. This Gnostic writing contains a series of visions Jesus gave to Peter. Jesus issued warnings against the heretics who were the bishops and deacons of the more orthodox churches and their false teaching that Jesus was the Christ who suffered a literal death on the cross. The author claims this teaching is laughable, and he labels its proponents as being blind. Even though Jesus' flesh was killed, Christ himself was far removed from suffering. The living Christ was laughing at the whole proceeding. Jesus was merely an outward appearance just as simple minded Christians are nothing but outward appearances of the living ones who have been fully enlightened by the spiritual truth of the immortal Christ.

Jesus said he is an intellectual spirit filled with radiant light. Our intellectual pleroma unites perfect light with the pure spirit. There will be no grace in any one who is not immortal. Grace will only be in those chosen from an immortal essence that has shown it is able to accept him who gives his abundance. The book ends by stating that when the Savior said these things, Peter came to his senses.

The Second Treatise of the Great Seth. In this Gnostic book Christ himself gives a first hand experience of how he descended into the man Jesus' body, occupied it for a time, and then died only in appearance. Simon the Cyrene was mistakenly crucified in the place of Jesus while Jesus stood by and laughed. The false believers are the more orthodox Christians, who foolishly believe the Jewish Scriptures are true, and that the Creator of the world is the Almighty. The ancient Jews and their God are a laughingstock. Those without gnosis are like dumb animals. They are totally ignorant.

These are just a few excerpts of the type of literature involved in those writings dealing with the gospels that are not included in the canon of Scripture. The uninformed, who do not accept Scripture, because they say there were other writings kept out of the Bible, believe these writings should be on the same level as Scripture. Most readers when informed, are able to see the obvious, and they understand why those gospels are not included as Scripture.

These texts are excluded because they were labeled with an heretical perspective completely out of step with the apostle's teachings. Many of them were also considered fanciful. Sometimes these scriptures are called the *Pseudepigrapha* based on a Greek word that means written under a false name. For example the Gospel of Thomas and Peter were not written by Thomas or Peter. Others call these books the *Apocrypha* meaning hidden books.

This concludes the study of the Gospels. The volume to follow will be titled *Reading and Understanding the Acts of the Apostles, the New Testament Letters, and the Beginning of the Church*. It will be the last volume of the series that begins with *Reading and Understanding the Old Testament: The Foundation of Judaism, Christianity, and Islam*. This is a project to help beginning students read and better understand the content of Scripture, to begin to think about those Scriptures and apply them to daily life, to see scholarship applied in a practical manner without getting swallowed up in scholarship terminology and debates, and then finally to advance their study to a higher level of scholarship.

BIBLIOGRAPHY OF SOURCES

Achtemeier, Paul J. *Inspiration and Authority: Nature and Function of Christian Scripture.* Peabody, MA: Hendrickson Publishers, 1999.

_____. *Jesus and the Miracle Tradition.* Eugene, OR: Wipf and Stock Publishers, 2008.

Achtemeier, Paul J, Joel B. Green, and Marianne Meye Thompson. *Introducing the New Testament: Its Literature and Theology.* Grand Rapids: Wm. B. Eerdmans, 2001.

Achtemeier, Paul J. and Robert J. Karris, George W. MacRae, and Donald Senior. *Invitation to the Gospels.* Mahwah, NJ: Paulist Press, 2002.

Aland, Kurt, ed. *Synopsis Parallels of the Four Gospels.* New York: United Bible Societies, 1985.

Alter, Robert. *The Five Books of Moses.* New York: W. W. Norton, 2004.

Aguilar, Jose Victor, and Miguel Cavada. *Ten Plagues of Globalization.* Trans. by Kathy Ogle. Washington, DC: Epica, 2002.

Armstrong, Dave. *The Catholic Verses.* Manchester, NH: Sophia Institute Press, 2004.

Bailey, Kenneth E. *Poet and Peasant: a Literary-cultural Approach to the Parables in Luke*. Grand Rapids: Wm. B.Eerdmans, 1976.

_____. *Through Peasant Eyes*. Grand Rapids: Wm B. Eerdmans, 1980.

Baillie, D. M. *God Was in Christ*. New York: Charles Scribner's Sons, 1948.

Baker, Mark W. *Jesus the Greatest Therapist Who Ever Lived*. New York: HarperOne, 2007.

Barbour, Ian G. *Issues in Science and Religion*. London: SCM, 1966.

Barth, Karl. *Church Dogmatics*. 4 vols. Edinburgh: T. & T. Clark, 1936-1969.

Beasley-Murray, G. R. *Jesus and the Kingdom of God*. Grand Rapids: Wm. B. Eerdmans, 1986.

Beach, Waldo. *Christian Ethics in the Protestant Tradition*. Atlanta: John Knox, 1988.

Bellah, Robert N., Richard Madsen, William M. Sullivan, Ann Swidler, and Steven M. Tipton. *Habits of the Heart: Individualism and Commitment in American Life*. Updated Edition. Los Angeles,and Berkeley: University of California Press, 1996.

Berkhof, Hendrikus. *Christ and the Powers*. London: SPCK, 1966.

Bohr, David. *Catholic Moral Tradition*. Huntingdon, IN: Our Sunday Visitor, 1990.

Borg, Marcus J. *Jesus, A New Vision: Spirit, Culture, and the Life of Discipleship*. San Francisco: HarperCollins, 1987.

_____. *Reading the Bible Again for the First Time: Taking the Bible Seriously but not Literally*. San Francisco: HarperCollins, 2001.

Borg, Marcus J., and N. T. Wright. *The Meaning of Jesus: Two Visions.* San Francisco: HarperCollins, 1999.

Bowley, James E. *Living Traditions of the Bible: Scripture in Jewish, Christian, and, Muslim Practice.* St. Louis, MO: Chalice Press, 1999.

Brettler, Marc Zvi. *How to Read the Jewish Bible.* New York: Oxford University Press, 2005.

Brown, Raymond E. The Gospel According to John. 2 vols. Garden City, New York: Doubleday,1966.

_____. *The Critical Meaning of the Bible.* New York: Paulist Press, 1981.

_____. *A Risen Christ in Eastertime: Essays on the Gospel Narratives of the Resurrection.* Collegeville, MN: Liturgical Press, 1991.

_____. *An Introduction to Christology.* Mahweh, NJ: Paulist Press, 1991.

_____. *The Birth of the Messiah: A Commentary on the Infancy Narratives in the Gospels of Matthew and Luke.* New York: Doubleday, 1993.

Brown, Robert McAfee. *The Spirit of Protestantism.* New York: Oxford University Press, 1965.

Brueggemann, Walter. *The Prophetic Imagination.* Philadelphia: Fortress Press, 1978.

Bultman, Rudolf. *The History of the Synoptic Tradition.* ET Oxford: Blackwell, 1963.

Burgess, John P. *Why Scripture Matters: Reading the Bible in a Time of Church Conflict.* Louisville: Westminster John Knox Press, 1998.

Caird, G. B. *Principalities and Powers.* Oxford: Clarendon Press, 1956.

_____. *The Language and Imagery of the Bible.* London: Duckworth, 1980.

Catholic Study Bible of the New American Bible. Edited by Donald Senior, et al. New York: Oxford University Press, 1990.

Charlesworth, J. H., ed. *Jesus and the Dead Sea Scrolls.* New York: Doubleday, 1992.

Childs, Brevard S. *Biblical Theology of the Old and New Testaments: Theological Reflection on the Christian Bible.* Minneapolis: Fortress Press, 1992.

Cohen, A. *Everyman's Talmud.* New York: Schocken Books, 1975.

Collegeville Bible Commentary. Edited by Dianne Bergant, and Robert J. Karris. Collegeville, MN: The Liturgical Press, 1989.

Cone, James. *Risks of Faith: The Emergence of a Black Theology of Liberation.* Boston: Beacon Press, 1999.

Corley, Jeremy. *Unlocking the Gospels: Five Keys for Biblical Interpretation.* Collegeville, MN: Liturgical Press, 2004.

Countryman, L. William. *Biblical Authority or Biblical Tyranny?* Harrisburg, PA: Trinity Press International, 1994.

Crossan, John Dominic. *The Historical Jesus: The Life of a Mediterranean Jewish Peasant.* San Francisco: Harper, 1991.

Dodd, C. H. *The Founder of Christianity.* New York: Macmillan, 1970.

Dunn, James D. G. *Unity and Diversity in the New Testament.* London: SCM, 1990.

_____. The Theology of Paul the Apostle. Grand Rapids: Wm. B. Eerdmans, 1998.

_____. *Christianity in the Making: Jesus Remembered.* Grand Rapids: Wm. B. Eerdmans, 2003.

Ehrman, Bart D. *The New Testament: An Historical Introduction to the Early Christian Writings.* 2nd ed. New York: Oxford University Press, 2000.

_____. *Lost Scriptures: Books that Did Not Make It into the New Testament.* New York: Oxford University Press, 2003.

Fackre, Gabriel. *The Christian Story: A Narrative Interpretation of Basic Christian Doctrine,* vol. 1. Grand Rapids: William B. Eerdmans, 1978.

_____. *The Christian Story: Authority of Scripture in the Church for the World,* vol. 2. Grand Rapids: William B. Eerdmans, 1987.

Fee, Gordon D., and Douglas Stuart. *How to Read the Bible for all its Worth.* Grand Rapids: Zondervan, 2003.

Fitzmyer, Joseph. *A Christological Catechism* (New Edition). New York: Paulist Press, 1977.

Ford, Richard Q. *The Parables of Jesus: Recovering the Art of Listening.* Minneapolis: Fortress Press, 1997.

Forell, George W. *The Protestant Faith.* Philadelphia: Fortress Press, 1975.

Frank, Harry Thomas. *Atlas of the Bible Lands.* Maplewood, NJ: Hammond Incorporated, 1990.

Goergen, Donald. *The Mission and Ministry of Jesus.* Wilmington: Michael Glazier, 1986.

Grady, John F. *Models of Jesus Revisited.* Mahweh, NJ: Paulist Press, 1984.

Grassi, Joseph A. *Rediscovering the Impact of Jesus' Death: Clues From the Gospel Audiences.* Kansas City: Sheed & Ward, 1987.

Greenleaf, Robert. *Servant Leadership.* New York: Paulist Press, 1977.

Gregg, Steve, ed. *Revelation: Four Views A Parallel Commentary.* Nashville: Thomas Nelson Publishers, 1997.

Griffith-Jones, Robin. *The Four Witnesses: The Rebel, the Rabbi, the Chronicler, and the Mystic.* San Francisco: HarperCollins, 2000.

Gross, David C. *1001 Questions and Answers About Judaism.* New York: Hippocrene Books, 1990.

Groothuis, Douglas R. *Jesus in An Age of Controversy.* Eugene, Oregon: Harvest House Publishers, 1996.

Gula, Richard M. *Reason Informed by Faith: Foundations of Catholic Morality.* Mahweh, NJ: Paulist Press, 1989.

Gustafson, James M. *Protestant and Roman Catholic Ethics: Prospects for Rapprochement.* Chicago: University of Chicago Press, 1978.

Hare, Douglas R. A. *The Son of Man Tradition.* Minneapolis: Fortress Press, 1990.

Harper Collins Study Bible: New Revised Standard Version With the Apocryphal/ Deuterocanonical Books. Edited by Wayne A. Meeks, et al. New York: Harper Collins Publishers, 1993.

Harrington, Donald J. *Interpreting the New Testament.* Wilmington, Delaware: Michael Glazier, Inc., 1983.

Hays, Richard B. *The Moral Vision of the New Testament: A Contemporary Introduction to New Testament Ethics.* San Francisco: HarperCollins, 1996.

Hauer, Christian, William A. Young. *An Introduction to the Bible: A Journey Into Three Worlds.* Englewood Cliffs, NJ: Prentice Hall, 1994.

Hauerwas, Stanley. *Unleashing the Scriptures: Freeing the Bible from Captivity to America.* Nashville: Abingdon Press, 1993.

Hendricks, Obery M., Jr. *The Politics of Jesus.* New York: Doubleday, 2006.

Hertzberg, Arthur. *Judaism*. New York: Simon & Schuster/ Touchstone, 1991.

Hill, Brennan R. *Jesus The Christ: Contemporary Perspectives*. Mystic, CT: Twenty-Third Publications, 2004.

Hooker, Morna D. *The Signs of a Prophet: The Prophetic Actions of Jesus*. Harrisburg, PA: Trinity Press International, 1997.

Horsley, Richard A. *Archeology, History, and Society in Galilee: The Social Context of Jesus and the Rabbis*. Valley Forge: Trinity, 1996.

_____. *Jesus and Empire: The Kingdom of God and the New World Disorder*. Minneapolis: Fortress Press, 2003.

_____. *The Liberation of Christmas: The Infancy Narratives in Social Context*. New York: Crossroads, 1993.

_____. *Covenant Economics: A Biblical Vision of Justice for All*. Louisville: John Knox Press, 2009.

Jeremias, Joachim. *The Parables of Jesus*. Trans. by S. H. Hooke. London: SCM Press, 1963.

_____. *Jerusalem in the time of Jesus: An Investigation into Economic and Social Conditions during the New Testament Period*. Philadelphia: Fortress Press, 1969.

Johnson, Elizabeth A. *Consider Jesus: Waves of Renewal in Christology*. New York: Crossroads, 1990.

Johnson, Luke Timothy. *Sharing Possessions*. Minneapolis: Fortress Press, 1986.

_____. *Faith's Freedom*. Minneapolis: Fortress Press, 1990.

_____. *The Real Jesus: The Misguided Quest for the Historical Jesus and the Truth of the Traditional Gospels*. San Fransisco: HarperCollins Publishers, 1996.

_____. *Religious Experience in Earliest Christianity*. Minneapolis: Fortress Press, 1998

_____. *The Writings of the New Testament: An Interpretation*. Minneapolis: Fortress Press, 1999.

Kasper, Walter. *Jesus the Christ*. New York: Paulist Press, 1976.

Kee, Harold Clark. *Medicine, Miracle, and Magic in New Testament Times*. New York: Cambridge University Press, 1986.

Kugel, James L. *How to Read the Bible: A Guide to Scripture: Then and Now*. New York: Free Press, 2007.

Kung, Hans. *On Being a Christian*. Garden City, NY: Doubleday, 1984.

Lane, Edmund. *Do Not Be Afraid, I Am With You*. New York: Alba House. 1991.

Lane, Thomas B. *Reading and Understanding the Old Testament; The Foundation of Judaism, Christianity, and Islam*. Parker, CO: Outskirts Press, 2010.

Latourette, Kenneth Scott. *A History of Christianity Volume 1: to AD 1500*. Revised Edition. New York: Harpercollins, 1975.

_____. *A History of Christianity Volume 2: 1500-1975*. Revised Edition. New York: Harpercollins, 1975.

Lewis, C. S. *Mere Christianity*. New York: The Macmillan Company, 1970.

Malina, Bruce. *The Social Gospel of Jesus: The Kingdom of God in Mediterranean Perspective*. Minneapolis: Fortress Press, 2001.

Marsden, George M. *Fundamentalism and American Culture*. NY: Oxford University Press, 2006.

BIBLIOGRAPHY OF SOURCES

Marty, Martin E., and R. Scott Appleby. *The Glory and the Power: The Fundamentalist Challenge to the Modern World*. Boston: Beacon Press, 1992.

_____. eds. *Fundamentalisms Comprehended*. Chicago: University Chicago Press, 1993.

Macquarrie, John. *Christology Revisited*. Harrisburg, PA: Trinity Press, 1998.

Mc Brien, Richard P. *Catholicism*. New York: HarperCollins, 1994.

McFague, Sallie. *Models of God: Theology for an Ecological, Nuclear Age*. Philadelphia: Fortress Press, 1987.

McLaren, Brian D. *The Secret Message of Jesus*. Nashville: Thomas Nelson Publishers, 2006.

Meier, John P. *A Marginal Jew: Rethinking the Historical Jesus*. 3 vols. New York: Doubleday, 1991-2001.

Most, William G. *The Thought of St. Paul: A Commentary on the Pauline Epistles*. Front Royal, VA: Christendom Press, 1994.

Mott, Stephen Charles. *Biblical Ethics and Social Change*. New York: Oxford University Press, 1982.

Mouw, Richard. *Politics and the Biblical Drama*. Grand Rapids: Wm B. Eerdmans, 1976.

Muggeridge, Malcom. *Something Beautiful for God*. New York: Harper & Row, 1971.

Murphy, Frederick J. *The Religious World of Jesus: An Introduction to Second Temple Palestinian Judaism*. Nashville: Abingdon Press, 1991.

National Council of Catholic Bishops. *Economic Justice For All: Catholic Social Teaching and the U. S. Economy*. Washington, DC: USCC Publications, 1986.

Nelson, James B., and Jo Anne Smith Rohricht. *Human Medicine: Ethical Perspectives on Today's Medical Issues.* Minneapolis, MN: Augsburg, 1984.

Neusner, Jacob. *A Rabbi Talks With Jesus.* Montreal: McGill-Queen's University Press, 2000.

New Interpreter's Bible: A Commentary in Twelve Volumes. Edited by Leander E. Keck. Nashville: Abingdon Press, 2003.

New Interpreter's Dictionary of the Bible. Edited by Katharine Doob Sakenfeld. Nashville: Abingdon Press, 2008.

New Jerome Biblical Commentary. Edited by Raymond E. Brown, Joseph R. Fitzmyer, and Roland E. Murphy. Englewood Cliffs: Prentice Hall, 1990.

New Oxford Annotated Bible With the Apocryphal/Deuterocanonical Books. Edited by Bruce M. Metzger and Roland E. Murphy. New York: University Press, 1991.

New World Dictionary-Concordance to the New American Bible. Iowa Falls, IA: World Publishing, 1990.

NRSV Exhaustive Concordance: Includes the Apocryphal and Deuterocanonical Books. Nashville: Thomas Nelson Publications, 1991.

New American Bible: The Catholic Study Bible. New York: Oxford University Press, 1990.

New Bible Dictionary. 2nd edition. Wheaton, IL: Tyndale House Publishers, 1987.

O' Brien, David, and Thomas A. Shannon. *Introduction to Roman Catholic Social Theology. Renewing the Earth: Catholic Documents on Peace, Justice, and Liberation.* Garden City, NJ: Doubleday, 1977.

_____. *Catholic Social Thought. A Documentary Heritage.* Maryknoll, NY: Orbis Books, 2010.

O' Connell, Timothy E. *Principles For a Catholic Morality.* San Francisco: HarperCollins Publishers, 1990.

O'Collins, Gerald. *Interpreting the Resurrection:Examining the Major Problems.* New York: Paulist Press, 1988.

O' Donnel, Thomas J., S J. *Medicine and Christian Morality.* New York: Alba House, 1976.

O'Donovan, Oliver. *The Desire of the Nations: Rediscovering the Roots of Political Theology.* Cambridge: Cambridge University Press, 1996.

Ogletree, Thomas W. *The Use of the Bible in Christian Ethics.* Philadelphia: Fortress Press, 1983.

Otto, David. *The Miracles of Jesus.* Nashville: Abingdon Press, 2000.

Pelikan, Jaroslav. *The Emergence of the Catholic Tradition (100-600), Vol 1* of *The Christian Tradition: A History of the Development of Doctrine.* Chicago: University of Chicago Press, 1971.

Pentateuch and Haftorah. Edited by J. H. Hertz. London: Soncino Press, 1968.

Perkins, Pheme. *Reading the New Testament.* Mahwah, NJ: Paulist Press, 1988.

Pilch, John J. *Choosing a Bible Translation.* Collegeville, MN: Liturgical Press, 2000.

Plotz, David. *Good Book.* New York: HarperCollins, 2009.

Pope Benedict XVI (Joseph Ratzinger). *Jesus of Nazareth.* New York: Doubleday, 2007.

_____. *Saint Paul the Apostle.* Huntingdon, IN: Our Sunday Visitor, 2009.

Presbyterian Understanding and Use of Holy Scripture. Louisville, KY: Office of the General Assembly, 1983.

Pontifical Biblical Commission. *The Interpretation of the Bible in the Church.* Washington, DC: U.S. Catholic Conference, 1994.

Raush, Thomas P. *Who is Jesus?* Collegeville, MN: Liturgical Press, 2003.

Richards, H. J. *The First Christmas: What Really Happened?* Mystic, CT: Twenty Third Publications, 1986.

Robinson, George. *Essential Judaism.* New York: Pocket Books, a division of Simon & Schuster, 2000.

Rogers, Jack B., and Donald K. McKim. *The Authority and Interpretation of the Bible: An Historical Approach.* San Francisco: Harper & Row, Publishers, 1979.

Sanders, E. P. *Jesus and Judaism.* Philadelphia: Fortress Press, 1985.

SBL Handbook of Style: For Ancient Near Eastern, Biblical, and Early Christian Studies. Edited by Patrick H. Alexander et al. Peabody, MA: Hendrickson, 1999.

Schnackenburg, Rudolph. *Jesus in the Gospels: A Biblical Christology.* Trans. by O.C. Dean, Jr. Louisville: John Knox Press, 1995.

Schillebeeckx, Edward. *Jesus: An Experiment in Christology.* New York: Crossroads, 1979.

Schreck, Alan. *Catholic and Christian: An Explanation of Commonly Misunderstood Catholic Beliefs.* Ann Arbor, MI: Servant Books, 1984.

Scott, James C. *The Moral Economy of the Peasant.* New Haven: Yale University Press, 1977.

Segundo, Juan L. *The Historical Jesus of the Synoptics.* Maryknoll, NY: Orbis, 1985.

Senior, Donald. *Jesus: A Gospel Portrait*. Mahah, NJ: Paulist Press, 1992.

Sider, Ronald J. *Rich Christians in an Age of Hunger*. Nashville: Word Publishing, 1997.

Sleeper, C. Freeman. *The Bible and the Moral life*. Louisville: Westminster/John Knox Press, 1992.

Sloyan, G. S. *Jesus in Focus: A Life in its Setting*. Mystic, CN: Twenty-Third Publications, 1983.

Sobrino, Jon. *The True Church and the Poor*. Maryknoll, NY: Orbis Books. 1985.

Soelle, Dorothee and Luise Schottroff. *Jesus of Nazareth*. Trans. by John Bowden. Louisville: Westminster John Knox Press, 2002.

Spohn, William C. *What Are They Saying About Scripture and Ethics?* Mahwah, NJ: Paulist Press, 1995.

Stackhouse, Max L., ed. *On Moral Business: Classical and Contemporary Resources for Ethics in Economic Life*. Grand Rapids: Wm B. Eerdmans, 1995.

Stemberger, Gunter. *Jewish Contemporaries of Jesus: Pharisees, Sadducees, Essenes*. Minneapolis: Fortress Press, 1995.

Stott, John R. W. *Basic Christianity*. Grand Rapids, MI: Wm. B. Eerdmans Publishing Co., 1966.

_____. *Issues Facing Christians Today*. Grand Rapids, MI: Zondervan, 2006.

Sweet, Leonard I. *Quantum Spirituality: A Postmodern Apologetic*. Dayton, OH: Whaleprints for SpiritVenture Ministries, 1994.

Thielman, Frank. *Theology of the New Testament*. Grand Rapids: Zondervan, 2005.

Throckmorton, B. H., ed. *Gospel Parallels.* New York: Thomas Nelson, 1967.

United States Catholic Conference. *"Health and Health Care: A Pastoral Letter to the American Catholic Bishops."* Washington D C: USC Publications, 1982.

Vatican Council ll: Dei Verbum (The Dogmatic Constitution on Divine Revelation). *The Documents of Vatican ll,* ed. W. M. Abbot. New York: Herder and Herder, 1966.

Vanderkam, James C. *The Dead Sea Scrolls Today.* Grand Rapids: Eerdmans Publishing, 1994.

Verhey, Allen. *Remembering Jesus: Christian Community, Scripture, and the Moral Life.* Grand Rapids, MI: Wm. B. Erdmans Publishing Co., 2002.

Vine, W.E. *Vines Expository Dictionary of Old and New Testament Words.* Nashville: Thomas Nelson, 1996.

Wakefield, Dan. *The Hijacking of Jesus: How the Religious Right Distorts Christianity and Promotes Prejudice and Hate.* New York: Avalon Publishing, 2006.

Wallis, Jim. *Agenda for Biblical People.* New York: Harper & Row, 1976.

_____. *God's Politics: A New Vision for Faith and Politics in America.* San Francisco: Harper Collins, 2005.

_____. *The Great Awakening: Reviving Faith & Politics in a Post-Religious Right America.* New York: HarperOne, 2008.

Westermann, Claus. *The Parables of Jesus in the Light of the Old Testament.* Trans. by W. Golka Friedemann and Alastair H. B. Logan. Minneapolis: Fortress Press, 1990.

Wink, Walter. *Naming the Powers: The Language of Power in the New Testament.* Philadelphis: Fortress Press, 1984.

_____. *Unmasking the Powers: The Invisible Forces That Determine Human Existence.* Philadelphia: Fortress, 1986.

_____. *Engaging the Powers: Discernment and Resistence in a World of Domination.* Minneapolis: Fortress Press, 1992.

_____. *Jesus and Nonviolence: A Third Way.* Minneapolis: Fortress Press, 2003.

Witherington, Ben, III. *Jesus the Sage: The Pilgrimage of Wisdom.* Minneapolis: Fortress Press, 1994.

_____. *Women in the Ministry of Jesus: A Study of Jesus' Attitudes to Women and Their Roles as Reflected in His Earthly Life.* New York: Cambridge University Press, 1984.

_____. *The Christology of Jesus.* Minnepolis: Fortress Press, 1990.

Wolterstorff, Nicholas. *Until Justice and Peace Embrace.* Grand Rapids: Wm. B. Eerdmans, 1983.

Wright, N. T. *Jesus and the Victory of God.* Minneapolis, MN: Fortress Press, 1996.

_____. *The New Testament and the People of God.* Minneapolis, MN: Fortress Press, 1998.

_____. *The Challenge of Jesus: Rediscovering Who Jesus Was and Is.* Downers Grove, Ill: Inter Varsity Press, 1999.

_____. *The Contemporary Quest for Jesus.* Minneapolis: Fortress Press, 2002.

_____. *The Resurrection and the Son of God.* Minneapolis: Fortress Press, 2003.

_____. *The Last Word: Beyond the Bible Wars to a New Understanding of the Authority of Scripture.* San Francisco: HarperCollins, 2005.

Yancey, Philip. *The Jesus I Never Knew.* Grand Rapids: Zondervan Publishing, 1995.

Yoder, John. *The Politics of Jesus.* Grand Rapids: William B. Eerdmans, 1972.

FROM THE AUTHOR

The author's teaching of the Bible, Religious Studies, and Theology over a forty year period has been done ecumenically in a public university, Penn State at Altoona; two Roman Catholic colleges, Mt Aloysius, St Francis of PA; and Northeastern Christian College; a public and Catholic high school; and in the United Church of Christ, the Christian Church (Disciples of Christ), and the Roman Catholic Church.

If we understand the Scriptures, there is room in Christ's church for all who believe and attempt to relate their imperfect lives to him. Life is a struggle to the Word and Spirit that comes from God and continues to work in the world. There is no group who perfectly understands. First Corinthians 13:12-13 says, For now we see in a mirror, dimly, but then we will see face to face. Now I know in part; then I will know fully, even as I have been fully known. May God's mercy and grace bless all of us who struggle in our understanding and spiritual growth along life's journey.

My prayer is the prayer of Jesus in John 17:17-23. Sanctify them in the truth; your word is truth. As you have sent me into the world, so I have sent them into the world. And for their sakes I sanctify myself, so that they also may be sanctified in the truth. I ask not only on behalf of these, but also on behalf of those who will believe in me through their word, that they all may be one. As you, Father, are in me and I am in you, may they also be in us, so that the world may believe that you have sent me. The glory that you have given me I have given them, so that they may be one, as we are one, I in them and you in me, that they may be completely one, so that the world may know that you have sent me and have loved them even as you have loved me.

A BRIEF BIOGRAPHY

EDUCATION

- DMin, Pittsburgh Theological Seminary: Reformed Theology with an Emphasis in Comparative Christian Theology. Dissertation: Protestantism, Roman Catholicism, and the Orthodox: A Comparison of Christian Theology. Dissertation Directors: Dr. Charles Partee and Dr. John Mehl.

- PhD, Clayton University: Religious Studies/Counseling Psychology. Dissertation: Using Programmed Instruction in Teaching Religion and Counseling. Dissertation Directors: Dr. Harry Cargas, Roman Catholic author of 31 books and 2000 published articles, Dr. Barbara Finn, and Dr. Richard Foster. (Clayton University associated with the Menninger Foundation closed it doors in 1989. Until that time it was listed in the United States Department of Education Handbook of Accredited Colleges and Universities.)

- MAT, Harding University: Biblical Studies.

- MEd, University of North Florida: Counseling.

- BSEd, Lock Haven University: Social Studies and English.

- Post Graduate Studies in Religion and Counseling Psychology at the University of Texas-El Paso, David Lipscomb University, Penn State University, and Indiana University (PA).

EMPLOYMENT

- Instructor of Religious Studies, and Chaplain in the Campus Ministry Program at Penn State University (Altoona Campus) teaching the following courses: Old and New Testaments, Comparative Christian Religions, World Religions, and Religion in America.

- Adjunct Professor of Scripture and Theology at Mt Aloysius College.

- Adjunct Professor of Scripture and Theology at St. Francis University (PA).

- Catholic High School Teacher, Counselor, and Basketball Coach, teaching the following courses: Biblical Studies, Psychology, World History and Cultures, American History, Government, Economics, and English. Head basketball coach for the 1970 Bishop Guilfoyle High School (PA) state champions.

- Public High School Teacher, Counselor, Basketball and Baseball Coach teaching the following courses: Biblical Studies, World History and Cultures, American History, and English.

- Peace Corps in Senegal, French West Africa. Helped train their Olympic basketball team for the 1964 Olympics in Japan.

- Played professional baseball in the Cleveland and Minnesota minor league systems. On the Altoona (PA) NABF national championship team, getting the team's only hit in the tenth inning in a 1-0 win. The team was inducted into Blair County (PA) Hall of Fame.

- Certified Psychologist, Teacher, and Counselor by the state of PA.

- Certified Counselor by the National Board of Certified Counselors.

- Over 40 years of teaching within the Roman Catholic Church, United Church of Christ, and the Christian Church (Disciples of Christ).

- Book Publication: *Reading and Understanding the Old Testament: The Foundation of Judaism, Christianity, and Islam*. Denver: Outskirts Press, 2010. The book is a text book for first level college students and a source for anyone desiring to expand their understanding.

- Book Publication: *Reading and Understanding the Gospels: Who Jesus Is, What He Teaches, and the Beginning of Christianity*. Denver: Outskirts Press, 2011. This book is a text book for first level college students and a source for anyone desiring to expand their knowledge and understanding.

- Book publication: *Reading and Understanding the Acts of the Apostles, the New Testament Letters, and the Beginning of the Church*. Denver: Outskirts Press, 2012.